Also by Daniel Benjamin and Steven Simon

The Age of Sacred Terror:
Radical Islam's War Against America

THE NEXT ATTACK

THE

NEXT

ATTACK

The Failure of the War on Terror
and a Strategy for Getting It Right

DANIEL BENJAMIN
and STEVEN SIMON

TIMES BOOKS

HENRY HOLT AND COMPANY / NEW YORK

Times Books
Henry Holt and Company, LLC
Publishers since 1866
175 Fifth Avenue
New York, New York 10010
www.henryholt.com

Henry Holt® is a registered trademark of
Henry Holt and Company, LLC.

Library of Congress Cataloging-in-Publication Data
Benjamin, Daniel, date.
    The next attack : the failure of the war on terror and a strategy for
getting it right /
    Daniel Benjamin and Steven Simon—1st ed.
        p.   cm.
    Includes index.
    ISBN-13: 978-0-8050-7941-8
    ISBN-10: 0-8050-7941-6
    1. War on Terrorism, 2001–   I. Simon, Steven.   II. Title.

HV6432.7.B425 2005
973.931—dc22

                                                    2005051444

Henry Holt books are available for special promotions
and premiums. For details contact: Director, Special Markets.

First Edition 2005

Designed by Victoria Hartman

Printed in the United States of America
1   3   5   7   9   10   8   6   4   2

For Henrike

———————

For Virginia

CONTENTS

Part Three   /   The Road Not Taken

A NOTE ON SOURCES

While researching this book, we were fortunate to speak with a large number of current and former government officials as well as with individuals who work closely with the administration in various capacities. We are grateful that they were so forthcoming with their experiences and observations and so generous with their time. Some of these interviewees allowed themselves to be identified by name. A number felt they could not do so for various reasons, the most common one being that their candor would endanger their positions. We regret not being able to identify all of our sources; the use of blind sources is one of the necessary evils of reporting in Washington. In the current environment, it would be impossible to write about policy deliberations and government actions without such sources.

PROLOGUE

We are losing.

Four years and two wars after the attacks of September 11, 2001, America is heading for a repeat of the events of that day, or perhaps something worse. Against our most dangerous foe, our strategic position is weakening. Inspired by Usama bin Laden's boldness and outraged by America's recent actions, more Muslims are sympathizing with the radical Islamists and joining their movement. Individuals who hitherto had no significant ties to radical organizations are enlisting themselves in the struggle and committing acts of violence, sometimes without any support from existing networks. In disparate places around the globe, from Indonesia to the Caucasus and from Pakistan to Western Europe, the jihadist ideology has become the banner under which an array of grievances is being expressed, and often that expression is violent. In many of these regions, local and global grievances are merging into a pervasive hatred of the United States, its allies, and the international order they uphold. Within parts of the Muslim world, social and religious inhibitions on violence are weakening, and the notion is gaining acceptance that an attack on infidels involving weapons of mass destruction would be justified.

The United States—and certainly its leadership—appears not to have comprehended the dynamic, ideologically driven insurgency whose heralds were four hijacked commercial jets. Instead of taking a comprehensive view of the phenomenon of radical Islam, only two indicators are used to show the measure of our progress in the war on terror: the number of days since 9/11 in which we have not experienced a second catastrophic attack, and the number of al Qaeda members who have been apprehended or killed. While it is true that bin Laden's group has been seriously hurt by the capture of many of its leaders and the disruption of many of its cells, the administration's focus on numbers feeds the widespread belief that the terrorist enemy is finite in quantity and destructible in the near term. The failure to look beyond al Qaeda and to recognize the multiplying forms that the jihadist threat is taking represents a serious failure of vision. We are repeating the errors of the time before 9/11 in believing, first, that what terrorists do abroad has little consequence for national security, and, second, that only states can truly threaten us. Unwittingly, we are clearing the way for the next attack—and those that will come after.

Not only are we not attending to a growing threat, we are stoking the fire. America's invasion of Iraq has turned that long-suffering country into the central theater of the jihadist struggle. We destroyed one of the hated secular dictatorships of the Arab world that jihadists had been unable to dent but left an open field for radicals from outside the country and within to cause havoc. The terrorists have found in Iraq a better sanctuary, training ground, and laboratory than they ever had in Afghanistan. They have also been given what they desire most: American targets in close proximity. They can now demonstrate their valor and resolve to bleed America, and in doing so, to build momentum for their cause. We have slain the chimera of Saddam Hussein's Iraq, but we are nourishing the all-too-real dragon of radical Islam.

It is unlikely that even in his most feverish reveries, Usama bin Laden could have imagined that America would stumble so badly and wound itself so grievously. By occupying Iraq, the United States has played into the hands of its opponents, affirming the story they have been telling to the Muslim world and adding to their aura as true warriors in defense of Islam. America's image in the Muslim world has never been more battered, and the jihadist claim that the United States seeks to oppress Muslims has never seemed more plausible—no matter how noble we view our own sacrifices in the liberation of Iraq. There is, as has so often been said, a war of ideas going on, a battle for hearts and minds. Unfortunately, America has wound up on the wrong side.

We and our friends are paying a price for these errors. As this is being written, investigators are pursuing leads from the British Isles to Pakistan in connection with the July 7 bombing of three Underground trains in London and a double-decker bus. The attacks, carried out with the al Qaeda hallmark of multiple simultaneous blasts, appear to have been the work of three Britons of Pakistani descent and a Jamaican immigrant who had converted to Islam. It is not clear yet whether, as alleged, they benefited from bomb-making instruction in a jihadist training camp in Pakistan, but that is entirely plausible. Nor do we know what was going through their minds when they planned the incident that killed fifty-six people. But if they are anything like other recent terrorists, then their anger was fired by the presence of Americans, Britons, and others in Iraq. "Our military is confronting the terrorists, along with our allies, in Iraq and Afghanistan so that innocent civilians will not have to confront terrorist violence in Washington or London or anywhere else in the world," Vice President Dick Cheney said in September 2003.[1] It has not turned out that way.

We have compounded these mistakes by squandering the chance to build defenses against a new kind of enemy. The successes we have notched against the leadership of al Qaeda have bought us time, but the time has been wasted. When American political leaders wish to show seriousness they first declare war on a problem, then they decree a bureaucratic reorganization. Since 9/11, we seem to be caught in a perpetual loop of reorganizing our homeland security authorities and our intelligence community. The possibility that we need something other than a sweeping organizational fix seldom gets taken seriously. Lawmakers feel any other response would be incommensurate with the original cataclysm, and if they chose such an avenue, they would be showing a lack of seriousness. But while the legislation mandating a great conglomeration of agencies has been enacted, the leadership, vision, and resources to make that "rationalization" effective have been missing. Particularly in the realm of homeland security, the last three years have witnessed an extraordinary amount of wheel-spinning. These were years we could not afford to lose.

More disturbing, the signs are growing that the jihadist threat is a diminishing concern for the nation. Despite clear evidence of an increase of jihadist activity abroad, a recent decline in threat reporting against domestic U.S. targets has led Terrance W. Gainer, the chief of the Capitol Police, to remark in May 2005, "The imminence of a threat seems to have diminished. We're just not as worried as we were a year ago, but we certainly are as vigilant." This from a man whose officers guard a known al Qaeda target, and who is regularly briefed by the FBI and CIA. John O. Brennan, then acting director of the new National Counterterrorism Center, agreed, saying, "Progress has been made."[2] The declining sense of urgency has been apparent in President George W. Bush's rhetoric, too. As one observer has noted, Bush mentioned the war on terror or some variant of the phrase more often in the thirty days prior to the 2004 election (seventy-one times) than in the six months after (sixty-six times).[3] Before the London attacks in July 2005, only 12 percent of Americans thought of terrorism as the nation's top priority, behind the economy, Iraq, health care, and Social Security—almost a 40 percent drop from the time of the November 2004 election.[4] If past experience holds, this most recent moment of horror will be another brief peak in a downward-moving average.

An argument is now heard that the destruction of the World Trade Center was a once-in-a-millennium lucky shot, that everything broke the hijackers' way. Others observe that the Muslim world has shown itself unwilling to hitch its wagon to bin Laden's mad star, forgetting that acts of jihadist violence are increasing in number and that small opinion changes at the margins of a population of 1.2 billion people can have enormous effects. Although the bad news from Iraq continues to dominate the airwaves, in some ways, Washington in the summer of 2005 feels much as it did in the summer of 1999, when talk of the challenge from China was a dominant theme. Then the question was whether China had stolen satellite technology and interfered in American elections. Now it is China's regional ambitions, its undervalued currency, and its military buildup. Though he has not spoken much of the global terrorist threat of late, Secretary of Defense Donald Rumsfeld wondered in a major address in June, "Since no nation threatens China, one must wonder: Why this growing investment? Why these continuing large and expanding arms purchases?"[5]

The focus has shifted. Few people are better bellwethers of the zeitgeist than *New York Times* columnist Thomas Friedman. His latest book, *The*

World Is Flat, a paean to globalization, shot to the top of the bestseller lists when it appeared in April 2005. But for Friedman the globalization that counts is the outsourcing of information technology jobs to Bangalore, manufacturing to China, and the computerization of the Third World— "Everyone in Mali uses Linux," he exclaims.[6] While Friedman recognizes (on page 391) the threat that al Qaeda poses to the benefits of globalization, he makes no acknowledgment of the parallel globalization going on, in which the Internet has accelerated the spread of everything from radical Islamist ideology to the minutiae of bomb making for a growing community of jihadists around the world. The wired world is bringing lightning change to the global security landscape, but all eyes are on how technology is again revolutionizing the marketplace.

At a time when we should be well into our planning for a long conflict, our attention is drifting from the greatest threat we face. It is a recurrent theme in radical Islamist writings that we in the West have a short attention span while the holy warriors of jihad will carry on their fight for as long as they have breath. They look forward, they say over and again, to the day when America returns to its slumbers. If we are indeed doing that, then the true lessons of 9/11 will not be learned until after the next attack.

PART ONE

Since September 11:
The Evolution of the Threat

1

TERROR'S NEW RECRUITS

It was 5:30 in the morning when the men emerged from the farmhouse. They climbed into three cars and, departing the Spanish hilltop town of Chinchón, headed north on the switchback road. In the lead vehicle, a white Renault van, the men turned on a tape of verses from the Quran. As they wound through the predawn gloom, they listened to the third Sura, to God's instructions for upbraiding those who do not accept the prophecy of Muhammad. "Say to the unbelievers: 'You shall be overthrown and driven into Hell—an evil resting-place!'" And they heard again of the Battle of Badr, the climactic military event in the early history of Islam, when of two armies, "One was fighting for the cause of God, the other being a host of unbelievers. The faithful saw with their very eyes that they were twice their own number. But God strengthens with His aid whom He will. Surely in that there was a lesson for the discerning."[1] It was Thursday, March 11, 2004.

An hour later, they pulled into Alcalá de Henares, the medieval village where the institution that would become Madrid's university was founded. Eighteen miles from the Spanish capital, the village now lies in its belt of suburbs. The men parked a couple of hundred yards from the commuter rail station, and then, clad in wool caps and scarves, made their way to the platforms, where morning commuters were awaiting the trains that would take them into the city. When train 21431 pulled away from the station at 7:01, four of the men who had driven from Chinchón were on board. They sat in separate cars, each near a door. Each man slid a cloth bag under his seat. At 7:04, train 17305 left the station, taking four more of the men; they were positioned exactly like the others, near the door, bag under the seat. Six minutes later, a third train, 21435, departed with four more men inside, and at 7:14, train 21713 rolled out of Alcalá de Henares with the last member of the crew inside.[2]

The men got off the trains one by one at different stops. At 7:37, the first of the trains arrived at Atocha Station, the patchwork of nineteenth- and twentieth-century buildings and canopies that is one of Madrid's two rail hubs, where commuter lines and intercity trains converge. With the train stopped and commuters shuffling out, three of the four bombs went off— one each in the fourth, fifth, and sixth cars. Seconds later, when train 17305 was just 500 yards from the station, the four bombs planted aboard it blew up. Over the next two minutes, two bombs detonated aboard train 21435, a double-decker, which was stopped in El Pozo Station, in a blue-collar neighborhood about three miles from Atocha, and one more blew up on train 21713, in the Santa Eugenia Station, two stops farther out.

As envisioned by the bombers, the trains would be both targets and delivery vehicles. The devices were timed to detonate in the stations so the concussion from the blast and the hail of glass and metal shrapnel would engulf the morning crowds on the platforms as well as the passengers still on the trains. Though three of the thirteen bombs failed to explode, the strategy worked as planned on three of the four trains. Had the commuter line been as efficient as the terrorists, the bloodshed would have been much greater. Because train 17305 was running late, the explosives on board detonated outside Atocha Station. Had it been on time, the multiple blasts might have brought down the station's walls or ceilings, killing hundreds more. In all, 191 people died in the four blast zones, and more than 1,800 were wounded.

The damage stretched far beyond the train stations. Three days after the bombings, the ruling Popular Party of Prime Minister José María Aznar suffered a surprise defeat in a long-scheduled general election. The attacks had suddenly given Spaniards a reason to punish their rulers. The previous year, Aznar had committed Spanish troops to the American-led occupation of Iraq, against the wishes of an overwhelming majority of his countrymen. According to surveys, as many as 98 percent of Spaniards opposed the military action, but until March 11, Aznar's decision carried few costs and had not significantly affected his political standing.[3] Many, however, saw the Madrid attacks as retribution by radical Islamists for Spain's support of the United States, and, perhaps more important, Aznar himself had seemed determined to avoid that conclusion. Only hours after the blasts, he issued a statement declaring that they were the work of the Basque terrorist group Euskadi Ta Askatasuna (ETA). Aznar maintained that ETA, which has carried out a campaign of terror in Spain for forty-five years, was to blame, even though early indications—the discovery just three hours after the bombings of the Renault with the Quran tape and several detonators inside—pointed clearly to jihadists. The appearance of trying to put one over on the Spanish people doomed Aznar's party at the polls.

The final reverberation came the day after the election, when José Luis Rodríguez Zapatero, the leader of the Socialist Party and the prime minister-elect, announced that he would fulfill his campaign pledge to withdraw Spain's troops from Iraq. The bombs not only wrecked trains and killed Spanish commuters; they also helped trigger the fall of a Western democratic government and opened a rift between Spain and its ally, the United States.

THE MADRID BOMBINGS had all the qualities of an al Qaeda operation. Multiple simultaneous bombings have been a hallmark of al Qaeda since its debut attacks in August 1998 on the U.S. embassies in Nairobi, Kenya, and Dar es Salaam, Tanzania. Though separated by hundreds of miles, these bombings were carried out within ten minutes of each other. Jihadists conceived of this tactic as a way to exponentially increase the horror of a terrorist attack and to draw attention to their capabilities. On March 11, the terrorists may have confined their operations within a radius of less than ten miles, but otherwise, they outdid themselves; no terrorists had ever set off ten bombs at once.

The strikes were carried out with the kind of precision timing that Khalid Sheikh Mohammed could admire. Mohammed, the mastermind of the demolition of the World Trade Center, had helped design a plan in the mid-1990s to destroy a dozen 747s nearly simultaneously over the Pacific—Operation Bojinka, it was called. Although the plan was disrupted by U.S. authorities before it could be executed, its promise of simultaneity remained a touchstone for jihadists around the world. The lethality of the Madrid bombings was also worthy of al Qaeda. The death toll placed March 11 in the same class as the October 2002 attacks of nightclubs in Bali, Indonesia, where Jemaah Islamiya (JI), an organization closely tied to al Qaeda, slaughtered 202 people, and the 1998 East Africa embassy bombings, which killed 224 people. Like those incidents and al Qaeda attacks in general, the Madrid bombings were designed to kill as many people as possible, as the choice of Atocha Station as the central target demonstrated.

But the Madrid bombings were not designed, funded, or executed by al Qaeda operatives. They were carried out by Muslim men, none of whom had ever been to al Qaeda's camps in Afghanistan, and only one of whom had anything that could be called terrorist training. Moreover, the planning and decision making in the conspiracy in no way resembled what goes on in typical terrorist organizations: No one, it appears, ordered the Madrid bombings. There was no single leader behind the attack; rather, several individuals collaborated on the operation, and the foot soldiers followed their lead.

The Madrid attack was originally seen to be another display of al Qaeda's global reach. In the public mind, Europe had become another territory marked by al Qaeda—together with Southeast Asia, East Africa, North Africa, and, of course, the east coast of the United States. Yet the bloodshed in Spain was not the handiwork of Usama bin Laden. Instead, it was an homage—both honor and emulation—to him and his ideas. The bombers chose the al Qaeda calling card of multiple simultaneous attacks as their own, killing as many people as they could to show that they shared an address spiritually, if not physically, with bin Laden. Madrid demonstrated the global reach of bin Laden's ideas, not his operations.

In important ways, this fact is far more disquieting than would be the discovery of a cell of terrorists who had trained together in the camps of Afghanistan, migrated to Spain, and carried out the killings. It underscores that this kind of terrorism is not the exclusive province of the membership of al Qaeda and its affiliated groups, that it requires no special al Qaeda training, equipment, indoctrination, or experience. All that is necessary are the most portable, least detectable tools of the terrorist trade: ideas. And Madrid shows all too plainly that people who hold these ideas and want to act on them live in the heart of the West. Their number is growing, and so too is the danger they pose.

TO GRASP JUST how improbable the Madrid bombings were from the perspective of traditional terrorist operations, it is worth considering the actors and their plot. The conspiracy emerged not from an organization but a milieu. Spain's modern Muslim community is only a few decades old; before the death of the country's longtime dictator, Francisco Franco, in 1975, there had been no Muslim presence to speak of since the end of the *Reconquista,* the Christian campaign to reclaim Iberia from Islam that culminated in the capture of Granada in 1492. The Muslims who have come to Spain in recent years are predominantly laborers from Morocco and other North African countries seeking to take advantage of European opportunities and wages.

The man who might be said to have brought radical Islam to Spain came from farther afield. Imad Eddin Yarkas, who goes by the nom de guerre of Abu Dahdah, was one of a wave of fugitives from the Middle East's internal strife who brought radical Islam to the West—much like Omar Abdel Rahman, the "Blind Sheikh," who fled Egypt and found refuge in the New York City area, where he inspired the first attack on the World Trade Center in 1993. Abu Dahdah had escaped from Syria, where a brutal campaign was waged in the 1980s against the Muslim Brotherhood, the fundamentalist group that sired most of today's Islamic extremists. After several years of wandering in the Arab world, he settled in Spain in 1993.

In Madrid, Abu Dahdah quarreled with the leaders of the main mosques and became the center of a circle of extremists, which included several mujahedin, veterans of the Islamic resistance to the Soviet Union in Afghanistan in the decade before. He devoted himself to recruiting young Muslims from Spain's burgeoning population of North African immigrants to fight in Afghanistan, Bosnia, and Chechnya. Selling clothes or the occasional used car to get by—and receiving money from the Islamic charities that funded the budding movement—he was in touch with some bin Laden associates in Europe. Within his suburban Madrid community of Lavapies, Abu Dahdah enjoyed the status of an imam. To his followers, he extolled the virtues and necessity of the holy warfare of jihad, distributing copies of Usama bin Laden's messages and pamphlets from the Palestinian group Hamas and other Islamist organizations.

After September 11, 2001, American and European investigators traced the path of Muhammad Atta, the leader of the cell that carried out the attacks on the World Trade Center and the Pentagon, and discovered that it ran through Spain, where he had met with Ramzi bin al-Shibh, a Yemeni jihadist who was originally supposed to be part of the Atta operation but had not been able to gain entry to the United States. From this lead, Spanish investigators came to believe that Abu Dahdah helped arrange the meeting and plan the 9/11 attacks. In the fall of 2001, he and ten others were arrested, thereby, the Spanish authorities believed, shutting down al Qaeda in Spain.[4]

But left at large were a number of individuals—acolytes and hangers-on—who had been influenced by Abu Dahdah. They had sat with him at the Alhambra restaurant in Lavapies, and they had drunk in his view of history as a battlefield between believers and infidels. Abu Dahdah's arrest served as confirmation of the worldview he espoused, which held that Christians were determined to destroy Islam's truest soldiers. It deeply angered the circle around him, and their resentment only grew with time.

One who was incensed was Sarhane Ben Abdelmajid Fakhet—a young follower often called El Tunecino because of his Tunisian origins. Sarhane was a figure much like Muhammad Atta. Just as Atta seemed to have escaped the narrow confines of life in Egypt when he moved from his native Cairo to Hamburg to study city planning, Sarhane had come to Madrid in 1996 to pursue a doctorate in economics. Like Atta, though, the move to Europe would lead not so much to a personal liberation but rather a profound radicalization. After Abu Dahdah's arrest, Sarhane became increasingly drawn to extremist ideas, and he decided that he needed to do more as a Muslim than just pray. He picked up some of the work left behind by Abu Dahdah, recruiting soldiers for jihad. Together with other young Muslims, he spent long hours talking about the war against Islam and watching videos of fighting from Afghanistan, Bosnia, and Chechnya.

By April 2003, Sarhane had lost interest in his studies and took a position selling apartments. He started off well, outselling his colleagues in the Arconsa Real Estate Agency in his first few months on the job. But around him, events were moving quickly. American troops had invaded Iraq on March 20 and toppled Saddam Hussein's regime just three weeks later. On May 16, jihadists in Casablanca bombed five targets, killing forty-two people. Among those later apprehended were three Moroccan radicals who had been part of Abu Dahdah's circle—there was always a great deal of back and forth between Spain and North Africa for the recent immigrants. The arrests of the Casablanca gang compounded the sense of beleaguerment that had set in after Abu Dahdah's incarceration.[5] By fall, Sarhane stopped showing up for work altogether.

Among the Lavapies set, the acute feeling of living in a hostile environment created a bond more powerful than class, nationality, or education. One of Sarhane's closest friends was a Moroccan named Jamal Ahmidan, nicknamed El Chino because of his narrow eyes. He had arrived in Europe in 1990 and worked as a drug trafficker, specializing in the hashish trade that runs from Morocco in the south to Amsterdam in the north. He spent time in jail in Morocco from 2000 to 2003 for a murder committed in Tetuán, his family's hometown. A drinker, smoker, and a frequenter of nightclubs before he went to prison, Ahmidan emerged a believer. He now prayed the required five times a day, though his newfound piety did not stop him from dealing drugs, at least to non-Muslims. He slipped back into Spain illegally and resumed business, selling hash and Ecstasy.

Ahmidan, like Sarhane, was filled with rage by the events in Iraq. He spoke of his desire to go there to fight the Americans, and he insisted that the Spanish government be punished for supporting the United States. He would love, he said, to "blow up the Bernabeu," Madrid's most famous soccer stadium, home of the legendary Real Madrid team. He was also bringing along others who shared his views. Ahmidan became the cell's chief recruiter, introducing many of the petty criminals, construction workers, and minimum-wage employees who would make up a cell that ultimately grew to include fifteen members. Among them were the Oulad brothers, Rachid, who worked as a bricklayer, and Mohamed, four years younger, who had worked as a waiter, laborer, and messenger and had been in trouble for drug trafficking; Abdennabi Kounjaa, who worked in construction; and his friend Asrih Rifaat Anour. They were almost all Moroccans, bound by ties of kinship and friendship, all marginal men.

The only person in the group who appears to have had genuine terrorist experience was Allekema Lamari. An Algerian, Lamari had been convicted by a Spanish court in 1997 of being a member of the Groupes Islamique Armés (GIA), the terrorist organization that had fought Algeria's military government since 1992, when the regime canceled an election that would have brought an Islamist party to power. Sentenced to fourteen years in prison, Lamari was released in a bureaucratic mixup in 2002. In September 2003, he turned up in Madrid, and there he made contact with Sarhane and Ahmidan. Exactly how much terrorist know-how Lamari brought with him remains unclear, but the growing circle of radicals in Madrid accorded him considerable respect.

About the time Lamari joined the group, it received the decisive bit of inspiration. On October 19, bin Laden released two audiotapes, which were broadcast on al Jazeera, the Arabic satellite news network. The first, addressed to the Iraqi people, congratulated them on their fast-growing post-invasion insurgency, in which they "have indeed slaughtered the enemy and have pleased the hearts of all Muslims. . . . Be glad of the good news: America is mired in the swamps of the Tigris and Euphrates."[6] The second tape, addressed to the United States, was classic bin Laden: a mixture of delight in America's difficulties in Iraq, a tirade against George W. Bush, and a vow to fight on. After mocking Bush for "begging the world to come to [his] aid" by providing troops in Iraq, he threatened those who supported the occupation: "Let the transgressors know that we reserve our right in responding when and where we see appropriate against all the countries that participate in this unjust war [in Iraq]—especially Britain, Spain, Australia, Poland, Japan, and Italy."[7] Spain had not appeared in previous statements, and its inclusion was not lost on the Madrid jihadists. According to a senior Spanish official, the cell went to work the next day planning its attack.

Around this time, Ahmidan was introduced to José Emilio Suárez Trashorras, a small-time drug dealer from the Asturias region in northern Spain. Suárez had worked in the area's clay mines, which supply the porcelain industry, and he still had friends who were miners. Meeting at a McDonald's in Madrid, Ahmidan and Suárez cut a deal to swap hashish for explosives and detonators, which Suárez's miner friends would pilfer.

The backdrop for this meeting was a world turning more violent as jihadists elsewhere became increasingly active. In Istanbul, terrorists carried out two sets of bombings in five days in November 2003. First, two synagogues were attacked virtually simultaneously, killing twenty-three people. Then, car bombs detonated outside the British consulate and the Turkish headquarters of the British HSBC Bank, claiming more than fifty lives. Finally, on November 29, insurgents in Iraq ambushed cars carrying eight Spanish intelligence officers, killing seven of them. A video of the attack was soon posted on the Internet and was viewed widely in jihadist circles—in Madrid, the group gathered to watch it on Ahmidan's VCR.

The first transaction with Suárez took place in early January 2004. Suárez sent a friend with a bag containing a sample of Goma-2, a kind of dynamite, and detonators, which Ahmidan and the others immediately took for testing at a farmhouse they had rented in Chinchón. Over the next two months, through a series of amateurish and nearly botched transfers, Ahmidan received close to 200 kilograms of explosives from Suárez. He drove the last 60 kilograms from Asturias to Chinchón himself and was pulled over for speeding on the way. The policeman did not notice that Ahmidan's papers were forged and did not check inside the car.

During the next week, the remaining supplies were purchased: cellular telephones; SIM cards, which hold the personal information, phone settings, and network authorization for a mobile phone; and bags of nails and screws that would be packed into the explosive devices for shrapnel. Then the men began disappearing from Madrid.

Early on Wednesday morning, March 10, the bomb building began in Chinchón. Each device consisted of a blue cloth sports bag with two brown leather handles, twenty-two pounds of Goma-2, and the shrapnel. A detonator was attached to the explosive and connected to the cell phones by copper wire. Fearing that a wrong number might set off the devices, the men turned the phones off and instead set the built-in alarm clocks to send the charge to the detonator.

They were done by early evening. Then, instead of resting, they spent the night reviewing the plans and praying. This was the same kind of intensely focused spiritual and practical preparation that was outlined in the document known as Muhammad Atta's "Last Will and Testament." The

document, which was found after the 9/11 attacks in the hijackers' belongings, is presumed to recount their last night:

> One of the Companions said the Prophet commanded us to read it before
> the raid, so we read it and we were victorious and safe.
>
>   The last night:
>   1. Mutual pledge to die and renewal of intent . . .
>   2. Thorough knowledge go [through] the plan in all its facets, and
>   the expectation of reaction or resistance from the enemy . . .
>   5. Staying awake through the night and pleading in prayer for vic-
>   tory, enablement, clear triumph, ease of matters, and discretion
>   upon us.[8]

Then they got into the cars and drove to Alcalá de Henares.

IN ONE SIGNIFICANT respect, Madrid deviated from the al Qaeda
script: The terrorists did not carry out the bombings as a "martyrdom operation," a suicide attack. Sarhane and Ahmidan did not even participate
in placing the bombs on the trains; instead, they stayed behind at the
farmhouse. The cell did not use all of its explosives, and other attacks were
planned. On April 2, a twenty-six-pound bomb was found on the track of
the high-speed Madrid–Seville train—it appeared not to have been
armed, suggesting that the bombers had fled before they finished their
work.

Al Qaeda has traditionally relied on suicide operations for several reasons: They can be relied on to bring the bomb very close to the target, they
rarely fail, and the key operatives are no longer around for interrogation.
The Madrid cell, by contrast, conceived of the March 11 attacks as the beginning of a campaign, and it therefore could not afford the loss of many
members. The cell seems to have regarded itself as an independent organization that would launch additional attacks in the future, which suggests
that affecting the outcome of the Spanish election—if they actually
thought they could—was not the only thing they cared about.

A protracted campaign of bombings, however, was beyond their capabilities. In a Madrid police station at 7:40 P.M. on March 11, precisely twelve

hours after the bombings, an alarm sounded from within a gym bag that lay in a pile of unclaimed belongings from El Pozo Station. When the police opened it up, they saw a cell phone attached to ten kilograms of Goma-2 dynamite and the same kind of detonators that had been found in the Renault—a faulty connection had apparently prevented the bomb from exploding. (The police had discovered the two other undetonated bombs aboard the trains and, for safety, blew them up.) By tracing the cell phone chip in the intact device, investigators were able to locate the store where the phone had been purchased. By the next afternoon, three of the bombers had been arrested, and the police were closing in on the rest of the cell.

On April 3, the police received a tip that the terrorists were in an apartment in the suburb of Leganes, south of Madrid. After a standoff that lasted several hours, with Sarhane, Lamari, Ahmidan, and four others in the apartment raking the courtyard with machine-gun fire to hold off the police, they began to discuss surrender. Police officers climbed the stairs to the second-floor landing of the apartment, set off a small charge to blow open the door to the apartment, and threw in a gas grenade to force the cell members out. The terrorists then opened fire and detonated their remaining explosives, killing a special agent and themselves and wounding fifteen others.

THE MARCH 11 OPERATION raises large questions. Classic terrorist operations typically involve strategists, logistical planners, couriers to move money and instructions, procurement specialists for delivering explosives, and finally, the operators who execute the attack. Who funded the attacks? Who provided the demolition expertise? Who decided on timing?

The evidence suggests that once they heard bin Laden's voice on the al Jazeera broadcast, the terrorists either did it all on their own or found assistance and guidance in essentially unprecedented ways. So far, for example, no indication of any outside financing has turned up. The major costs—the Goma-2 and the detonators—were covered by sixty kilograms of hash that Ahmidan provided from his drug business. Other expenditures such as the cell phones, the rent on the farmhouse, and phony license plates were paid for by the terrorists out of their own pockets. In all, the plot is estimated to have cost about $50,000—very little money for a remarkable amount of destruction.

Who taught the inexperienced Sarhane and the others how to build a bomb? Perhaps it was Lamari, but the evidence is anything but clear. Devices that incorporate cell phones are now commonly used by terrorists—they have been employed by Palestinian terrorists against Israeli targets, and they are used frequently in Iraq. The Madrid cell may have had contacts that have not yet been uncovered. Or one of its members may have taken the design off the Internet, where information on bomb assembly is easily available. That three of the thirteen bombs did not explode suggests that those fabricating the explosives were relatively inexperienced. But if they succeeded in setting off ten devices on the basis of a design with which none of them had any experience, handling materials that few or none of them had worked with before, then their success is chilling—and underscores just how accessible basic terrorist technology has become.

Finally, who guided the terrorists to attack when they did? They should not be given full credit for toppling the Spanish government—Aznar's blunder in blaming ETA was the decisive misstep that cost him the election. But if luck favors the prepared, it took some insight for the terrorists to have paved the way for the Popular Party's disaster. Again, the Internet may have played a role. No later than December 2003, two documents were posted on an Islamist message board associated with al Qaeda by a group calling itself "The Information Institution in Support of the Iraqi People."[9] The first, a four-page "A Message to the Spanish People," rehearsed the grievances of the Iraqi people against the United States: the support Washington gave to Saddam Hussein during the Iran-Iraq War; Operation Desert Storm; the sanctions regime of the 1990s; and the current occupation. The message lauded the Spanish people for demonstrating against the occupation, but complained that "we have not sensed any serious effort to drop the government of the war criminals. . . . Therefore we declare that the responsibility for the occupation lies upon the participating armies and their people. If the Spanish people wishes to save the blood of its sons let them withdraw from Iraq alive before we send them as burned corpses to their families." The message included a vague threat against "Spanish national security in the future."

The lengthier of the documents—more than forty pages long—was entitled "Jihadi Iraq—Hopes and Risks." It provided an in-depth examination of the strategic importance of the struggle in Iraq against the

American-led occupation. For the jihadist movement, it contended, Iraq was the key battleground, and much of the document was devoted to identifying the occupation's points of vulnerability. Following on a theme that al Qaeda spokesmen have focused on since September 11, it asserted that the way to damage the United States was by inflicting enormous economic costs. The tract observed that U.S. forces would not be driven from the field, but if America's coalition partners were to withdraw their troops from Iraq, the burden on Washington would become intolerable. The document presented an insightful evaluation of domestic political support in Britain, Poland, and Spain for those countries' troop deployments, and it concluded that Spain was America's weakest partner. Spanish public opinion, it noted, was overwhelmingly against the war, and the government of José María Aznar was far out on a limb. The anonymous author of "Jihadi Iraq" concluded:

> Therefore, we say that in order to force the Spanish government to withdraw from Iraq, the resistance should deal painful blows to its [i.e., the Spanish] forces. This should be accompanied by an information campaign clarifying the truth of the matter inside Iraq. It is necessary to make utmost use of the upcoming general election in Spain in March next year.
>
> We think that the Spanish government could not tolerate more than two, maximum three blows, after which it will be forced to withdraw as a result of popular pressure. If its troops remain in Iraq after these blows, then the victory of the Socialist Party is almost guaranteed, and the withdrawal of the Spanish forces will be on its electoral programme.[10]

The document predicts that a Spanish pullout would create a domino effect that the British and other governments would be unable to withstand.

"Jihadi Iraq" is a sophisticated analysis of a kind that has been appearing with greater frequency over the past five years. What is not clear is whether any of the Madrid jihadists ever saw it. No statements to that effect are known to have been made by any of the conspirators who were captured. The document has not been found downloaded on any computer belonging to the Madrid cell.

Still, the possibility that strategic guidance like this could be so easily provided in the open—it is believed that no intelligence service detected "Jihadi Iraq" before the attacks—indicates another dimension of the changing threat. If terrorist groups are now emerging from the ground up, and not through the extension of a network, they may be far more effective if they are guided by strategic thinkers who can operate from a safe distance. In short, the operator's intelligence—almost any operator's, in fact, not just that of a petty criminal—becomes much less of a limitation when he is part of a virtual organization. His destructive capability becomes dramatically enhanced when deployed at the right time against the right target. Shrewd guidance can make the difference between the thuggery of the disgruntled and a strategic attack.

It may yet be discovered that the jihadists of Madrid had more outside help than we know. But certain facts about their work are already clear: A group of men changed from being angry but passive members of Europe's immigrant Muslim community into highly capable terrorists in virtually no time. From the moment they heard bin Laden's voice summoning them to action until March 11 was a period of less than six months—and from the time they acquired their first shipment of dynamite until they used it was little more than two months. In the world of terror, this is a blink of an eye. Al Qaeda took six years to carry out its first attacks in East Africa, and it took two and a half years to carry out the September 11 operation after bin Laden gave Khalid Sheikh Mohammed the green light—the plan had already been gestating in Mohammed's mind for years. The kind of speed demonstrated in Madrid can make it vastly more difficult to foil attacks since it greatly reduces the chances that police and intelligence officers will catch wind of an operation.

A swelling cohort of radicals with boundless anger and a belief in unbounded war, a growing ability to prepare a terrorist attack quickly, the prospect of guidance and technical assistance from a distance—all these add up to a changing threat that may be turning more abundantly dangerous and more difficult to defeat.

2

FROM NEW YORK TO BAGHDAD

On September 11, 2001, Usama bin Laden staked his claim to be the leader of global Islam. The Twin Towers were ignited as a signal that he and his followers were everything that the established political leaders of the Muslim world were not: bold, imaginative, decisive, and prepared to do anything to end the historic humiliation of Islam. Bin Laden made this clear after the attacks, when in his first words to the world he declared, "What the United States tastes today is a very small thing compared to what we have tasted for tens of years. Our nation has been tasting this humiliation and contempt for more than eighty years. Its sons are being killed, its blood is being shed, its holy places are being attacked, and it is not being ruled according to what God has decreed."[1] The catastrophe that inaugurated this age of shame was the abolition of the caliphate in 1924, not quite eighty years earlier. That institution, whose incumbent reigned as pope and king, had symbolized the unity of Islam for 1,300 years. Kemal Atatürk, the secularist leader of the Turkish state that emerged from the ruins of the Ottoman Empire, ended the caliphate, and afterward, Muslim clerics from around the world were unable to agree on how to resuscitate it.

Bin Laden's goal was much more than self-promotion: He also sought acceptance of his religious ideology and his political strategy. Though it may be hard to conceive of mass slaughter as an instrument of proselytization, September 11—along with all of al Qaeda's "spectaculars" or mass-casualty terrorist strikes—aimed at winning converts to its worldview. It is through this prism that the phenomenon of jihadist violence must be seen.

At the core of bin Laden's thinking is an understanding of history as an unending conflict between Islam and "World Infidelity." Drawing on the work of the twentieth-century Egyptian Islamist Sayyid Qutb, the medieval Muslim commentator Taki al-Din ibn Taymiyya, and a group of contemporary Saudi apocalypticists, bin Laden and his fellow radicals believe that waging this battle is the highest activity man can undertake, and they argue that this is part of the original message of Islam. Their struggle is therefore also about returning the faith to its original state and purifying it of all that has corrupted it in the centuries since the time of the Prophet Muhammad and his immediate successors, known as the four "Rightly Guided Caliphs." In this reformed Islam, jihad—understood as driving non-Muslim forces from Muslim lands—belongs at the sacramental center of life. As more Muslims embrace this vision and join the struggle against World Infidelity, not only will the heterodox innovations that have crept into the faith be eliminated, but the believers will turn the tide against the infidels. Reform and revival will be rewarded when a global order is established with Islam triumphant.

To achieve such sweeping change, bin Laden espouses a strategy that turns on one premise: The believers must attack World Infidelity, in the form of the United States and its allies, head-on. This approach is a departure from that of earlier jihadists, who assassinated Egyptian President Anwar Sadat in 1981 and who fought unsuccessful running battles in the 1980s and 1990s against the authorities in many Arab countries. That first generation of radicals considered these regimes to be apostate because of their insufficient piety and inclination to secularism and, calling these governments the "Near Enemy," deemed them an appropriate target for their violence. Bin Laden, however, reversed the strategy and argued for striking the "Far Enemy," the United States, as a more effective way to topple the authoritarian regimes of the Muslim world. He reasoned that because all these governments rely on U.S. support to stay in power, convincing America to disengage itself from the Muslim world is the best approach. The concomitant requirement for such a strategy is that violence against the United States has to be catastrophic; pinprick attacks that cause a few casualties here and there will never force America to detach itself from its proxies in the Muslim world. The killing must be on a grand scale.

After the end of the jihad against the Soviet occupation of Afghanistan in 1989, bin Laden worked to line up radical Islamist groups around the world behind his vision and leadership. He stitched together a network of organizations by subsidizing them financially, providing them with materiel, and training their members in the camps of Afghanistan. His al Qaeda organization established its bona fides with breathtaking violence by destroying two American embassies in East Africa in 1998, and then by nearly sinking the destroyer U.S.S. *Cole* in October 2000. The attacks of September 11 were meant to propel this effort to another level, to galvanize al Qaeda's allies and the rest of the Muslim world to join the fight against the Far Enemy. The thunderclap of approval al Qaeda expected for history's greatest terrorist attack would end the debate about tactics and demonstrate to Muslims just who had the courage to stand up to the West.

Any honest assessment would have to conclude that bin Laden achieved much of what he set out to do. (He was undoubtedly helped by the fact that the damage to the Twin Towers exceeded his expectations; bin Laden thought that only the areas above the impact zones would be destroyed, not the entire structures.) It has been amply documented that 9/11 earned bin Laden considerable acclaim among a significant minority in the Muslim world: According to polling in 2003 by the Pew Research Center, respondents in Indonesia, Jordan, Morocco, Pakistan, and the Palestinian Authority considered bin Laden one of the three world figures most likely to "do the right thing."[2] Since that poll, confidence in bin Laden has diminished in Lebanon, Turkey, Morocco, and Indonesia. Whether this is because he is increasingly seen as having failed to deliver, or because he is associated with growing violence between Muslims, is hard to say. At the same time, bin Laden's popularity has gone up in Pakistan and Jordan, despite large numbers in Pakistan who think that extremism is a danger to their country.

Those who were inclined to commit jihadist terror were clearly energized by the example of September 11. The wave of incidents that followed the attacks on the World Trade Center and the Pentagon has been the most intense, sustained global campaign of terror in modern history: In April 2002 a suicide bomber detonated a truck with a cargo of propane on the Tunisian island of Djerba, killing sixteen, most of them German tourists; in October 2002 the Indonesian group Jemaah Islamiya, al Qaeda's Southeast Asian affiliate, detonated car bombs in Bali that killed more than 200 people, most of them Australian tourists; in November 2002, al Qaeda operatives in Kenya attacked an Israeli-owned hotel and attempted to shoot down an Israeli charter plane; in May 2003, the Saudi affiliate of al Qaeda attacked three housing complexes for foreigners in Riyadh, killing thirty people; in August 2003, Jemaah Islamiya bombed the Marriott Hotel and the Australian Embassy in Jakarta; in November 2003, Turkish jihadists carried out two double-bombings in Istanbul in a week, destroying two synagogues on one day and a British bank and the British consulate on another day. And beginning in 2004, the violence moved into the cities of Western Europe with the attacks in Madrid that year, which killed 191, and in London in July 2005, when four bombs killed fifty-six people in the Underground and on a double-decker bus. In a parallel development, Chechen terrorists in Russia have become increasingly jihadist in their outlook and methods. Their attacks have become more brutal and spectacular. This was evident in their seizure of a Moscow theater in October 2002, the destruction of two passenger jets nearly simultaneously in August 2004, and the taking of more than 1,000 hostages in a school in Beslan in September 2004, which led to at least 330 civilian deaths, no fewer than half of them children. (In Moscow and Beslan the botched rescue attempts of Russian forces added to the death toll.)

Statistics do not reveal—but any serious measure of the jihadist movement must also include—the scores of thwarted attempts. Some of these would have caused monumental bloodshed, such as the conspiracy to destroy four Western embassies and U.S. warships at harbor in Singapore, which was discovered in December 2001, or the 2003 plot to destroy a passenger jet at London's Heathrow Airport using a shoulder-fired missile, or the effort to build a large fertilizer-and-fuel-oil bomb in Britain in 2004, in which young British Muslims acquired 1,300 pounds of fertilizer before being caught. Others would have caused extraordinary panic, such as the conspiracy that was foiled in London in which jihadists produced the toxin ricin, which they planned to put in tins of face cream for sale in drugstores.

The cataclysm of September 11 did not turn all the world's jihadists into card-carrying members of al Qaeda, eager to take on the United States. Regional agendas remain—militants in Southeast Asia, for example, still seek the creation of a Southeast Asian caliphate, a single state incorporating Indonesia, Malaysia, and the southern Philippines. Central Asian radicals still want to establish something similar in their region. Many North Africans living in European cities continue to think first and foremost about the corrupt, authoritarian rulers of their home countries. This is probably not a great source of unhappiness to al Qaeda's top planners, since persistent discontent and violence serve their strategic interest in overtaxing the capacities of their enemies. But the cumulative effect is unmistakable: The jihadists have been emboldened, and a broad reorientation involving the targeting of the United States and its allies has occurred.

A Spiritual Catastrophe

September 11 galvanized the global jihad but also splintered it, because bin Laden miscalculated. He fully understood that the attacks would elicit a harsh response from the United States; indeed, for bin Laden, American retaliation was something to look forward to, for it would inevitably kill innocents and demonstrate to Muslims the ineffable hatred that World Infidelity bore for them. The bombing runs of American warplanes would add another chapter in the history of Western brutality, alongside the subjugation of the Palestinians, the occupation of Kashmir, and the sanctions on Iraq; bin Laden's jihadist argument would be all the more irresistible. In exactly these sorts of terms, the al Qaeda leader celebrated the U.S. air strikes against Afghanistan in a December 2001 video appearance: "These events have revealed extremely important things to Muslims. It has become clear that the West in general, led by America, bears an unspeakable Crusader grudge against [Muslims]. . . . Those who lived these months under the continuous bombardment by the various kinds of the U.S. aircraft are well aware of this. Many villages were wiped out. . . . Millions were made homeless."[3]

But bin Laden did not foresee how effective the U.S. campaign in Afghanistan would be. He may have thought that the United States, fearing a repetition of the Soviet Union's experience in the 1980s, would merely arm the Taliban's opposition, the Northern Alliance, and give it air support. If he believed this, he may have taken too seriously his camp's rhetoric, which depicts Americans as cowards who hide behind their technology, unwilling to fight on the ground and suffer losses. Or he may have believed that the mujahedin would humiliate the invading Americans as they had humiliated the Russians. (Jihadist historiography habitually emphasizes the valor of the mujahedin but gives little credit to the $3 billion in arms and training that the United States and Saudi Arabia gave the Afghan resistance.) Bin Laden thought he was covering his bases when, days before the attacks on Washington and New York, he had al Qaeda operatives assassinate Ahmed Shah Massoud, the charismatic military leader of the Northern Alliance.

But the jihadists were unprepared for the Americans' ability to combine ground movements by local forces and bombing with precision-guided munitions. The militants were fortunate when they needed it most: At Tora Bora, al Qaeda outbribed local warlords who had been enlisted to close the noose around the terrorist group, and bin Laden, the world's most wanted man, slipped away on foot. The jihadists also surprised U.S. forces in battle during Operation Anaconda, especially at Shah-i-Kot, where al Qaeda outmaneuvered U.S. forces and secured the high ground, pinning down the Americans and surprising a unit of Army Rangers. As one military analyst described it, "The ferocity and capability of the al Qaeda fighters came as a shock to the Army troops." American firepower won out, but the engagement "must be regarded for the Americans as a humbling experience."[4]

Still, neither bin Laden nor his followers expected the Taliban regime to be destroyed with such ease or al Qaeda to be swept so quickly from the field, a fate that occurred in no small measure because the Taliban arrayed themselves in long trenches that made for easy targeting. The defeat devastated radical Islamists. Many of them believe that in order to spread the true faith and retake the Muslim world, they must first control a state, and

Afghanistan was seen as just such a beachhead. The loss was not just a military setback but also a spiritual disaster for those who thought the Afghan theocracy was the starting point from which the dominoes of the apostate regimes would tumble. How could one interpret this event except as an abandonment by God? The Center for Islamic Study and Research, an al Qaeda mouthpiece, admitted this on its Web site: "When retreat followed retreat in Afghanistan . . . despair began to creep among many . . . and feelings of impending defeat and the end of the mujahidin there began to overtake them. During the course of these feelings, mutterings began here and there that the mujahidin had made a mistake in their calculation, and that they were taken by surprise by something they had not expected, and that they had been overhasty, and forced themselves into an unequal conflict."[5]

The historian David Cook has written about how the loss of Afghanistan led many radical Islamists into a period of deep doubt and soul-searching in which they sought scriptural precedents for such setbacks. They looked for accounts of engagements in which the believers were defeated—the Battle of Uhud, which came a year after the heroic experience at Badr and where some Muslim forces deserted, is the outstanding example—and interpreters allied with al Qaeda explained that such reversals were trials designed by God for his faithful. They took refuge in apocalyptic visions in which the believers suffered catastrophes that were a prelude to God's—and their—ultimate triumph. And they emphasized that the destruction in Afghanistan truly did demonstrate the state of war between the West and Islam.[6] But the wounds were nonetheless real and not to be glossed over.

The Fate of the Core

The American invasion of Afghanistan robbed al Qaeda of its sanctuary and put its members on the run. In the course of the fighting, al Qaeda's number-three official, operations chief Abu Hafs al-Masri, also known as Muhammad Atef, was killed by a missile fired from a Predator drone. In the months that followed, the United States scored more significant victories against al Qaeda than anyone in the field of counterterrorism would have imagined after September 11. American intelligence and law enforcement agencies, along with those of other nations, were driven by a common understanding of the terrorist threat that had not existed before 2001 and disrupted numerous plots and captured one major terrorist after another: Ramzi bin al-Shibh, who met with Muhammad Atta in Spain, was captured in Karachi. Ali Qaed Senyan al-Harthi, a high-level al Qaeda official, was killed with five others in a remote area of Yemen by a missile fired from a Predator drone. Abd al-Rahim al-Nashiri, a Saudi who served as al Qaeda's operations chief on the Arabian Peninsula, was apprehended in the Persian Gulf region. Walid Baattash, another operative involved in the World Trade Center and Pentagon attacks, was arrested in Karachi.

The triumphant moment in this campaign, however, arrived on March 1, 2003, when a disheveled Khalid Sheikh Mohammed appeared on television screens and front pages around the world following his predawn arrest in Rawalpindi, Pakistan. The man who had brought the idea of using planes as cruise missiles to bin Laden, "KSM," as he is called, is also the uncle of Ramzi Yousef, who engineered the first bombing of the World Trade Center in 1993. Uncle and nephew had plotted together in 1995 on the Bojinka conspiracy to blow up a dozen 747s over the Pacific. Mohammed had eluded capture for almost a decade.

Al Qaeda has taken a punishing. Yet the true state of the organization remains unclear. Although the Bush administration has spoken of 3,000 terrorists captured or killed, it is not known how many of those were actually terrorists, as opposed to the irregular troops who made up much of al Qaeda's strength in Afghanistan and who were unequipped to operate outside that country as terrorists.[7]

The picture has been further clouded because the Bush administration has repeatedly increased its claims regarding the number of top al Qaeda officials who have been taken out of action. Barton Gellman of the *Washington Post* has observed that when the pace of captures slowed, the administration has still claimed improving results. At the beginning of 2003, top officials said that more than one-third of the most-wanted terrorists had been apprehended or killed. In the closing stages of the 2004 presidential campaign, President Bush claimed that "75 percent of known al Qaeda leaders have been brought to justice." Yet when reporters pressed the White House for documentation to support that number, they were stonewalled.[8] Asked about this figure, senior terrorism analysts from the CIA, the FBI, and the Terrorist Threat Integration Center (which has now been turned into the National Counterterrorism Center) all confess that they have no idea what the basis for the figure is. "It's a White House number," says one analyst, reflecting a common view. The White House has never explained the figure beyond saying that it is based on the number of al Qaeda members in the top echelons of the organization on September 11. The claim is hard to comprehend. No intelligence agency is known to have fully mapped al Qaeda's leadership then or now, and many terrorism analysts would question whether that was even possible or meaningful given the fluidity of the group and its impressive ability to replace its losses by promoting from within.

At least two groups of top al Qaeda managers escaped the fighting in Afghanistan. One centers around Saif al-Adel, a highly skilled former Egyptian army colonel. Together with a small number of others, Adel made it to Iran and has reportedly been living in the southeastern corner of that country. The group's status is puzzling. While Iranian authorities have claimed that these operatives are now under "house arrest," officials within the Bush administration say that the al Qaeda veterans were being used as a bargaining chip. The deal envisioned would have called for Washington to disarm a group of Iranian exiles based in Iraq called the Mujahedin-e Khalq, which opposes the Iranian regime and conducted attacks against it from Iraqi bases during the reign of Saddam Hussein; in return, Iran would hand over Adel and his colleagues. No agreement was ever reached because the Bush administration was riven by disagreements over whether to negotiate with Iran's mullahs. Whether Adel's group is being restrained by Iranian officials in any significant way is difficult to gauge. Saudi counterterrorism officials blame Adel's group for directing attacks by "al Qaeda in the Arabian Peninsula," as the local affiliate calls itself, including the May 2003 bombings in Riyadh that killed thirty people, including eight Americans.[9]

Then there is the top tier of the leadership: Since 9/11, Usama bin Laden and his deputy, Ayman al-Zawahiri, have eluded capture for a period longer than it took the United States to fight World War II. It is not known if they are together, but Pakistani and American experts believe they are somewhere in the "Tribal Areas," the semi-autonomous region along the border with Afghanistan, or the densely wooded, largely roadless areas in Pakistan's far northwest. It is even occasionally suggested that the two men might be in Karachi, Pakistan's most lawless, jihadist-infested city.

Numerous reasons have been adduced for the failure to catch bin Laden and Zawahiri. One explanation is that the hunt for bin Laden after his escape from Tora Bora was so halting that bin Laden and those with him had time to assemble an effective early-warning system that relies on the sympathetic inhabitants of the region and allows the al Qaeda leaders to move to another hideout when word comes of the approach of hostile forces. Another theory is that Pakistani authorities, for all the help they have rendered in the war on terror, are none too eager to deliver up bin Laden because they fear that Washington would soon forget about Pakistani needs, as happened in the early 1990s after the Soviets were driven from Afghanistan. Whatever the case, bin Laden's ability to remain free has enhanced his status. To his followers around the world, he seems to enjoy an otherworldly protection and to have the divine wind at his back. His aura as the emir of the jihad has grown, strengthening his claim to leadership of the Muslim world.

Even so, it is uncertain whether bin Laden and Zawahiri are capable of much operational activity. Most experts believe that the need to attend to their personal security, the remoteness of their hideouts, and the damage done to the rest of the network has meant that the two leaders are constrained from playing the hands-on role that they did before 9/11. But that is not the same as saying that the core of al Qaeda is out of business, as some have suggested. Estimates of the number of operatives at al Qaeda's disposal around the world today vary wildly—the numbers range from a few hundred to many thousands and reflect continuing uncertainties about where al Qaeda leaves off and other organizations begin. Moreover, the total number of al Qaeda operatives at large is only one consideration in evaluating the strength of the group—indeed, it is a mistake to place too much emphasis on numbers when an individual cell, if skilled and uncompromised, can do enormous damage. A hint of that potential surfaced in the summer of 2004, when U.S. officials announced that surveillance material had been found on the computer of an al Qaeda operative in Pakistan, and nine men in Britain were arrested. The targets of the surveillance included the Citigroup Center and the New York Stock Exchange in New York City; the Prudential Financial Center in Newark, New Jersey; and headquarters of the International Monetary Fund and the World Bank in Washington. The information was not new—the actual casing had been done in 2000 and 2001—but it was said to have been recently accessed and to be of unusually high quality. Al Qaeda operatives had apparently gained entrance to at least some of the buildings and had mapped security cameras and traffic patterns. According to one White House official familiar with the material, there was no indication of a live conspiracy to attack the targets, but the episode itself was sufficient to force some government analysts to revise their thinking on the current state of al Qaeda and its capabilities.

Self-Starters

Amid the many al Qaeda–related attacks of the period since 2001, the phenomenon of self-starting terrorists began to appear. As we have seen, the Madrid bombings demonstrate one way that the sparks thrown off by September 11 are catching. Inspired by bin Laden's example and convinced that America is waging a merciless campaign against Islam, Sarhane, Ahmidan, and Lamari followed the jihadist argument to its conclusion.

Madrid was the most destructive but by no means the only example of the new breed of self-starting terrorist cells. It was not even the first: That distinction belongs to the operatives who carried out five bombings in Casablanca on May 16, 2003. These attacks killed forty-five people, including twelve operatives, and injured more than a hundred others. Here, too, the power of al Qaeda's example was evident. The bombings all occurred within thirty minutes, and the terrorists were, unlike in Madrid, on martyrdom missions. The Casablanca crew had not fought in Afghanistan, not had they experienced the kind of character-altering training that alumni of the Afghan camps and other terrorist groups have described. Rather, they were inhabitants of Casablanca's Sidi Moumen slums, members of a group called Salafiya Jihadiya—the Jihad of the Righteous Ancestors.[10] The group, and the network of other North African organizations it was tied in to, had historically singled out Moroccan targets for their occasional and haphazard violence. Now, however, the Far Enemy was in the crosshairs.

This time, however, the terrorists' lack of training showed. The May 2003 attacks, though bloody, were inept, resembling in no way the perfectionism of bin Laden's group. They chose as targets Le Positano, a Jewish-owned Italian restaurant near the Belgian Embassy and frequented by Europeans; a Jewish community building; a Jewish cemetery; a bar called Casa España; and the Kuwaiti-owned Safir Hotel. The bombs were fairly crude devices, explosive-filled backpacks that the individual operatives hand-detonated with plungers. The bombers assigned to attack Le Positano failed to get past the doorman, so they blew themselves up outside, killing a parking lot attendant and a couple of Moroccan policemen stationed outside the Belgian Embassy. Since it was a Friday night, the beginning of the Jewish sabbath, the community building was empty; two bombers detonated their devices outside, killing two more policemen and a night watchman. The cemetery had not been used for Jewish burials in decades, and it too was empty except for three young Moroccans sitting by a fountain and smoking. The terrorists were more successful at the Casa España and the Safir Hotel—they gained entry to the first by slitting the doorman's throat—where most of the casualties occurred. But out of all the blasts, the only Westerners killed were two Frenchmen, two Spaniards, and one Belgian; none of Casablanca's Jews were among the victims. The overwhelming majority of the dead and injured were Moroccan Muslims, marking the operation as a botch.

How much outside guidance and instruction the Casablanca bombers received remains unclear. Al Qaeda operatives from Saudi Arabia have been found in Morocco—in 2002, three were captured with plans to use bomb-packed speedboats to blow up U.S. and NATO ships in the Strait of Gibraltar—and Moroccans have turned up in al Qaeda operations in other countries, including Zacarias Moussaoui, the Frenchman of Moroccan origin arrested in August 2001 because of the suspicions he aroused at a Minnesota flight school. But as one Spanish investigator put it, Casablanca appears to have been "99 percent local."[11]

The fact that the Madrid and Casablanca bombings seem to have been carried out without much outside assistance does not mean other self-starter groups will not find their way to the global jihadist network and receive help from it. Early information about the London Underground bombing of July 2005 underscores this point. It is not clear whether the perpetrators—Mohammad Sidique Khan, Shehzad Tanweer, Hasib Hussein, and Germaine Lindsay—had contacts with radical groups in Britain, but it is certainly possible. The first reports give no suggestion that they were recruited; rather, the indications are that they stepped forward and committed themselves to violence. They may well have sought to pursue their mission as mujahedin by acquiring training in Pakistan, which two or more of them visited in the year before the attacks and where three of the four conspirators' families had originally come from. (The Jamaican-born Germaine Lindsay was a convert to Islam.) This, after all, is similar to what Muhammad Atta and his fellow members in the Hamburg cell that carried out the 9/11 attacks did, though they traveled to bin Laden's camps in Afghanistan. The Pakistan connection illustrates two points about the self-starter phenomenon: First, in an era in which it is relatively easy to travel anywhere, a cell in one country may not be connected to others in the same region but could be linked to radicals on another continent. Second, self-starters do not need to have the independence of the Madrid cell. There is potentially a wide range of relationships with other groups, cells, and networks. There *is* still a network, with multiple byways and channels, and to the extent that the global jihad's new recruits make contact with it, the danger they pose can be enhanced.

Multiple bombings remain one of the most telling signs of allegiance to bin Laden's creed. Another group, also thought to be self-starters, attacked two targets in Egypt's Sinai peninsula in October 2004 nearly simultaneously. Two car bombs partially collapsed the ten-story Hilton Hotel in Taba, while two bomb-laden pickup trucks detonated in a holiday village in nearby Ras a-Satan, killing thirty-four people. Most of the victims were Israeli tourists who had gone to the beach for the Jewish holiday of Succoth. Much remains obscure about the attack, and although Egyptian authorities rounded up hundreds of people for interrogation, little information on the plot has been released to the public. The attacks were the first in Egypt since 1997 and a sobering intimation that radical Islamism could reappear in countries where it had been stamped out and its advocates had been jailed, executed, or driven into exile.

One astonishing aspect of the self-starter phenomenon is that it arises even in countries that have well-established jihadist networks. In Pakistan, authorities report that more than two dozen essentially independent terrorist cells have emerged even though groups such as Lashkar-e-Tayba (LeT) and Harakat ul-Mujahedin (HuM), which have their own training camps and several thousand members, still operate in the open. HuM and LeT, like a number of other radical groups, are believed to still be funded by the Pakistani military's Inter-Services Intelligence (ISI), which supported them to aid the insurgency in Kashmir. With relations somewhat improved with India, and the United States watchful for state-sponsored terror, LeT and HuM have, for now, reduced their activity in Kashmir and across the border in Afghanistan. The new terrorist cells appear to be motivated by a hatred for Islamabad's military regime, which they view as having become a creature of American policy in the aftermath of September 11, and they presumably view the militants of HuM and LeT as sellouts. Following the pattern seen elsewhere, they reportedly formed in the aftermath of a series of high-profile arrests of al Qaeda members in Pakistan, including that of Khalid Sheikh Mohammed in March 2003.

The best known of the new groups illustrates the dimensions of the danger. Called Jundullah, or Army of God, it was founded by Attaur Rehman, a middle-class native of Karachi with a master's degree in statistics who received training as a guerrilla in Afghanistan in the 1990s. He was arrested in June 2004 after an attempted assassination of the Karachi Corps commander, the most senior military officer in the region, which missed its target but left eleven others dead. Jundullah's membership— and, Pakistani officials say, that of other such groups as well—is composed of people just like Attaur Rehman: children of the educated middle class, not the impoverished alumni of madrassas (Islamic religious academies) that most think of as the face of Pakistani extremism. Other operatives who have been arrested include two brothers—one a cardiologist, the other an orthopedic surgeon. The appearance of highly educated, prosperous terrorists such as these is a disturbing development: They are likely to be technically capable and able to design and execute large attacks that could include biological and chemical agents. Like its European and North African cousins, Jundullah has at least partially accepted al Qaeda's focus on the Far Enemy. When Rehman was arrested, the group was preparing an attack against the American consulate in Karachi.[12]

As a class of terrorist groups, the jihadist self-starters pose a further challenge for the intelligence and law enforcement agencies. They are likely to be smaller, comparatively self-contained, and, if well run, more difficult to penetrate than the larger terrorist groups, which are already hard targets. (Some, like the Madrid cell, might be relatively easy to disrupt, because their inexperienced members are less disciplined and less likely to keep their activities secret. But the militants have shown an ability to learn from one another's experiences, and no one should bank on sloppiness.) In addition, when discovered, they may yield little in the way of intelligence if they have few of the links to other radicals that investigators need in order to disrupt other cells and networks—it will all depend on their "connectivity" with other parts of the radical Islamist movement.

The Jihad Comes to Iraq

The global jihad that burst into flames on September 11 would not have died if the United States had never invaded Iraq, but the future of the threat would look far less daunting. The full effects of the decision to go to war in Iraq will not be known for years. But it is already clear that America's actions have dramatically reshaped and energized the jihad in ways that have surprised even those who warned of the consequences of invasion.[13]

The foremost effect of the invasion was inadvertently to affirm the jihadist argument. The conflict between radical Islam and the West—like all ideological struggles—is ultimately about competing stories and about the reaction of an audience whose sympathies are up for grabs. In this case, the audience is the global community of Muslims. Many, and probably the vast majority of Muslims, will never be persuaded to embrace a worldview that has violence at its core. But tiny differences at the margins of a community of 1.2 billion people can make a profound difference in the terrorist threat. And even if most Muslims reject the radicals' call to arms, they may take to heart arguments about the intentions of America and the West in ways that will further poison relations between Muslims and non-Muslims for years to come.

The opposing stories can be crudely summarized: America portrays it-self as a benign and tolerant force that, with its Western partners, holds the keys to modernization, progress, and prosperity for the Muslim world. Radical Islamists declare that the universe is governed by a war between Is-lam and World Infidelity, which comes as a violent intruder into the realm of Islam wearing different masks—secularism, Zionism, capitalism, global-ization. World Infidelity, they argue, is determined to occupy Muslim lands, usurp Muslims' wealth, and destroy Islam. So much was evident already in the Quran's account of the trials of the Prophet's fledgling community in the seventh century, and the pattern was recapitulated through centuries of warfare between Islam and Christendom, from the Crusades to the battles of Lepanto (1571) and Vienna (1683) to the collapse of the Ottoman Empire after World War I. Islamists tell the history of the past century as a relentless effort to destroy the unity of the Muslim world, first by drawing the borders of the Middle East in a way that divided the Ottomans' Arab lands into a patchwork of phony states that were then handed over for the European powers to rule. The next affront was the creation of Israel in 1948, which is seen as an alien imposition, a spike driven into the heart of Islam. The de-cades since are portrayed as an extension of that effort to divide, subjugate, and destroy the realm of Islam.

These injuries inflicted on the community of believers are felt to have caused more than just geopolitical weakness; they have also frustrated Muslims in their effort to carry out the task God gave them of spreading the faith and bringing enlightenment to the nations. If the world turns to Islam—as Muslims believe it must—then justice and equality, core values of the religion, will reign, and the global order will be set aright.

That sense of exceptionalism and global mission finds its mirror reflec-tion in the self-image of many Americans. Most Americans sincerely be-lieve that the U.S. armed forces entered Iraq with benign, even generous, intent and that the invasion would eventually be seen in that light. Of course there were hard security concerns: Saddam Hussein had commit-ted aggression against two neighboring states, threatened Israel, spon-sored terror, and produced weapons of mass destruction. But he had also treated his own people with extraordinary viciousness, and once America removed him from power, the road would be clear for the emergence of a new and free Iraq. This would be a liberation—the latest in a series of beneficent interventions by the United States to save Muslim lives that included the liberation of Kuwait and the defense of Saudi Arabia in 1990–91, the humanitarian mission to Somalia in 1992–93, and the military actions to protect Muslims in Bosnia and Kosovo in 1995–99.

But radical Islamists had interpreted these events differently: They viewed Operation Desert Storm as an excuse for America to occupy and defile the holy soil of Saudi Arabia; the sanctions that were placed on Iraq afterward, which they blamed for widespread malnutrition and higher child mortality, represented another cunning effort to harm Muslims. The Somalia deployment was depicted as a prelude to the destruction of the Islamist regime then in power in Sudan—where bin Laden and his followers then enjoyed safe haven—and it was only thwarted by al Qaeda's assistance to the Somali warlords. The wars in the Balkans were seen as American stratagems to kill Bosnian and Kosovar Muslims. For years, the militants had made these arguments and told this story of ceaseless depredations by America. Inevitably, any U.S. move on Iraq was bound to be taken as the most dramatic confirmation of their narrative and, given the low level of trust for the United States in the Muslim world, an unparalleled opportunity for the Islamists to win converts to their cause.

Thus bin Laden would declare in February 2003, "We are following up with great interest and extreme concern the crusaders' preparations for war to occupy a former capital of Islam, loot Muslims' wealth, and install an agent government, which would be a satellite for its masters in Washington and Tel Aviv. . . . Needless to say, this crusade war is primarily targeted against the people of Islam."[14] Ayman al-Zawahiri likewise insisted in his own audio message on the eve of the invasion that "after dividing Iraq, Saudi Arabia, Iran, Syria, and Pakistan will come next. They would leave around Israel only dismembered semi-states that are subservient to the United States and Israel. O Muslims, these are the facts that have been made clear to you."[15]

History's Opportunity

Every jihadist statement is woven on this framework of surpassing grievance. But the flip side of the rhetoric of oppression is the chance for heroic opposition. In the 1998 fatwa that has become the most famous of jihadist texts, bin Laden declared, "The ruling to kill the Americans and their allies—civilians and military—is an individual duty for every Muslim who can do it in any country in which it is possible to do it, in order to liberate the al-Aqsa Mosque and the holy mosque [Mecca] from their grip, and in order for their armies to move out of all the lands of Islam, defeated and unable to threaten any Muslim. This is in accordance with the words of Almighty Allah."[16] By invading Iraq, the United States provided the jihadists with the ideal opportunity to fulfill their obligations and drive an occupying army out of the lands of Islam. There would be roughly 150,000 Americans spread thinly over a wide-open country. This was an entirely different picture from the U.S. deployment in Saudi Arabia, where just 5,000 troops were stationed, most of them in remote desert camps where ordinary Saudis would never see them.

From the perspective of the jihadists, the targets were being delivered for the killing. The American occupation of Iraq gave the radicals an unprecedented chance, in bin Laden's words, to help "establish the rule of God on earth."[17] They have been making the most of it through the insurgency, turning Iraq into an unrivaled theater of inspiration for the jihadist drama of faith.

The Iraqi insurgency puzzles many people. In May 2005, James Bennet of the *New York Times* observed, "The insurgents in Iraq are showing little interest in winning hearts and minds among the majority of Iraqis, in building international legitimacy, or in articulating a governing program or even a unified ideology or cause beyond expelling the Americans. . . . This surge in the killing of civilians reflects how mysterious the long-term strategy remains."[18] But the failure is one of American comprehension, not insurgent strategy. The jihadists have been clear about their simple goals: Kill Americans, kill any foreigners allied or supporting them, kill Iraqis working with the Americans, and ensure that the American project of reconstructing Iraq fails. Over time, as U.S. forces became harder to hit, the militants have shifted their efforts from targeting Americans to targeting the new Iraqi forces—"cutting out the middleman," as Bennet put it—but they were making startling headway just the same.[19]

What matters for the jihadists is to stick with their narrative, and the presence of Americans and their supporters from other countries requires

that the radicals put up a relentless armed opposition. The desired outcomes are driving American forces out of Iraq, preventing the emergence
of a moderate, Western-oriented government, and, possibly, igniting a
civil war between Sunnis and the majority Shiites, who are having their
first taste of power in Iraqi history. Though the jihadists are not the only
ones in the insurgency—they are joined by Sunni nationalists, former
Baathists, and more moderate Islamists—their maximalist stance has
strongly influenced the course of those who are violently opposing the
United States and the new Iraqi government.

The radical Islamists' prominence in the insurgency may owe in part to
their early start. Before the U.S. invasion, much was made of the presence
in Iraq of the Jordanian jihadist Abu Musab al-Zarqawi—Secretary of
State Colin Powell and others pointed to Zarqawi as evidence of cooperation between al Qaeda and the regime of Saddam Hussein.[20] That story
was later undercut by the CIA, which concluded that there was little evidence of a relationship between the two men.[21] Moreover, intelligence officials from several Western services privately say that until recently,
Zarqawi was more of a rival to bin Laden than anything else, an assessment that American officials now endorse. And as a former military officer
who served as one of the Pentagon's top intelligence officials now notes, it
appears that Zarqawi was in Iraq assembling a force to attack U.S. in-
vaders. "One thing we didn't read right," he says, "was Zarqawi being in the
country before the fight." The Jordanian was traveling the length and
width of Iraq, and "the reporting I was reading at the time was
consistent—he was going to be there fighting Americans once we got
there." This former officer admits, "We knew he was a big guy" in the jihadist world, but no one believed that the radicals would get much of a
foothold in Iraq, which was considered to be too secularized, a "country of
accountants" as some said before the war. "In terms of predicting a jihadist
insurgency, we flat out missed that," he adds. "We thought it would be a
Baathist/Sunni [nationalist] insurgency that would be easily contained."

As the violence has engulfed Iraq, the jihadists have scored impressively.
It is impossible to provide an accurate breakdown of those killed by jihadists as opposed to those slain by other insurgents, and the composition
of the insurgency has been frustratingly opaque for U.S. intelligence analysts. According to one British analyst, 60 percent of all the attacks carried

out by the insurgency are committed by former members of the Iraqi security services, yet it is also clear that not all attacks are equal, and the major vehicle bombs, for example, have had an outsized impact.[22] In any
case, from the jihadists' perspective, too-sharp distinctions are beside the
point. If their success is measured by the number of dead Americans, then
they could count in July 2005 more than 1,600 GIs and roughly 100 contractors killed since the end of "major combat operations" on May 1, 2003.
That is, of course, more than half as many Americans as perished on September 11, 2001. They might also argue that killing a U.S. soldier has a
greater value since, in their view, no true Muslim could have qualms about
killing an infidel combatant, though some feel uneasy about killing noncombatants. In addition to those deaths, the jihadists can claim 93 British
troop deaths, 101 fatalities from other coalition partners, and more than
7,000 soldiers wounded so badly they could not return to duty.[23]

Just as radical Islamist grievances must be constantly aired to advance
the argument, so must their accounts of valor in battle be broadcast to
demonstrate their virtue. Thus, the jihadist organizations incessantly post
claims of responsibility on the Internet, often with video files showing
their attacks—sometimes before U.S. military authorities make any statement about an engagement. For the fighters, every individual kill, every
blast-battered Humvee or downed helicopter, is a boast and a confirmation of their resolve to stand up to America.

Targeting Americans may be their highest goal, but the U.S. effort to reconstruct Iraq and install a working democracy has given the insurgents a
myriad of other targets worth their firepower. It is impossible to present a
full record of the violence. U.S. authorities tally only their own casualties,
the new Iraqi government makes infrequent estimates, and much goes un-
reported entirely, according to Americans on the ground in Iraq. But just a
few examples suffice: More than 2,600 Iraqi policemen were killed in the
insurgency, more than half that number in the first six and a half months
of 2005.[24] The lower-end estimates for the number of civilian Iraqi deaths
since the American invasion—which include only confirmed civilian
deaths—are in the vicinity of 24,000, or more than one-tenth of 1 percent
of the population, and in 2005, the monthly death rate was rising.[25] If
America were to sustain comparable losses, total deaths would be approximately a quarter of a million. A more controversial estimate was made by

distinguished public health scholars from Johns Hopkins University, who used statistical sampling techniques. Their work suggested that 98,000 more deaths occurred between March 2003 and September 2004 than in a comparable prewar period. To ensure a conservative result, they excluded data from Fallujah, which saw some of the worst fighting during this period.[26]

Other indicators fill out the picture: Beginning in June 2003, insurgents in Iraq began targeting the country's oil and gas pipelines as part of their effort to undermine the reconstruction effort, which was essential for building acceptance for the American-led occupation. The attacks since then have been unrelenting. By mid-July 2005, there had been almost 250 recorded attacks.[27] Thus, despite $2 billion in American investment, Iraq's oil production hovers around 2 million barrels a day, half a million barrels below prewar levels.[28] According to Gal Luft of the Institute of the Analysis of Global Security, the sabotage has cost Iraq more than $10 billion, or more than 50 percent of its total 2004 oil revenue.[29] The insurgents have reveled in their successes, publishing pipeline maps on the Internet and urging all mujahedin to join in the destruction. Similarly, although the United States has spent at least $1.2 billion to improve Iraqi electrical production, the insurgency has repeatedly attacked the power infrastructure, and the national grid puts out on average only 4,000 to 4,200 megawatts a day, still below the prewar level of 4,400 megawatts.[30] For a group determined to depict America as a predator and to undermine its credibility with ordinary people, this disruption of basic services has a double effect: Not only are Iraqis enduring hardship because of the U.S. occupation, they are also prodded to wonder how a military that could destroy Saddam's forces so rapidly could fail to turn the lights on. Of course, the implication is that the Americans don't want Iraqi lights on.

Perhaps not surprisingly, jihadists who were downcast and perplexed in 2002 about the rapid defeat of the Taliban now feel exuberant about their accomplishments in Iraq. A 2004 article in al Qaeda's *Voice of Jihad,* an online magazine, makes the case that the United States has a greater strategic mess on its hands in Afghanistan and Iraq than the Soviet Union did in Afghanistan in the 1980s. The author describes how America has stumbled badly by getting itself mired in two guerrilla wars at once and argues that U.S. forces are now "merely trying to 'prove their presence'—

for all practical purposes, they have left the war." Zarqawi described things in a similar way. "There is no doubt that the Americans' losses are very heavy because they are deployed across a wide area and among the people and because it is easy to procure weapons," he wrote in a communiqué to his followers that was posted on several radical Web sites. "All of which makes them easy and mouthwatering targets for the believers." Among the recurrent motifs on the Web are that Iraq will be for America what Afghanistan was for the Soviet Union. "We believe these infidels have lost their minds," was the analysis on a site called Jamaat ud-Daawa, which is run out of Pakistan. "They do not know what they are doing. They keep on repeating the same mistake." And, naturally, the insurgency is credited with foiling America's worst designs. "If there was no jihad, Paul Bremer would have left with $20 trillion instead of $20 billion," one Web site declared, referring to an amount that the Arabic media had said was the amount of lost oil revenue during the occupation.[31]

This is not just the bluster of the hard core. On jihadist message boards, elation has been in evidence. One writer in the fall of 2004 saw events in Iraq bringing dramatic changes to the Muslim world. "Al-Qaeda," he wrote, has "gained a new land: The Country of Two Rivers [Iraq]. The distances separating the black banners [of al Qaeda in Iraq] and Jerusalem became shorter." This writer saw age-old rifts in the jihadist world, and in the Muslim world more broadly, healing. "The Jihad in the world has united under the banner of al-Qaeda: Although the names have not been unified, the thoughts [ideologies] have come close enough to the degree of unification. This was noticed in Chechnya, Algeria, Kashmir, Iraq, and Allah willing, in Palestine."[32]

One question often asked about the insurgency in Iraq is how much of a role foreign jihadists are playing. The answer should give some sense of the temperature of the global jihad, showing how militants have been seized by events in Iraq and how much of a threat they pose within the country. Certainty on the matter has been difficult because of a lack of good evidence. Only a small number of foreign insurgents are ever captured, and after a suicide attack it is difficult to tell an Iraqi limb from a foreign one. U.S. military spokesmen have usually provided low estimates, suggesting at times that fewer than 1,000 foreign fighters had come into the country. By contrast, in September 2004, interim Prime Minister Iyad

Allawi (who, it is true, had an interest in magnifying the size of the threat) exclaimed that "foreign terrorists are still pouring in."[33] In one interview, he estimated that foreign fighters constituted 30 percent of insurgent forces.[34] Fragmentary reporting from many countries suggests that there is a growing flow of young men toward Iraq, and in May 2005 the London-based newspaper *Al Hayat* put the number of Saudis who have gone to fight—widely agreed to be the largest group—at more than 2,500.[35] According to officials in the intelligence community, foreigners continued to make up by far the largest group of suicide bombers in Iraq through the middle of the year. Roughly 400 suicide bombings have been carried out in Iraq since the U.S. invasion in 2003. The number of such attacks has also been skyrocketing: In April 2005 alone, there were sixty-nine suicide operations, more than in the entire year preceding the June 2004 transfer of sovereignty to the Iraqis.[36] In May 2005, there were an estimated ninety suicide bombings—nearly as many as the Israeli government has documented in the conflict with the Palestinians since 1993.[37] The figure indicates how the nature of the struggle is becoming more jihadist with each passing month.

It is also clear that the large majority of fighters coming into Iraq are not the hardened warriors of Afghanistan or even the veterans of terrorist groups in other countries. Instead, these young men are new recruits to the global jihad who have been drawn to Iraq by the fighting underway there. According to a study by the Israeli scholar Reuven Paz, who analyzed the biographies of 154 foreigners who died in Iraq, "The vast majority of [non-Iraqi] Arabs killed in Iraq have never taken part in any terrorist activity prior to their arrival in Iraq."[38] In other words, this is a new generation of fighters who have taken up arms because of the developments of their time—which they consider to be part of a war on Islam, as Paz points out—not individuals acting on the basis of a lifelong commitment to a cause. A study that the young Saudi scholar Nawaf Obaid has made for the Center for Strategic and International Studies indicates that most Saudis who have gone to Iraq to fight were moved to embrace radicalism by the events taking place in the country next door. Saudi authorities gave Obaid access to interrogation material and other information relating to nearly 300 Saudis captured in Iraq and some three dozen others who were killed in suicide attacks. What he found was that "the largest group is young kids who saw the images [of the war] on TV and are reading the stuff on the Internet. Or they see the name of a cousin on the list or a guy who belongs to their tribe, and they feel a responsibility to go."[39]

While Iraq's appeal to foreign jihadists is a major aspect of the insurgency, an equally important story has been the emergence of a large indigenous Iraqi jihadist movement. Although the face of the insurgency may belong to Abu Musab al-Zarqawi, most of the fighters are native Iraqis. Alongside Zarqawi's "al Qaeda in the Land of Two Rivers," two of the best known and most active insurgent groups are Ansar al-Sunna and the Islamic Army of Iraq, both of which are homegrown.[40] Even in the category of suicide bombings, the Iraqis are catching up, according to U.S. military and intelligence officials.[41]

Where did they all come from? It is fair to say that most of these fighters did not become radicalized overnight. Although much has been made of U.S. intelligence failures regarding weapons of mass destruction, the lack of any sense of the strength of radical Islamist sentiment in the country may yet be deemed an error of the same magnitude. The "country of accountants" turned out not to be.

Instead, elements of the Sunni population of Iraq had been undergoing something like the Islamization that has swept the rest of the Arab world in recent years. Many of the audiocassettes of radical preachers that have circulated through the Arabic-speaking world have long been available in Iraq. Much as the autocrats of the Arab world have used Islam in the past to burnish their credentials or create a hedge against domestic opponents, Saddam and his Baath Party began a "Faith Campaign" in 1993. As Amatzia Baram, one of the world's leading experts on Iraq, has written, this happened because of two developments: "First, the [Baath] Party lost much of its confidence in its own ideology; and second, party and regime sensed that a new zeitgeist was filling the horizon—Islam. Saddam knew that large segments of the Iraqi public were 'returning' to religion. As a result, he decided to jump on the bandwagon."[42] Although most of those who became more religious did not espouse radical views, a minority did. Despite its secularist roots, the regime allowed these groups to exist because they were anti-Saudi and thus politically useful for Saddam.[43]

Exactly what portion of the Iraqi Islamists now fighting in the insurgency are true jihadists, ready to wage a global war, is impossible to know.

But it seems a safe bet that even if the large majority of Sunnis decide that their future lies with a united democratic Iraq, it will be many years before the jihadist element in the country can be controlled and wiped out. Anbar Province, the vast western part of the country that is dominated by Sunnis and that has often been a no-go zone for Coalition forces, will likely be a jihadist enclave for a long time to come. The reasons are simple: The cities and towns of Anbar, some of which have been ruled by Taliban-like councils since the American invasion, have been deeply hostile to American forces and the new authorities in Baghdad. Voting participation in the January 2005 elections ran at 2 percent, and while that is not an ideal indicator of support for the new Baghdad regime—it is impossible to tell how many stayed away from the polls because of genuine opposition and how many because of intimidation—it still tells a vivid story about attitudes in the province. U.S. forces have found that they can root out the insurgents with costly, bloody military operations, but the militants are soon back in town—as they were in Fallujah and Ramadi. Indeed, reports in the summer of 2005 suggest that the insurgency had gained so much ground in Anbar that the rebels were becoming more organized. As one analyst wrote in July, "The most ominous implication of this revolves around the very real possibility of insurgents cohering into organized guerrilla formations and possibly inflicting serious casualties on the U.S. military in Iraq."[44]

Expelling the terrorists for good will require a tough and proficient intelligence service, which is necessary to penetrate the radicals' operations, identify their leaders, and arrest or kill them. Reportedly, some Iraqi leaders have complained that today's Iraqi intelligence service is heavily dependent on the assistance of the CIA.[45] It could take five years or longer before the service is up to the task of confronting insurgents in Anbar Province, or longer still if its members remain so overwhelmingly Shiite and Kurdish that they lack the roots in the region or the tribal connections necessary to work effectively. In the meantime, Iraqi security forces have made ample use of torture, extrajudicial murder, and lesser forms of abuse in dealing with the Sunni resistance or individuals rounded up in connection with the insurgency. These measures could well alienate as many Sunnis as they succeed in taking off the street.[46] Moreover, the terrorists are not so foolish that they will make themselves targets for air strikes by opening up large training camps with neat rows of tents, obstacle courses, firing ranges, and closed road tracks for evasive driving practice. Instead, they can plan operations from inside apartments and houses.

Anbar will likely be the last part of the country brought under central control, and that bodes ill for all of Iraq. Many of the suicide attacks in Baghdad are carried out by operatives who drive their explosive-laden vehicles in from Anbar.[47] The question will be whether its jihadists will continue to focus on targeting the new Iraqi regime and its supporters or whether militants with more global ambitions will make use of the sanctuary Anbar offers to plan operations farther afield. Neither possibility is encouraging.[48]

Spoils of War

Iraq has given violent Islamists more than an arena in which to dramatize their cause and bravery: It has provided them with a country-sized training ground and a laboratory for innovating the tactics and operations of the future. The loss of Afghanistan and its camps hurt the jihadists badly, but the on-the-job training they have received in Iraq has more than made up for that setback.[49]

The distinguished military analyst Anthony Cordesman recently assessed the Iraqi insurgency and listed thirty-two "major adaptations that insurgents and terrorists in Iraq made in terms of tactics and methods of attack."[50] They include using "mixed attacks" in which one explosive device is set off and then, when rescue personnel or military forces are dispatched, other explosives are detonated; complex ambushes using small arms, automatic weapons, and rocket-propelled grenades; "swarming" techniques in urban and road ambushes; improved sniper skills; better surveillance; and a wide array of better techniques for evading U.S. signals and human intelligence. They have also become proficient at penetrating the young Iraqi military, police, and intelligence services. These improvements could not be made sitting in Afghanistan, and they will be useful to the current generation of jihadists and their followers for a long time to come.

Just how fast the insurgents have learned is clear from advances in their

bomb making. According to Roger Davies, a former British military officer who ran his country's bomb unit in Northern Ireland and now con-
sults with several U.S. agencies, there is a progression in the type of
improvised explosive devices that show up in areas of terrorist activities. It
begins with simple wire-detonated devices and then develops through different kinds of radio-activated models to "off-route projectiles" (rockets
and propelled grenades that are fired at vehicles from a distance), and on
to weapons with more complicated fusing. A process of evolution occurs
when U.S. or Iraqi government forces deploy countermeasures against the
insurgents' bombs, and the insurgents improvise to overcome those
countermeasures. Once the Coalition forces in Iraq started using jammer
technology to defeat one class of radio-controlled bombs, the insurgents
developed another kind. In late spring and summer of 2005, the insurgents
began using weapons called Explosively Formed Projectiles that, as Davies
puts it, "have been done before but only in interesting places—the Gaza
Strip and southern Lebanon." These bombs are set back from the road
and remotely triggered. They will penetrate Humvees, Bradley Fighting
Vehicles, and even tanks. These innovations are taking their toll. In June
2005, more U.S. troops were killed by improvised explosive devices—
thirty-six—than in any previous month. In addition, a class of Iraqi mid-
dlemen has now emerged to sell improvised explosive devices to whoever
will buy them—Shiite radicals, Baathists, Iraqi Sunnis, foreign jihadists.[51]

There has been an enormous amount of bombing in Iraq, and the consequence, in Davies' view, is that terrorist capabilities have developed
there with unprecedented speed. Technical strides that required eight
years in southern Lebanon, six years in Chechnya, and three years in Gaza
have been achieved in just twelve months—the jihadists have mastered the
full repertoire. "Iraq is a melting pot for terrorists," Davies says. "Much of
what they can do is because there has been a pooling of experience of
fighters from Afghanistan, Chechnya and the Middle East."

The insurgency in Iraq is producing not only the operatives for the
next decade of terror, it is also sorting out the leaders. Armies have long
known that the best method for producing field commanders is to fight
wars. Likewise for the jihadists, there is no substitute for operational activity, which Iraq has in unrivaled plenitude.

The emergence of Abu Musab al-Zarqawi proves the point. If bin

Laden is the Robin Hood of jihad, Zarqawi has been its Horatio Alger, and Iraq his field of dreams. The son of a Jordanian army officer, Zarqawi had a history of drinking and drug abuse when he came under the influence of a Jordanian radical imam, Abu Muhammad al-Maqdisi. He gravitated to Pakistan and Afghanistan in the early 1990s but missed most of the fighting. Together with Maqdisi, he hoped to bring the jihad to Jordan, but he was caught in 1994 with an arms cache in his house and spent the rest of the decade in jail. After being released in the amnesty granted after the death of King Hussein in 1999, he returned to Afghanistan with the hope of training mujahedin for action in Jordan. Zarqawi met bin Laden and, with his assistance, established a training camp and started running terrorist operations through his Tawhid w'al Jihad (monotheism and jihad) network. That did not mean that the two men saw the Islamist struggle in exactly the same way: Although both bin Laden and Zarqawi place the same emphasis on jihad as a central obligation of Muslim men, Zarqawi has been more interested in focusing his efforts on the Middle East while bin Laden sought a more global campaign.

When the Taliban was toppled, Zarqawi relocated to the Kurdish enclave in northern Iraq, a zone that was independent of Baghdad's control, and joined up with the radical Islamist Ansar al-Islam group.[52] By this time, he was well known to American intelligence, and he would later be identified as the architect of the assassination of American diplomat Lawrence Foley in Amman in October 2002. He appears to have gotten such a fast start in Iraq after the American invasion that it may have even surprised bin Laden; reports are entirely plausible that the al Qaeda leader wanted someone else to run jihadist operations in Iraq and even tried to send a replacement for Zarqawi.[53]

Ultimately, the two men found it advantageous to join forces. For Zarqawi, getting the imprimatur of the emir of jihad added to his stature, and bin Laden, who was holed up somewhere on the Pakistan-Afghan border while the action was in Iraq, was able to show he was engaged in the insurgency. Hence, in 2004, Zarqawi's Tawhid w'al Jihad became "al Qaeda in the Land of Two Rivers." An additional concern for bin Laden, according to one senior member of the intelligence community, was financial. "Among the financiers in Saudi Arabia, there has been a reluctance to give to the core al Qaeda," this official said, because it does not seem to be able to mount significant operations. "They are more inclined to give to Zar-qawi now, and that [redistributing funds to bin Laden] might have been a piece of the merger." It remains unclear how much of a "merger" this really is. "There are still difficulties over money," the official adds, "and it's un-clear how closely they're cooperating."

In Iraq, Zarqawi has distinguished himself as a terrorist planner and implementer of genius, and his fingerprints are on many of the most spec-tacular incidents, including the destruction of the UN headquarters in Au-gust 2003, which killed senior diplomat Sergio Vieira de Mello and drove most UN personnel out of the country, and the massive vehicle bombs in the Shiite shrine cities of Karbala and Najaf and at the Jordanian Embassy in Baghdad. Zarqawi's visceral hatred of Shiites—in a letter captured by Coalition forces, he wrote that they are "a greater danger and their harm more destructive to the nation than that of the Americans" and called them "the most cowardly people God has created"—is representative of a large segment of the jihadist movement. (Bin Laden, while hardly ecu-menical, at least says publicly that the struggle is open to all good Mus-lims.) His eagerness to slaughter Shiites, who constitute the majority of the population in Iraq, makes him perfectly suited for the insurgency. As he has made clear in his writings, a key part of his strategy is to inflict so much harm on the Shiites that they fight back against the Sunnis.[54] This would lead either to the United States intervening against the Shiites or withdrawing from a hopeless civil war, in a replay of the events in Leba-non in the early 1980s. While the Shiites have shown remarkable en-durance throughout the jihadist attacks, in the summer of 2005 the violence was turning even more sectarian as killings of Shiite and Sunni clerics increased. To a disturbing degree, Zarqawi has been advancing his strategy toward a civil war, which might well destabilize the surrounding region. Shiite Iran appears to be involving itself more deeply in Iraqi af-fairs, and the prospect of unrest among Shiites in the Eastern Province of Saudi Arabia and in the Gulf state of Bahrain, while not imminent, is nonetheless all too real.

Zarqawi's notoriety has probably earned him credit for some attacks that were not his, just as a number of conspiracies in Europe have been falsely attributed to him. But his capabilities speak for themselves. Already, there have been a number of arrests in Germany and Spain of operatives who were said to belong to Zarqawi's network, and European intelligence services are watching anxiously for more signs of his expanding operations.

Zarqawi's potential as a threat outside the war zone is already considered significant and growing. Undoubtedly, now, if the U.S. government had the choice of removing either Zarqawi or bin Laden's deputy Ayman al-Zawahiri, Zarqawi would be the more desirable target. It is telling that bin Laden reportedly asked the Jordanian in March 2005 to attack the United States.[55] It suggests that bin Laden believes that al Qaeda may be incapable of doing so anytime soon and that Zarqawi has or could develop the resources to do so. For the time being, American counterterrorism experts rate such an attack as unlikely. "Whatever was suggested is probably not very far along," says one government expert. "He [Zarqawi] will want to attack the U.S. because that is the gold standard, but he's got his plate full in Iraq." Zarqawi would have developed into a formidable threat whether there was a war in Iraq or not. But Iraq provided him with a unique opportunity to build networks, acquire allegiances, innovate tactics, and, it appears, become bin Laden's heir apparent.

The invasion of Iraq has provided the ideological fuel and the weaponry for a vastly expanded terrorist campaign. In October 2004, the *New York Times* reported that 380 tons of the high explosives HMX and RDX had disappeared from an Iraqi weapons site called al Qaqaa, which had been identified as a possible location for weapons of mass destruction. With the U.S. presidential election in its closing days, the news caused a stir, and for good reason: HMX can be used as a detonator for a nuclear weapon. RDX was the type of explosive used in the bombing of the U.S.S. *Cole*—600 pounds of the material came close to sinking the destroyer. A few simple calculations suggest that the amount lifted from al Qaqaa would be enough to sink the entire U.S. Navy twice over.

The discussion about the missing explosives turned into a proxy debate within the presidential campaign over the management of the war effort, but the focus on the 380 tons distorted the discussion. Military analysts knew before the war that Saddam Hussein had amassed an enormous stockpile of conventional military weaponry. Few, though, were prepared for what they found after the Baathist regime was toppled. David Kay, who led the Iraq Survey Group's effort to locate weapons of mass destruction, noted in his report of October 2003 "the almost unbelievable scale of Iraq's conventional weapons armory. . . . For example, there are approximately 130 known Iraqi Ammunition Storage Points (ASP), many of which exceed 50 square miles in size and hold an estimated 600,000 tons of artillery shells, rockets, aviation bombs and other ordnance. Of these 130 ASPs, approximately 120 still remain unexamined."[56] The unsecured storage points, which were bigger than towns, offered enough weaponry to conduct an insurgency or an international terrorist campaign for years, if not decades. "There is an almost unlimited number of artillery rounds in an almost unlimited number of places," says Roger Davies, the British bomb expert. "It would be impossible to control the sites." Artillery rounds have been the key component for improvised explosive devices used in Iraq. While they are unlikely to be transported to Europe or the United States, they could be smuggled into neighboring countries. On the other hand, explosives like RDX and HMX might be moved longer distances, and no one can say if the al Qaqaa stocks were much or all of what Iraq had.

Right now, jihadists are concentrating their efforts on Iraq. But radical message boards regularly light up with discussions of the need to strike elsewhere to show America that it is fighting a global war. If even the smallest fraction of these weapons is transferred out of Iraq—and it is likely that some movement has already occurred—the consequences could be grim.

Spillover

Though no one knows how many foreign fighters have migrated to Iraq, it is also true that no one is looking forward to any of them coming home. The backbone of al Qaeda and the network it created was composed of veterans of the fighting in Afghanistan in the 1980s and 1990s, who turned up in countries around the world—from Spain, where some belonged to the circle of Abu Dahdah, to Indonesia, where they formed the nucleus of Jemaah Islamiya, the group responsible for the bombings in Bali and Jakarta. Arab regimes tended to recognize the threat posed by the veterans of Afghanistan, and they often imprisoned them or harassed them until they fled and settled in the more hospitable West. While the insurgency in Iraq is far from over, intelligence and law enforcement officials around the world are already bracing for the jihadists' return. In France and Germany, authorities have been monitoring the Muslim communities, trying to keep track of those who depart for Iraq and working especially hard to keep tabs on the few who have returned thus far. The U.S. intelligence community has set as one of its top priorities the effort to plan for the spread of the veterans and deter future terrorist violence.

The problem may still be around the corner for Europe and the United States, the impact of the insurgency is already being felt among Iraq's neighbors. Syria, which has acted as a gateway for foreign fighters, is witnessing its own Islamist revival. A new online magazine, *Message of the Mujahidin,* dedicated to promoting radical Islam and opposition to what it calls the "Christian Baathist" regime of Bashar al-Assad, appeared in December 2004. Islamist preachers have become increasingly emboldened and are establishing a higher profile—some, in fact, have taken the opportunity of the fall of Saddam to increase sales of their audiocassettes in Iraq. For a country that within living memory massacred Islamists by the thousands—as the longtime strongman Hafez al-Assad, Bashar's father, did in 1982—this is a striking development.

Antipathy to the U.S. occupation is also providing radicals throughout the Gulf region with new energy, and it appears that the contents of the Iraqi cauldron are spilling over. In Saudi Arabia, for example, al Qaeda affiliates began carrying out attacks against foreigners in 2003. A car bomb attack in early 2004 against the Interior Ministry, home of the kingdom's top counterterrorism officials, also indicated that the radicals were learning new tricks from the insurgency next door. According to Roger Davies, Saudi jihadists have relied on charges made of ammonium nitrate and aluminum in the past. This time, they used artillery shells, just as insurgents in Iraq do. "A lot of incidents in Saudi Arabia—and there have been more than are reported—are being blamed on terrorists who have gained experience in Iraq," he says.

Another country to feel the impact of the fighting is Kuwait, which in the past had largely been spared from Islamist violence. In early 2005, police raids led to five gun battles with radicals who were planning attacks; eight suspected terrorists were killed and more than thirty were arrested.[57]

In another crackdown, eight members of the military were arrested, including several officers, for planning attacks on U.S. forces in Kuwait.[58] To Davies, the connection is clear: "It has also been reported that Iraqi-type devices are showing up in Kuwait, where there have been a number of attempted terrorist attacks, and we've just seen the first VBIED [vehicle borne improvised explosive device] in Qatar, where we've never seen one before." The attack in Qatar on March 19, 2005, which killed one Briton, occurred outside a theater where Shakespeare's *Twelfth Night* was being staged for a mostly Western audience. The attacker was an Egyptian employee of the state-run Qatar Petroleum.

Bombs are one sign of the spread of jihadist violence; innovations in targeting provide another. One illustration is the growing desire to disrupt the flow of oil from the Gulf region. Before September 11, when jihadists spoke about oil, it was to complain about how the Saudi royal family and other leaders of oil-rich Arab nations were squandering the patrimony of the Islamic people, selling it cheaply to the West and pocketing the profits. Out of an apparent concern about harming the oil infrastructure, bin Laden never called for attacks on oil facilities.

All that changed after the attacks on Washington and New York. On October 6, 2002, Yemeni operatives affiliated with al Qaeda drove a boat bomb alongside the French supertanker *Limburg*, which was carrying almost 400,000 barrels of oil off the coast of Aden. The attack killed one sailor but failed to sink the ship or start the inferno the terrorists hoped for. It seems likely that in the aftermath of the September 11 attacks and all the discussion of the economic harm it caused, al Qaeda had overcome its previous reluctance because of its desire to continue targeting the economies of the West.

With the insurgency's determined effort to blow up pipelines in Iraq and cripple the country's economy, the interest in targeting oil facilities elsewhere has grown. In May 2004, terrorists stormed the offices of a multinational oil contractor in the Saudi port city of Yanbu, killing six Westerners and a Saudi. On May 29 came an attack against an oil company and a residential compound in Khobar, killing twenty-two people, nineteen of them foreigners. The violence then subsided—or was directed elsewhere, such as the American consulate in Jiddah, which was attacked in December 2004—but the idea of driving out the foreign workforce that has been essential for the Saudi oil industry is clearly an attractive one for the radicals.

In 2004 and 2005, jihadist Internet message boards have featured numerous discussions about the targeting of oil as a way of harming America and driving it out of Iraq. Although the recent rise in oil prices owes to numerous causes, the political and economic impact on the West is undoubtedly something jihadists are watching closely. With rising Islamist violence in the Gulf, intermittent disruptions from Venezuela and Nigeria—where Islamist violence has not yet been directed at oil but cannot be ruled out for the future—the possibility is increasing that terrorists will seek to use their own "oil weapon." Doing so would fit in well with their goals of inflicting broad damage on American society, and, with the forces and weaponry at their disposal as a result of the botched occupation of Iraq, they may yet have the wherewithal to carry it off.

THE UNITED STATES moved rapidly after September 11 to eliminate the sanctuary al Qaeda had enjoyed for so long in Afghanistan. In "phase two" of the global war on terror, however, the jihadist movement recovered many of its losses. The new battlefield that is Iraq has given the radicals a place to train, experiment with tactics, and select the most capable fighters. They have acquired access to almost limitless caches of arms, and in the ungovernable regions of the country they have gained a new sanctuary in which to plan attacks. As valuable to them as all this, they have also been able to advance their story, first by illustrating the perfidy of their infidel enemy and, second, by demonstrating their own bravery and determination. This chance to show their dedication at arms—it smacks almost of medieval chivalry—is invaluable to the jihadists, and, making use of modern communications technology, they are ensuring that their feats are known. The new heroes of jihad and those who are won over by their story are, the movement knows, the means to get beyond Baghdad, perhaps even to reach again as far as New York.

3

JIHAD IN THE AGE OF GLOBALIZATION

The consequences of America's invasion of Iraq would be disturbing enough if the threat of violence were confined to its immediate neighborhood. But the occupation of Iraq has taken on a vastly greater significance because it came at a moment of profound change in the global Muslim community, one that has thrown the relationship between Islam and the West into question in a way unprecedented in modern history.

As never before, the identity of millions of Muslims is in flux. Old ties of tribe and clan, of national origin and local religious custom, are eroding. The practice of Islam itself is evolving at a rate that rivals anything seen in the past. Many factors have contributed to this trend, among them the decline of Arab nationalism and the growth of a large Muslim diaspora in Europe and the United States. The strongest underlying cause is the powerful religious revival called Islamization, which began in the 1960s and then was strengthened in the 1970s and 1980s, when Saudi Arabia's leaders put some of their new petrodollar wealth into missionary activity, in part to check the influence of the revolution in Shiite Iran. The most dramatic transformation wrought by Islamization has been to strip away national and ethnic distinctions, so a Jordanian of Bedouin descent from the country's eastern desert, an Algerian immigrant in a Parisian *banlieue,* and an Indonesian from Sulawesi now increasingly view themselves as part of a singular community with common interests. Everything else is secondary. When the Pew Research Center surveyed the state of Muslim identity in 2003, its researchers found that large majorities in Indonesia, Pakistan, Lebanon, Nigeria, and Jordan agreed with the statement "I feel more solidarity these days with Islamic people living around the world," and that sizable pluralities concurred in Kuwait, Morocco, and the Palestinian Authority.[1] In the Muslim diaspora, the picture is even starker: To take one example, according to another poll 80 percent of British Muslims say they view themselves as Muslims first and foremost.

A consequence of this deepening of personal religious identity and the greater solidarity with fellow Muslims is an increased hostility to those who are perceived to be the enemies of the believers. Atop the enemies list for most Muslims is the United States. (Israel is also cited for slot number one, but an increasing number of Muslims consider America and Israel to be a single entity.) During the 1980s and 1990s, America's standing in the Muslim world had been in a slow decline because of the nation's strong support for Israel and the widespread belief that it is only through American assistance that the unpopular autocracies of the Muslim world maintain their grip on power. But these attitudes were complex, and it was often observed that the only thing Muslim protesters want more than to see America humbled is to get a green card and move to the United States. Since the September 11 attacks, and especially since it became clear that the United States intended to invade Iraq, what little approval there was for America has collapsed.

Public opinion surveys paint an extraordinarily grim picture: In Jordan, on which the United States relies as a buffer for Israel's eastern border, favorability ratings for the United States have been volatile, dipping to 5 percent in 2004 but climbing no higher than 25 percent in 2005. In Pakistan, a nuclear power upon which America depends to prevent a resurgence of al Qaeda, the number dropped to 10 percent in 2002 and has slowly climbed to 23 percent in 2005. In Turkey, a non-Arab NATO ally that maintains a close relationship with Israel, the portion of the population voicing a positive perspective on the United States fell to 15 percent in 2003 before floating back up to 23 percent in 2005. Pew pollsters conclude their analysis of the 2005 survey returns by saying, "With the exception of

Christian opinion in Lebanon, views of the U.S. in other predominantly Muslim nations are more negative and have changed little."[2] Though in the past this feeling was balanced by the long-standing positive view of America as a land of economic opportunity and a haven from persecution in their own countries, the sweet notes have now disappeared, leaving behind a hardened residue of resentment, disgust, and fear.

In Muslim eyes, America is a nation of hypocrites. Roughly two-thirds of Turks and Moroccans and almost as many Pakistanis believe we are using the campaign against terror to mask other objectives. Majorities of those polled in Morocco, Turkey, Jordan, and Pakistan say that the United States wants less democracy in the world, not more. More than 60 percent of Moroccan respondents think that the United States aims to control Middle East oil, or simply to "dominate the world." In 2003, about half of those surveyed in Morocco, Kuwait, Jordan, and Lebanon said they were worried about a potential U.S. military threat to their countries; in Turkey, Nigeria, Pakistan, and Indonesia, threat perceptions ran higher still, peaking at 74 percent. These figures show both how little the populaces of these countries understand American strategy—what American leader would want to occupy Turkey or Morocco?—and how much public opinion has come to parallel Usama bin Laden's own argument about American intentions. There may be no causal link, but the similarity is unnerving. To be sure, polling is a problematic science, especially in some Muslim countries, where people may be reluctant to express their real views for fear of repression, or for cultural reasons related to gender and age. But these results have been repeated over and again, in country after country.[3] They are buttressed by the open hostility voiced toward America and all its works, including by those in the Western-oriented elites and the media, much of which are controlled by governments that know how to pander to popular prejudices.

Now newspaper editorials and mosque pulpits overflow with often unbelievably vicious language and imagery relating to the United States, but the best indication of the mood in the street is to be found in popular culture. In the summer of 2004, Egypt's most prominent film director, Youssef Chahine, released a movie called *Alexandria . . . New York*. It is an allegory for U.S.–Egyptian relations, in which an aging filmmaker returns to New York and meets an old flame and the son he had unknowingly fathered. The encounter turns bitter. Father and son reject each other. Tellingly, the elderly filmmaker denounces his son, saying, "The violence which started in Hiroshima is in you."

Such themes are not just the province of cinema. Khalid Sawi, leader of the Haraka Theater Group, had a smash hit with his play *Messing with the Mind*, which begins with actors dressed as Marines rushing into the theater shouting, "You have the right to remain seated and die. And turn off your cell phones." The play ends when the main character, an American general named Fox News, screams, "I hate Arabs!" before being shot in the head. Sawi was elated over the play's success, exclaiming, "We had our first hit in fifteen years thanks to Bush!" The airwaves now reverberate with popular songs that mock or deplore America. Shaaban abd al-Rehim, a singer whose dance tunes are ubiquitous in Cairo, acquired a huge following with songs like "Attack on Iraq" and "I Hate Israel." As tempting as it is to question the validity of recent polling, the fact is that the intensification of anti-Americanism is evident in everyday life.[4]

None of this would matter much were it not for the danger that some of those who hate us will be moved to act, to become terrorists. The overwhelming majority of Muslims will no doubt be content to dislike or even hate America as they have before—passively or at least nonviolently. We can even cope with the occasional individual whose sense of outrage causes him to snap, like Hesham Mohamed Hedayet, the Egyptian who shot several bystanders at the Los Angeles International Airport in July 2002, killing three people.[5] It is another problem entirely if there is a sizable and growing pool of people whose beliefs orient them toward violence and a movement prepared to absorb and arm them.

That, unfortunately, is exactly what is happening in parts of the Muslim world today. Religious revivals have been underway in every major faith and in every region—with the exception of Western Europe—for several decades, and they often lead to a loosening of traditional attachments in favor of imported and financially well-supported creeds. As the Islamic revival has deepened, the dominant trend has been toward salafism, a fundamentalist school that emphasizes the emulation of the *salaf*, "the men of old," of the time of the Prophet and the earliest generations of Islam. (Because it has been predominantly fueled by Saudi money and doctrine, the new *salafis* are often inaccurately called Wahhabis, after those who follow the teachings of the eighteenth-century Arabian cleric Muhammad ibn abd al-Wahhab. Not all *salafis* are Wahhabis.) Salafism insists on the inerrancy of Muslim scripture and what might be called a strict constructionist brand of sharia or religious law. For rootless immigrants and disaffected second-generation youths in Europe, salafism provides the attraction of the authentic. For those living in the squalid metropolises of the Middle East, it offers an emotionally rich alternative to the bankrupt slogans of Arab nationalism. Throughout the Third World, in the myriad places where the state has failed to provide the basic needs of its citizens, it is the banner under which medicine and education are provided. Salafism appeals to younger Muslims as a way to differentiate themselves from their parents and grandparents because it is seen as pure, stripped of the local, superstitious, and customary usages of their families' countries of origin. It confers a sense of moral superiority while its strictures offer welcome constraints, especially in the diaspora, where the surrounding culture is viewed as irredeemably licentious.

Salafism has a potent appeal because it underscores Islam's universality. Its dictates echo the Quran's demand that the inhabitants of Arabia abandon local gods and give their allegiance to a single transcendent deity, and they serve as a set of ties among believers much as the Arabic language became a unifying bond—Muslims may be of many different tribes or nations, but they speak to God with a single tongue. Even when warfare between rival dynasties in the eighth century prompted the caliphate to migrate from Damascus to Baghdad and then again in the thirteenth century to Constantinople, the move was taken as a sign of Muslim unity; the caliph could rule from anywhere, it was said, since the community of believers, the *umma,* was undifferentiated. Muslims have long been encouraged to think of themselves as a unitary community of the faithful, despite their differences in race, ethnicity, and nationality. The hajj, the annual pilgrimage to Mecca, which brings together millions of Muslims from every corner of the world, demonstrates in the most tangible way every year and across countless generations that such an *umma* exists.

The belief among Muslims that they are part of a global community and share an identity, a history, and a way of life provides comfort for the millions who now live as scattered minorities in non-Muslim lands, an almost unprecedented condition in history. In one of the ironies of history, the notion of the *umma* functions in the same way for Muslims in the twenty-first century as the concept of *'Am Yisrael* (the people of Israel) has for Jews, who have considered themselves to be part of a transnational *qahal qadosh*, a holy congregation. These beliefs have helped preserve the cohesion of peoples who have left their homeland for an arduous exile. In a *salafi* universe, a Muslim can feel with some conviction that his beliefs and way of life are shared in practical, temporal detail with like-minded Muslims everywhere. He or she is then a member of the *umma*, a community in which the ethnic, ritual, linguistic, and political differences that sundered the realm of Islam after the golden age of the early caliphs have been utterly dissolved. They might not be where they came from, but they are home.

In a world that offers ever fewer physical boundaries—where the borders between the historic *dar al Islam* (the realm of Islam or submission) and *dar al harb* (realm of war) appear to have dissolved—the salafist approach to Islam provides boundaries of another kind of community, diet, dress, comportment, and daily routine. Traditional Jews would recognize much in this way of life, since rabbinic Judaism has fostered a similar approach through *halakha*—the law, literally "the way"—which regiments life and creates a daunting array of impediments to close relations with non-Jews and non-observant Jews. The emphasis on specific actions intimately tied to everyday life and on a simple irreducible doctrine that is believed to be pure makes a globalized identity possible.

The trouble, however, is that with the transnational Muslim identity comes a sense of universal grievance. The local and the global can no longer be distinguished. Now, the sufferings of Muslims everywhere have become even more palpably the responsibility of every Muslim. Oppression in Chechnya, Palestine, Kashmir, or Iraq is seen as part of a larger conflict pitting Muslims against their persecutors everywhere and simultaneously. The struggle of Kashmiri Muslims is the jihad of British Muslims. The conflict in Palestine might appear to be a local shepherds' war to American policy makers, but from the perspective of a certain kind of *umma* member, the battle is taking place not just in Gaza, but also in Paris, Casablanca, and Mombasa. (On a trip to Indonesia in 2003, George W. Bush found this out the hard way; in a meeting with Indonesian clerics, he was shocked to find that they did not want to talk about Indonesia and its tradition of tolerance but preferred to berate him about the sufferings of Palestinians.)[6] For many Muslims, the world is increasingly becoming a single undifferentiated battlefield.

Globalization—especially the "abolition of distance," as *The Economist* has called it—gets much of the blame or praise for this development. But religious doctrine is feeding it as well, and for *salafis,* the sense of beleaguerment is acute. Like all fundamentalists, they see themselves as an embattled, chosen few who must defend against hostile encroachments of secularism, materialism, and what they see as a pervasive anti-Muslim conspiracy. The force behind these menaces is held to be the United States, Israel, the West—in short, the infidel. For many young Muslims who have inherited an aversion to the United States from parents and teachers angered by U.S. support for Israel and apparent indifference to the sufferings of the Palestinians, clothing their hatred with religion only strengthens their identity.

Since the emphasis is on action, two kinds of response are available to the *salafi.* One is *dawa,* or preaching. This can mean many things, but the generally accepted sense of it is to invite non-Muslims to embrace Islam or to enjoin fellow Muslims to greater piety. The other category of action is jihad. This too can mean many things, including the struggle for self-mastery and submission to God, or participation in combat against infidels on behalf of Muslims. Many *salafis* take the route of *dawa* and shun violence. But among those with a deepening preoccupation with membership in the new *umma,* the decisiveness and drama of jihad is compelling—and bin Laden's example speaks powerfully. It is hardly surprising, therefore, that the war in Iraq has inflamed the sense that Muslims are under attack everywhere; that hatred of America, already a constitutive part of the new transnational identity, has deepened; and that more young Muslims are prepared to commit their lives to violence.

Before U.S. forces even rolled into Iraq, a senior American intelligence officer observed that "an American invasion of Iraq is already being used as a recruitment tool by al Qaeda and other groups. . . . And it is a very effective tool."[7] By the end of 2003, the flow of fighters was already considerable. Before the outbreak of hostilities, an underground railway had helped al

Qaeda and Taliban fugitives get out of Afghanistan to relative safety in Europe. As the insurgency began, the train went into reverse, sending fighters to the new Iraqi field of jihad. Recruiters in Italy, Germany, France, Spain, Britain, and Norway provided false documentation, training, and travel funds, and pointed the routes into Iraq. About a dozen arrests were made in 2003 of these "travel agents." It may be that some of Abu Musab al-Zarqawi's success in the Sunni resistance owes to his entrepreneurship in moving fighters to the battle. Investigations have shown that he was in contact with an operative in Milan who had helped coordinate the movement of kamikazes, as some radicals referred to them, to Syria and then on to Iraq.[8] One of those who got into Iraq in this way was Morchidi Kamal, who came from Italy and reportedly helped launch the October 2003 rocket attack aimed at the Baghdad hotel where Deputy Secretary of Defense Paul Wolfowitz was staying.[9] As CIA Director Porter Goss told the Senate in February 2005, "Those who survive will leave Iraq experienced in and focused on acts of urban terrorism. They represent a potential pool of contacts to build transnational terrorist cells, groups and networks."[10]

No one can say how far the radicalization will go or how many young men—and perhaps soon women—are on the road to violence. Even if we had far better numbers for those going off to fight in Iraq, we would still have only a partial picture since not all of those who choose jihad will head to Iraq. Some may go to Chechnya, some will travel to Pakistan for training in camps for redeployment elsewhere, some will stay where they are in the expectation of committing violence in the future. Olivier Roy, the French scholar who has done more than anyone to describe the globalization of Islam, maintains that the jihadist phenomenon will be contained by Muslim communities because they recognize it as a danger to their well-being. If that means that jihadists are not likely to be the dominant element in Muslim society, the prediction is probably true. In addition to the communities' prudence about where their interests lie, the militants' killings of Muslims often undercuts their appeal and creates a barrier to wider acceptance of their ideas and acceptance of their leadership. But the key issue is not whether jihadists are going to dominate communities. We should not fall victim to the fallacy of numbers. Relatively small increases in the number of terrorists can make a major difference in the dimensions of the threat in an era when explosives are widely available or easily produced and more dangerous technologies are becoming rapidly accessible. The American invasion of Iraq has undoubtedly enhanced the pull of jihad. And there is one good reason to believe that the dynamic of radicalization is more powerful and threatening than anything we have seen in the past: the Internet.

Jihad Wired

The link between advances in communications technology and social change is a well-mined historical theme. Just as writing allowed the priesthoods of the great religions to eclipse local cults and the printed book enabled people to think beyond tribal boundaries and conceive of themselves as nations, the Internet has spawned a universe of new communities. The early prophets of the World Wide Web, certain that it would promote American-style free markets, predicted that its spread would lead to the riotous bloom of democracy and "the creation of a new civilization, founded in the eternal truths of the American Idea," as Newt Gingrich's Progress and Freedom Foundation put it in 1994.[11]

Information technology may be revolutionizing modern life, but American values and free marketeers have hardly been the only beneficiaries. For individual Muslims, the Internet has provided the means to transcend their surroundings and participate in the new *umma*. It is the delivery vehicle par excellence for a set of powerful ideas, which now ricochet around the world with light speed. Sermons from Saudi Arabia, communiqués from the jihad, instruction on proper Islamic behavior, history lessons, Quranic exegesis—all these flicker onto millions of computer screens or land in e-mail in-boxes daily. Where there are few computers, adherents wait their turn in the Internet café or print the message and circulate it that way. Without the Internet, bin Laden still could have taken his jihad global—videotapes and compact discs were already spreading the word before Netscape—but its growth would be at a comparative snail's pace. In fact, the Internet is driving the creation of the new transnational Muslim identity and, with it, a hatred of America.

For those who wish to deepen their devotion, the Islamist Web provides a slippery slope that may easily lead to the embrace of violent jihad. There is an abundance of sites that provide religious guidance in the form of sermons given in Saudi mosques, fatwas issued by important and not so important clerics, and question-and-answer-format Web pages on every conceivable issue of religious observance. But these sites typically include content related to the plight of Muslims in Palestine, Chechnya, Kashmir, and Iraq and exhortations about the duties these travails impose on all Muslims. Indeed, if someone looking for guidance on an issue of observance regarding food or dress follows one link or another, he will soon be confronted with the imperative of jihad in terms like those posted on Islahi.net in a scolding letter from a Saudi sheikh: "You who shirk Jihad. . . . How can you enjoy life and comfort while your noble sisters are being raped and their honor is defiled in the Abu Ghraib prison. . . . You who shirk jihad, what excuse can you give Allah while your brethren in the prisons of Abu Ghraib and Guantanamo and ar-Ruways and al-Ha'ir [prisons in Saudi Arabia] are stripped naked? [W]hat are you waiting for?"

In just a few years, the radical Islamist Web has exploded in size. According to Gabriel Weimann of Haifa University in Israel, the number of Web sites related to terrorist groups—including non-Muslim ones, which are a small fraction of the total—has grown from twelve in 1998 to about 4,400 today. Countless other sites espouse radical Islamist views without being associated with particular violent groups. Many of the sites have flashy graphics, compelling content, and frequent updates. Chat rooms serve to establish personal contacts and provide space for views that are too extreme for posting to the site itself.

To grab the attention of children, some sites present cartoons, interactive games, fables, adventure stories—as well as images of children with real weapons playacting as terrorists. For adolescents, there are rap videos, like Sheikh Terra's *Dirty Kuffar* (infidel), which flashes images of Marines cheering as one of them shoots an Iraqi on the floor; a rolling list of the fifty-six countries that are said to have been the victims of American aggression since World War II; a Russian soldier being blasted by a Chechen guerrilla with an AK-47; and pictures of Colin Powell and Condoleezza Rice with the words "still slaves" superimposed on them. As the heavy beat goes on, the rappers guffaw in the background while on the screen the destruction of the Twin Towers is replayed. For those a little older, there are applications for recruitment accompanied by background "investigation" forms, job listings, and links to stores where books and pamphlets that glamorize jihad can be bought.

To grasp the impact the Internet is having, it is worth recalling how a different medium revolutionized attitudes in another time and place. In the America of the 1960s and 1970s, television brought the Vietnam War, as it was so often said, into the nation's living rooms. The images and reportage caused an unprecedented revulsion in a population accustomed to trusting its government and supporting its armed forces. It was a war that President Lyndon Johnson said was over when he heard that the anchorman Walter Cronkite had come out in opposition. The pictures removed the heroic sheen from the fighting and helped create a bond of opposition to the war. Without the coverage, it is hard to imagine the antiwar movement gathering strength or the chain of events that ultimately led to the U.S. pullout from Indochina. Certainly no other war in American history was brought to an end—and closed in defeat—because of public opinion.

For many Muslims who are experiencing events in Iraq as a virtual war, the experience is the inverse: Instead of a tragedy, the scenes are part of a heroic epic. A new video is posted every few days, if not more frequently. The clips tend to be relatively short—most a few minutes—though compilations are made by both the jihadists in the field and the home audience. The scenes are more varied and often more kinetic than those filmed by the embedded American crews that operated with the U.S. military in Iraq in 2003. Indeed, the filming is an integral part of the overall operation—the footage is dramatic precisely because the cameraman is part of the combat unit, there to document a planned attack or execution, not a journalist waiting for something to happen nearby. The effect they strive for is exaltation, not disenchantment. What, after all, was the tape of four American contractors being trampled and hacked to death in Fallujah in April 2004 but a downmarket version of Hector being dragged before the gates of Troy?

The most common subject is the rocketing of Humvees, but scenes that have been posted include: mujahedin shooting down a helicopter with a shoulder-fired missile and then dispatching the one surviving passenger with a bullet; a clump of men, purportedly American soldiers, who have emerged from their damaged vehicle only to be blown up, presumably by a rocket-propelled grenade; car bombings near buildings or against other vehicles, presumably with Coalition or "converter"—Iraqis who support the occupation or work in the new Iraqi regime—personnel inside; the suicide attack on the U.S. base in Mosul in December 2004, which caused the greatest single-day death toll among American forces. The clips almost invariably begin with the logo of the group responsible—Ansar al-Sunnah's calligraphy-with-rocket-propelled-grenade; al Qaeda's Iraqi assault rifle emerging from an open book (presumably a Quran) superimposed on a globe; the Islamic Army's Kalashnikov and a jihadist's face framed by the map of Iraq—as though they were team insignia to spark the fan's sense of belonging.

For most viewers, the videos are a dramatic change from what they are accustomed to. A longtime jihadist sympathizer is likely to have seen videos that show mujahedin in Afghanistan running through an obstacle course and firing weapons, with perhaps a shot of the damaged U.S.S. *Cole* as a closing image. If the individual is someone who ordinarily sticks to Arab television or Muslim news sites, then he is probably used to images of defeat and horror—for example, the iconic picture of Muhammad al-Durra, the young boy who was shot and killed, allegedly by Israeli forces, while cowering at the Netzarim junction with his father at the outset of the second intifada in 2000. After decades in which Muslim armies were routinely humiliated—in the Middle East repeatedly, in Iraq, even in South Asia, where Pakistan has lost four wars to India—these new images of Muslims destroying military targets and enjoying dominance over their captives must be inspiring. In some of the compilation videos, the images of retribution and of an enemy rendered powerless are juxtaposed with images of the humiliation of Muslims and the killing of children like al-Durra.

Of Sacraments and Bandwidth

There may not be any focus group data on the strengths and weaknesses of jihadist Web sites, but we can get some idea of what is going on in the minds of some members of the new *umma* by looking at the most popular—and grisly—of the downloads. Nothing else has lit up the Web like the videos of beheadings, and nothing else demonstrates how an archaic practice has taken on the aspect of a public sacrament with the help of modern technology.

The appeal of decapitation is grounded in its earliest connection with Islam: "When you encounter the unbelievers on the battlefield, strike off their heads until you have crushed them completely; then bind the prisoners tightly" is an injunction delivered in a discussion of the laws of war in the forty-seventh Sura of the Quran. According to Ibn Ishaq, the Prophet's earliest biographer, Muhammad ordered the decapitation of 700 men of the Jewish Banu Qurayza tribe in Medina for plotting against him, and as a result the practice has had the aura of authenticity for centuries. Beheading has been the culmination of many a tale of Muslim warfare, and it remains a form of capital punishment in Saudi Arabia to this day. Along with its variant throat-slitting, decapitation has also been used in modern times in the Algerian war of liberation in the 1960s, when it was the punishment for informers and collaborators. The practice reached gruesome proportions in the 1990s again in Algeria, when it became the signature method of killing for the radical Islamists, who murdered thousands of their countrymen with a justification—apostasy—much like the one bin Laden cites for killing Muslims who collaborate with the West. In 1994, Egypt's Nobel laureate novelist Naguib Mahfouz was stabbed in the throat by extremists who sought to punish him for his writings. In the late 1990s, Chechen rebels began to cut throats, too.

When a terrorist kills today by slitting the throat or cutting off the head of his victim, it underscores his identity as a jihadist and acts as a kind of sacrament, a way of making the violence holy. This has been clear since the discovery of the document that was found in the baggage of several of the 9/11 hijackers, often called "The Last Will and Testament of Muhammad Atta." The document describes how in the course of taking over the airplanes, the hijackers will slaughter those who get in their way. The Arabic word used is the same one for the ear-to-ear cutting of a sheep that reenacts the biblical sacrifice of Isaac on the Muslim holiday of Eid al-Adha. Severing the infidel's head from his body thus becomes an act redolent with the sense of sacrifice and the literal execution of God's law, which to the jihadist means death for infidels and apostates.

To seize their aircraft on September 11, the hijackers carried out their instructions and killed members of the flight crew by slitting their throats. Ever since, the practice has been spreading. The abduction and murder of *Wall Street Journal* reporter Daniel Pearl in January 2002 made decapitation virtually de rigueur in jihadist killings of individuals or small groups. Pearl's murder was videotaped, copies were widely sold, and it was posted on the Internet. The market for such carnage has exploded since then. When the American civilian contractor Nicholas Berg was kidnapped and beheaded in Iraq in May 2004, so many people tried to download the file that it had to be posted on dozens of different sites to prevent servers from crashing.

According to MIT's *Technology Review,* demand for the beheading videos has been overwhelming. Dan Klinker, webmaster of Ogrish.com, a non-jihadist site that specializes in gore and posts the videos, says that each beheading video has been downloaded from his site several million times; the Berg video was downloaded 15 million times from his site alone.[12] Undoubtedly, plenty of the hits come from non-Muslim devotees of snuff films, but these videos are also posted on numerous Arab-language sites as well. These sites have a habit of either crashing from overuse or being shut down because of their terrorist content, and as result, it seems likely that some who are clicking on Ogrish.com are doing so because of their jihadist sympathies. "During certain events (beheadings, etc.) the servers can barely handle the insane bandwidths—sometimes 50,000 to 60,000 visitors an hour," Klinker says. An Associated Press report in September 2004 observed that decapitation videos were outselling pornography in Baghdad.[13] Berg was the first of three Americans to be decapitated in Iraq; the number of Iraqis who have been killed this way is unknown but certainly exponentially larger.

Jihadist message boards attest to the delight of those who watch the beheadings. At one point in 2004 during a lull in the killing, one writer posted a message urging the insurgents on, saying that they were not only making history but helping their supporters' physical health.

> O Mujahideen! . . . You have marked our faces with joy after they had forgotten laughter. You have lifted up heads that were covered with humiliation. . . . Yes, by Allah, you are the men of the era. You are the pro-

tectors of the religion and the guards of the ideology. . . . We used to start our day by watching a slaughter [beheading] scene, for it is no secret to the knowledgeable that it stimulates and appeases the contents of the chests. . . . By Allah, many of those who suffer from high blood pressure and diabetes, have complained about the cease of these operations, for they were tranquilizing them. . . . Someone even told me, and I believe he speaks the truth, that he does not eat his food until he has watched a beheading scene, even if it were replayed or old.[14]

For some who download the decapitations, these are not just spectacles for ogling; they are a kind of participatory event that binds the distant Web surfer with the triumphant killers. One well-known case involved a series of executions: The insurgents had captured two American contractors and a Briton. After American Eugene Armstrong was beheaded in September 2004, someone posted a message on a jihadist message board suggesting that the most dramatic way to proceed would be to place the British hostage, Kenneth Bigley, next to the second American, Jack Hensley, and to film his horrified reaction during the beheading. The captors accepted the suggestion. It was the Web at its most interactive.

Given the popularity and the sense that beheading is what a jihadist does, the spread of the tactic to countries beyond Iraq was inevitable. In Saudi Arabia, Paul Johnson, an American engineer for Lockheed, was kidnapped in June 2004 by al Qaeda in the Arabian Peninsula and decapitated by his abductors.

The Changing Rules of War
and the Death of Restraint

Islamic authorities have historically set clear boundaries on the use of violence. Regarding the laws of war, for example, clerics of the various schools of the Sunni establishment have traditionally insisted that local battles between Muslims and their enemies be fought locally and not as a jihad, in which all able-bodied Muslims would be required to participate. They would also argue, as many still do, that such a jihad requires the leadership of a caliph, an office that currently does not exist. Indiscriminate violence—the killing of noncombatants, women, and children—as well as the killing of fellow Muslims has been almost universally condemned throughout history.

One of the "achievements" of Usama bin Laden and his lieutenant Ayman al-Zawahiri has been to forge an ideology that loosens the shackles on jihad and justifies indiscriminate violence, including the killing of Muslims. They have done so on the basis of medieval Islamic jurisprudence; the writings of Sayyid Qutb, the enormously influential Islamist thinker of the past century, and the arguments of the first generation of jihadists, the killers of Egyptian President Anwar Sadat. The al Qaeda leaders have been able to win a following for this ideology in part because of its obvious affinity for some Muslims' feelings about the West and because of the crumbling authority of the traditional clerical establishment, which might have discredited bin Laden's claims. Al Qaeda's arguments and the popularity among some Muslims of jihadist terror is effectively reducing the inhibitions on violence.

The example of the response to the 9/11 attacks is indicative: Establishment clerics were virtually unanimous in condemning the attacks on religious grounds. Muhammad Sayyid al-Tantawi, the head of Egypt's al Azhar University, declared, "Attacking innocent people is not courageous, it is stupid and will be punished on the day of judgment. . . . It's not courageous to attack innocent children, women and civilians." This view was echoed by other preachers who insisted that Islam prohibits "all forms of attacks on innocents."

The violent wing of the salafist movement had other ideas. On April 24, 2002, a group called Qaidat al-Jihad that supports radical Islamists issued a carefully reasoned justification for the use of violence in pursuit of Muslim interests. This manifesto, "Regarding the Mandates of the Heroes and the Legality of the Operations in New York and Washington," served two objectives: first, to establish the religious qualifications of the neo-imams while undermining the establishment clerics' claim to authority; and second, to show conclusively that the Quran and the Prophet's own actions provided ample support for the use of violence against civilians.

The authors of the manifesto heaped scorn on the scholarly elite, using the same strategy Islamist radicals have employed for decades of tarring them as the stooges of the West. "These great events," they wrote, "which changed the face of history on such a grand scale occurred in the *umma*, and it will be a great regret to anyone who blames those who brought about the operation in September. Those ignorant ones do not speak with legal evidence or reasonable logic. Rather, they speak their masters' languages and in the concepts of the enemy of the *umma*." The "ignorant ones," of course, are the "sultan's parrots," the clerics on the state's payroll, as the overwhelming majority of establishment clergy are. Their "master" is Saudi Arabia, and the "enemy of the *umma*" is the United States. The radical *salafis* levy the further charge of hypocrisy against the establishment clerics, noting that while they deem suicide bombings carried out against Israelis as permissible, the September 11 attackers are condemned. According to the radicals, there can be just one reason for this blatant inconsistency and that is the clerics' desire to defend ties between the regimes that pay them and the United States.

These accusations, coupled with growing popular anti-Americanism, are driving clerical opinion to the extreme in much of the Muslim world. If a decade ago only outliers like the Blind Sheikh, Omar Abdel Rahman, might issue a fatwa explicitly calling for the killing of Americans, the situation now is far different. Moderates who are fearful of seeing their influence wane are moving to the extremes to preserve their fraying authority.

The example of one famous cleric, Sheikh Yusuf al-Qaradhawi, is instructive. Qaradhawi, who is widely considered a moderate imam, is based in Qatar and has an international standing that has made him a source of guidance to Muslims worldwide on a wide array of issues. Qaradhawi has flatly condemned the September 11 attacks. But in 2004, he issued an opinion endorsing attacks on Americans—including civilian contractors—in Iraq. (He later dampened the furor by insisting that whatever he said, it was not in the form of a fatwa and thus was not binding.) His shift was not unique. At about the same time, a dozen sheikhs at al Azhar University, the preeminent seminary of the Sunni world, bastion of the clerical establishment, expressed similar views.[15]

The erosion of the authority of the established clerics is one of a constellation of changes that suggest that Islam might be at the very early stages of some sort of reformation.[16] A new breed of religious authorities is emerging that is not the product of the religious establishment. The phenomenon began in the nineteenth century with the growth of literacy, which gave ordinary people access to sacred scriptures, and colonialism, which sidelined clerics as a source of authority and empowered those with the secular skills to support a European administration. As a result, individuals with Western-style educations who are not steeped in the traditions of Islamic thought have taken it upon themselves to interpret scripture and, in essence, to declare their insights on a par with the great commentators of the past. Salafism, which was itself founded in the late nineteenth and early twentieth centuries by Muslim reformers, abets this inclination by emphasizing the individual's understanding of the Quran and the hadith, the stories of the Prophet, over the teachings of centuries of clerics, whose conclusions are often viewed as "innovation" and therefore intolerable.

The challenge to the authority of establishment clerics over such central issues as the legitimate use of force—and over the right to deliver binding religious rulings in general—comes not just from al Qaeda but from a swelling cohort of upstart imams. These clerics are typically not as well trained as their formally schooled opponents—they are likely to be self-taught, inspired by the imam at their local mosque, which might be no more than a basement or an apartment in a tenement, or by pamphlets and Web sites that endorse jihad. They are also more likely to pick and choose which traditions or trends in scholarly opinion to follow.

One example of the new breed of imams is Saad al-Faqih, a Saudi physician and self-appointed religious authority who lives in London, where he runs the Committee for the Defense of Legitimate Rights, a group that opposes the Saudi regime. He believes that advances in information technology have superseded the customary religious hierarchy. As al-Faqih sees it, any Muslim armed with a basic understanding of Islamic methodology and a CD-ROM that contains all the essential texts can hurdle the "knowledge gap" between himself and the clerical establishment. Al-Faqih acknowledges that he is "not an *alim* [credentialed scholar], but with these tools I can put together something very close to what they would produce when asked for a *fatwa*."[17] Another member of this group is Sheikh Abu Hamza al-Masri, a former Soho club bouncer who until last year was the popular preacher at London's radical Finsbury Park Mosque. Al-Masri has dismissed centuries of learning by saying, "What's the use of all this Islamic knowledge if it's not bringing anything positive to Muslim people or Islam?" On the Web, where the new *umma* is most palpable, "the sheikhs of al Azhar are totally absent," as one commentator put it. By contrast, "the enterprising young mullah who sets himself up with a colorful Web site in Alabama suddenly becomes a high-profile representative of Islam for a particular constituency."[18]

The notion that an ordinary individual can pronounce on issues of religious law has been absorbed widely, and Abu Hamza al-Masri is not its most extreme example. Though it risks caricature to say so, the danger of this trend is apparent in the pronouncements of some self-empowered thugs, such as an unnamed insurgent in Iraq who engineered a kidnapping in November 2004. His captive was a fellow Iraqi named Rasool, who worked for a European organization that removes unexploded ordnance from schools and public buildings. Rasool had been promised by some of the kidnappers that he would be freed if he spoke honestly, but the gang leader explained that, instead, he would be beheaded because "I have issued a fatwa that you should be beheaded." With Rasool lying facedown on the floor and the executioner's sword at the ready, the leader simply halted the proceedings and for no clear reason ransomed Rasool off to his family.[19]

With growing frequency, legal justifications are being offered for attacks against civilians—and, in particular, children—who were historically treated as "inviolable." In late 2001, al Qaeda spokesman Suleiman Abu Gheith issued a statement that specified that the war against the United States would not be over until Muslims have fulfilled their "right to kill four million Americans—two million of them children—and to exile twice as many and wound and cripple hundreds of thousands. Furthermore, it is our right to fight them with chemical and biological weapons, so as to afflict them with the fatal maladies that have afflicted the Muslims because of the [Americans'] chemical and biological weapons."[20] At the time, he and bin Ladin were among the few public Muslim personalities who advocated such unrestricted warfare.

Now others have caught up with him. By arguing that in democracies, citizens vote for their governments and thus are implicated in their actions, these advocates contend that all Americans provide vital support for U.S. military operations. (Bin Laden himself has addressed this notion of the "implied consent" of American civilians repeatedly, underscoring how seriously he takes the issue of satisfying Muslims' requirement for a legal basis for mass killing.)[21] Consequently, the entire notion of the noncombatant is disappearing. The emphasis on killing children is justified by a law of proportionality. As one Palestinian preacher put it, "If the infidels target Muslim women, children, and elderly, then it is permitted for Muslims to repay them in kind and kill [their women, children and elderly] as they killed. This is because of the word of Allah the Supreme, 'Anyone who attacks you, attack him as he attacked you.'" Statements like these are typically coupled with images of Muhammad al-Durra, or references to the enormous numbers of Iraqi children who are said to have died because of United Nations sanctions. Additional arguments are based on necessity: At a time when the United States and Israel command overwhelming conventional military might, suicide bombing and attacks against "soft targets" are permitted because of the lack of alternatives. As this material proliferates, it is lowering the social barriers to participation in the jihad and indiscriminate violence. It is preparing radical Muslims, and especially those who live in the new online *umma,* where so much of it circulates, to set themselves the goal of causing massive violence.

Not all the social inhibitions regarding such killing have been destroyed, but there always appears to be someone who will attack even the most sacrosanct. In September 2004, when nearly 200 children were killed in Beslan by Chechen terrorists (and by the Russian security forces who bungled their rescue attempt), most radical commentators said little about the debacle. One who did was Omar Bakri Mohammed, an influential extremist imam in London, who opined, "If an Iraqi Muslim carried out an attack like that in Britain, it would be justified because Britain has carried out acts of terrorism in Iraq." By way of clarification, he added, "As long as the Iraqi did not deliberately kill women and children, and they were killed in the crossfire, that would be okay."[22]

The expansion of combatant status to include people who are usually considered civilians has not gone unchallenged by influential salafists. Some have argued that al Qaeda's tactics violate Islamic standards of honorable combat. Others, including even Omar Bakri Mohammed, argue that only the caliph can declare jihad. Since the caliphate is defunct, there can be no jihad. He also asserts that the Prophet was "pro-life," and prohibited the killing of women, children, and the elderly, unless, as he says above, it is unavoidable or accidental. Omar does, however, think that a certain kind of killing is necessary, just not under the rubric of jihad. He therefore approves attacks against the American and British governments, including their embassies.[23]

Abu Musab al-Zarqawi's killing spree in Iraq, which has claimed so many Sunni and Shiite lives, has generated salafist opposition as well. The kidnapping and murder of Egypt's ambassador to Iraq in July 2005 was denounced by Egyptian radicals with plenty of violence in their past, including al Gama'a al Islamiyya, which butchered fifty-eight people, most of them tourists, in Luxor in 1997. Their argument had less to do with honor, Muhammad's "pro-life" values, and the status of the caliphate, and more to do with concerns about the way such murders may discredit the jihad in the eyes of ordinary Muslims. One critic complained that the killing of Muslims by jihadists "makes the average Muslim opposed to Islamist groups and casts doubt on their credibility in changing their societies for the better." Even Sheikh al-Maqdisi, Zarqawi's mentor, has challenged his protégé's targeting of Muslims, including Shiites. Others reject indiscriminate jihadist violence because it has led "to the killing and expulsion of members of Islamist groups in general—and of al Qaeda in particular—[and] to the fall of Muslim Afghanistan and the occupation of Iraq."[24] This combination of ethical and utilitarian concerns and the salafist credentials of those who voice them hints at the potential for a split on the legitimacy of violence against civilians. This debate, however, has only just been joined. But as in earlier periods in Islamic history, the extreme views of a minority can challenge the mainstream to define its position on contentious issues. It is too early to say how this process will play out in the twenty-first century. Much depends on the outcome, however, because it will determine the durability of the jihadists' creed.

The most worrisome sign that massive violence is becoming morally acceptable for some individuals is the discussion that surrounds the use of historically taboo weapons. The most striking case involves nuclear weapons. In 2003, Sheikh Nasir bin Hamad, a well-regarded young Saudi cleric, produced "A Treatise on the Ruling Regarding the Use of Weapons of Mass Destruction Against the Infidels." The work aimed to settle the question of whether Islamic law allowed the use of weapons of mass destruction in jihad. Hamad, relying on an argument of proportionality, concluded, "If a bomb was dropped on them [i.e., the Americans] that would annihilate 10 million and burn their lands to the same extent that they burned the Muslim lands—this is permissible, with no need to mention any other proof. Yet if we want to annihilate a greater number, we need further evidence."[25] (After he was arrested by Saudi authorities later in 2003, Hamad recanted his views on television.) While his current status is unknown, it is assumed that he has been released. Michael Scheuer, the former CIA official and counterterrorism expert who, as Anonymous, wrote *Imperial Hubris* and *Through Our Enemies' Eyes,* has suggested that the treatise might have been written at the behest of al Qaeda as a way of providing "sufficient Islamic grounding," which hitherto had been lacking, as a way of preparing the Muslim public for a nuclear event.[26] The episode is telling and mortifying in its illumination of where the religious discourse is going and the fantasies of violence now in circulation. Among those who already wish to kill Americans, there are no limits to the violence that can be inflicted. And, as such arguments gain wider circulation— and amplification by those who express in chat rooms and on message boards their yearning for attacks with weapons of mass destruction—we can expect the number of those drawn into these visions of boundless slaughter to increase.

The Cult of Martyrdom

Perhaps nothing demonstrates as clearly the changes underway in Islam as the growing cult of martyrdom. Although Sunni warriors have fought bravely and without regard for personal safety in countless wars, suicidal attacks have not traditionally been esteemed in large measure because of the Quranic injunction against suicide. Today, however, the veneration of the "martyrdom operation" is one of the distinguishing characteristics of radical Islamic rhetoric, whether in print, on the Web, or anywhere else. With its deep support among salafists, the cult of martyrdom is an extraordinary example of how a community that sees itself as pursuing only the oldest of practices can embrace a total historical novelty. The rise of the suicide operative could hardly be more dramatic: According to the authoritative RAND Corporation's chronology of terrorism, three-quarters of all suicide bombings since 1968 have taken place between September 11, 2001, and the middle of 2005.[27] (Prior to 1968, the practice was essentially unknown.)[28] The overwhelming majority of these recent suicide attacks were carried out by Sunnis.

Many social scientists resist the argument that religious motivation has anything to do with suicide terrorism. Citing the example of the Sri Lankan Tamil Tigers, who were pioneers of the practice, these experts argue that the key factor is the presence of a powerful organization capable of identifying and motivating operatives to carry out the attacks. But the analysis overlooks the need for an ideology that can be used to convince the individual to sacrifice his or her life. The fact that the Tigers could provide such motivation indicates that divine approval is not the only kind that works. Radical Islam has proven to be especially effective at providing this motivation, and the new media are helping it to do so.

The origins of the jihadist cult lie in Shiism, not Sunni practice. For Shiites, the suicidal fight waged by Hussein, the grandson of the Prophet, against the superior forces of his adversary, Yazid, at Karbala in the year 680 is considered the model of righteous self-sacrifice. Hussein's death is re-enacted every year in the festival of Ashura, in which the injustices of the past and present are collapsed into a tableau of oppression and grief. But the appeal of sacrifice like Hussein's had never been established in the Sunni world, whose mainstream jurists argued that suicide was explicitly forbidden in the Quran by the verse "And do not kill yourselves; verily God is compassionate unto you."[29]

It was the astonishing successes of the 1979 Iranian revolution in bringing a religious regime to power that caused the Shiite preoccupation with martyrdom to impress Sunni youths who were living amid the stagnation and repression of the Arab world. They were struck, for example, by the success of Iranian-backed suicide bombers in Lebanon in driving out the U.S. forces that had been dispatched there by the Reagan administration. The key crossover came among Palestinians, who began to carry out suicide attacks in 1993, and by the mid-1990s, a "martyropathy," as the French sociologist Farhad Khosrokhavar has called it, began to take hold. Hamas and Hezbollah went to great lengths to encourage suicide bombers since they were ideal weapons: cheap, devastatingly effective, and unavailable for interrogation after the attack. The martyrs used the one weapon available to them against the juggernaut of the Israeli army, their bodies. They made videotaped statements prior to their attacks, and their testaments were distributed via the Internet and by Hezbollah's al Manar television to Muslim viewers around the world. The message came across that while Muslim youths outside of Palestine passively accepted the degradation of their culture and loss of independence, here were heroes who fought back.

Now, the cult seems to have won broad acceptance, and the story of one of its more recent stars indicates how it has cut across boundaries of class, education, age, and gender. Hanadi Jaradat was a twenty-nine-year-old lawyer from a prominent Palestinian family. In June 2003, she had seen her brother and his friend gunned down by Israeli soldiers who were attempting to arrest them. One night a few months later, she had a bite to eat at the Maxim restaurant in a mixed Arab-Jewish neighborhood in Haifa, Israel. When she was finished, she walked to the register, paid her bill, returned to her table, and detonated a large, shrapnel-laced bomb that had been strapped to her body. Since she was standing, the seated patrons absorbed in their skulls the full force of the nails, ball bearings, and metal scraps. For her, as for many, victory over the enemy was not the point. "I know," she conceded in her videotaped will, "that I shall not bring back Palestine. I fully know this. However, I know that this is my duty for Allah. Believing in the principles of my faith, I respond to the call."

Jaradat's attractive face now adorns Web sites as the most glamorous of the martyrs, who like her do not yearn for death because it will necessarily bring victory. Rather, it is the only way they can really live. A French Muslim terrorist, caught before he could act and subsequently interviewed in prison, described feeling that the closer he got to staging a self-destructive attack, "the more alive he felt." The alternative was death in life, caused by a surfeit of humiliation.[30] Farhad Khosrokhavar has developed a typology of the humiliation these individuals feel in their everyday lives, whether by the subtle racism in Europe, or, as in Jaradat's case, by the Israeli occupation. Or they may feel "humiliation by proxy" because of the relentless stream of images on television or the Internet of Muslims being humiliated by India, Russia, America, and Israel. This humiliation is internalized and compounds the loss of dignity at home. For a small minority of Muslims in the West, there is also the humiliation that comes from living in comfort while your coreligionists suffer. Honor and dignity are themes that occur repeatedly in the vast array of last testaments. In their absence, death becomes preferable to life, especially if it entails the slaughter of an enemy that regards life as precious and, for the self-sacrificing warrior, guarantees the pleasures of paradise.

The violence of the suicide bombers not only restores honor, it also establishes the reality of their existence within societies that do not value them. These martyrs are bearing witness to the greatness of their faith and meaning of their lives in the face of realities that deny Islam its primacy and Muslims their self-worth.

When pollsters asked individuals in six Muslim countries in May 2005 whether they approved of suicide bombings against Americans and other Westerners in Iraq, about 50 percent in Lebanon and Jordan and 56 percent in Morocco said yes. Majorities in Turkey, Indonesia, and Pakistan disagreed. One wonders how majorities in Egypt, Syria, and Saudi Arabia would have responded if the researchers had been allowed to survey these countries. It is no wonder that one of the most repeated mantras in jihadist rhetoric—it appears in communiqués without number from Iraq—is the taunting apostrophe to Westerners, "You love life, and we love death."

E-Operations

For all of its power as a means of radicalizing potential jihadists, the Internet's significance goes beyond spreading propaganda. It has become a key operational tool and is transforming how terrorists do their business.

At the simplest level, e-mail has added another channel of communication for jihadists, alongside phones, faxes, written and oral messages, and the availability of sophisticated encryption programs has benefited terrorist operatives. But this may be the smallest part of the Internet's impact. What is transforming jihadist violence is the ability to disseminate tactics, technical know-how, and strategy. As a result, aspiring terrorists can increasingly find what they need with a few keystrokes instead of undertaking a long journey to a remote corner of Pakistan, the Philippines, or the Caucasus. The availability on the Internet of training materials and targeting guidance independent of any vetting process allows volunteers to "contribute" to the cause immediately. In short, the requirement for joining up is reduced to a simple process of self-selection.

The distance learners of jihad have a wealth of material to choose from. If they visit the right Web sites, they can learn, for example, how to construct mines and hand grenades; build incendiary bombs; make RDX; rig a bomb for detonation by cell phone—much as was done in Madrid—train to be a sniper; mix chemical weapons; culture botulism; fire a Stinger-type missile; and launch rocket-propelled grenades (RPGs), large ground rockets, shoulder rockets, and mortar bombs. (According to the SITE Institute, which monitors online jihadist material, there was a sudden spate of inquiries on radical message boards both shortly before and after the July 7 London bombings for a video that showed how to assemble an explosive belt for suicide bombings.) From online periodicals such as *Camp al-Battar* and *Sawt al-Jihad* (*The Voice of Jihad*) they can learn a range of ways to attack "Targets Inside Cities," a posting in which the late head of al Qaeda in the Arabian Peninsula, Abd al-Aziz al-Muqrin, carefully lists four types of targets, the intended effect of each type of attack, and their hierarchy based on potential impact.[31] This material demystifies terrorism and allows those who are sufficiently motivated to prepare and carry out actual attacks, something relative novices might otherwise be deterred from doing without a more involved process of indoctrination. The Internet has also made it possible for terrorist organizations to empower low-level operatives to have a direct impact on the type and targeting of jihadist violence. For some aspiring operatives with general technical know-how or a willingness to carry out suicide operations, it may even do away with the need for terrorist training camps. It could also make it that much easier for, say, the single experienced mujahed to leverage his own ability to prepare others for attacks.[32]

To gauge how useful the World Wide Web has been for those carrying on the fighting, consider some of the uses to which it apparently has already been put. In February 2002, eight months before the bombing of the French tanker *Limburg,* an online article appeared about the advantages of bombing tankers because "it is also well known that the American economy will not be able to endure whatsoever the rise in oil prices."[33] As it became clear in 2002–2003 that the United States was going to invade Iraq, military-style "After Action Reports" from fighters in Afghanistan were posted on the Web for those who would be confronting the Americans in Iraq. They described American tactics and the importance of hanging tough through bombing campaigns because the militants would have far better prospects in the ground fighting. Islamist Web sites routinely post translated works of U.S. military doctrine. By contrast, U.S. intelligence and law enforcement are so strapped for Arabic and other language translators, it can hardly keep up with the demand from interrogations and intelligence intercepts alone.

Few people in the West are studying Islamist Web sites for their insights into war-fighting techniques. According to Aimee Ibrahim, a thirty-year-old American of Egyptian parentage who works for DFI International, a Washington firm that contracts with the federal government, there are huge amounts of material to digest. Ibrahim, who studied Islamic jurisprudence in Cairo and holds an American law degree from Catholic University, tracks the development of bomb technology on the Web. Among the different kinds of designs she has seen posted are various chemical and radiological devices and a wide array of conventional bombs. Many of the recipes or instruction sets are tried and true and trace their lineage back to *The Anarchist Cookbook,* a manual published in 1971 for opponents of the war in Vietnam. Others are more recent innovations, and it appears that there is a considerable amount of testing of new methods going on, to judge by the postings on various forums. During the runup to the war in Iraq, Ibrahim noticed a spike in participation in jihadist message boards, and there has been no decline since. These forums are buzzing with discussions of how to improve detonation techniques or increase the size of charges, and endless questions about possible innovations. "A lot of people write in with suggestions," she notes, "like, 'Hey, guys anyone ever think about poisoning the head of an RPG?'"

Throughout its history, the jihadist movement—which has always included a large number of university graduates in science in its ranks—has sought to increase the technical expertise at its disposal.[34] It is a common theme in jihadist discussions that Americans hide behind their technology and use it to make up for a lack of courage. (It is a mistake to think that just because bin Laden and his followers espouse ideas that strike some as primitive and are prepared to live in caves, they are unlikely to master sophisticated technologies.) According to Ibrahim, "A lot of people are willing to train others [in electronic technology and other skills] and say, 'It's the tool of the enemy and we need to be better at it.' "

The Internet has allowed the radicals to attract talent on a much greater scale. Ibrahim once found a notice in a jihadist forum from someone we will call Hani asking for experts in chemistry, physics, electronics, mathematics, and computer programming. Among the responses were one from a regular member of the forum who had skills useful for explosives work, surveillance, and computer operations:

1) Chemistry, pretty good in the science of explosives and the use of light- and medium-sized weapons and small military munitions.
2) Considerable experience with the program 3-D StudioMax, not to mention programs like Flash Photoshop, Photo packet software etc.
3) Experiences in constructing computer equipment and repairing interruptions/breakdowns
4) Experience in oceanography.
   That's enough. . . .

Hani rejoiced, citing this respondent as a brother "with capabilities to serve the religion of God," and asked everyone to ask themselves the question: "When I want to help the mujahideen in their war against the infidels, what knowledge of the natural sciences do I have to offer them?" Shortly afterward, a female member of the forum, whom we will call Rana, offered her skills in microbiology and cytology and in the English language. Her posting, which noted that she was writing from Canada, elicited a gleeful response from Hani: "Wow, oh sister Rana! I thought you had left the forum, and I said, Our sister, where did she go? And thank God that we finally found you."

For the most part, the tone among the participants in such discussions is warm and collaborative; though, on occasion, Ibrahim notes, a question will be posted and the answer will come back, "I'm crashing on a deadline to build a device. I'll have to get back to you." Different ways of transferring information over the Internet have been evolving rapidly. It is not just a matter of sending written instructions: Now, bomb makers send digital pictures and digital videos showing how to carry out particular ways of mixing chemicals or assemble bomb components. They can use live chat or new Voice Over Internet technology to walk one another through problems in real time. Counterterrorism experts are deeply concerned by the increase in the number of password-protected sites and forums and the possibility that two or more people will connect in a forum and then establish contact among themselves by e-mail, away from any potential prying eyes. Another unsettling trend Ibrahim has observed is the growing migration of members of jihadist forums to the Arabic-language professional Web sites that deal with subjects such as electrical engineering and chemistry, where they will ask for help solving problems that the members of the jihadist forums could not. "For the most part," she says, "people are willing to help. They'll say, 'Do this and this and go with God.'" These responses suggest that jihadists are able to draw on a wide range of highly skilled experts and that a significant number of Muslim scientists are prepared to help out those they know who oppose America by violent means. As a result, know-how that previously could be acquired only through years of study or considerable hands-on experience can now be transferred easily across vast distances.

In talking about the virtual jihadist world, Ibrahim calls it "The New Base," a play on al Qaeda, which means "The Base." She says it is clear that the master bomb makers are now scattered around the world and are able to collaborate with operatives and one another without having to run the risk of being in a conflict zone. This goes a long way toward eliminating the need for terrorist training camps and even for sanctuaries. One could argue that because they can be detected by satellites and spies, camps are too vulnerable to be valuable anymore. "For all I know," Ibrahim says, speaking of the master bomb makers, "these guys could be chemistry professors at major universities."

4

RADICAL ISLAM'S STRATEGIC DEPTH

Islamist activism is global in scope but has always been diverse, with the specific concerns that animate political action varying from country to country. Muslim communities relate their religious identity and beliefs to the practical problems of everyday life, whether in their relations with neighbors or to the state, in a bewildering variety of ways. In many countries, Muslim minorities feel themselves to be beleaguered and have chosen to confront the governments or majority populations. In some countries, Islamist movements are the political opposition to governments that define themselves as Muslim, too.

Despite the importance of local issues, there has been in recent years a detectable trend toward the globalization of these grievances. Increasingly, local resentments are being displaced onto the United States and its allies, under the influence of a jihadist perspective that has spread throughout the Muslim world.

Why should we care? Two reasons: First, though the analogy is rough, local militants are the strategic reserve for al Qaeda and the global jihad. They might be convinced to carry out attacks against Western interests around the world—embassies, pipelines, companies, schools. Many, perhaps most, of them will be unsuitable for operations that require them to move to another part of the world. But some of them will be capable, and they pose a threat to us. Second, these local conflicts can generate instability and upheaval that have the potential to disrupt our day-to-day lives. Some of the dangers are already obvious:

- Conflict between Muslims in Europe and the wider society there may interfere with America's key alliances as the Europeans turn inward to deal with these tensions. Divisions between us and our allies could widen if our policies toward the Middle East further radicalize Muslim communities in Europe.
- In Chechnya, an insurgency with a growing jihadist element has roiled Russia, diverted its transition to democracy, and now threatens to destabilize a sizable region.
- An Islamist insurgency in Saudi Arabia would play havoc with a volatile oil market and the global economy and could spill over into neighboring countries important to our security, including Iraq and Jordan.
- Jihadist fervor in Pakistan, a country with nuclear weapons, has inflamed the country's rivalry with India and is creating a huge cohort of angry, anti-American young people.
- In Southeast Asia, strategic interests including oil and vital sea-lanes are at stake, as well as the continuing vitality of several vulnerable regional economies.

The churn of local conflicts is providing soldiers for the global jihad. It may not be long before substantially more extremists from these five regions—Europe, Chechnya, Saudi Arabia, Pakistan, and Southeast Asia—are participating directly in the war against America.

Europe

It is an unwelcome irony that Europe, which emerged from the Cold War more united, peaceful, and prosperous than at any time in history, may be threatened by jihadist violence as much as any part of the world outside Iraq. Europe, as home to the world's largest Muslim diaspora, is at the heart of the battle over Muslim identity. Its experience with jihadist terror is already a long one: It served as the logistics and planning base for the September 11 attacks, which were prepared principally in Hamburg, and it has been a haven for many Islamists like Abu Dahdah, who fled repression in Syria. In the 1990s the Continent was jolted by fighting between Muslims and Christians in the Balkans. The conflict was primarily ethnic, but it was exploited skillfully by jihadists for operational and propaganda purposes.

The March 2004 Madrid bombings affected Europe profoundly, puncturing the feeling that many shared after September 11 that the United States was the primary target and that Europeans had little to fear. But the awakening came not because of a change in jihadist targeting but because the terrorists had failed repeatedly in their earlier attempts. In 2001 they had tried to bomb the Strasbourg Cathedral and the U.S. Air Force base in Kleine Brogel, Belgium; a cell in London was broken up in 2003 for conspiring to produce the toxic agent ricin, while another in Germany was planning a series of attacks against Jewish targets. European intelligence services estimate that radical Islamists have planned as many as thirty "spectaculars" since September 11.[1] As one British official put it before the July 7, 2005, bombings in the London Tube, "We've been very, very lucky." That verdict is probably still just, given the amount of radical activity in Europe.

Much of Europe's problem owes to the fact that the individual Muslim's identity is sharply tested there. Most of the Continent's Muslims arrived in the 1950s and 1960s as workers to fill postwar Europe's labor shortage, and they stayed on in countries that, for the most part, neither expected nor wanted to integrate them into their societies. It soon became apparent, however, that there was no easy way to send these workers back or to stanch the flow of family members seeking reunification with loved ones—let alone to stop them from having children. As a result, Europe has sleepwalked into an awkward multiculturalism. Its Muslim residents, many of them now citizens, live for the most part in ghetto-like segregation, receive second-rate schooling, and suffer much higher unemployment than the general population. Those who do work are more likely than their non-Muslim counterparts to have low-wage, dead-end jobs.

Indeed, it is this marginality that helps to explain the appeal of radicalism. The Madrid cell was composed of a host of men on the margins—

drug dealers, part-time workers, students—and this has been a pattern among jihadists for some time. The Hamburg cell that carried out the September 11 attacks was financially better off, and its members tended to come from higher income families. But they too were drifting through Europe as their hatred deepened. L'Houssaine Kherchtou, a Moroccan al Qaeda member in the 1990s, described in a U.S. court how he had floated around the Continent, working episodically and often illegally, before finding his way to Milan and recruitment for jihad.[2] This class of potential terrorists could well be around for as long as Europe absorbs cheap labor from across the Mediterranean in North Africa.

A parallel development has arisen out of the Continent's ongoing political and economic unification, which has undercut the power of traditional national identity, especially among young people. The citizens of the various member states of the European Union still consider themselves to be French, or Polish, or British, but with the emergence of a single currency and EU passports, a world in which individuals choose from among multiple identities has come to be taken for granted.

European Muslims have the same sense of choice when it comes to identity, and many are picking religion as their determining trait. For example, according to a 2002 survey of Muslims in Great Britain, 41 percent of the respondents under thirty-five years of age described themselves as solely "Muslim" rather than "British and Muslim," which was one of the other choices on the questionnaire. (One out of three respondents over the age of thirty-five felt this way, too.)[3] Much the same trend has been documented in France, where the proportion of Muslims who identified themselves as "believing and practicing" increased by 25 percent between 1994 and 2001.[4] Given the inclination that Christian Europeans feel toward a broader, transnational identity, it is not surprising that many Muslims also want to feel that they are part of something bigger. Identification with the new *umma* and its predominantly salafist orientation has become an attractive alternative. This trend has not gone unnoticed by non-Muslim Europeans. According to May 2005 Pew polls, solid majorities in the United Kingdom, Germany, France, and the Netherlands say they see a growing Islamic identity among their Muslim neighbors. In Spain, nearly 50 percent share this perception. Three-quarters of respondents in France, Germany, the Netherlands, and Spain, and a smaller majority in the UK, see this as a bad thing, with many citing fear of violence or, more generally, the ill effects that a failure of Muslim integration might yield. Large majorities in all these countries now worry about Islamic extremism.[5]

The spread of salafism in Europe has been further facilitated by a shortage of homegrown clerics. The number of mosques has grown dramatically in the past decade along with the sharp increase in the Muslim population, but Europe does not have the thousands of clerics needed to meet this need. There are no privately endowed institutions for religious training, as are commonplace in the United States, and, for Muslims, there have been no state-funded seminaries, as are provided for officially recognized faiths. European governments are now wrestling with the complex issue of providing religious training and licensing preachers, but it will be years before such a system begins to graduate the imams needed to meet the spiritual needs of Europe's Muslims. In the meantime, Muslim communities in Europe must rely on clerics from the Middle East and South Asia for religious guidance and leadership in prayer. Saudi Arabia, Egypt, North Africa, and Pakistan have been producing a surplus of imams, but many of them are imbued with a salafist perspective and hostility toward secular European values. The result is that salafist clerics wield an outsized influence on the debate over the evolving shape of Islamic belief and practice in Europe.

Their impact is clear in the story of boys like Salah, who was the subject of a report in the *Los Angeles Times* in April 2005. The son of immigrants from Mali who lived in a tidy immigrant neighborhood in Paris's ethnically mixed nineteenth *arrondissement*, Salah set off for jihad in Iraq at the age of thirteen. The preacher whose rhetoric inspired Salah, Farid Benyettou, was himself only in his early twenties, but his oratory brought crowds of 1,500 worshipers to his Friday sermons in one of the city's largest mosques. His most impassioned speeches, however, were reserved for the special classes he taught in Arabic and Islamic religion. These were held at his apartment, where acolytes would gather to hear the turbaned cleric analyze world affairs, the situation of Muslims, and the logical imperative of jihad.[6] When Benyettou was arrested on terrorism charges as he prepared to send another two boys to Iraq, his lawyer described Benyettou's approach to recruitment, saying that he "would talk to his [disciples] about Abu Ghraib, the abuse of Muslims and say, 'What are you going to do about it?' He was like a . . . guru who claimed to know the sacred texts . . . and he convinced them that the texts said it was their duty to go to Iraq to fight for the cause." One boy from Salah's neighborhood was killed in 2004 carrying out a car bombing in Iraq. Two others, aged nineteen and twenty-four, were killed in the Sunni Triangle. One other friend was captured by U.S. forces in Fallujah. Salah himself appeared not to have made it to Iraq but was working as a middleman in Syria, preparing others for the jihad there.[7]

Although the news media have paid much attention in recent years to the re-emergence of European anti-Semitism, a burgeoning anti-Muslim sentiment may yet become the bigger and more troubling phenomenon; it is already helping to drive the deepening alienation of European Muslims. In France, researchers found that 24 percent of those they spoke with conceded a dislike of North Africans, the largest Muslim group in the nation, and 62 percent told pollsters that Islamic values were incompatible with the French Republic.[8] A larger percentage said that they considered Islam to be an intolerant religion, and over half of the respondents stated that there are too many immigrants in France—"immigrants," of course, being code for Muslims.[9] The situation in Germany is similar. A 2004 survey showed that 70 percent of Germans believe that "Muslims do not fit in Western society," and over 80 percent associate Islam with the word "terrorism."[10] In Britain, one in ten people think that peaceful coexistence of non-Muslims and Muslims in Britain is impossible. One in three disagreed with the statement "In general, Muslims play a valuable role in British society," and two-thirds thought that Britain's Muslims do "little" or "nothing" to promote tolerance.[11]

Not surprisingly, Britain's Muslims are not happy with how they are treated by the wider society. One-third of them say that either they or someone they personally know has been subjected to abuse or hostility because of their religion; over half say that the position of Muslims has worsened since the Iraq war began in March 2003. Two in three stated that antiterrorism laws are applied unfairly against Muslims, nearly half would oppose an oath of allegiance to Britain, and 70 percent think that Muslims are politically underrepresented.[12] When some of the British government's top civil servants met after the Madrid bombings to discuss how to defeat al Qaeda domestically, the picture that confronted them was deeply unsettling. Muslims had three times the unemployment rate of the entire population—only 48 percent of the Muslim population was working, well below the 68 percent figure for the population as a whole—and Britain's ten most underprivileged districts were home to three times as many Muslims as non-Muslims. Although terrorists rarely come from the poorest sectors of society, their sense of grievance is often nourished by the impoverishment of their fellow Muslims. In all, the Home Office estimated, "There may be between 10,000 and 15,000 British Muslims who 'actively support' al Qaeda or related groups."[13]

The sense of antipathy Muslims encounter in Europe is not just a matter of quiet slights at work or on the street. In recent years, a number of European leaders have made comments that display a remarkable hostility. In 2001, Italian Prime Minister Silvio Berlusconi set off an international furor when he declared the superiority of European civilization to that of Islam. "We should be confident of the superiority of our civilization, which consists of a value system that has given people widespread prosperity in those countries that embrace it, and guarantees respect for human rights and religion," Berlusconi said. "This respect certainly does not exist in Islamic countries." The West "is bound to occidentalize and conquer new people," he said. "It has done it with the Communist world and part of the Islamic world, but unfortunately, a part of the Islamic world is 1,400 years behind. From this point of view, we must be conscious of the strength and force of our civilization."[14] More recently, the Queen of Denmark announced flatly, "We are being challenged by Islam these years—globally as well as locally. It is a challenge we have to take seriously. We have let this issue float about for too long because we are tolerant and lazy. . . . We have to show our opposition to Islam and we have to, at times, run the risk of having unflattering labels placed on us because there are some things for which we should display no tolerance."[15]

This is more than a matter of a bad atmosphere: Europe's right-wing political parties have profited significantly from popular antipathy to Islam and have made real inroads by stressing anti-immigration politics. In the 2002 presidential election in France, Jean-Marie Le Pen of the National Front won a place in the runoff against incumbent Jacques Chirac. Belgium's Flemish Bloc, Denmark's People's Party, Italy's Northern League, and Switzerland's People's Party have all registered gains, though none has actually come to power. In Britain, the Conservative Party leader Michael Howard centered much of his 2005 election campaign against Prime Minister Tony Blair on an anti-immigration theme. The ascendancy of nativist sentiment has pushed political discourse to the right. As the center has moved, popular support for the liberal policies that have long characterized the relationship between state and society within Europe has diminished. Among the first fruits of the rightward shift has been the ban on headscarves in French schools and the Dutch decision to expel 26,000 asylum seekers from the Netherlands. The next steps will likely be in the realm of tightened law enforcement and immigration controls. European Muslims will naturally interpret these measures as being directed against them and may well become even more defensive and less interested in assimilation. Thus accelerates a dynamic of alienation, with the Christian Europeans becoming increasingly hostile to the self-segregating Muslims.

These tensions will worsen in the coming years as Europe's demographic crisis and its antipathy to outsiders sharpen—as Christian Europe continues to shrink and Muslim Europe grows.[16] Approximately 1 million Muslims arrive in Western Europe annually, about half seeking family reunification and half in search of asylum. As many as another half million are believed to be entering the EU illegally each year.[17] More important is the fact that the fertility rate among these immigrants is triple that of other Europeans. Consequently, the Muslim population is younger than the non-Muslim population, and Europe's Muslim population is likely to double from about 15 million in 2005 to 30 million by 2025. At the same time, current demographic projections show that Europe's non-Muslim population is stagnant or shrinking. Europe could well be 20 percent Muslim by 2050. Bernard Lewis, the renowned historian of Islam, may be right in his prediction that by the end of the twenty-first century the European continent would be "part of the Arabic west, the Maghreb."[18]

Tensions in Europe between Muslims and non-Muslims are likely to escalate as these demographic changes take hold and anti-immigration policies become more commonplace. Larger youth populations tend to be associated with higher levels of criminal activity, which will further rankle the non-Muslim population. Some of the greatest irritants will be over matters of religious practice: wearing headscarves, obtaining halal meat—ritual slaughter is controversial in several European countries and is banned in Switzerland because it is seen as inhumane—and the provision of workplace facilities for prayer five times a day. The socioeconomic problems that make the lives of many Muslims in Europe miserable—ghettoization, unemployment, lower wages, unequal access to education, discrimination in the workplace—are unlikely to disappear, and the resulting discontent is likely to be expressed in religious terms. Against this background of anomie, jihad can be attractive to young European Muslims. It is empowering, promising the chance to do something dramatic, to assert oneself and punish one's tormenters.

Europe has already had a premonition of how this future may look. At 9:00 on the morning of November 2, 2004, a man wearing a white robe and baggy coat was riding his bicycle on an Amsterdam street, approaching Theo van Gogh, an artist and filmmaker, who was on foot. The bicyclist fired six rounds from a handgun, dismounted, and, in an act of pure ritual, knelt over van Gogh and slit his throat with a butcher knife. He then plunged a second knife into van Gogh's chest, pinning a note to his body. After kicking the corpse, he walked away, according to witnesses, as though nothing had happened.

The killer, Mohammed Bouyeri, was a twenty-six-year-old dual citizen of Morocco and the Netherlands. If one had encountered him three years earlier, he would have appeared to be an immigrant success story. From a working-class family of immigrants, Bouyeri had graduated from the Dutch secondary school system and the local Mondrian college and had worked in social services within Amsterdam's Muslim community. He appeared to be a responsible, concerned citizen—not especially religious or discontented. He was the sort of person who was expected to navigate through Dutch society successfully, establish a family, build a career.

According to Dutch intelligence, Bouyeri's moment as an upstanding citizen was preceded by a rowdy adolescence and, at some point between 2000 and 2002, seven months in a Dutch jail for a "violence related crime."[19] It was there that he may have embraced the kind of Islamic observance that he had spurned on the street before his arrest. In any case, he emerged from jail with a commitment to community service and a strong Muslim identity. Things, however, did not go well for long. During 2002, his worldview began to harden. The causes cannot be known with any certainty. His mother died of breast cancer, and he failed to win municipal funding for two community centers he hoped to build for Muslim immigrants. Bouyeri began to spend time with a Syrian immigrant known as Abu Khaled and a local high school student named Samir al-Azzouz, both of whom had a history of radical activity.[20] Abu Khaled had spent time in jail in Syria, where he had been active in the Muslim Brotherhood, and he made his way to the Netherlands after having been granted political asylum almost a decade earlier by Germany. Al-Azzouz, a Dutch resident, had been intercepted in the spring of 2002 and returned to the Netherlands by Ukrainian authorities while he was en route to join Chechen rebels in their battle against Russia. Shortly thereafter, Bouyeri moved out of his boyhood home into his own small apartment in a quiet residential section of western Amsterdam, outside the usual immigrant orbit.

There, he was primed for transformation through his entry into the Internet's virtual *umma*. His initial foray was in the online debate about the appropriate status of women in Islam. Later, he moved on to jihadist Web sites. His recruitment to battle, however, did not take place in a mosque or through direct exposure to a fiery imam calling young men to war. It occurred in late-night bull sessions with other committed young men and apparently without the involvement of any other organized group or authority.

In his new apartment, Bouyeri, Abu Khaled, al-Azzouz, and about ten others conspired to carry out a string of attacks against the Dutch Parliament, Schiphol Airport, and a nuclear reactor. Jason Walters, the son of an American employee of the U.S. military and a Dutch woman, was another member of the group. His participation is worth noting because he was not a Muslim by birth, was not a stranger to American or European culture, but was a classic self-starter, attracted to radical Islam because it gave him an outlet for his alienation and anger. He saw his personal plight reflected in the social exclusion of Muslims and identified with their impulse to fight back. At age sixteen, Walters had traveled to Afghanistan and Pakistan for training, an experience that gave him enormous credibility with other would-be jihadists.

Because of the company Bouyeri was keeping, Dutch police took notice of him. Wiretaps were installed in his apartment in 2003, and it was subsequently raided. Bouyeri and several others were taken into custody after materials that could be used to make explosives were found, along with a "martyr's will" and, of course, videotapes of beheadings and other gruesome acts. At that time, however, conspiracy to commit terrorist acts was not a crime, and the Netherlands did not have the legal framework in place to hold suspects without charge for more than a brief period. The men were released after ten days, but surveillance continued on and off until the middle of October 2004. Unbeknownst to the Dutch security services, the aspiring jihadists had a mole in the police station who kept them informed about those who were watching them. Bouyeri knew when to strike because he had been tipped off when the police suspended their surveillance.

His target was the bad boy of Dutch cinema. Theo van Gogh, a distant relative of the painter Vincent van Gogh, had produced a movie written by Ayaan Hirsi Ali, a Somali immigrant to the Netherlands who had risen to become a member of the Dutch Parliament. Her short screenplay for the film, *Submission,* dealt with the mistreatment of women in Islam. (Ali had undergone genital mutilation as a child in Somalia and barely escaped from an arranged marriage before winning asylum in the Netherlands.) The central image of the film was the back of a woman clad in a transparent gown; written on her back were Quranic verses.

For van Gogh, a professional provocateur who equated vulgarity with authenticity and delighted in ethnic abuse, the shocking imagery was the surest way to get the attention of an audience. Van Gogh had been an admirer of Pim Fortuyn, a leading Dutch politician who had gained notoriety by characterizing Islam as primitive, misogynistic, and anti-democratic. (Fortuyn was murdered in 2002, but by an animal rights activist, not a Muslim radical.) Van Gogh deplored the political left for failing to challenge a fundamentally illiberal religion, and he did not hesitate to condemn those he thought supported the Muslim cause. He had recently derided Amsterdam's mayor, Job Cohen, for his efforts at fence-mending, accusing the mayor of siding with the "fifth column of goat fuckers" that threatened to undermine the customary tolerance of Dutch society.

The paper that Bouyeri pinned to van Gogh's torso contained a long note addressed not to the dead man but to Hirsi Ali, saying that she had betrayed Islam and threatening her life. He then advanced arguments that have become typical of "new *umma*" jihadists. Bouyeri quotes the Quranic verse in which Muhammad is reported to have said that there can be "no aggression unless against the aggressors." This passage is usually deployed by moderates to show that mainstream Islam endorses violence only as a last resort. Bouyeri acknowledges this but insists that he had killed van Gogh in self-defense, because he and his ilk had "terrorized Islam." The note then advances the familiar theme of a Jewish conspiracy to control the Netherlands and subjugate Muslims, citing a half-dozen passages from the Talmud that purport to show that the rabbis considered non-Jews to be subhuman. An apocalyptic poem composed of verses from the Quran follows this "exposé" of Jewish racism.[21] This vision of the end of time ends with Bouyeri's declaration of certainties:

I surely know that you, O America, will be destroyed
I surely know that you, O Europe, will be destroyed
I surely know that you, O Holland, will be destroyed
I surely know that you, O Hirsi Ali, will be destroyed

The strangest thing about this diatribe is that it fails to mention the film *Submission*. Hirsi Ali's crime, according to Bouyeri, is her legislative proposal that Muslim job applicants in the Netherlands be screened for their ideological leanings, a move designed to put pressure on radical Islamists by making it harder for those who do not subscribe to European values to find work. Bouyeri saw this proposal of an ideological litmus test as being somehow linked to the global battle against Islam. In Bouyeri's mind, the global and the local were fused; the war in Iraq, the struggles of the Palestinians, Chechens, and Kashmiris, and Dutch administrative procedure and *Submission* were all of the same tissue. Van Gogh became the object of his response to all these affronts. "What moved me to do what I did was purely my faith," he said at his trial in July 2005, adding, "I was motivated by the law that commands me to cut off the head of anyone who insults Allah and his prophet." At the close of the proceedings, he declared, "If I were released and would have the chance to do it again . . . I would do exactly the same thing."[22]

Van Gogh's murder came at a moment of flux in Dutch politics. De-mographic projections showing that in a few years, non-Muslims will comprise less than 50 percent of the population in Amsterdam, Utrecht, and Rotterdam had put many Dutch residents on edge. Anti-immigration sentiment in the Netherlands was already on the rise in a nation where 900,000 of its 16 million people are Muslim. (Muhammad is now the most commonly registered first name in Amsterdam.) Some Dutch voters began to gravitate to the right, and many identified van Gogh's death with the death of a way of life defined by multiculturalism, mutual toler-ance, and a kind of sunny hedonism.

The chief political beneficiary of this anxiety and sense of loss was a previously marginal politician named Geert Wilders. Before the van Gogh murder, polls showed that Wilders's party—which advocates immigration controls, law and order, and denying EU membership to Turkey—would win 9 of the 150 seats in the lower house of Parliament. Immediately after the killing, polls showed that it would capture 28 seats, Wilders's base of support having broadened to include nearly every sector of the electorate. As a candidate with a single cause, it was easy to infer from his rocketing popularity what the country's leading concern had become. Local opinion surveys showed that 40 percent of the respondents hoped that Muslims in the Netherlands would no longer feel at home, and that 80 percent favored more restrictive immigration laws.

Within a week there were at least twenty reported cases of arson in the Netherlands involving Muslim schools and mosques. Wilders himself came under a death threat posted on the Internet, where he was accused of idolatry and mocking Islam and was sentenced to death by decapitation. The sense of crisis led to a wide-ranging public debate and the adoption of laws designed to discourage immigration and provide police with greater powers. Immigrants can no longer get automatic citizenship for wives they bring to the Netherlands, and citizenship now requires a working knowledge of the Dutch language. Police are now able to detain suspects longer and charge them with conspiracy. Newspapers reported that a kind of "white flight" may have begun, as Dutch citizens are emigrating to other EU countries or to North America.

As a group, the London bombers of July 2005 bear a striking res-emblance to Mohammed Bouyeri's circle. The oldest of the bombers,

Mohammad Sidique Khan, was a man involved in his community, much like Bouyeri. He had been a teacher's assistant in the Hillside Primary School in Beeston, a town close to Leeds, and was well known and well liked because of his commitment to the children who lived in that tough neighborhood—he would, for example, persuade youngsters to stay in school and take them on camping trips into the Yorkshire Dales. A thirty-year-old graduate of Leeds University, he had drawn the attention of the media for his community service—he had been interviewed by the London *Times* educational supplement—and his local member of Parliament had invited Khan to London for a tour of the House of Commons in October 2004. Khan was more even tempered and meticulous in his habits than Bouyeri and seemed to be a good example of how someone of recent immigrant stock could turn into a fine young Briton.

But at some point in 2004 he began to change. It could have been the stresses of raising a young family—Khan had a wife and young daughter—in a rough area on a salary of about $25,000 a year. Or, it could have been that events in Iraq had angered him. An imam from the Beeston mosque confirms that the issue was one of deep concern for his congregants: "A big thing is Iraq and Afghanistan. Lots of youngsters, whether they have Islamic knowledge or not get automatically affected. It triggers something."[23]

Two of Khan's accomplices, twenty-two-year-old Shehzad Tanweer and eighteen-year-old Hasib Hussein, were, like him, of Pakistani descent, and they idolized him. Tanweer had graduated from Metropolitan University in Leeds with a degree in sports science. His family owns a small fish-and-chips shop and had enough money to buy him a used Mercedes sedan when he was about to get his degree. He had a brush with the law in 2004, when he was arrested for disorderly conduct, but people who knew Tanweer thought of him as apolitical and quiet, "a nice lad" who got along with everyone. Hussein, by contrast, had a belligerent streak and a reputation as a delinquent. Like Tanweer, he was a devotee of martial arts, but he was having a harder time fitting in. Hussein had dropped out of high school in 2003 and the next year he was arrested for shoplifting. Only days before the London bombings he had been seen smoking a joint with friends in a Leeds park. The fourth member of the group, nineteen-year-old Jamaican-born Germaine Lindsay, had converted to Islam about five years earlier and adopted the name Lindsay Jamal. Unlike the others, Jamal was intensely religious. He often recited the Quran in Arabic at the local mosque, where his chanting was much admired, as was his piety. He married another convert to Islam, Samantha Lewthwaite—she changed her name to Ashrafiya—who was expecting their second child at the time of the attacks.[24]

Marc Sageman, a psychiatrist and former CIA case officer, has observed that ties of friendship and kinship play a vital role in motivating radical Islamist terrorists to carry out their attacks. In his influential book, *Understanding Terror Networks,* he has shown that the willingness to carry out suicide attacks depends heavily on a dynamic within a cell in which members feel an increasing pressure to meet one another's expectations.[25] Through their interactions, the members raise the stakes and bind each other in a shared commitment to violent action that individually they would be unlikely to undertake. Sageman believes that such a dynamic developed in Madrid, and something similar might have been underway in the Netherlands when Bouyeri decided to distinguish himself. The same pattern appears to recur in the London attacks. Three of the four bombers shared an ethnic and religious background and had been shaped by the same blighted and gritty neighborhood. It is also known that they were not drawn together and indoctrinated by a radical imam at the local mosque. (In fact, when Khan began to show signs of radicalization, fellow worshipers at the local mosque made it clear they were concerned, not pleased.) Instead, it was in a bookstore, the al Iqra Learning Centre in Leeds, where they held the intense discussions that led to the decision to attack. And it was in a small empty storefront, jammed between a takeout chicken place and an electrician's shop, that they planned their operation and stored the materials.

From the first reports following the bombing, the timeline of the men's radicalization remains unclear. Much attention has been focused on the fact that some, and possibly all of them, traveled to Pakistan in the year before the attacks—it seems it was there that Lindsay, who came from Buckinghamshire, met the others—and it is possible that meetings there with hardened extremists were pivotal in turning the four to violence. Some news accounts suggest that they may have received indoctrination and training from Pakistani jihadist groups, such as Lashkar-e-Tayba, whose terrorist camps have hosted other non-Pakistani radicals. After

Khan's November 2004 trip to Pakistan, his second trip in two years, he quit his teaching job and began spending more time with his two Leeds friends, who would become his co-conspirators.

It is, however, equally possible that the dynamic of radicalization began in Britain. The three men from Leeds could have been in touch with al Muhajiroun or Hizb ut-Tahrir, extremist groups that operate in the country. Such an interaction toward radicalism might have provided an impetus in the same way that Abu Khaled and Samir al-Azzouz appear to have influenced Bouyeri. We may also find that the London bombers were genuine self-starters, individuals who are attracted to the jihadist ideology because of the sense of grievance they have developed in their everyday lives. It is easy to imagine that as a result of a growing interest in the global jihad, the men decided to visit Pakistan, seeking out radicals there and acquiring the training they needed. In the era of globalization, the pathways of radical influence and attraction can run in any number of directions. To assume that there is a single source of trouble is to make a dangerous mistake.

"Islam has bloody borders," Samuel Huntington wrote famously in his 1996 book *The Clash of Civilizations and the Remaking of World Order.* In light of the evidence of Madrid, Amsterdam, and London, the bloodiness may not be confined to the borders—it is now in the heart of the West. The challenge this will pose for a continent that has struggled nobly over half a century to build for its citizens a "paradise," as Robert Kagan half-ironically put it, will likely be as great as any Europe will face in the coming century.

Chechnya

Islamist radicalism thrives on war. Atrocities help to create and attract new militants, and the experience of the fight expands their capabilities, giving them skills and inspiration for the next battle. This has been the case in Afghanistan, Bosnia, Kosovo, Kashmir, and Chechnya. All of these conflicts, to some degree or another, started out with religion playing a relatively small role, but eventually the question of religious identity moved to the center, driving the parties to greater violence. In the Balkans, hundreds of thousands died; in Afghanistan, the tally has run into the millions. The jihad lives off these conflicts—they are, in a way, the undersea plumes that nourish monsters. They also tend to expand, overflowing their boundaries, spreading destruction.

The war in Chechnya began as a conflict over autonomy between Russia and one of the peoples who had been conquered by the czars and badly mistreated during the Soviet era. For over a century the Chechens had been one of the most restive ethnic groups in the Russian/Soviet dominion. During World War II, Stalin accused the Chechens of being pro-Nazi and deported the population en masse to Central Asia. Tens of thousands died from the hardship. In 1994, war broke out between Chechen rebels and the Russian government, leading to the devastation of the region. A 1996 agreement gave Chechnya substantial autonomy, though not independence. While there was an elected local government, the area was never reconstructed and became a zone of lawlessness and warlordism.

Although by the late 1990s most Chechens were weary of violence, the situation was ideal for radical Islamists eager to foment more trouble. Chechens are Muslim, but at the outset of the conflict few were particularly radical in their beliefs. Two extremists became particularly notorious: Shamil Basayev, a Chechen, and Khattab, an Arab and a bin Laden associate from the border region of Jordan and Saudi Arabia. The two set up training camps to attract aspiring fighters, and in 1999 they promoted an insurrection in neighboring Dagestan. When Russian forces reacted, the fighting spilled back over into Chechnya. The Russians gained control of the ruined capital, Grozny, but they have been fighting a counterinsurgency against the Chechen forces ever since. From early on, the conflict captured the attention of the jihadist world. Muhammad Atta originally planned to make his way from Hamburg to Chechnya to fight when, in 1999, an al Qaeda recruiter persuaded him to go to Afghanistan, where he had his fateful meeting with bin Laden.[26] And according to a 2005 estimate by Mark Kramer of Harvard University, as many as 400 to 500 jihadists have been fighting alongside a Chechen force that often numbered less than 2,000 guerrillas.[27]

Russian incompetence has done much to inflame Chechen hatred and to drive the rebels to greater violence. But the influence of the jihadists on the fighting has been unmistakable. There has been a dramatic increase in the number of terrorist attacks since 1999, and the insurgents in Chechnya have demonstrated an ability to wire complex explosives, to use vehicle-borne improvised explosive devices, to target oil and gas pipelines, and to carry out effective sniper attacks. Kramer reports that the dynamic interplay of radicalization and technical advance led Russian officials "to worry that Chechen guerrillas will seek to blow up a water reservoir, chemical waste dump, or nuclear power plant—a concern that prompted the tightening of security at all nuclear energy installations in August–September 2004."[28]

The most distinctive aspect of the turn to terror is the use of suicide bombings, which were largely unknown during the first Chechen war. In 2003, there were nine suicide bombings in Moscow alone, killing scores of people, and in December of that year, a bomb in a commuter train in southern Russia killed forty-one people. In August 2004, the killing continued spectacularly when two Chechen women on separate airplanes nearly simultaneously detonated explosive belts they were wearing, causing the planes to crash—an attack so effective that al Qaeda probably wished it had orchestrated it. Shortly afterward came the attack on Middle School No. 1 in Beslan, claiming the lives of at least 330 of the 1,000 hostages—more than half the dead were children—and almost 30 members of the Russian security forces. Chechens have taken captives for years, but the peculiar horror of taking hostage hundreds of schoolchildren represented a new level of barbarism—one reached, perhaps in part, because of the theorizing about mass killing of noncombatants that is in the jihadist ether.

For many in the West, Chechnya and the North Caucasus represent "a quarrel in a far-away country between people of whom we know nothing," to use Neville Chamberlain's notorious phrase about Czechoslovakia in 1938. Yet the violence is a matter of concern for outsiders because of several facts. The first is that Russia's handling of its problems in the region has become a central issue in the presidency of Vladimir Putin and has damaged his relationship with the West. After Beslan, Putin increased central control in Russia by eliminating elected governors, a move that elicited criticism from Europe and America that the Russian president was destroying his country's fledgling democracy. Another outstanding issue is that the violence is spreading. Fighting has taken hold in Dagestan, North Ossetia, and other nearby republics, and the insurgents have announced their intention to carry out attacks in the predominantly Russian areas of Stavropol Krai and Krasnodar Krai.[29] The scholars Rajan Menon and Peter Reddaway speculated in March 2005 that "these deep-rooted problems could lead to the progressive crumbling of Russia's authority along its entire southern border. That would undermine Putin, or even cause his fall from power. It would also transform Russia's geostrategic position."[30] Also important, the extremists may follow in the terrorist tradition of trying to strike their enemy in foreign settings. In 2002, a group of Algerian jihadists who had fought in Chechnya were arrested for conspiring to attack the Russian Embassy in Paris. Nine suspects were detained in the matter for possessing the ingredients for a large bomb and materials that were thought to be for building chemical weapons. (One of those arrested, Menad Benachelli, is the brother of another jihadist who had been captured in Afghanistan and is now an inmate at Guantánamo.)[31] That a group of Algerians was eager to strike a blow for a struggle taking place a thousand miles away tells us much about the internationalization of grievance in the Muslim world. It also suggests that we would be naive if we thought that something similar will not happen again in the future.

Saudi Arabia

In the aftermath of the September 11 attacks, in which fifteen of the nineteen hijackers came from Saudi Arabia, concern among U.S. policy makers for the stability of the Saudi regime—and America's oil supply—was exceeded only by the sense among many Americans that this longtime friend of the United States was deeply complicit in the catastrophe. There was some justification on both scores. Although most of the formative intellectual influences on jihadist ideology were from Egypt, Saudi money and Saudi individuals, Usama bin Laden among them, did much to promote this creed. In particular, the Saudi royal family spent hundreds of millions of dollars on missionary activity to spread Wahhabi-style Islam in the 1980s and 1990s, and some of the support that went to jihadist groups was funneled through charitable foundations that had their imprimatur.

Since the early 1990s, Saudi preachers, many of whom worked outside of the ranks of the state clergy, became leading propagandists of jihad, replacing the earlier generation of Egyptian writers who sparked the Sunni radical movement in the 1960s. Their sermons and religious opinions, which demonize the United States and its presumed ally, the Jews, are propagated widely via the Internet in Arabic and in translation. Michael Doran, formerly of Princeton University and now an aide on the National Security Council staff, calls Saudi Arabia the "cultural hub" of the jihad, pointing out that the Manichean and puritanical ideology of many Saudi clerics reaches Muslim communities far beyond its borders. Abu Muhammad al-Maqdisi, the former Jordanian mentor of Abu Musab al-Zarqawi, studied in Iraq but has been deeply influenced by Saudi preachers and has written about the apostasy of the Saudi royal family. Similarly, Abu Bakr Bashir, the spiritual leader of the Indonesian terrorist organization Jemaah Islamiyah, studied in Saudi Arabia and works to spread the values of Wahhabism in his native country, even though the indigenous Muslim customs and beliefs of Indonesia are very much at odds with his message.[32] Moreover, money from individual Saudis continues to find its way to terrorists. Although U.S. officials give the Saudi government credit for trying to shut down the pipeline to radicals, it may never be possible to shut the spigot entirely.

Contemporary jihadist agitation in Saudi Arabia originated in the first Gulf war. That conflict revealed the inability of the Saudi royal family to defend the land of Muhammad, despite the vast sums it had spent on American weapons. This brought suspicions of royal corruption to the surface, even as American (i.e., non-Muslim) forces were flooding into the kingdom. An opposition movement coalesced, among which were those who rejected the legitimacy of the royal family and sought, above all, to remove the American prop that kept it in power. These radicals first committed violence in 1995 with the deadly bombing of the U.S. Army office in Riyadh that managed training programs and the sale of American equipment to the Saudi Arabian National Guard. A year later came an even more audacious attack: the bombing of the Khobar Towers in Dhahran, a U.S. Air Force residential complex, a massive attack that killed 19 Americans and wounded 400. This strike was the work of Iranian agents working with Saudi Shiites, not Sunni radicals, but it set the standard for future attacks.

The next wave of violence commenced in 2003, at the behest of Abd al-Aziz al-Muqrin, a young Saudi jihadist who disagreed with bin Laden's "Far Enemy" doctrine of attacking the United States as the means to undermine the Saudi royal family. His view was hotly debated within the movement. For many jihadists, not only was bin Laden's strategic focus correct, but the Americans had done the jihadists a great favor by delivering targets for destruction to Iraq, which greatly simplified the job of killing them. This, so far as most Arabian radicals were concerned, was reason enough to carry the jihad to Iraq and not waste lives, resources, and reputation attacking targets within Saudi Arabia. Moreover, attacks that would inevitably endanger ordinary Muslims in the kingdom were bound to sacrifice the moral high ground the jihad needed to grow—and win.

Though he professed to revere bin Laden, al-Muqrin rejected these concerns. In an interview in the first edition of the online publication *Sawt al-Jihad,* he said, "I did not go to Iraq, and I will not go to Iraq. I swore to clear the Arabian peninsula of polytheists. We were . . . born in this country so we will fight the Crusaders and Jews in it until we have expelled them."[33] This sentiment helped to mobilize a group of local jihadists, and under the banner of al Qaeda of the Arabian Peninsula (QAP), al-Muqrin set his followers in motion. In March 2003, as they prepared for their first strike, members of the group inadvertently detonated a bomb in a safe house, thus alerting Saudi authorities, who raided the location and discovered an enormous arms cache. Conscious of the rising threat, Saudi police raided another safe house in early May, but they botched the operation and allowed the cell that had been hiding there to escape. That same month, twelve jihadists from QAP detonated three car bombs virtually simultaneously in residential compounds in Riyadh, killing 30 and wounding 200.[34]

The intensity and indiscriminate nature of the attack were unprecedented in recent Saudi experience. It shook the public and drew a coordinated, massive response from the government. Assaults on safe houses were carried out all over the country—in Mecca and Medina in the west, in Riyadh and elsewhere in the center, and in the southern border region of Jizan—which in turn demonstrated that the insurgency had a nationwide presence. The raids were punishing. The jihadists lost large arms caches and mid-level commanders as well as their operational leader,

Yusuf al-Ayiri. In all, perhaps a dozen cells of five to twenty jihadists each were dismantled.

Despite these losses, the QAP had the manpower, weapons, ammunition, and second-tier leaders to press on with its campaign. In November 2003, QAP members in police uniforms drove vans loaded with explosives into a residential compound in Riyadh; the blast claimed 17 lives and wounded 120 people, including many children. Here the jihadists showed themselves to be *takfiri,* those who believe that it is justified to kill Muslims who commit apostasy and who collaborate with the enemy. (Zarqawi is just such a *takfiri.*) But they soon found that in the battle to win over "hearts and minds" among the Muslim population, the indiscriminate savagery of the *takfiri* approach was self-defeating. As 2003 drew to an end, these attacks had begun to erode QAP's public support.

That winter saw the continued attrition of QAP ranks. Political pressure on the Saudi government to act decisively and effectively remained strong. An indication of the seriousness with which the Saudis viewed this was the changed attitude of Prince Nayef, the interior minister, who had long been associated with a live-and-let-live attitude toward jihadists as long as they fought their battles outside of the kingdom. By March 2004, insurgents were being caught in small groups while on the run, indicating that their access to safe houses had been cut off. In April, after the bombing of the police headquarters in Riyadh inspired more public disgust, al-Muqrin revised his instructions to emphasize the priority of striking "the Jews, Americans, and Crusaders in general." In May, QAP attacked the offices of a Swiss pipeline services company in Yanbu on the Red Sea coast— the first attack on an oil-related target in the kingdom—and a residential compound in Khobar that had many foreign residents. By June, however, much of QAP's battered command structure, including al-Muqrin, was dead, killed at the hands of Saudi forces.

During the following six months the scattered remnants of QAP lay low, slowly regrouping. They were determined to show that they were still a force to be reckoned with. The truth was that the dynamic leadership that had set them in motion was gone, their arms caches had been discovered, and they could no longer communicate safely and consistently. Their final attacks, which were meant to be spectacular, instead demonstrated their dramatic decline. In December 2004, the group assaulted the U.S.

consulate-general in the western city of Jeddah, one of the most heavily defended installations in the kingdom. In this show of bravado, five attackers in a single car attempted to gain entry to the consulate grounds. Armed only with pipe bombs and small arms, they succeeded in stunning the Saudi perimeter guards and, at the end of the day, killing four non-American consulate employees. Four of the attackers were killed during the assault or died afterward from their wounds. They seemed to have no idea of the layout of the interior of the compound—where the key structures were, how its defenses were configured, or what kinds of weapons would be needed to penetrate the hardened core of the post. They never succeeded in entering the consulate building itself. With no advance surveillance or reconnaissance before the attack, no clandestine contacts within the consulate, insufficient numbers, and inadequate weaponry, the attack was doomed—QAP's audacity was matched only by its incompetence. It may be that after so many attacks in which mostly Muslims were killed, QAP felt compelled to show its determination to kill Americans, even if it was unable to do so.

The second and, it seems, last attempt to make a dramatic statement came on December 29. Militants launched coordinated, nearly simultaneous, car bomb attacks against the Ministry of the Interior in the mistaken belief that Prince Nayef, the minister, was on the premises, and against the special forces recruiting office. The attack was rushed because Saudi security had uncovered the plot and were on the verge of taking down the cell. Although the attacks drew blood, the vehicles bearing the explosives could not get close enough to the targeted buildings to inflict significant damage. Ten more radicals were shot in police raids immediately following the botched car bombings, including two of the remaining operational commanders.

As of the summer of 2005, all that remains of QAP is its propaganda machine, the online publications *Sawt al-Jihad* and *Camp al-Battar,* which remain dedicated to the job of keeping jihadists motivated and supplying them with the concepts and skills needed to wage a long war. The continued existence of these publications—and their producers—show that QAP elements are capable of eluding Saudi security while intermittently putting out a publication of forty or more pages that is disseminated to a global audience.

The Saudi government's success in rolling back its domestic jihadists may be owed in part to the war raging next door in Iraq, which has attracted hundreds and possibly thousands of Saudis who might otherwise be inclined to oppose their own government. The Saudi regime has also adopted a comprehensive strategy, which called for delegitimizing QAP even as it worked to destroy the group's networks. The first step was to enlist the official clergy to issue edicts condemning QAP. Given the eroded credibility of clerics in the pay of the state, it is not clear how effective this was. A second step was to compel three of the most notorious jihadist preachers, including Nasir bin Hamad al-Fahd, the author of the fatwa justifying the use of weapons of mass destruction, to recant publicly their radical ideas. This may have been effective in persuading some supporters of QAP to back off. The regime also persuaded its critics on the religious right, including Safar al-Hawali, a cleric who spearheaded the criticism of the regime in the early 1990s and wrote a virulently anti-American apocalyptic tract, "The Day of Wrath," to condemn the use of violence. The Saudi leadership made good use of the media under their control by depicting explicit imagery of the bloodshed that QAP had wrought on Muslim civilians, showcasing grief-stricken relatives of victims and mangled children. They appealed to parents to monitor their children and report on activities that showed the influence of extreme Wahhabi thinking, such as destroying televisions, which are viewed by militants as sinful instruments. Finally, the leadership acted behind the scenes to pressure violent groups outside the kingdom that benefit from Saudi largesse, such as Hamas, to condemn the terrorist attacks.

Whether the victory over QAP will last will depend, first, on the commitment of the Saudi leadership to a reform process that expands political participation, strengthens the job market, and visibly reduces royal corruption. Persistent divisions within the Saudi family and the opposition raise doubts about the viability of this course. Moreover, the Saudi regime typically changes slowly, and the country faces enormous demographic problems in the near future. The average Saudi woman has four children, which generates a population growth rate of 2.3 percent per year.[35] Current unemployment is conservatively estimated at 14 percent, and it is difficult to imagine how the economy will create enough jobs to employ such large numbers of young people. Unemployment among the young can be destabilizing, even in one of the world's richer countries.

Another key factor will be how events in Iraq unfold and what Saudi Arabia's veterans do when they return from the jihad. It has been rumored that Saudi officials and clerics have at least tacitly supported the migration of jihadists to Iraq as a way of defusing domestic tensions. If so, this will be another case in which pursuing short-term interests could cause long-term harm: Those who return will be even more radicalized and battle-hardened, representing a real threat to the regime. And their ability and willingness to carry on the struggle at home may depend on the Saudi leadership's reforms and on the capacity of the economy to absorb them. These are large and ominous uncertainties.

What makes the issue of a resurgent jihadist underground in the kingdom so worrisome is that there may be no country on Earth as poorly understood as Saudi Arabia. Because the government has kept the barriers to foreigners high, social scientists, journalists, and intelligence services have not developed the detailed understanding of popular attitudes in Saudi Arabia that they have in other countries. Is Saudi Arabia the "aircraft carrier for the jihad," as one recently retired senior intelligence official thinks it might be, or is the country ultimately stabilized by a young middle class committed to reform within existing institutions, as some Saudis have argued? At a time when serious scholars debate such fundamental issues as whether the Saudi elite is essentially unified or divided into opposing camps, a large question mark hangs over the future of the kingdom.

Pakistan

Pakistan hangs in the balance. President Pervez Musharraf, dubbed the "minimal satisfier" by the Brookings Institution scholar Stephen Cohen because of his tendency to provide the barest concessions on political issues, has done very little to alleviate the conditions that have made his country a center of the jihad. In January 2002, in the aftermath of September 11 and the removal of the Taliban from power in Afghanistan, Musharraf delivered a stirring speech broadcast to the nation in which he vowed hard punishment for anyone responsible for extremism in Kashmir or involved in religious intolerance within Pakistan.[36] "Violence and terrorism has been going on for years," he observed, "and we are weary and sick of this Kalashnikov culture." He deplored religious groups that had supported the Taliban in Afghanistan. Within Pakistan itself, he went on, rampant religious intolerance between Sunnis and Shiites has meant that "we started slaughtering each other in mosques, the houses of God." He stressed the need for continued reform of Pakistan's religious schools or madrassas, which had served as conveyor belts feeding the jihad, and he warned that if the schools did not act responsibly, they would have their "freedom taken away."[37]

Musharraf won credit for correctly identifying Pakistan's problems and for choosing to side with the United States, which had presented him with an ultimatum after September 11 demanding that he support the overthrow of the Taliban and crack down on al Qaeda. He made good, for the most part, on those top-of-the-list requirements, though many in the U.S. government and outside have expressed impatience at the sluggishness with which Pakistani authorities confront terrorists—the occasional, well-staged arrest of a militant has come to seem like a ritual designed solely to remind American officials that Islamabad is on the case.

Musharraf's post–September 11 actions entailed more peril than the general probably knew. He was reversing key aspects of the policy of the 1990s, when the Pakistani intelligence service had nourished many of the jihadist groups so they could fight in Afghanistan in support of the Taliban or carry out terrorist attacks in Indian-controlled Kashmir. Pakistani intelligence could exercise a degree of restraint on its longtime clients, but some of the more extremist splinter groups considered Musharraf's switch to the American side to be traitorous, and they targeted him for assassination. At least two and possibly as many as six attempts were made on Musharraf's life over the next four years. One of these attacks in December 2003 involved radicals within the Pakistani army and was a very near miss.[38] The detonation of the large bomb that had been planted on his motorcade route in Rawalpindi, just outside of Islamabad, was delayed by an electronic jamming device, giving Musharraf's vehicle just enough time to get out of range. These efforts are said to have sharpened Musharraf's determination to crack down on radicals, but he has done little to address the broader ills that beset Pakistan and feed jihadist sentiment.

Each religious sect has its own political party and armed wing. On the

Sunni side, the major parties have been identified with internal violence and international terrorism as well. In 2005 the former interior minister, Faisal Saleh Hayat, asserted that the leadership and rank and file of the two leading Sunni parties, Jamaat e Islami (JI) and Jamiat Ulema i-Islami (JUI), key players in Pakistani politics, are directly tied to terror networks outside of Pakistan. The fact that Khalid Sheikh Mohammed was arrested in March 2003 in the home of a JI operative symbolizes the close connection between domestic and foreign terrorism. After a spate of international attacks, including against the Indian Parliament in December 2001, the activities of many of the largest jihadist groups such as Lashkar-e-Tayba appear to have been restrained, but their training camps continue to operate, and a number of non-Pakistanis have become equipped for the global jihad there.[39] Reports that some of the men who bombed the London Underground in July 2005 had been to LeT camps highlights this concern. They would not have been the first individuals to have plotted terrorist attacks after passing through the camps. Willie Brigitte, a French citizen born on the island of Guadeloupe in the Caribbean, was arrested in Australia in 2004 for plotting terrorist attacks. Brigitte, who had converted to Islam in 1998, had trained at LeT's facility near Lahore, a city that some of the London bombers visited.

Pakistan's jihadist infrastructure represents a major long-term problem because it is not clear that Islamabad wants to disarm the militants. The country is awash in a sea of weapons and rife with *lashkars,* or private armies in the service of warlords, religious party leaders, or both. The interior ministry estimates that in addition to the millions of legal weapons in the country, there are 18 million illegal arms. The government's response to the problem of militias has thus far entailed huge subsidies for the worst offenders in return for their quiescence. This can backfire; in one case, the JUI engineered a deal with a tribe in northwest Pakistan whose leaders promptly turned the funds over to al Qaeda.[40]

The organizations themselves are only the tip of the problem. The pervasiveness of sectarian violence is directly linked to growth of the madrassa system and the corresponding decline in public education. The religious parties foster this trend by funding madrassas directly from their party coffers. These schools isolate students from society while teaching them that their religion is under threat and must be defended at all costs, at home or in Kashmir or Afghanistan. It is a self-sustaining, vertically integrated system designed for waging war against similarly structured movements. Its ultimate objective is to win new adherents and obliterate competitors.

The incentives are huge for sectarian parties to expand this system for churning out future adherents on an industrial scale. When Pakistan was established in 1947, there were 137 madrassas. In 1988, following the anti-Soviet jihad and waves of tribal and sectarian fighting in Afghanistan, there were 3,000. The most reliable estimates for 2005 put the number at over 10,000. Not all are militant, but more than enough are dangerous. Musharraf's pledge to tame the madrassas was codified in legislation in 2001 to register and regulate them, but the pledge was never fulfilled. Rather than press the political parties that control the madrassa system to comply with the law, Musharraf backed off, urging voluntary compliance in return for massive government financial assistance. The total package of budgetary support for the madrassas came to $100 million, a figure that does not include private charitable contributions to schools in the system. This is a lot of money and, predictably, it had the opposite of its intended effect. With so much government money available, it made sense for the parties to set up even more madrassas. In the meantime, the diversion of resources needed to bribe sectarian leaders further starves a dying public education system. The government is on the defensive: Musharraf's former minister of education, Zubaida Jalal, was forced by a mob organized by sectarian party leaders to announce that she was a fundamentalist and to condemn schoolbooks that did not contain Quranic injunctions to wage jihad.

What makes this picture so dismal is that the Pakistani people are becoming ever more passionately anti-American. In the words of Stephen Cohen, Pakistan is "probably the most anti-American country in the world right now, ranging from the radical Islamists on the one side to the liberals and Westernized elites on the other," an assessment largely borne out by survey data.[41] Although Musharraf remains popular, with a favorable rating of 65 percent, Usama bin Laden is viewed favorably by about the same margin.[42]

The hatred of the United States is evident in the language radicals use to energize their followers. Where, before September 11, extremists focused their hatred on India and the issue of Kashmir, now they seek to mobilize support by inciting others against America.[43] The radicals' ties to the Taliban are one reason for the growing antipathy; Iraq is the other. The militant group Lashkar-e-Tayba, for example, has used its online Urdu publication to call for sending holy warriors to Iraq to take revenge for the torture at Abu Ghraib prison as well as for what it calls the "rapes of Iraqi Muslim women." One notice on its site reads "The Americans are dishonoring our mothers and sisters. Therefore, jihad against America has now become mandatory." The organization's postings speak of an "army" of 8,000 fighters being mustered from different countries bound for Iraq.

Despite its rhetoric, there is thus far little evidence that Lashkar-e-Tayba has gone global. But the shift in language is indicative. Although the discourse of outrage does not necessarily signify the will to act soon and might even be a substitute for action, the virulence of the language used about America provides one signpost to a violent future. At some point, the group may well feel it needs to make good on its rhetoric.

Pakistan's social and political problems have seemed intractable for decades, and the weakness of its institutions offers little hope. The West has placed its hopes in Musharraf, but the general has done little to strengthen any forces for moderation outside himself and the army. Democracy remains a promise perpetually postponed, as Musharraf has reneged on his pledge to give up his office as chief of the army staff and hold fair elections. He has maintained his control by acquiescing in the maneuvers of Sunni extremist parties, who had their biggest breakthrough in electoral politics in 2003, and flirting with the traditional political parties. The net result is that Musharraf and the state are increasingly indistinguishable, an unhealthy situation for Pakistan and a world dependent on the defusing of the jihadist threat.

Southeast Asia

Islam in Southeast Asia has medieval roots.[44] In the late nineteenth century and most of the twentieth century, religious identity took a radical turn in parts of Indonesia and the Philippines for complex reasons. The shrinking cost of long-haul travel by steamship meant that greater numbers of believers from Indonesia, in particular, could make their way to Mecca on pilgrimage, where they were exposed to a puritanical form of Islam unlike the more eclectic, tolerant approach of their native Sufism. The interconnectedness of Southeast Asia and the Middle East also brought more students to the large seminaries there, especially al Azhar in Cairo, where visiting students imbibed the thought of the new Muslim revivalists who rejected the relaxed religious observances that characterized popular Islam in their homeland.

Cultural crosscurrents were not the only factor. Colonial occupation by Britain, the Netherlands, Japan, and the United States stirred resistance that found expression in religious terms. In the Philippines, Muslim rebels fought a bloody but losing battle against the U.S. Army in the waning years of the nineteenth century. The descendants of these fighters picked up the torch after World War II, when they embarked on a guerrilla war in Mindanao that still goes on. A separate, major insurgency got underway in Indonesia in the early 1900s, aimed at imperial Dutch rule in the archipelago. The Japanese exploited the mobilizing qualities of Islam after the Dutch surrendered to them in 1942 through a tactical alliance that preserved the structure of the prewar resistance, keeping it alive to fight another day. This day came after Indonesian independence was recognized by the Netherlands in 1949, when a part of the anticolonial insurgency reignited under the banner of Dar ul-Islam (Domain of Islam), this time against the secular rule of Sukarno, the insurgent leader turned authoritarian ruler who governed the country until 1967. It was not until 1962 that the regime in Jakarta managed to crush the rebellion, execute its leader, and imprison the fifteen top commanders of the insurgency. In the 1990s, the progeny of the Dar ul-Islam generation of fighters took up the cause again under the rubric of Jemaah Islamiya (JI), this time against the regime of Suharto, the general who overthrew Sukarno, and then against Megawati Sukarnoputri, his successor. JI's battle now grinds on against the administration of Indonesia's new president, Susilo Bambang Yudhoyono. Like its parent organization, JI espouses a wide variety of aims that do not constitute an especially coherent program. Some activists want to establish a caliphate in Southeast Asia or impose Islamic law in Indonesia; others are separatists in pursuit of political independence from the authorities in Jakarta, while still others want more influence within the existing order.

Incoherence, however, has its own virtue; since there is something in the movement's agenda for everyone to agree upon, JI enjoys a larger following than might otherwise be the case. This proved to be a vital advantage when the Indonesian government tried to move against the group's leadership in 2004.

Muslims in Malaysia and Thailand have had a restless and occasionally violent relationship with their respective governments, as well. In Thailand, where 6 to 9 percent of the population—about 2 million people—are ethnically Malay and Muslim by religion, there has long been discontent. The southern provinces in which most Muslims live have been neglected by the central government of this largely Buddhist country for decades. Isolation and impoverishment have fueled both crime and political grievance, which have become intertwined as criminal kingpins cloaked their operations in the mantle of principle and opposition forces turned to crime to finance their political maneuvers and recruitment efforts. As in other countries in the region, Muslim resentment against the government's failure to deal with social and economic problems was framed in the language of religion. Violence sputtered there throughout the 1990s and erupted in large-scale battles with police in 2004. The government of Prime Minister Thaksin Shinawatra responded brutally, without discriminating between militants involved in terrorism and other, nonviolent activists, thus driving moderates into the radicals' camp. In Malaysia, Muslims who have become enmeshed in the jihadist underground do not hail from remote or neglected provinces of a large country, but are mostly urban, integrated individuals, schooled in nearby Singapore, and are, in some instances, veterans of Singapore's military. Malaysia has also served as the strategic haven for Indonesian radicals on the run from Indonesian authorities, including Abu Bakr Bashir, who founded JI in Indonesia in the 1970s, and Abdullah Sungkar, who created JI in Malaysia in 1993–94.[45]

The evolution of these movements since 9/11 roughly parallels the developments in Europe, the Caucasus, and Central Asia. While al Qaeda's leadership was still largely intact, it worked with JI on plans to attack targets in Indonesia, Malaysia, Singapore, the Philippines, Taiwan, Vietnam, and Cambodia to coincide with the one-year anniversary of the 9/11 attacks. This information, derived from the interrogation of captured al Qaeda operations coordinator Omar al-Farouq, led to the closure of embassies in

Asia in September 2002 and the simultaneous change of the Department of Homeland Security's color code system in the United States from yellow to orange. The Singapore conspirators planned to attack the American, Australian, and Israeli embassies and, in an echo of the assault on the U.S.S. *Cole,* strike U.S. naval vessels or personnel. These attacks had been conceived in Afghanistan by al Qaeda's war council. During this period, it became apparent that the leading Indonesian radical Riduan Issamudin, known also as Hambali, had an al Qaeda connection dating back to the 1990s.

With the arrests of al-Farouq in Indonesia in June 2002, Khalid Sheikh Mohammed in Pakistan in March 2003, and Hambali in Thailand in June 2003, the umbilical link between jihad in Southeast Asia and the old guard of Afghan Arabs weakened, and was replaced by a looser, qualitatively different relationship based more on the transfer of technical expertise than on command and control.[46] On their own now, the militants began to target Western assets. The firebombing of the Bali resort in October 2002, which killed 200 people, mostly Australian vacationers and Indonesians, was a transitional operation; the ringleader, Samudra, had links to al Qaeda, but the local group did the planning and target selection. The choice of the Bali resort as a target was meant to hurt an American ally.[47] The attack showed that a regional group had adopted al Qaeda's global agenda and was pursuing attacks against the "Far Enemy" but now without hands-on steering from the al Qaeda leadership in Afghanistan.

The bombing of the Marriott Hotel in central Jakarta in August 2003 also reflected a turn to targets associated with the "Far Enemy," and another departure from the localized jihad that had been typical of Muslim activism in the region.[48] A host of lesser-known attacks have also fit this pattern: The bombing of the U.S. consulate in Bali and the Philippines consulate in Sulawesi in the fall of 2002, the spring 2003 bombings of the UN building and of Soekarno-Hatta International Airport in Jakarta, and the fall 2004 bombing of the Australian Embassy in Jakarta.[49] Ironically, the degree to which the local jihadists had adopted al Qaeda's global agenda and fixation on the United States as its own became a problem for the al Qaeda leadership, at least according to Khalid Sheikh Mohammed's statements to his American interrogators. As far as the leadership was concerned, JI and its affiliated groups were endangering the potential of their regional operations by taking on the United States, which in turn put unwanted pressure on Jakarta to suppress jihadist networks in Indonesia.[50]

The generational shift to a younger, indigenous cadre of leaders has been fostered by a small number of *pesantren,* or religious boarding schools. Probably no more than five out of the 14,000 such schools in Indonesia, indoctrinate their students with a harsh and confrontational form of Islam and provide them with the religious justification for violence in pursuit of religious goals, as they have defined them. Although the *pesantren* form only a small part of the broader system of religious education in Indonesia, they graduate large numbers of students. The most well-known radical *pesantren,* al Mukmin, has 1,800 full-time students and is considered to be an efficient transmission belt for recruits to the Southeast Asian jihad. Its alumni carried out the attacks against the Bali resort, the Marriott Hotel, and the Australian Embassy.

The ascendancy of local jihad leaders and the expansion of attacks to include Western targets are not the only things the jihad in Southeast Asia has in common with militant activity in other regions. While the "Far Enemy"—the United States and its allies, including Australia, Singapore, and Israel—has been targeted in addition to the "Near Enemy," whose churches, shopping malls, and businesses in regional capitals and rural areas of the Philippines continue to be attacked, local jihadist groups have tightened their links, engaging in joint planning and operations. These connections have gotten so close that law enforcement and intelligence analysts find it difficult to distinguish among them.[51] Members of these groups roam freely around the region. For planning sessions, for example, the jihadists have favored some areas, like Thailand, where tourist-friendly policies and weak law enforcement make their movements more secure, or Malaysia, because it allowed visa-free entry to most Gulf passport holders. For training purposes, Mindanao in the Philippines has been the preferred location for teaching Indonesian militants how to fight. For access to Western targets, Singapore, Jakarta, and the popular beach resorts in Thailand have assumed a magnetic quality.

By 2005, the jihad was well established in Southeast Asia. In Thailand, where Muslim separatist violence had been rife from the late 1960s through the 1980s, successive governments had finally gotten the upper hand, largely through conciliatory policies that relieved some of the misery of life in the southern provinces. But such progress has been lost more recently, as incompetent and unfair administrations of Muslim provinces, against a backdrop of pervasive and persuasive jihadist propaganda, have led to intensified violence. The pattern resembles the evolution of the jihad in Chechnya, where government repression and indiscriminate violence transformed an ethno-nationalist resistance motivated by local grievances into a jihad with global overtones.[52] Since early 2004, casualties from the fighting have mounted and, despite vague indications that the Thai government understands that its policies are inflaming opinion in the south, the conflict is expected to widen.[53]

Violence in the Philippines continues even as the government is engaged in negotiations with the Moro Islamic Liberation Front over granting Muslims a degree of autonomy in their "ancestral domain."[54] The problem is the Abu Sayyaf Group (ASG), which will not be reconciled to a cease-fire and has deepened its ties to JI. As a result, while the Philippine government is negotiating with one set of Islamists, it is fighting another, which inevitably entails noncombatant casualties, perpetuate Muslim animosities, and provide the jihadists with the propaganda they need to prosper. At the same time, the partnership between Abu Sayyaf and JI is supplying the latter with remote camps for the training of recruits, while it confers on Abu Sayyaf crucial skills for combating both the Philippine armed forces and the "Far Enemy." According to Gamal Baharan, an Abu Sayyaf detainee whose training included ship demolition, the thinking of the group is inclined toward the global jihad, not just killing Philippine infantry. The chief of the U.S. mission in Manila told an interviewer early in 2005 that Mindanao had become "the new Mecca for terrorism."[55] Although that may be an exaggeration, the potential is certainly there.

In Indonesia, the jihad continues as well. It is dispersed, just as Indonesian jurisdiction itself is scattered throughout thousands of islands. Many militants are from jihadi families, where parents and grandparents participated in the resistance to the Dutch and the Sukarno and Suharto regimes. They follow double lives, working at their trades while offering their combat skills on a clandestine basis to the cause. In the judgment of Sidney Jones, a renowned expert on the Indonesian jihad who was expelled from the country in 2004 for her reporting on the state of the war, the jihadists are not going to achieve their goal of independence, let alone a regional caliphate, but their success in regenerating lost cadres and their broad popularity will make them impossible to eliminate. As JI turns toward a globalized jihad and works to professionalize other regional jihadist groups, Jones's verdict carries stern implications for the United States and its friends in the region.

5

MUSLIMS IN AMERICA

Why has there been no second September 11? In the weeks and months following that day, it was universally proclaimed that more attacks were on the way that would wreak even greater devastation. Obviously, this has not happened. There are a number of possible explanations.

The first is that America has simply become too difficult a place for terrorists to operate, in part as a result of changes the U.S. government has made. An important one has been the tightening of immigration controls, which make it considerably more difficult to gain entry to the United States, especially for individuals from Muslim countries. (However, the government has hardly begun to grapple with the threat of Islamist radicals entering from Europe and the five countries that are on the "visa waiver" list that allows their citizens to enter the United States without visas.) But more significant is the greater consciousness of the threat that now animates the nation's law enforcement personnel, public officials, and private citizens. This vigilance, a dividend of al Qaeda's attacks, is valuable beyond any reckoning, and has made America a much harder target.

Another partial explanation is that the jihadists are getting what they need elsewhere. By bloodying America in Iraq, they are fulfilling their requirement to demonstrate to the *umma* that they are what they claim to be: the champions of Muslim rights. As we have seen, a deluge of propaganda underscores their bravery and success in every conceivable medium. Iraq is now undoubtedly the main show, the foremost "field of jihad." But this provides limited comfort. Islamist message boards continue to speak of the need to strike the United States, if only to demonstrate the ability to do so. The letter Usama bin Laden sent to Abu Musab al-Zarqawi in March 2005 asking for help in launching an attack in the United States underscores this desire.[1]

A third reason, the one most often cited by counterterrorism experts, is that the jihadists perceive a need to outdo what they have done before when striking the "Far Enemy." As one former senior intelligence official observes, "Why haven't they smuggled ten people into the country to carry out suicide attacks at malls? We know they're trying to do something bigger and better." Mounting an operation that will kill thousands can take a long time, especially for a group that is averse to failure. The patient "perfection freaks," as they have been dubbed, of al Qaeda spent five years preparing the August 1998 attacks against the U.S. embassies in East Africa. Mindful that they are playing on God's chessboard, they have the patience to plan and drill until they are certain of success.

Alongside these considerations must also be a recognition that the American Muslim community has been inhospitable to jihadists and, thus far, largely immune to the radicalization going on elsewhere. One of the stunning contributions of the *9/11 Commission Report* was its documentation of the solitary path of the hijackers while they were in America. They appear to have had more contact and support with individuals from foreign embassies than with American Muslims.[2] If the Commission is correct, their operations were pathbreaking in that they were able to live off the land and stage their attacks without having a cell of local activists to prepare the ground for them. That they could pull off such attacks is obviously bad news. That no local network was found to support them is good news.

In the years since 9/11, the Justice Department's massive dragnet has turned up remarkably little in the way of a terrorist presence. A number of fund-raisers for the Lebanese group Hezbollah and the Palestinian group Hamas have been uncovered, and these have led to important prosecutions. People who raise money for Hamas have often been implicated in doing the same for jihadist groups such as al Qaeda—the streams of money are often mixed—so these prosecutions are critical.[3] But beyond those cases, the haul has been slim. In June 2005, President Bush announced that "federal terrorism investigations have resulted in charges against more than 400 suspects, and more than half of those charged have been convicted." Yet a *Washington Post* investigation has shown that only thirty-nine people were convicted of crimes tied to national security or terrorism. Of those, only fourteen had any link to al Qaeda. Among these were John Walker Lindh, the Californian who fought with the Taliban, Zacarias Moussaoui, the would-be hijacker, and Richard Reid, who tried to ignite a shoe bomb aboard an airplane over the Atlantic in December 2001.[4] Beyond these well-known cases, law enforcement officials point to one bona fide case of an al Qaeda operative, Iyman Faris, who was caught in the United States while plotting a crime. Whether Faris was genuinely criminal or simply insane is still unclear. A truck driver from Columbus, Ohio, Faris was arrested in 2003 for plotting to bring down the Brooklyn Bridge by cutting its suspension cables with blowtorches. The possibility of actually causing enough damage to endanger the bridge before detection verged on nil, and Faris, who had a license to haul hazardous materials, could easily have killed many more people had he just dispersed the contents of an appropriately filled truck. A higher-profile case occurred in Lackawanna, New York, where six Yemeni-Americans who had traveled to Afghanistan, attended a training camp, and met bin Laden were arrested in September 2002. But even in this case the hype was extraordinary. The group was described in a briefing to the president as the most dangerous cell in the country. In reality, they were doing nothing throughout the time the FBI observed them. The possibility that they would be handed over to the Defense Department for internment probably helped convince them to agree to plea bargains on charges of providing material support for terrorists and to years of jail time.[5]

That is not to say that there are no terrorists in the United States or that the nation has been fully protected from the virus of the jihadist ideology. Some of those closest to the intelligence and law enforcement efforts of the last four years are convinced that the FBI is still far from mastering the job of domestic intelligence gathering and is failing to find the trail of operatives who are here. Says one former White House official, "If you listen to the director of the FBI, there was no support structure for 9/11, and there is

no support structure here now." This, he believes, is at odds with the practice of jihadist terrorists since the time they first emerged from training in
Afghanistan and carried out the 1993 attack on the World Trade Center.
Expressing a sentiment that is heard from many in the intelligence community, he adds, "I think they are getting their resources in place. I think
things are happening in America. And I don't think we're seeing them."

Even so, in the large majority of cases, those arrested had no contact at
all with any foreign jihadist group. Given the availability of terrorist
know-how on the Internet, it is possible they would have developed into
dangerous operatives, but most were nowhere near such capability at the
time of their arrests. Reviewing the record of 119 terrorism-related prosecutions, New York University's Center on Law and Security concluded that
"the legal war on terror has yielded few visible results. There have been relatively few indictments, fewer trials, and almost no convictions on charges
reflecting dangerous crimes. Either the government is focused primarily
on using arrests to obtain information rather than conviction, or the legal
war on terror, as fought in the courts, is inconsequential."[6]

The chief reason why American Muslims have been relatively immune
to the call of the new *umma* is that their community does not resemble its
counterparts in Europe.[7] America has, for the most part, integrated Muslims in much the same way it has integrated other immigrant groups. The
first wave of Arab immigrants to America were primarily Christians from
Lebanon, and many of the Muslim Arabs who arrived here afterward were
middle class, relatively well educated, and worldly in their outlook. Later
Muslim immigrants from South Asia were less prosperous, but many
came equipped with some English-language skills and often a background
in trade. These groups followed a well-established path of adaptation and
integration, and their children spoke English, attended public schools, and
made their way in American society. By contrast, the majority of Muslim
immigrants to Europe came in search of work after World War II, when
the project of repairing the war's damage was underway. Europeans (with
the exception of the British) did not make much of an effort to integrate
these migrants, who were expected to go back to their countries of origin
when the job was complete. European countries had homogeneous societies unfamiliar with the habits of social integration, and the first two generations of Muslim immigrants kept to themselves, retaining their native

languages and customs, a situation that engendered an alienating atmosphere for their children.

The degree of Muslim integration in America is revealed by their average household income, which is higher than that of the general population. Two-thirds of Muslim households earn more than $50,000 per year, as compared to a median U.S. household income of $42,158, and a quarter of Muslim households earn $100,000 or more. This is undoubtedly both a cause and effect of their high level of educational attainment: More than a third of Muslim Americans have advanced degrees, compared to 8.6 percent for the population as a whole. Unlike their ghettoized fellow Muslims in Europe, American Muslims tend to live in improving neighborhoods in central cities and in the suburbs. On the whole, residential segregation is low, although it appears to be increasing as Muslims begin to gather more in their own enclaves. It is unclear whether this represents a durable trend, but it could be that integration of Muslims into American society is slowing down.[8]

Perhaps the starkest contrast between the Muslim communities on the two sides of the Atlantic involves political activity. While Muslims in America have yet to be represented in Congress, the electoral importance of this increasingly organized community has grown tremendously. In the 2000 and 2004 elections, the Muslim community in Michigan was identified as a key constituency in a battleground state that could conceivably affect the outcome of the presidential vote.[9] Senior political operatives of both parties lined up to meet with community leaders in a way that would be unimaginable in most of Europe. Similarly, there has been growth in political activism, in the form of grassroots organization, lobbying, voter registration, and the number of delegates to national conventions and candidates for office. This is a good news story. Even though the period since September 11 has been the most difficult one in the history of the American Muslim community, with a wave of anti-Muslim sentiment and 1,500 reported hate crimes in 2004 alone, many Muslims clearly feel that there are political solutions for their concerns, which means that these individuals are unlikely to withdraw from American society or, worse, lash out at it.[10]

Muslims, like other Americans, take their religion seriously. Nearly half attend Friday prayer every week. The number of mosques and the number of worshipers is growing—there are believed to be about 1,300 mosques in the United States and upward of 300 religious schools—a trend driven by immigration and, to a far lesser extent, conversions.[11] As in Europe, the younger generation seeks a more authentic form of Islam than the one their parents practice. This can have a positive effect, by strengthening identity and insulating young people from the subtler forms of discrimination they encounter as a minority. As one Chicago student explained, "I am more religious than my father because I have the luxury of thinking about my faith. I discovered Islam when I became involved in the campus mosque. . . . Our new awareness is also a reaction to the treatment of Muslims in this country. After September 11, the older generation who ran the show thought it best to lie low. . . . As that happened, the younger generation was uncomfortable with this, especially at colleges and universities. We decided we must become active."[12] The religious revival also has its downside. According to Marcia Hermansen, a Muslim professor of Islamic studies at Loyola University, "Quite a number of Muslim youth in America are becoming rigidly conservative and condemnatory of their peers, their parents, and all who are not within a narrow ideological band."[13] The trend in this direction was already evident before 9/11, and the Muslim Brotherhood was reported to have been secretly recruiting on campuses, warning that violence would become inevitable if Muslims in America were to be persecuted.[14]

How religious identity and Muslim Americans' sense of their place in the society evolves will directly affect America's domestic security. The more disaffected individuals, the greater the danger that jihadists will gain a foothold in the United States. While the danger of radical outsiders coming into the country will always exist, the chance of a successful attack will be magnified if American citizens link up with them or if groups of American self-starters emerge. The question now is whether conditions are developing that would make those events more likely.

There is good reason to worry. The same government dragnet that demonstrated the low level of terrorist activity has created a new uncertainty and even animosity on the part of Muslim Americans. In the climate of the period, a major law enforcement effort to find terrorists was inevitable. But more than 760 immigrants were secretly arrested and detained, some for many months. They were denied visits from family members and lawyers. According to human rights organizations, seventy men, all but one of them Muslim, have been jailed for weeks or months as "material witnesses" since 9/11, without having been charged with crimes.[15] These and other actions, like the wholesale and seemingly random interrogation of thousands of American Muslim men, sent shock waves through the community. One of the sorest points for American Muslims has been the aggressive prosecution strategy set by former Attorney General John Ashcroft. This led to a series of shoddy cases and a succession of dubious sting operations. Americans may have been given the impression that law enforcement authorities now possess the zeal that had evaded them before September 11, but it is questionable whether the Justice Department's efforts have made us safer, given how much antigovernment sentiment they have spurred and how few actual terrorists have been apprehended.

A striking example of the botched investigations was the case against a supposed "sleeper operational cell" in Detroit in 2002. The hapless immigrants caught up in this fiasco were suspected of having had prior knowledge of the September 11 attacks, and they were also said to possess targeting information on the MGM Grand Hotel in Las Vegas and the *New York Times* headquarters in New York. In announcing the arrests, Ashcroft declared that it was "a defining day in America's war against terrorism," and applauded the action as "a textbook example of the central role that cooperation with local, state and federal enforcement officials— plays in the prevention of terrorist attacks."[16] The only conviction obtained was for an immigration offense, which was overturned shortly thereafter. (Ashcroft himself was given a rare public admonishment by the judge in the case for twice violating a gag order in the proceedings— during press conferences, the attorney general repeatedly praised a government witness. He later apologized for his interventions.)[17] The charges, it later emerged, were based on the misinterpretation of some key pieces of evidence and the exclusion of others. Internal Justice Department communications revealed that the agency was riven by internal dissent over the case and that officials involved knew all along that the case was weak at best.[18] Despite the Detroit experience, FBI agents arrested a Muslim American lawyer in Portland, Oregon, on May 6, 2004, on suspicion of collaboration in the Madrid bombing two months before. The suspect, Brandon

Mayfield, was kept manacled and shackled for two weeks while the FBI puzzled over Spanish-language documents in his possession that turned out to be his son's homework.[19]

Incidents like these have engendered a sense of vulnerability and resentment among many Muslims and have succeeded in instilling a fear of Muslims among the general population. Opinion surveys show that one in four Americans holds a negative stereotype of Muslims. About a quarter of the respondents in a July 2004 poll believed that Muslims "value life less than other people" and "teach their children to hate unbelievers." Fully half did not believe Muslims had been as vigorous in condemning terrorism as they should be.[20] More disturbing is the fact that nearly half of those queried in a December 2004 poll believe that the U.S. government should curtail Muslim civil liberties, with a quarter stating that Muslim Americans should be required to register their whereabouts with the federal government.[21]

Such opinions could initiate a dynamic of alienation and hostility of the kind found in Europe. Significant numbers of American Muslims, polls show, feel that they receive neither respect nor tolerance. According to one survey, nearly 75 percent of Muslims "either know someone or have themselves experienced an act of anti-Muslim discrimination, harassment, verbal abuse or physical attack since September 11."[22] The incidents include pulling the headscarves off girls' heads, spitting, and verbal epithets. Of course, large majorities of Muslims already strongly disagree with U.S. policies in the Middle East and toward the Muslim world in general, a fact that cannot be overlooked in gauging the potential for greater alienation.[23]

For a number of reasons—some having to do with the political sensitivity of the subject—there is little good social science on the American Muslim community. One journalist who is working on surveying this landscape is Geneive Abdo, who has written authoritatively about Islam in Iran and Egypt and is now at work on a book about Muslims in America.[24] Her extensive interviews have led her to conclude that the 9/11 attacks and the suspicions that have been directed at Muslims in their wake have fundamentally changed the way American Muslims relate to their country. Abdo says that before September 11, Muslim immigrants to the United States were focused on traditional immigrant goals: work, housing, and education for their children. As practitioners of Islam and migrants from the Middle East and South Asia, they were not swept into the mainstream of American society, but like other non-Christian immigrants, held at arm's length. Their partial exclusion from American culture was mirrored by an impulse among many of them toward seclusion, as they sought to preserve and transmit to their children the customs of their homeland and the values of Islam.

Since 9/11, Abdo relates, a significant number of younger American Muslims have been reeling from the outbreak of prejudice. The reason, she says, is that after the attacks "it became respectable to express anti-Muslim views." The changed atmosphere has had a dislocating effect and has led to a retreat from the society around them into Muslim enclaves, where their sense of self-worth is not under attack. "Many of these young adults," she concludes, "are going to withdraw and avoid participating in a culture that looks down on their religion and reflexively equates their way of life with violence." Although she emphasizes that none of her subjects has suggested violence as an option for American Muslims, she foresees that "the isolation of American Muslims will increase unless there's a sea change in the administration's approach to the war on terrorism at home and its failure to take the foreign policy concerns of American Muslims seriously, especially the occupation of Palestinian territory."

Other experts have made similar observations. John Tirman, an expert on immigration policy at MIT who works closely with the Muslim community, notes that "in surveys, interviews, and meetings Muslims and Arab-Americans describe strong feelings of isolation and alienation from the American mainstream, disrespect for their views on the wars in Iraq and Afghanistan as well as the Palestinian question, and a sense of hopelessness about finding a place for Islam in American society." He adds that "at a gathering of national and local leaders of Muslim and Arab-American communities at the Social Science Research Council in Washington this fall, a few voiced concern about [the possibility of] internment should another act of terrorism befall America."[25] Such fears are indicative of a community perilously on edge.

Irritants abound. Charity is one of the five pillars of Islam and as such is taken seriously by American Muslims, who traditionally have been generous donors to charities that funnel money to Islamic causes abroad.

Lebanese-Americans gave to Hezbollah and its related organizations, and donations from Palestinian immigrants flowed to charities that were linked to Hamas. Others gave to funds operated by groups that have been linked indirectly to al Qaeda. Though some of this money undoubtedly went to support terrorism unbeknownst to most donors, the bulk of it funded legitimate charitable causes. Yet many American Muslims lack alternative distributors for charitable donations. The U.S. government, which has designated twenty-seven charities worldwide as supporters of terrorism, has seized or frozen large sums that have already been donated, and when the American Muslim community asked Washington to provide an approved list of charities to which Muslims could contribute, or to select a third party to distribute the frozen funds to recipients unconnected to radical groups, both of these proposals were rejected. The result, ironically, has been that donations are now being collected by trusted individuals in cash, to be spirited out of the country to unregulated charities—exactly the kind of underground mechanism that brought so much U.S. pressure on Saudi Arabia, where money collected in this fashion found its way to al Qaeda and affiliated groups.[26]

The elements already exist for the development of a radical sensibility among some American Muslims. Extremist sentiment on college campuses has been well documented, and small groups are known to have raised money for mujahedin and to have celebrated the anti-American sentiments of visiting radical sheikhs.[27] In March 2002, a Saudi graduate student, Sami Omar al-Hussayen, was charged with raising funds for terrorist organizations, including Hamas, and managing Web sites that supported terrorism. Though at trial the jury decided that he was guilty only of committing free speech, his acquittal was soon followed by his deportation for immigration violations, presumably because of the effect his free speech might have in radicalizing American Muslims. In Northern Virginia, a well-known preacher named Ali el-Timimi was convicted in April 2005 and later sentenced to life in prison for persuading a group of young men to do their Muslim duty by joining the global jihad. According to at least one witness, he told a small group of admirers on September 16, 2001, that "the time had come for them to go abroad and join the mujahidin engaged in violent jihad in Afghanistan." For government prosecutors, this qualified as "soliciting others to levy war against the United States and contributing services to the Taliban." Of the eleven young men initially charged along with el-Timimi, nine were convicted and given sentences ranging from four years to life imprisonment. (Five of these nine were born in the United States; the others were naturalized citizens or visa holders.) Some of them actually traveled to Pakistan and trained with Lashkar-e-Tayba, the terrorist group that believes that India occupies Kashmir illegally, and which has carried out hundreds of attacks against that country. Others had sought out Taliban contacts in Pakistan during the combat phase of the U.S. operations in Afghanistan.[28]

Such prosecutions will continue, and acts of violence arising from the world that el-Timimi and al-Hussayen inhabit are likely to disrupt the brittle equilibrium that now exists in America in the post–September 11 atmosphere of fear and mistrust. The question, though, will be how the project of integrating Muslims into American society continues in an age of terror. This, as the European example amply demonstrates, is not something that can be left to chance.

6

THE MEASURE OF THE THREAT

It is simply no longer possible to maintain that the United States is winning the war on terror. The number of terrorists is growing, as is the pool of people who may be moved to violence, and the means and know-how for carrying out attacks, including catastrophic ones, are becoming more readily available.

In thinking about terrorism, it is useful to keep in mind a simple image: two concentric circles, one very small, one very large. The inner circle represents those who are committed to carrying out acts of terror or actively supporting those who do—through fund-raising, propaganda, recruitment, and the like. The outer circle represents the universe of those who might migrate into the inner group. In the case of jihadist terror, those in the inner circle include members of al Qaeda, its affiliated groups, the new self-starters, fighters in Chechnya, some of Pakistan's radical Islamists, and an array of others scattered around the world. The outer circle is composed of those who might be susceptible to the virus of the jihadist ideology. It encompasses those Sunnis who might be convinced by Usama bin Laden's argument that the United States seeks to destroy Islam and oppress Muslims. At a minimum, the outer circle includes millions of people who might support the jihadist movement, some fraction of them by committing violence.

Unfortunately for the world's intelligence services, there is no census authority for the global jihad. Because of the war on terror, some of those in the inner circle are being arrested, deported to countries where they will be tried or at least carefully watched by the authorities, or killed in Iraq and Chechnya. Nonetheless, the consensus among Western intelligence services and independent analysts—whether they are judging by the activity of Muslim groups in Europe, the fighting in Chechnya, or the expanding activity of radicals online—is that a significant and growing migration is taking place from the outer circle to the inner circle. The attacks of September 11 and, perhaps even more dramatically, the invasion of Iraq have caused the ranks of the jihadists to swell. The long-term danger of terrorism is growing.

Numbers are not the only index of danger. Organization, capability, and opportunity are also key factors. If the core of al Qaeda has been damaged as seriously as U.S. government officials contend, then the likelihood of the most spectacular kinds of attacks is probably lower, at least for the moment. Operations experts like Khalid Sheikh Mohammed are few in number and, if there are any remaining in al Qaeda, they are constrained by problems of communications and the attrition of cells in the field. In May 2005, Pakistani and U.S. authorities engineered the capture of Abu Faraj al-Liby, who was, in the words of one top intelligence official, "the switchboard," the person who was rebuilding the al Qaeda leadership's ties to cells and other organizations around the world, which had been frayed or cut over the past four years. Al-Liby had been connected with the plot against U.S. financial institutions that was broken up in 2004, and this apprehension represents another important step in degrading the threat from al Qaeda itself. One or two capable cells might still inflict catastrophic damage if they remain undetected. But, for now, the probability of that happening has been lowered.

On the other hand, the growth in the number of jihadists and, in particular, the rise of the self-starters increases the chances of attack. Their violence may be less exotic, but it will still be lethal. Madrid may well be the touchstone—in the next few years, we will likely see more 3/11s than another 9/11. This, too, is a judgment based on probability. Most self-starter groups are likely to be less competent than terrorist organizations with long track records and established standards of tradecraft. In other words, low-quality attacks like the one in Casablanca could become common, and plenty of conspiracies will be detected early and prevented. But if only one in fifteen of the self-starters is competent and technically capable—if we use as a standard the European ratio of major conspiracies to success-fully executed attacks—the results could be devastating. What Sarhane, Ahmidan, and Lamari put together in a few months was not extremely difficult to do, and, if others act with the same kind of speed, they may be able to avoid detection by law enforcement authorities. With the addi-tional element of fighters returning from Iraq, the odds move significantly in favor of the self-starters or others carrying out attacks that kill in the triple digits. It cannot be ruled out that a self-starter group on its own or with al Qaeda remnants could carry out a genuine "spectacular," possibly involving a weapon of mass destruction. Although many of those who are drawn to the new *umma* are young, radical Islamism continues to attract well-educated, often scientifically trained adults—as was the case with the Jundullah activists in Pakistan, whose members include physicians and university-trained statisticians. Among the fifteen terrorists that Farhad Khosrokhavar interviewed in French prisons, most had studied in univer-sities and many had mastered multiple languages—four of them spoke three or more. Two were scientists, and another had a business degree. These are dangerous men.

In the coming years, the threat will be greater in Europe, where more individuals are being won over by the attractions of the new *umma* and the moral clarity of its worldview, than in the United States. But Ameri-cans would be foolish to be complacent because of the absence of attacks since September 11 and the relative comity of the American Muslim com-munity. Surely one of the lessons of September 11 is that the rise of ex-tremism outside the United States threatens Americans at home, and no immigration system or set of shipping inspections can fully insulate us. This is all the more true in a world in which it seems every day's headlines play into al Qaeda's propaganda. As the Pakistani journalist Najam Sethi has observed, Guantánamo is seen in the Muslim world "as evidence of how America and the West make the war against terrorism synonymous with the war against Islam"; Abu Ghraib and the purported flushing of a Quran down the toilet have likewise become potent symbols.[1] Moreover, given the images coming out of Iraq, the incitement on the Web, and anti-Muslim sentiment at home, we need to recognize the growing possibility that radicalism will expand its foothold in the United States. While the heavy hand of American law enforcement may have deterred some would-be terrorists, it could well have enraged others.

Different kinds of violence could also emerge. Iraq, an unparalleled laboratory for terrorist innovation, has renewed the jihadists' understanding of the value of retail violence; we could see a rise in assassinations, kidnappings, and beheadings in different parts of the world, to name the most obvious possibilities. The question is often posed why al Qaeda has not simply planted bombs in half a dozen Midwestern shopping malls, something that, it has been argued, would create pandemonium in the United States. Beyond the possibility that it does not have the operatives in place to do so, the best answer is that a plan like this does not meet al Qaeda's standards—it would not be the kind of event that would move the nation to change course, pull its troops and business interests out of the Middle East, and allow radical Islamists to come to power there. In the jihadist mind-set, such attacks would have neither the symbolic weight nor create the necessary carnage to achieve historic, world-altering goals.

But we should not expect al Qaeda's version of a meaningful act to be a lasting constraint on the jihadist movement. According to one rumor, Khalid Sheikh Mohammed told his interrogators that in the fall of 2002, al Qaeda members were fascinated by the paralysis that beset the Washington, D.C., area when a series of random individuals were killed by the snipers John Allen Muhammad and John Lee Malvo. If al Qaeda does not—or cannot—carry out such attacks, others may.

Jihadist terror is becoming a wide-open field. The emerging threat of cyber terror is another case in point. After September 11, many experts were skeptical about the possibility of jihadist cyber attacks aimed at disrupting key sectors of the economy that are driven by computers, like banking or telecommunications. The belief was that this would not interest jihadists because of the unlikelihood that it would cause the bloodshed that seemed a prerequisite of the new terror. But that judgment may have been premature. Now, online forums have appeared devoted to "e-jihad." There has been some hacking of the Web sites of Jewish organizations, and those who frequent Islamist message boards express a desire to improve jihadist cyber skills, which some presumably are.

*   *   *

HOW BIG A threat is all this? What is the potential damage to society? A strong argument can be made that even if there are more Madrid-sized attacks, and even if they become more frequent, we will get used to it. Although terrorism will never have the same "it's part of life" quality that, say, automobile accidents or cigarette smoking do, it is also true that terrorism on this scale will not cause as many deaths as these phenomena do. Despite the special horror that attaches to mass killing, Israelis have gotten accustomed to the permanence of terror, and we may do so, too. This is not something to look forward to: Israel has suffered terribly from the persistence of a terror that has made ordinary life, at least in its cities, a permanent ordeal, and many confess the sense of relief they feel when traveling abroad, away from the danger. The point is only that such terror would not cause the societies of the West to quake or cause fundamental institutions to be called into question.

The problem is that there is no certainty that Madrid-scale attacks represent an upper limit on the terrorism we face. On the contrary: A distinctive, almost unique characteristic of jihadist terror is its interest in genuine catastrophic attacks, with no meaningful boundaries on violence—witness Sheikh Nasir bin Hamad al-Fahd's "Treatise on the Ruling Regarding the Use of Weapons of Mass Destruction Against the Infidels," which allows the use of nuclear weapons so long as no more than 10 million people are killed. In the view of its practitioners, violence is sanctified, and therefore the more, the better. When terrorists like the self-starters of Madrid hear bin Laden's voice urging them to attack, they will consider how they can kill the most people. Some of them may figure out how to kill more than the number that died on March 11, 2004—perhaps many more.

There are two routes available. The first and, for now, easier one is to use "conventional" means—for the most part, available explosives—to strike targets whose destruction will cause mass casualties and, potentially, far-reaching economic disruption. That is what happened on September 11, and while it would be much harder today to gain control of wide-body airplanes because of the invasive searches of passengers and locked cockpit doors, terrorists nonetheless have other options. Another class of targets that could cause vastly more bloodshed if attacked are America's chemical plants. One hundred twenty-three chemical facilities in the United States are located in or near major metropolitan areas; any of these could put more than 1 million people at risk if it were to suffer a "toxic release." Approximately 700 plants could threaten populations of roughly 100,000 each; another 3,000 facilities could endanger 10,000 people apiece.[2] One plant in northern New Jersey alone threatens the safety of 12 million people in the New York metropolitan area. It is widely agreed that security in most of these plants is inadequate.

What is true for the chemical plants is even truer for the trucks, trains, and ships that transport chemicals. As Richard A. Falkenrath, formerly the deputy homeland security adviser in the Bush White House, recently wrote,

> Of all the various remaining civilian vulnerabilities, one stands alone as uniquely deadly, pervasive and susceptible to terrorist attack: industrial chemicals that are toxic when inhaled, such as chlorine, ammonia, phosgene, methyl bromide, and hydrochloric and various other acids. . . .
>
> The federal government has the authority to regulate the security of chemicals as they are being transported on roads, railways and waterways. With only one minor exception, the administration has not exercised this authority in any substantial way since Sept. 11. There has been no meaningful improvement in the security of these chemicals moving through our population centers.[3]

A variation on the theme of catastrophic killing is catastrophic disruption—less bloodshed but massive economic damage. One possibility would be the use of a radiological dispersion device—a "dirty bomb"— in a central, economically vital location. These devices pack together conventional explosives like dynamite with radioactive material, such as cesium-137, which is commonly used in industry and for medical purposes. A bomb with thirty kilograms of cesium-137 would release the same amount of radioactivity as the Chernobyl reactor did in 1986.[4] Most of the deaths from such a blast would result from the explosives, not the radioactivity. But the area contaminated by the radioactivity—the actual size would depend on the amount of explosives—would likely be uninhabitable for an indefinite period of time. The economic consequences of, say, losing a square mile of real estate in lower Manhattan would be overwhelming.

The other alternative for terrorists as they seek to raise the level of violence is to acquire or create a weapon of mass destruction. It is fair to say that the aspiration to use weapons of mass destruction is a constitutive element of the global jihad—it has been there since the very beginning. Bin Laden has been open about his desire for such weapons, and in the mid-1990s al Qaeda sought to buy the material for a nuclear weapon.[5] For $1.5 million—a large sum for any terrorist group, even al Qaeda—it negotiated to buy a cylinder of weapons-grade uranium of South African origin from a former Sudanese government official. Al Qaeda had the material tested and then bought the cylinder, but the deal turned out to be a swindle. Instead of highly enriched uranium, the terrorists found themselves in possession of a lump of some other, non-fissile radioactive material, possibly irradiated scrap metal. Bin Laden also dispatched one of his closest aides, Mamdouh Mahmud Salim, to shop for nuclear weapons components in Germany in late 1998, where he was arrested. These experiences may have instilled some caution in the group about the possibility of acquiring a nuclear weapon, but that did not deter them from pursuing other unconventional weapons programs. In the same period, bin Laden invested in the Sudanese government's effort to produce VX nerve gas.[6] (Intelligence reports on that effort led to the destruction of the al-Shifa chemical plant in Khartoum in August 1998.) An al Qaeda defector testified in federal court in 2001 that the group was working with the Sudanese government to produce chemical weapons.[7]

After the fall of the Taliban, more evidence of al Qaeda's ambitions was found. Technical documents discovered at al Qaeda safe houses in Afghanistan indicate that the organization has focused attention on nuclear weapon design issues. Many of the documents suggest that those involved with these matters had a crude understanding of the physics involved; other documents, however, were quite detailed.[8] What expertise al Qaeda lacked, it sought from like-minded scientists: In the summer of 2001, bin Laden met with two capable Pakistani nuclear scientists and discussed the challenges of producing nuclear weapons and other types of WMD. The Pakistanis provided al Qaeda with a blueprint for developing a nuclear bomb and discussed uranium mining in Afghanistan.[9] According to the 9/11 Commission, al Qaeda members discussed—though it is not clear how seriously—the idea of storming a Russian nuclear base and forcing personnel there to launch a missile at the United States.

It is unlikely that al Qaeda or any other jihadists currently possess a nuclear weapon, because if they did, they almost certainly would have used it quickly. But so long as there are 600 tons of poorly secured nuclear materials in the former Soviet Union—enough for more than 2,000 bombs—and many tons of highly enriched uranium in research reactors around the world, some with weak defenses, the specter of nuclear terrorism will remain real. Under the most optimistic circumstances, America's bilateral effort to secure fissile material in Russia will be complete in three years. A more likely scenario is that most of the work will not be done for five or more years, and even then, some Russian facilities will remain unimproved because of Moscow's unwillingness to allow foreigners into them. Nor is Russia the only potential source; there is a possibility of "leakage" of material from Pakistan, where jihadist sympathizers might insinuate themselves into the nuclear weapons establishment, and there is the remote chance of a sale or supply of such material by North Korea or Iran. For many of the same reasons that such a transfer from prewar Iraq to al Qaeda was extremely unlikely, these last two scenarios are somewhat implausible as well. But they are not impossible.

Acquiring the fissile material is the key step. Turning that material into a weapon would require complex engineering, but if it is not already within the capabilities of radical Islamists, it probably will be soon. When the Center for Strategic and International Studies canvassed a group of leading scholars of radical Islam and nuclear weapons experts in 2005, a third of the respondents believed that the terrorists already had the capability to make a bomb, while the average of the other respondents' estimates put the necessary skills in the terrorists' hands in about five years.[10]

Nuclear terrorism can be avoided, as Graham Allison has written in his 2004 book *Nuclear Terrorism: The Ultimate Preventable Catastrophe*. The key is securing loose nuclear material, but current efforts along this path need to be invigorated enormously, something that does not look likely in the near term. When Steve Coll of the *Washington Post* asked sixty nuclear and terrorism experts at the Los Alamos National Laboratory about the likelihood of a nuclear terrorist attack on U.S. soil in the next several decades, only three or four thought the chance was negligible.[11]

The use of other kinds of weapons of mass destruction will be harder to prevent. In the coming years, for example, the technology for making chemical weapons is likely to become more accessible. The development of "micro reactors," machines that are only a bit larger than an average bread basket, will allow chemical companies to produce chemicals in smaller quantities on short order. This serves the needs of "just-in-time" manufacturing, but the same technology in the wrong hands will make it easier to produce some of the most dangerous nerve agents, such as VX and sarin.

Horrible as chemical weapons are, their use would probably be less than cataclysmic for three reasons: Large amounts are required to kill significant numbers of people; the environment can make dispersal difficult; and the area of contamination is usually small. Biological weapons, by contrast, pose a greater threat, because small quantities can go further—one kilogram of anthrax spores could kill 10,000 people under the right conditions—some agents are infectious, and detection is often slow. Most worrisome of all is the galloping technological progress that is putting the means for producing biological agents in the hands of more and more people. Biological weapons development is not easy: Producing anthrax spores that are the right size so that they are inhaled into the lungs is quite difficult, as is drying the agent and dispersing it. Technology, however, will soon lower these hurdles considerably, and, at the same time, the number of people with the training to prepare dangerous biological agents is growing rapidly. Today, there are no more than 10,000 individuals in the world with the experience in government programs necessary to produce military-quality biological weapons. But the number of people who are capable of taking a biological agent and aerosolizing it for widespread dispersal is perhaps a hundred-fold greater. And the number who have the basic scientific skills to culture pathogens and even perform some of the genetic manipulations to make these agents more dangerous runs into the hundreds of thousands and possibly millions.[12] Thanks to the revolution in biotechnology, the number of facilities where such work could be done is undoubtedly in the thousands, and genuine global oversight is impossible.

Hence, at the center of the counterterrorism challenge of the coming decades is a race to limit the spread of the jihadist ideology before the technological barriers to producing biological weapons fall so low as to be meaningless. We have one advantage in that the jihadists got a late start in the field. One of the more curious discoveries after the fall of the Taliban concerns al Qaeda's changing attitude to biological weapons. Although bin Laden and the other leaders have shown an enduring interest in chemical weapons, they had no interest in biological agents until 1999. In a memo found on a computer in Kabul, Ayman al-Zawahiri observed that "the destructive power of these [biological] weapons is no less than that of nuclear weapons." Al-Zawahiri, himself a surgeon, goes on to regret the group's late start in this area and confesses that "despite their extreme danger, we only became aware of them when the enemy drew our attention to them by repeatedly expressing concern that they can be produced simply."[13] This, much like the increased emphasis jihadists put on damaging the U.S. economy after they watched all the fretting about the economic consequences of September 11, is a powerful example of the feedback loop connecting our fears with the terrorists' ambitions.[14]

Other materials and information found in Afghanistan indicate that al Qaeda began building a biological weapons laboratory and received advice from a Pakistani microbiologist. The group tried, but failed, to obtain strains of anthrax that would be deadly for human beings.[15] The Pakistani scientists who advised bin Laden on nuclear weapons also provided diagrams for a balloon system for dispersing biological and chemical agents. Another jihadist, a member of the Indonesian group Jemaah Islamiya, was also reportedly dispatched to Malaysia to put together an anthrax program there. Little is known about his fate.

It is small consolation that the jihadists got a late start in pursuing biological weapons and wasted the period in which they had a sanctuary in Afghanistan. The problem, however, is that a sanctuary is hardly necessary any more. Indeed, terrorists are likely to soon value the anonymity and concealing density of a city, in which they can find new safe havens. In a city, they are also more likely to find the skills and services they will need to operate, and they will have the added protection of knowing that their enemies cannot target them with cruise missiles or Predator drones, as happened in Afghanistan. With the number of jihadists growing, they are gaining the advantage in a race we cannot afford to lose.

PART TWO

Self-Inflicted Wounds

7

THREAT ASSESSMENT

The events of the past three years have profoundly damaged the fight against radical Islam. As America's standing in the Muslim world has sunk, the migration from the outer circle of people who might be seduced by the jihadist argument into the inner circle of committed terrorists has accelerated. Usama bin Laden can certainly claim that some of the gains of the jihadist cause are the fruit of his bold strategy. Much of the radicals' success, however, is our own fault. Misguided U.S. policy—above all, the invasion and occupation of Iraq—has led to the growth of violent anti-Americanism, which is propelling us toward a future of more terrorist attacks in more places with increasing lethality.

Behind these failures lies the inability of the senior leadership of the Bush administration to comprehend the nature and dimensions of the threat of radical Islam. America's top decision makers have not recognized that we face a global insurgency, and they have ignored the jihadist movement's ideological appeal. Instead of working to undermine it, they inadvertently strengthened it through actions that effectively confirmed the radicals' argument. The Bush team's commitment to a worldview focused on states, which scants the danger of independent terrorist groups, and its determination to rely on military force in the fight against terror, have wrought lasting damage to America's strategic position. Today, there is no end in sight to the jihadist threat.

WHEN THE BUSH foreign policy team came into office in January 2001, its members brought long résumés and strong views. Vice President Dick Cheney had served as secretary of defense in the administration of George H. W. Bush. Secretary of Defense Donald Rumsfeld had held the same position in the Ford administration. Secretary of State Colin Powell had served as chairman of the Joint Chiefs of Staff and as national security adviser in the course of a distinguished career. Deputy Secretary of Defense Paul Wolfowitz and Deputy Secretary of State Richard Armitage both had decades of high-level Washington experience.

The group was not uniform in its outlook, and one of the central story lines of the first term of the Bush administration was the marginalization of Powell, Armitage, and the State Department. The rest, however, shared a powerful belief that states were the only actors in the world that could materially threaten U.S. security. A state could be a problem if it was a rising power, such as China, which threatened to erode American dominance in East Asia. Or it might present a menace to U.S. allies and economic well-being, as Iraq and Iran did with their known histories of producing weapons of mass destruction, geopolitical ambitions in the oil-rich Gulf region, and hostility to Israel. Or it could be a wayward, dangerous force foundering in the transition from communist dictatorship to democracy, as Russia was. The United States, the new team believed, had lost its way, because the Clinton administration had failed to meet the challenges such states posed head-on. In a *Foreign Affairs* article in 2000 that presented the Republican foreign policy manifesto for the upcoming presidential election, Condoleezza Rice chided the Clinton team for having failed to implement "a disciplined and consistent foreign policy that separates the important from the trivial." By contrast, Rice promised, a Republican administration under George W. Bush would "focus U.S. energies on comprehensive relationships with the big powers, particularly Russia and China, that can and will mold the character of the international political system."[1]

"Power matters," Rice wrote, and the power that matters most is America's overwhelming military might. The nation, the Republican argument ran, had allowed itself to be hemmed in by a raft of international treaties and agreements and a style of operating that deferred too much to the opinions of others, thus unwisely holstering America's advantage. With the Cold War over, the United States could achieve a great deal more in terms of safeguarding its interests and promoting democracy if it were unabashed about the exercise of its own power. In this "unipolar moment," as the neoconservative columnist Charles Krauthammer wrote in June 2001, "we now have an administration willing to assert American freedom of action and the primacy of American national interests. . . . An unprecedentedly dominant United States . . . is in the unique position of being able to fashion its own foreign policy. After a decade of Prometheus playing pygmy, the first task of the new administration is precisely to reassert American freedom of action."[2]

The new team came into office determined to move decisively on its three highest priorities. The first was to accelerate the development of a national missile defense, a goal that since the time of Ronald Reagan had aroused almost religious passion for conservatives. Even before George W. Bush's inauguration, his aides began consultations with members of Congress and traveled to foreign capitals to discuss their plans for moving forward with missile defense and withdrawing from the Anti-Ballistic Missile Treaty of 1972, which had committed the United States to forswearing such a system.

The other objectives at the top of the list were to readjust the U.S. relationship with China, which the new administration viewed as a dangerous rising power, and to complete the unfinished business of Operation Desert Storm by toppling Saddam Hussein. Concern about Iraq ran deep in the group. As far back as the 1970s, for example, Paul Wolfowitz had studied the potential threat that Iraq posed to America's energy supply. All the members of the Bush national security team except Donald Rumsfeld had been in government during Operation Desert Storm, and while they originally supported the first President Bush's decision not to send Coalition forces into Baghdad to overthrow Saddam, several had been surprised by the Iraqi despot's durability and had come to regret that choice. Wolfowitz, in particular, argued strenuously during the late 1990s that Saddam posed a serious threat to regional security and to the United States, and that he had to be removed from power. In 1998, under the banner of a group called the Project for the New American Century, an open letter was sent to President Clinton that stated, "The only acceptable strategy is one that eliminates the possibility that Iraq will be able to use or threaten to use weapons of mass destruction. In the near term, this means a willingness to undertake military action as diplomacy is clearly failing. In the long term, it means removing Saddam Hussein and his regime from power."[3] Among the signatories were Rumsfeld, Wolfowitz, Armitage, John Bolton (a future undersecretary of state), Elliott Abrams (a future senior director of the National Security Council), and Zalmay Khalilzad (a future ambassador to Afghanistan and Iraq). In their view, clearing the Baathist regime from the international stage would bring numerous benefits: First, a tyrant with unquenchable ambition and a documented record of producing weapons of mass destruction would no longer be able to threaten his neighbors, who possessed much of the world's proven oil reserves and were thus of the highest strategic importance. Second, after the Iraqi threat was eliminated, U.S. troops could be removed from Saudi Arabia, where they were seen as an irritant to many groups within the Saudi population and to Islamists around the world. Third, the long-frozen politics of the Middle East could be shattered with the removal of the last major Arab nationalist, a dictator who thrived on being the region's most rabid opponent of the United States and Israel. The notion that the Arab-Israeli conflict could be resolved or would fade away if Saddam were removed from power added an enticement to the idea of doing so.

In recent years, several formidable critics, including former Secretary of the Treasury Paul O'Neill and former Counterterrorism Coordinator Richard Clarke, have pointed to these statements to argue that the Bush administration was determined to attack Iraq and topple Saddam Hussein on whatever pretext was necessary. This claim has received a measure of confirmation from the "Downing Street memo," which came to light in the spring of 2005 and memorializes a July 2002 meeting of British Prime Minister Tony Blair with a group of his senior aides. In the document, British intelligence chief Sir Richard Dearlove, who had just returned from meetings in Washington, reported that U.S. military action against Iraq "was now seen as inevitable." George W. Bush, he observed, "wanted to remove Saddam, through military action, justified by the conjunction of terrorism and WMD." Dearlove warned Blair and his colleagues that "the intelligence and facts were being fixed around the policy."[4]

If Dearlove's assessment that the United States was committed to war as early as the summer of 2002 is accurate, then the high cost of the war—nearly 2,000 American lives and more than ten times as many Iraqi lives—makes it essential to know why the Bush team felt that removing Saddam was imperative, and what their understanding was of the threat he posed. Only then can we establish where the strategic errors were made and how we can avoid them in the future. This is a matter of our long-term national security.

BEFORE SEPTEMBER 11, 2001, THE terrorist threat did not factor prominently in the Bush administration's worldview. The president admitted to Bob Woodward that before the attacks, "I didn't feel that sense of urgency, and my blood was not nearly as boiling."[5] The administration's counterterrorism record before 9/11 has been thoroughly debated by, among others, Richard Clarke and Condoleezza Rice in their appearances before the 9/11 Commission, which afterward laid out its reconstruction of events in great detail. At this point, it is sufficient to note one fact: The first meeting of Bush's foreign policy cabinet, known as the Principals Committee, occurred within days of the new president's inauguration on January 20, 2001, and it dealt with the issue of regime change in Iraq. The Principals did not meet on the issue of al Qaeda until September 4, seven days before the attack.

Many reasons can be cited for that long interval. Until al Qaeda's strikes on New York and Washington, much of the foreign policy establishment of both parties viewed terrorism as a headline-grabbing problem but merely a second-tier national security threat, if only because so few people were likely to be affected and it was considered inconceivable that an act of terror could seriously alter the nation's strategic position. Another reason involved a more specific understanding of terrorism that the new foreign policy team brought with them into office, a view that was expressed at the first meeting on terrorism of the Deputies Committee, the interagency group of sub-cabinet officials who work through many aspects of an issue before the Principals confer about it. At this meeting, which was held in April 2001, in the White House Situation Room, Richard Clarke laid out the case for putting military pressure on the Taliban and al Qaeda forces in Afghanistan and targeting Usama bin Laden directly. After Clarke spoke, Paul Wolfowitz declared, "Well, I just don't understand why we are beginning by talking about this one man bin Laden." When Clarke answered that bin Laden and his network presented an "immediate and serious" threat to the United States, Wolfowitz retorted, "Well, there are others that do as well, at least as much. Iraqi terrorism, for example." CIA Deputy Director John McLaughlin interjected that the Intelligence Community knew of no Iraqi terrorist activity directed at the United States. But Wolfowitz was not persuaded. "You give bin Laden too much credit," he insisted. Returning to the possibility of an Iraqi connection, he declared, "He could not do all these things like the 1993 attack on New York, not without a state sponsor. Just because FBI and CIA have failed to find the linkages does not mean they don't exist."[6]

In suggesting an Iraqi link to terrorist acts like the first bombing of the World Trade Center, Wolfowitz was bucking years of investigative and intelligence work by the FBI and the CIA. Instead, he was embracing the theory of Laurie Mylroie, a researcher affiliated with the American Enterprise Institute, the neoconservative think tank with which many Bush administration officials and supporters—including Dick Cheney, former Defense Policy Board Chairman Richard Perle, and former Director of Central Intelligence James Woolsey—have been associated. In a series of books and articles in the mid- and late-1990s, Mylroie had spun an elaborate argument that Saddam was the hidden force behind the terrorist groups, including al Qaeda, that had attacked the United States numerous times in the course of a decade. She argued that the Iraqi leader was behind two bombings in Saudi Arabia and the bombing of the U.S. embassies in Kenya and Tanzania, though no hard supporting evidence was presented.[7] Her most dramatic claim was that Iraq had organized the 1993 bombing of the World Trade Center and that Ramzi Yousef, the leader of the group that carried out the bombing, was actually an Iraqi intelligence agent. As "proof" of the Iraqi government's involvement, she pointed to the participation in the conspiracy of Abdul Rahman Yasin, an Iraqi national who fled New York after the bombing and resurfaced later in Baghdad.

Mylroie's work has been carefully investigated by the CIA and the FBI, and in the 1990s she had presented her material to members of Richard Clarke's staff at the White House. The U.S. government devoted countless man-hours to investigating and prosecuting the perpetrators of the 1993 bombing, and, while many have marveled at the ingenuity of Mylroie's theory, the strong consensus among counterterrorism experts in and outside of the government is that the work is not credible. There is a broad agreement among intelligence and law enforcement authorities that Ramzi Yousef was not an Iraqi agent but rather a terrorist entrepreneur with ties to the radical Islamists of al Qaeda. No compelling proof of a connection between Yasin and Iraqi intelligence has been uncovered, either. (Several other participants in the plot, including Yousef, planned to escape to their homes in Egypt and Pakistan after the bombing. Yousef made it, others did not, but no one has claimed that Egypt or Pakistan backed the bombing.) The most knowledgeable analysts and investigators at the CIA and at the FBI believe that their work conclusively disproves Mylroie's claims. Her dogged insistence on her arguments, together with her assertion that Saddam was behind the September 11 attacks, have sealed her reputation as an ideologue. Nonetheless, she has remained a star in the neoconservative firmament. The dust jackets of her books boast effusive praise from leading neoconservatives, including Paul Wolfowitz; Richard Perle and James Woolsey have cited her work approvingly numerous times.[8]

The April 2001 clash between Wolfowitz, who had just re-entered government after eight years of academic life as dean of the Johns Hopkins School of Advanced International Studies, and the career civil servants Clarke and McLaughlin, who had been living in the world of classified intelligence, was a harbinger of things to come. Wolfowitz's belief that al Qaeda must have had a state sponsor expressed well the belief within the Bush team that states were what counted. Still, his rejection of the idea that nonstate actors had moved to center stage in international affairs was surprising. For more than a decade there had been a drumbeat of news stories and commentary on the waning power of the state as multinational companies, international crime syndicates, nongovernmental organizations, and drug cartels had shown how easily they could evade its grasp. Two members of the Bush team—Cheney and Rumsfeld—had been chief executives of large companies, and Wolfowitz and Rice had been at the pinnacle of political science, the academic discipline that had studied these developments. Yet this seems to have done nothing to shake the certainty that al Qaeda was little more than a front for someone else, and the leading suspect was Laurie Mylroie's archvillain, Iraq.

After September 11

The destruction of the World Trade Center marked a dramatic break in the history of American national security. No attack of notable magnitude had been carried out by a foreign force on the continental United States since the War of 1812; only the 1941 bombing of Pearl Harbor, in what was then the distant American possession of Hawaii, was comparable. No terrorist attack in history had caused anywhere near as many casualties. In the face of such an unprecedented event, some kind of reflection on first principles might have been expected. That did not happen.

As soon as they saw the television images from Lower Manhattan, many in the intelligence community suspected al Qaeda of having engineered the attacks. That day, most CIA personnel were quickly evacuated from the Langley headquarters and moved to the printing plant on the Agency campus. By choice, the staff at the Counter-Terrorist Center (CTC) stayed in their offices. Two hours after the attacks, an analyst from CTC ran over to the printing plant and told the CIA's senior leaders that he recognized a couple of names on the flight manifests of the hijacked planes as those of al Qaeda operatives.

In the hours and days that followed, while the intelligence community built the case against al Qaeda, most of the Bush inner circle focused immediately on making the connection to Iraq and, more broadly, dealing with the terrorist threat as a problem of recidivist states. As Bob Woodward noted in his book *Plan of Attack,* on the afternoon of September 11, Donald Rumsfeld brought up with his aides the possibility of striking Iraq and al Qaeda simultaneously, and the next day he asked in a White House meeting if the attacks offered an "opportunity" to move against Iraq. In his Oval Office address on the night of September 11, President Bush declared, "We will make no distinction between the terrorists who committed these acts and those who harbor them," and in the discussion afterward, Rumsfeld declared that the problem was larger than bin Laden and al Qaeda—states that supported terrorism, such as Iraq, also had to be addressed. Pressure, he argued, had to be exerted primarily on states. The president agreed, saying, "We have to force countries to choose." When the conversation resumed the next day, Vice President Cheney added, "To the extent we define our task broadly, including those who support terrorism, then we get states. And it's easier to find them than bin Laden."[9]

At a meeting of the national security team with the president at Camp David on the weekend of September 15–16, the discussion continued. Without any intelligence to support the claim, Paul Wolfowitz estimated there was a 10 to 50 percent chance that Iraq was responsible for the carnage in New York and Washington. At this meeting and at subsequent ones in Washington, Wolfowitz, with some backing from Rumsfeld, pressed for confronting Iraq immediately as a response to the 9/11 attacks. Secretary of State Colin Powell countered this line of thought, arguing that a move against Iraq without evidence of Iraqi complicity in the attacks would doom efforts to build a broad coalition against terror.[10] In a September 20 memo to Rumsfeld, Undersecretary of Defense Douglas Feith complained about the lack of good targets in Afghanistan and aired the idea of bombing Iraq in retaliation. (He added—astonishingly—that because U.S. attacks were expected in Afghanistan, an American attack on targets in South America or Southeast Asia might surprise the terrorists.)[11] In these internal debates, the Iraq hawks had a powerful ally; on September 17, President Bush had told his advisers, "I believe Iraq was involved."[12]

The president settled on a strategy of dealing with Afghanistan first, but it was evident to many that an invasion of Iraq was not far off. "It was clear since 9/12 or 9/13 that some in OSD [Office of the Secretary of Defense—the civilian leadership of the Pentagon] were aiming for Iraq," says Lieutenant General Greg Newbold, now retired from the Marines, who was then serving as chief of operations for the Joint Staff, which serves the chairman of the Joint Chiefs of Staff. Larry Wilkerson, a retired Army colonel who was Colin Powell's chief of staff, had a similar perception: "It became clear to me about a month after the Camp David meeting that half a million men beating the shit out of Saddam Hussein was one of the top two or three options on the table." On November 21, the president instructed Rumsfeld to begin preparing a war plan for Iraq.[13]

In their public statements, the president and his aides concentrated heavily on the issue of state complicity. Just days after the attack, Paul Wolfowitz made the startling pledge that the United States would focus on "removing the sanctuaries, removing the support systems, ending states who sponsor terrorism."[14] With seven countries—Iraq, Iran, Libya, Syria, Sudan, North Korea, and Cuba—on the State Department's list of state sponsors of terror, Wolfowitz appeared to be committing America to an immense military undertaking, since states rarely consent to be "ended." Colin Powell rebuked him for the remark, but the overall tendency in administration rhetoric was to draw a sharp line between those who assisted terrorists and those who did not and to suggest that those in the former group faced serious peril if they did not change their ways.

Framing the issue this way became a central part of the administration's discussion of terrorism, and the peak of the effort came on January 29, 2002. In his State of the Union address that evening, Bush declared that Iraq, North Korea, and Iran "and their terrorist allies, constitute an axis of evil, arming to threaten the peace of the world. By seeking weapons of mass destruction, these regimes pose a grave and growing danger. They could provide these arms to terrorists, giving them the means to match their hatred. They could attack our allies or attempt to blackmail the United States. In any of these cases, the price of indifference would be catastrophic."[15]

Saddam Hussein's Iraq was unquestionably one of the most troublesome countries on the map. The Iraqi dictator's past spoke for itself: He had begun work on nuclear weapons decades earlier, gassed his own people, invaded Kuwait, and ruled with utter barbarity. He had rejected the demands of the international community repeatedly on the issue of inspections to ascertain that he had no weapons of mass destruction. And he regularly sought to inflict a cost for the de facto partition of his country after the 1991 Gulf War that had created a Kurdish enclave north of the thirty-sixth parallel—Iraqi gunners continually shot at American and British aircraft patrolling the skies. Though there was little chance they could down one of the planes, the Americans and British periodically pounded Iraqi antiaircraft batteries and related targets to punish Baghdad.

Even so, virtually no serious military analyst believed that Saddam represented an imminent threat to the United States. His military was a shadow of what it had once been, and, compared to the other two members of the "axis of evil," there was little information to suggest that he was developing any weapons capabilities that would make him a near-term danger. By "near-term danger," most analysts meant one thing: nuclear weapons. Neither biological nor chemical weapons would have given Saddam the capability to impose his will on his neighbors or in any way challenge the United States and its allies. But nuclear weapons are different; they are the great equalizer. Unlike North Korea, which was already thought by the intelligence community to have enough fissile material for at least a couple of nuclear bombs, and Iran, which had a substantial nuclear program that was also poised to produce weapons material, there was no substantial proof that Saddam was rebuilding his nuclear program—though Vice President Cheney would repeatedly assert that it was a certainty, without providing evidence. The threat was longer term: Before 9/11, the UN sanctions regime against Iraq had shown signs of weakening, as Saddam put forward the claim that children in his country were starving as a result—a complaint that fell on sympathetic ears in many parts of the world. The fear was that sanctions would crumble, and a newly liberated Saddam would be able to rebuild his nuclear weapons program. Among the most thoughtful hawks, such as Kenneth Pollack, the former NSC staff member and author of the influential book *The Gathering Storm,* the possibility that Saddam could develop such weapons was the clinching argument for removing him from power. But as even Pollack acknowledged, if there was no evidence that Saddam was reconstituting his nuclear program, more pressing security needs, such as dealing with al Qaeda, should take precedence.

Against this backdrop, the contention that an alliance between terrorists and rogue states posed the greatest threat to the United States became the linchpin of the administration's argument for going to war against Iraq. Using one of several formulations, the political leadership invoked the claim that Bush himself made in October 2002, that "Iraq could decide on any given day to provide a biological or chemical weapon to a terrorist group or individual terrorists. Alliance with terrorists could allow the Iraqi regime to attack America without leaving any fingerprints." The hypothesis of cooperation between the nation's enemies became the engine of American foreign policy. The notion that the threat could be worse than the president's vision of chemical and biological attacks metamorphosed into the ultimate argument in Condoleezza Rice's assertion that "we don't want the smoking gun to be a mushroom cloud"—despite the paucity of credible intelligence showing that Iraq was in fact pressing ahead with its nuclear weapons program.[16] The beauty of seizing on the rogue state–terrorist nexus was that if the administration addressed it correctly, both malefactors would be undone. Strong action would prevent state sponsors of terror from advancing their hostile designs, while at the same time, in Douglas Feith's words, "Terrorist organizations cannot be effective in sustaining themselves over long periods of time to do large-scale operations if they don't have support from states." This, Feith reported, was the "principal thought underlying our strategy in the war on terrorism."[17]

State Sponsors and the New Terror

President Bush and his advisers cannot be faulted for either directing the intelligence community to investigate whether Iraq was involved in the attacks or for seeking to pressure states that sponsor terror. Faced with the devastation of September 11, any American leader would have done the same. In fact, the United States has a history of leaning on sponsors of terror in various ways, from UN sanctions, which ultimately compelled Libya to get out of the business of sponsoring terrorism in the mid-1990s, to the use of force—the 1986 air strike on Libya after its involvement in the killing of U.S. military personnel in a bombing at a Berlin discotheque; the missile attack on Baghdad in 1993 after Saddam Hussein's failed effort to assassinate former President George H. W. Bush; and the 1998 missile attacks on Afghanistan and Sudan after the East Africa embassy bombings.[18]

Any sensible counterterrorism policy will seek to pressure states to stop giving sanctuary, money, weapons, official documents, free passage, and other support to terrorists. Many terrorist groups have relied on state support, and al Qaeda's development was indeed aided by its relationships with states. Sudan harbored the group in the early 1990s, and Afghanistan gave it a home after Usama bin Laden was expelled from Sudan in 1996.

Compared with the kind of support that Hezbollah, for example, has received from Iran and Syria, the sustenance al Qaeda has received from states is relatively small. Al Qaeda's relationships with both Sudan and Afghanistan were unlike the traditional model, in which a state provides the lifeblood of money and materiel for a group. Bin Laden invested heavily in Sudan while he was there, and he appears to have lost a sizable amount of money when he was expelled. The Taliban gave al Qaeda sanctuary, which benefited the group greatly, but there too al Qaeda did not receive financial support from the Taliban. Instead, bin Laden helped the Afghans keep their Islamic Emirate going with money and even fighters. There is no evidence, moreover, that the Taliban provided weapons or official papers for al Qaeda, which likely had a better network of international contacts than the village mullahs of the Taliban could muster.

Pressuring state sponsors makes sense, but the administration erred by casting the terrorists of global jihad as a derivative problem of the phenomenon of rogue states. In fact, state sponsorship of terror against the United States has been waning for years. The three leading state sponsors of terror in the past two decades were Libya, Syria, and Iran. Libya's last act of terrorism was the 1988 bombing of Pan Am 103 over Lockerbie, Scotland; Syria has never directly targeted the United States, although Americans have been killed in attacks against Israeli targets by Syrian-backed groups; Iran's last attack on America was the 1996 bombing of the Khobar Towers in Saudi Arabia. Both Iran and Syria continue to support Palestinian rejectionist groups, but these, as a rule, attack only Israelis and have been loath to challenge America directly.[19]

On most experts' scorecards, Iraq under Saddam would have ranked as the fourth or fifth most active state sponsor of terror. (A strong argument could be made that Sudan had its hand in many more serious conspiracies in the past decade than Iraq.) Iraq's last conspiracy against the United States was the failed attempt to assassinate former President George H. W. Bush in Kuwait in 1993, a fact that was noted in the State Department's annual report "Patterns of Global Terrorism" in 2000.[20] President Bush declared in his 2002 State of the Union address that "Iraq continues to flaunt its hostility toward America and to support terror," but the two halves of the sentence were not connected. Iraqi terrorism since the failed 1993 effort had consisted overwhelmingly of three kinds of activity: efforts to kill Iraqi dissidents abroad; support for the Mujahedin-e Khalq, an Iranian opposition group based in Iraq that carried out terrorist attacks against the Tehran regime; and payments to the families of Palestinian suicide bombers. None of these presented a threat to the United States. Abu Nidal, the notorious Palestinian killer, lived in Baghdad until he committed suicide in 2002—as many as four bullet wounds were reportedly found in his body, making him an exceptionally talented suicide—but he was no longer active, and his group had dissolved from infighting.

A core part of the case that Bush and his advisers made was that Saddam might collude with terrorists because it would allow him to hurt the United States "without leaving fingerprints," but it appears that a large part of the reason Iraq—like Iran and Libya—stopped targeting the United States was the belief that it could not carry out an attack without detection. (Iran, under its newly elected president, Muhammad Khatami, may have also changed its policy after the Khobar Towers attack because terrorism was not advancing its goals. The Iranian regime appears to have supported the attack because of a desire to drive a wedge between the United States and Saudi Arabia, but the bombing's only effect was to cause Washington to move the troops stationed in Saudi Arabia to a more secure location.) Since detection carries with it a strong likelihood of retaliation, as Iraq learned in 1993, when U.S. cruise missiles destroyed the country's intelligence headquarters, the calculus did not make sense—it was just no longer worth the risk to attack America. That cruise missile strike was derided by conservative critics of the Clinton administration as a "pinprick," but Saddam seemed to have gotten the message.[21]

Beyond the matter of whether the Iraqi regime was likely to attempt a terrorist attack against the United States, the administration's argument raised the further question of whether Saddam Hussein and Usama bin Laden were likely to collaborate. In fact, Iraq and al Qaeda were anything but natural allies. A central tenet of al Qaeda's jihadist ideology is that secular Muslim rulers and their regimes have oppressed the believers and have plunged Islam into a historic crisis. Hence, a paramount goal of Islamist revolutionaries for almost half a century has been the destruction of the regimes of such leaders as Anwar Sadat and Hosni Mubarak of Egypt, President Hafez al-Assad of Syria, the military government in Algeria, and the Saudi royal family. To contemporary jihadists, Saddam was another in a line of dangerous secularists, an enemy of the faith who refused to rule by Islamic law and who habitually murdered religious leaders in Iraq who might oppose his regime. Perhaps the best summation of the jihadist view of Saddam's Iraq was given during the Persian Gulf War by Omar Abdel Rahman, the radical sheik now imprisoned in the United States. When he was asked what the punishment should be for those who supported the United States in the conflict, he answered, "Both those who are against and the ones who are with Iraq should be killed."[22]

The interests of Baathists and jihadists were too divergent for them to collaborate against America while Saddam was in power. But that does not mean they had no contact or did not at times sniff around each other to see if they might become allies. The Middle Eastern tradition of keeping tabs on all groups, friendly or not, persists, and the U.S. intelligence community was aware of a few meetings between bin Laden's men and Saddam's. Most of these contacts occurred in the first half of the 1990s, before al Qaeda's destructiveness had been demonstrated by the August 1998 Nairobi and Dar es Salaam bombings, though some meetings occurred as late as 1999. While bin Laden was still in Sudan, Hassan al-Turabi, the country's Islamist leader and bin Laden's local patron, brokered a truce between al Qaeda and Saddam.[23] But by the standards of state sponsors, there were few contacts between Iraq and al Qaeda. In reality, Iran had many more contacts with the jihadists, but these too seemed to be aimed primarily at giving Tehran some insight into what al Qaeda was up to. The conclusion of the intelligence community in the 1990s was that neither country had a collaborative relationship with al Qaeda. In 1998, in an effort to ensure that the U.S. government was not becoming complacent in this judgment, Richard Clarke asked his staff to evaluate the available intelligence to see if these conclusions were justified. After reviewing a large amount of intelligence, they too endorsed the intelligence community's verdict. After a lengthy investigation of its own, the 9/11 Commission arrived at the same understanding in 2004 and noted in its final report, "We have seen no evidence that [the contacts] ever developed into a collaborative operational relationship. Nor have we seen evidence indicating that Iraq cooperated with al Qaeda in developing or carrying out any attacks against the United States."[24]

The argument that all of our enemies will inevitably find common ground should be treated with caution. This is the kind of thinking that prevented American policy makers from recognizing the Sino-Soviet rift in the 1960s, a period in which the Soviet Union and China were more likely to wage war against each other than against the United States. But if the claim that Iraq and al Qaeda had cooperated or might collaborate was questionable, the idea that Saddam Hussein would give a weapon of mass destruction to al Qaeda was even more dubious.

About the underlying premise of this argument—that Saddam had such weapons—there was little doubt among the security professionals in the West.[25] Saddam had used chemical weapons against Iran in the brutal war of 1980–1988. He had also used them against his own people in the notorious case of the gassing of the Kurds of Halabja. He had failed to account for large stocks of nerve agents, such as VX, and biological weapons materials, such as anthrax, as required by the terms of his surrender in 1991 and subsequent UN resolutions.

Whether he had weapons of mass destruction was clearly an important question, but the critical issue was whether he would use them. In a sense, the question was whether it was true that September 11 had changed everything. The attacks certainly showed that catastrophic terrorism on American soil had become a reality. But that is not the same as saying that anyone other than al Qaeda or terrorist groups like al Qaeda would carry out such attacks. In a 2004 interview, Douglas Feith explained that, after September 11, the administration asked the question, "Was Iraq involved in 9/11? We found no hard link. What about Iraq–al Qaeda links in general? Well, there were some, but that wasn't the essence of the Saddam Hussein threat. The danger of Saddam's providing W.M.D. to al Qaeda or another terrorist group–there you had a real problem, because his record on W.M.D. was indisputable."[26]

But was it? Did Saddam's weapons pose a greater threat after September 11 than before? Did al Qaeda's attack tell us something new about Saddam Hussein's behavior? The answer to these questions is the same: no. Saddam is an execrable man and one of the most loathsome national leaders in a century in which there was plenty of competition. He had miscalculated badly on a number of occasions, most notably by invading Kuwait in August 1990. But he was not insane. He wanted to avoid obliteration.

As far as the United States and its vital interests were concerned, he was deterred.

The "indisputable" record on WMD does not prove what Feith believed. In January 1991, during the runup to Operation Desert Storm, Secretary of State James Baker had sent Saddam a message. In a meeting in Geneva with Iraqi Foreign Minister Tariq Aziz, Baker said bluntly:

> If the conflict involves your use of chemical or biological weapons against our forces, . . . the American people will demand vengeance. We have the means to exact it . . . this is not a threat, it is a promise. If there is any use of weapons like that, our objective won't just be the liberation of Kuwait, but the elimination of the current Iraqi regime, and anyone responsible for using those weapons would be held accountable.[27]

At that time, Iraq possessed enormous stocks of chemical and biological weapons, but Saddam never used them during the war. In the twelve years thereafter, he never used them, although, characteristically, he implied that he might use chemical weapons against Israel.

There is also no record of his having given such weapons to any terrorist group. The Bush administration's claim that Iraq had provided training to al Qaeda operatives in chemical and biological warfare has never been confirmed. When it was asserted, senior intelligence officials privately expressed discomfort with the report, suggesting that it was an overstatement. The 9/11 Commission noted that the source who made the most detailed allegations on this case later recanted them. Two top al Qaeda members who were subsequently captured—Khalid Sheikh Mohammed and Abu Zubayda—also adamantly denied that there had been cooperation between Iraq and al Qaeda.[28] Before the war, CIA Director George Tenet publicly declared that only when Saddam believed he faced the end of his regime was he likely to use weapons of mass destruction or give them to terrorists. Saddam obviously believed that James Baker's threat about overwhelming retaliation was one that remained in force after Baker left office in 1992. That he declined to back al Qaeda or any other terrorist group in conspiracies against the United States indicates that he believed prudence was his best course. And he remained true to the unwritten rules of state sponsorship of terror: Never get involved with a group that cannot be controlled and may get you into much more trouble than you want; never give a weapon of mass destruction to terrorists who might one day use it against you.

The lesson is important: In an age of catastrophic terror, deterrence remains a viable means of keeping rogue states in check. There are, of course, no guarantees; statecraft is not a natural science with immutable laws. North Korea, for example, has a record of provocative behavior, including involvement with drug dealing and counterfeiting, blowing up South Korean airliners, and killing South Korean cabinet members. It is hardly inconceivable that the Pyongyang regime, in its desperation for cash, might sell a nuclear device to al Qaeda. But the hypothesis that Iraq would do so was never a strong one.

Possibly the best explanation of what the Bush team did in developing its hypotheses about Iraq and al Qaeda collaborating in an attack with weapons of mass destruction is the one provided by the great historian of science Thomas Kuhn. He observed that when new data threaten established and strongly held theories, scientists tend to explain them away. Though the scientists "may begin to lose faith and then to consider alternatives, they do not renounce the paradigm that has led them into crisis. They do not, that is, treat anomalies as counter-instances, though . . . that is what they are."[29] In other words, they try to shoehorn new facts into old ways of understanding. In the same manner, when President Bush and his advisers were faced with an unimaginable attack by a terrorist group that was more capable than most states, they determined that a state must have been behind it. They did not allow the facts to dent their strategic understanding.

The Body Count

The move to war came fast—faster than has been reported. According to one diplomat who worked on the seventh floor of the State Department, where Colin Powell and his top aides had their offices, a small, secret meeting was held on the Martin Luther King Day weekend in January 2002 in the Old Executive Office Building, where most White House staff members have their offices, to plan for a conflict in Iraq. "The original idea was to go to war by Tax Day [April 15] '02," this official says. The meeting was chaired by retired General Wayne Downing, who had recently joined the National

Security Council staff as the top counterterrorism official, replacing Richard Clarke. The aim of the exercise was, as this individual puts it, "blue-skying" or considering at the most basic level "the proposition of getting under way in an operational mode by April 15." But exactly who was driving the effort was unclear. The draft paper that was distributed to attendees appeared to have been drawn up in the Office of the Vice President. "In that period, it really wasn't clear who was in charge," says another official who attended the meeting. One person who appears not to have known about the meeting beforehand was the national security adviser, Condoleezza Rice. When she was informed about the event after it had occurred, according to one attendee, "Rice ordered all the papers [that had been distributed at the meeting] destroyed. She was pissed."

Why the train slowed down is not clear, but it hardly came to a halt. Although President Bush would say throughout the fall of 2002, as the issue of confronting Saddam was debated by Congress and the United Nations Security Council, that there were no war plans on his desk, the decision had already been taken to confront Saddam. Richard Haass, the director of policy planning at the State Department and a close aide to Secretary Powell, recalled visiting Rice in her office in the West Wing of the White House in early July 2002 to discuss Iraq. "I raised this issue about were we really sure that we wanted to put Iraq front and center at this point, given the war on terrorism and other issues. And she said, essentially, that that decision's been made, don't waste your breath."[30] Not only had the Secretary of State not been consulted, the decision was made before a full, rigorous assessment of the Iraqi threat had been made. If the history of past administrations is any guide, there would have been a steady flow of intelligence making its way to the president, to Vice President Cheney, and to Secretary Rumsfeld. But these were likely fragmentary reports that dealt with limited issues concerning Iraqi actions and capabilities. Troubled by the growing momentum toward hostilities, in September 2002, congressional leaders requested a "National Intelligence Estimate" report on Iraq, the most comprehensive report that the intelligence community produces. But the decision itself had already been taken. It is often the case in Washington that political leaders use intelligence not so much to inform their decisions as to justify them. But for what has been rightly called America's first war of choice, this is a striking fact.

The speed with which everything moved left those who were concerned about the implications of a war out in the cold. Larry Wilkerson, Powell's chief of staff at the time, says that the essential decision making and planning "was not taking place in the statutory process of the NSC but in the parallel process run by Cheney." Another senior State Department official recalls that Deputy Secretary of State Armitage "would go into discussions and say we're going to play rope-a-dope," to try to slow things down. "Rope-a-dope" meant meeting with Bush and Rumsfeld and throwing up all the obstacles one could without seeming to be opposed to the policy. Thus, according to this official, Powell would say, " 'Yes sir, yes sir, we need to deal with Iraq,' but then he'd say we need to build a coalition and throw out twenty-five questions that Rumsfeld had to answer. The president would say, 'Now, well, Don, what about Uzbekistan and what about India?' But that didn't stop it." Powell, whose caution about deploying troops has been well known since Operation Desert Storm, had deep doubts about another war with Iraq and America's ability to see through the immense task of occupying the country and putting it back on its feet after a war and decades of decay under Saddam's leadership. As Wilkerson would recall, "My boss's view was that you'll be creating more problems than you're solving. If you're prepared to deliver the necessary resources, then I'm with you." At an August 2002 meeting with Bush at his ranch in Crawford, Texas, Powell and Armitage aimed to "restructure the dialogue" on Iraq within the government, says another State Department official, but "all I recall is that nothing happened."

In December 2002, the first deployment order was issued for the military buildup in Kuwait, Saudi Arabia, and the Gulf states. If one agrees with Napoleon's famous adage that an army can do anything with its swords but sit on them, this was the commitment point. An American president was not going to send tens of thousands of ground troops into the region and bring them home without fighting. "The deployments clinched it," says Wilkerson.

While the Iraqi threat was being played up at every opportunity by administration spokesmen, a strange kind of deflation of the jihadist threat was occurring. To judge by official rhetoric, al Qaeda was simply a gang of "evildoers," and what counted was how many were caught or killed. There is no question that al Qaeda is a group of brutal killers. But this does not eliminate the need for serious discussion of the group's ideology—beyond the assertion that "they hate freedom," as the president would say—or of the ideological bond it was forming with the Muslims who applauded September 11. It was to be expected that the struggle against al Qaeda would be cast this way, since the primary markers of success were the captures or kills, which the administration showcased. And, to be fair, a central part of the battle against al Qaeda involves a manhunt. But the language that officials used underscored their exclusive focus on the individuals and their lack of interest in undermining the terrorists' argument. Frances Fragos Townsend, who became the White House's top counterterrorism and homeland security adviser in May 2004, echoed other official pronouncements when she said that Bush's goal was to "decapitate the beast."[31] Some spoke of al Qaeda as a serpent; others used the metaphor of an army whose finite number of troops could be systematically destroyed—or "decimated," as Bush often put it.

After his September 2001 declaration that he wanted bin Laden "dead or alive" began to seem as if it would not soon be fulfilled, Bush stopped talking about the al Qaeda leader directly. According to a top-ranking adviser, however, "the president's overriding goal is to 'cut the head off the snake.' "[32] After the Riyadh and Casablanca attacks in 2003, *Time* magazine quoted a Pentagon intelligence official's assessment of the administration's rhetoric. "They keep likening [al Qaeda] to a snake," this official said, "but it's more like a deadly mold."[33]

Bush himself set the tone for dealing with the jihadists this way with his request for constant updates on the "high value target" lists of terrorists.[34] For the president, the fight against terror is a manhunt. He has been reported to hold daily half-hour meetings that are "extremely granular, about individual guys," according to Richard A. Falkenrath, who attended some of these meetings in his capacity as deputy homeland security adviser. Falkenrath added, "This is a conversation he's been having every day, more or less, with his senior advisers since September 11"; it covers "the same people, over and over again."[35] The administration currently claims that 75 percent of known al Qaeda leaders have been taken out of action, but, as noted in chapter 2, the White House has provided no substantiation for that number.[36] Despite that ambiguity, the constant reference to these achievements and the analogies to beasts that can be slain creates the illusion that, one day, with a few more captures, the United States can effectively end the terrorist threat.

The conviction that Iraq posed the greater threat to America was not confined to the White House. The campaign in Afghanistan, which has been lauded as a model of contemporary warfare because of the way it brought together U.S. Special Operations troops and airpower with indigenous forces, also neglected important counterterrorism objectives. The Taliban was toppled quickly and effectively, allowing U.S. forces and the Northern Alliance to capture Kabul and end nearly a decade of nightmarish rule. But eliminating al Qaeda did not seem to have the same priority. In November 2001, bin Laden's forces evacuated Kabul and moved toward Kandahar and the southwest part of the country. The hammer of the U.S. military had swung, but the war planning provided for no anvil on which to crush the terrorists and their paramilitary foot soldiers. At least three of the most senior officers on the Joint Staff saw what was unfolding and raised the issue of opening another front by interposing a blocking force in the south to face the fleeing al Qaeda forces. These generals convinced General Richard Myers, the chairman of the Joint Chiefs, to ask the general in command, Tommy Franks, to consider a southern option. The chain of command, however, ran directly from Secretary of Defense Rumsfeld to Franks, and the general was not taking advice from others, even from Myers. "It was predictable and inevitable," says one of the generals involved. "Franks opposed the notion that he would be supervised by the Joint Chiefs." Ultimately, Franks opened a second front by deploying a Marine Expeditionary Unit, but the number of troops was insufficient for the job of destroying the al Qaeda and remaining Taliban forces. The conclusion of this episode occurred at Tora Bora, where the shortcomings of light and mobile U.S. deployment that relied on local forces became clear, and bin Laden slipped away.

This was not the only instance in which the Pentagon allowed secondary considerations to get in the way of the mission. Another example came in the first months of 2002, when the CIA's small fleet of Predator drones shrunk because of crashes and malfunctions. When it was first flown in 2000, the Predator had provided surveillance imagery that astonished counterterrorism officials; some of the film was shown to President Bill Clinton and National Security Adviser Samuel R. Berger, who had been pressing for new means of tracking and targeting the terrorists. The Predator material had raised hopes that the intelligence community had finally found the instrument that would provide reliable information on the whereabouts of bin Laden and other al Qaeda leaders. At the urging of Richard Clarke and others, Predators were armed with Hellfire missiles so that a target could be struck almost instantly, once it was identified. This would obviate the need to fire cruise missiles from offshore submarines or launch aircraft that would take hours to reach the target.

Despite the optimism among counterterrorism experts for the Predator, it had been the subject of months of haggling between the CIA and the Defense Department before September 11, over issues of funding and questions about who had the authority to order the firing of a Hellfire missile from the drone. These quarrels kept the Predator from being used against al Qaeda. Almost immediately after the terrorist strikes, however, it was put into service and performed brilliantly, killing, among others, Mohammad Atef, al Qaeda's chief of operations, in November 2001. But once major combat in Afghanistan was finished and more craft were required to keep up the hunt for terrorists, Secretary Rumsfeld held up the transfer of the Predators. For roughly two months the Department of Defense demanded that the CIA accept a set of conditions under which the Agency would operate the drones, which affirmed the Pentagon's ultimate control of them, the terms of indemnification if one was damaged or lost, the cost of maintenance, and the like. According to one top military intelligence official, "When he [Rumsfeld] got an issue like that he could be pretty stubborn. He wanted to make sure everyone knew who owned them and was accountable. And with that kind of guidance, the lawyers had a field day."

The delay infuriated the terrorist hunters at the CIA. One individual who was at the center of the action called this episode "typical" and complained that "Rumsfeld never missed an opportunity to fail to cooperate. The fact is, the secretary of defense is an obstacle. He has helped the terrorists." The military intelligence official agrees that this was a low point. The Predator tug-of-war "went on for months. It probably had some operational impact. It got pretty nasty."

Making the Case

As combat preparations in Afghanistan wound down, the president and a small group of his advisers turned more of their attention to Iraq. In the many articles and books that have been written about the preparations for war, it has become clear that different members of the administration's inner circle viewed the coming conflict with Iraq differently and that there was no single, easily explicable set of war aims. Removing Saddam Hussein and ending his regime—not merely disarming him—was clearly the common denominator. Beyond that, however, there were varying ideas about what goals the United States should have for Iraq.

According to several former administration officials, Donald Rumsfeld focused heavily on the execution of the war but said little about postwar reconstruction or the political reconstitution of the country. His deputy, Paul Wolfowitz, had far greater ambitions. Wolfowitz viewed the terrorist threat as a product of a badly dysfunctional political environment in the Middle East and argued that the United States could create a viable democracy in Iraq and that in turn would have a profound impact on the region, leading other countries to move one way or another away from autocracy and toward free institutions. Wolfowitz's views got powerful support from outside scholars with whom the White House consulted. Among them was a former colleague of Wolfowitz's at the Johns Hopkins School for Advanced International Studies, the distinguished Middle East expert Fouad Ajami. The most influential of those who advised the White House, however, was Bernard Lewis, the retired Princeton professor who, in a career dating back to the 1940s, had been a dominant figure in the study of the Muslim world. Lewis counseled that Iraq could establish a democracy, but that strong American guidance was needed. In March 2003, Dick Cheney said in a nationally televised interview, "I firmly believe, along with men like Bernard Lewis, who is one of the great students of that part of the world, that strong, firm U.S. response to terror and to threats of the United States would go a long way, frankly, toward calming things in that part of the world."[37] President Bush appeared to embrace the vision of Iraq as a catalyst for wide-ranging, positive change in the region when he asserted in a November 2003 speech that "Iraqi democracy will succeed—and that success will send forth the news, from Damascus to Teheran—that freedom can be the future of every nation. The establishment of a free Iraq at the heart of the Middle East will be a watershed event in the global democratic revolution."[38]

But the issue of democratizing Iraq or remaking the Middle East was not the one the administration brought to the American people. Instead it became necessary to convince the American people that this was the necessary "phase two" in the war on terror. After September 11, Americans were prepared to accept the contention that the strategic environment had changed and that a new approach to security was required. Even so, as the administration recognized, a connection between the already demonstrated threat of terrorism and the less tangible threat of Iraqi weapons of mass destruction had to be established: The hypothetical case that Saddam would give such a weapon to terrorists such as al Qaeda had to be made credible. The problem they faced was that virtually no one from the permanent government—from the intelligence agencies or the civilian and military units that deal with counterterrorism issues— believed that Saddam would collaborate with al Qaeda in most foreseeable circumstances.

From the outset, the administration's leadership was determined not to be constrained by this disagreement. In practice, this meant conducting an informal evaluation to find out who within the government might be an ally and who would be an obstacle. One of the Pentagon's top counterterrorism officials experienced such a probe in a meeting with Paul Wolfowitz a few months after September 11. In the course of their conversation, Wolfowitz said to this official "something like 'Well, you know the Iraqi intelligence service was behind the first World Trade Center bombing.'" Like everyone in the counterterrorism community, this individual had been familiar for years with Laurie Mylroie's work and her contention that Saddam Hussein was the ultimate backer of jihadist terror. Her work, he thought, "read like an *Enquirer* article"—referring to the *National Enquirer*—"not preposterous but underwhelming in terms of veracity. You'd have to be willing to take a few blind steps." But Wolfowitz, he recalled, "was citing it like it was fact. He was almost quoting from it."

"You know, I've read her book, too," this official told the deputy secretary, "and I'm not convinced." Wolfowitz registered the dissent instantly. As this individual recalls, "At that point, the light went out and he just wasn't interested. And that's how it was for everyone. If you said you weren't convinced, you might as well have said, 'You guys are a bunch of liars.'" Voicing such opinions led to the marginalization of whole units of the defense bureaucracy, including Special Operations and Low-Intensity Conflict (SOLIC), the bureau in the civilian Office of the Secretary of Defense that deals with terrorism. The Pentagon's civilian leadership began working around SOLIC, assigning tasks to other bureaus with no background in the area and ignoring the memos and policy recommendations that SOLIC produced. "SOLIC was seen as a useless appendage," confirms one retired officer who served at that time on the Joint Staff.

"There was an inner circle of special assistants and cronies who worked the critical issues, and we were excluded," says the senior official who disagreed with Wolfowitz about Mylroie's work. For him, the absurdity of the situation became evident not long after his encounter with the deputy secretary. While working late one night, he was told by a colleague that a naval reserve officer was in the Crisis Coordination Center of the Office of the Secretary of Defense (a conference room near Donald Rumsfeld's office), mapping out connections among terrorists and their sponsors. The official went up to the room on the third floor of the Pentagon's E-Ring, where he found a large swath of butcher paper pinned on the wall and covered with a mass of lines and drawings that "looked like there was spaghetti all over it." At one end was written "bin Laden" and at the other, "Saddam Hussein." When he asked the officer what he was doing, the reservist responded, "I was asked to show the connections between Saddam and UBL."

"Were you asked to show if there was a connection?"

"No, I was told to show the connection."

The official was flabbergasted. "I gave him my reaction and said, 'I don't see much connection here even though you've drawn a lot of lines up here.' We were never involved or asked."

For the uniformed military, the story was much the same. One of the military's most senior intelligence officials recalls that the issue of connections between Iraq and al Qaeda came up frequently as the civilian leadership worked to advance its argument. "Regularly and consistently I was asked, 'Do we have a smoking gun?'" this official recalls. "And regularly and consistently I said we don't." Such responses had no impact on policy deliberations.

The Pentagon was not the only place where Bush political appointees bumped up against—and drove over—career intelligence officials. At the State Department, Larry Wilkerson, Colin Powell's chief of staff, recalls,

"We could find no links, no evidence" of a Saddam–bin Laden collaboration. But the Pentagon leadership and aides from Vice President Dick Cheney's office continued to press their argument in interagency discussions. Wilkerson cites a prewar meeting in the White House Situation Room that brought together policy makers and representatives of the CIA, the National Security Agency, which is responsible for collecting communications intelligence, and the Pentagon's own Defense Intelligence Agency. After the presentations were made by the intelligence officials, Wilkerson recalls, Undersecretary of Defense Douglas Feith "leapt to his feet, pointed at a certain National Intelligence Officer and declared, 'You people don't know what you are talking about.'" Feith held up a piece of paper and then read out loud "something about al Qaeda's ties with Iraq during the time it was in Sudan [1991–1996]. The item came from OVP [the Office of the Vice President] that came, ultimately, from a newspaper clipping and it was presented as intelligence." Among those in the room was Stephen Hadley, the deputy national security adviser, who "just sat there looking white and didn't say anything." Wilkerson was aghast. "Who knows how many other people they intimidated?" he wonders.

Few political appointees like to be told that their views are wrong, but the refusal of the Bush team to modify its opinions in the face of established evidence was remarkable. It was also a sign of the broad contempt in which they held the intelligence community and most of the senior civil servants and officers in the Pentagon. In this, they were at odds with the historic mainstream of the Republican Party but were representative of neoconservative opinion about these institutions.

Indeed, several of the members of George W. Bush's inner circle had established themselves as perennial critics of the nation's intelligence community. The roots of the disdain stretched back at least as far as the mid-1970s, when intelligence assessments of the Soviet Union sparked a debate about whether the CIA had gone soft and was underestimating the dimensions of the communist threat. The Director of Central Intelligence at the time was George H. W. Bush, and he sought to stem the criticism by creating a group of outside experts to evaluate the intelligence and draw independent conclusions about Soviet intentions and capabilities. The group, known as "Team B," was chaired by Harvard professor Richard

Pipes and included among its number Paul Wolfowitz, then a young civil servant working at the U.S. Arms Control and Disarmament Agency. Team B provided a sharply different portrait of the Soviet threat, one that was more ambitious and aggressive than the CIA's National Intelligence Estimates had suggested. In the mid-1990s, the experience was repeated when Republicans, then in the majority in Congress, alleged that the intelligence community was understating the threat from ballistic missiles and established another commission to evaluate the problem. The Commission to Assess the Ballistic Missile Threat to the United States was led by Donald Rumsfeld, the future secretary of defense. Rumsfeld's chief of staff on the commission was Steve Cambone, an academic who, in 2001, would become the special assistant to the secretary of defense and later undersecretary of defense for intelligence, a new position that Congress established at Rumsfeld's request in 2003. Paul Wolfowitz, who has spoken disparagingly of the intelligence community as a "priesthood," served on the commission as well.[39] The commission's report sharply criticized the intelligence community, and some of its conclusions were borne out when North Korea fired a Daepodong-1 missile over Japan in 1998, well before the intelligence community believed Pyongyang would have that capability. The latter experience appears to have left Rumsfeld, Wolfowitz, and many of their aides with little respect for the U.S. intelligence community. On the specific issue of how the intelligence community viewed Iraq and terrorism, Richard Perle, a leading neoconservative and a close adviser to Rumsfeld, may have been speaking for all of them when he declared, "I think the people working on the Persian Gulf at the C.I.A. are pathetic."[40]

Upon their assumption of power in 2001, the Bush appointees made no secret of their disdain. Joseph Collins, a deputy assistant secretary of defense in the first Bush term who had close ties to several members of the new Defense Department team—he had helped prepare Paul Wolfowitz for his Senate confirmation hearings—admits, "The incoming team, especially Doug Feith and [Deputy Undersecretary of Defense] Bill Luti, behaved as if some of the uniforms and civil servants were Clintonistas and were either soft on the threat or not tuned in to Administration priorities." In the early days, the new leadership removed many of the career officials it did not approve of, and Rumsfeld and his aides seemed determined to take the "uniforms" down a peg, openly deprecating the Joint Chiefs' expertise. Another former deputy assistant secretary says, "They had no respect for the Agency [i.e., the CIA] and very little for the military. The Joint Staff and the military—they were just dissed."

Former senior intelligence officials recount being asked incessantly to reexamine the relationship between al Qaeda and Iraq. There was "a relentless barrage of questions" on the subject, as one official put it, and others have described the interest, especially from the Department of Defense, as obsessive. One senior administration official recalls that among the crew of intelligence officers who conducted morning briefings of senior officials, "it was a joke that Wolfowitz's briefer came back every morning and hit F5, the save-get key on the computer that sent out the message saying, 'investigate al Qaeda–Iraq, al Qaeda–Iraq.'"

Unhappy with the intelligence community it had, the Pentagon leadership created its own intelligence cell in October 2001. The Counter Terrorism Evaluation Group (CTEG) was created as a two-person unit to review intelligence on terrorism within Douglas Feith's Office of the Undersecretary of Defense for Policy; the members were prominent neoconservatives—David Wurmser, a former fellow at the American Enterprise Institute, and Michael Maloof, a former aide to Richard Perle. The men trawled through raw intelligence reports from human sources, communications intercepts, and the like, with the aim of providing their own analysis.[41] Individuals who saw the group's briefing described a presentation that aimed to demonstrate the numerous connections between al Qaeda and a host of other terrorist groups and state sponsors. PowerPoint slides reminiscent of the butcher paper with the "spaghetti all over it" were meant to show the ties connecting bin Laden's group to secular Muslim states like Iraq and even to Shiite groups like Hezbollah. CTEG's work was intended, in the words of one senior defense official, to challenge the "conventional wisdom" that these groups and states did not work together.[42] In reality, the presentation appears to have embodied the view that all bad Muslims are bad together.[43]

Judged by the standard procedures of the U.S. government, the use to which CTEG's work was put was unusual. Those who sat atop the Defense Department's large intelligence apparatus were called to a meeting to discuss the work. A senior officer who was there remembers "a long session" with military officials refusing to concur in the findings. They did not feel under pressure, but "that was kind of stuff you dealt with." At the request of the secretary of defense, the CTEG people met with Director of Central Intelligence George Tenet and senior CIA analysts. According to one agency official who attended the briefing, the CIA was skeptical of the CTEG findings. "They did point out some individual facts that we hadn't focused on," this official said, "but I don't think anything they briefed to us fundamentally changed our bottom line on the issue."[44] Moreover, CTEG's work, unlike standard intelligence reports, was never circulated to the numerous component parts of the intelligence community. "We never saw anything Feith's people were writing," says one State Department official. "It wasn't disseminated through regular finished product channels." In effect, CTEG's work was not subject to criticism or review of any serious kind, and it was not, in Washington parlance, "coordinated" or cleared as a publication of the intelligence community. Coordination is typically a laborious process in which all the parts of the community voice their views on a work of intelligence. Some assessments are usually changed through a process of negotiation; dubious elements are thrown out; irreconcilable objections are noted.

Nonetheless, CTEG's briefings were given to two groups that are supposed to receive fully coordinated intelligence: the White House and Congress. To the chagrin of George Tenet, the briefing was provided, without his knowledge, to the Office of the Vice President and the National Security Council.[45] It was also presented on Capitol Hill to congressional committees. As a result of one of these briefings the amateurishness of CTEG became all too apparent: When a senior counterterrorism official from the CIA was called to discuss the Defense Department's version of the world of transnational terror, he and Senator Carl Levin discovered that they had been given different sets of PowerPoint slides—Levin had received a set meant to convince senators of two things: the ties between all the nefarious actors in question *and* the fecklessness of the CIA. The counterterrorism official had received a different set that omitted the sharp criticism of the CIA.

CTEG's work can be assessed without relying exclusively on the statements of those in government because a memorandum that packaged together some of the group's work was leaked in November 2003 to *The Weekly Standard,* the magazine edited by William Kristol that is the foremost expositor of neoconservative views. In a cover story entitled "Case Closed," parts of the classified memo were printed, including excerpts from fifty raw intelligence reports that were adduced as proof of the Department of Defense's arguments. (The original memo was a follow-up requested by members of the Senate Select Committee on Intelligence after a briefing by Douglas Feith.) The memo was said to demonstrate that al Qaeda and Iraq had a close, substantive relationship that involved "training in explosives and weapons of mass destruction, logistical support for terrorist attacks, al Qaeda training camps and safe haven in Iraq, and Iraqi financial support for al Qaeda—perhaps even for Mohamed Atta."[46]

Yet a serious intelligence review would have resulted in much of the material being quickly discarded. One report claimed that Usama bin Laden had visited Baghdad in 1998 to meet with Iraqi Deputy Prime Minister Tariq Aziz, but this is almost impossible to believe in light of how many intelligence services were tracking the movements of both individuals. Another report that has bin Laden traveling to Qatar in 1996 is almost as implausible. There are also glaring mistakes in the analytic material. What is referred to as bin Laden's "fatwa on the plight of Iraq" was in fact his well-known statement "Jihad Against Jews and Crusaders," which spoke of the suffering of Iraqis but only as proof of a U.S.–led global campaign to destroy Islam. Nor does the CTEG document prove what it set out to: It presents few verifiable assertions and does not illustrate a tie that was ongoing, cooperative, and operational. At best, it records expressions of various individuals' wish for a better relationship between the two sides—a desire that does not appear to have been consummated by the principals. Meetings between Iraqi officials and al Qaeda members began in the early 1990s, and there are reports that Iraq wanted to "establish links to al Qaeda." In 1993, "bin Laden wanted to expand his organization's capabilities through ties with Iraq." But in 1998, the Iraqis still "seek closer ties," and the sides are still "looking for a way to maintain contacts." Much seeking and wanting is referred to, but little more. The fact that meetings occurred has never been at issue, nor has it been disputed that some jihadists lived in or traveled through Iraq. (There were more meetings with Iranian authorities, as well as more terrorists living in or transiting through Iran.) What is disputed is that the meetings had any real-world effects. The findings of the 9/11 Commission, which came out well after CTEG had done its primary work, stated clearly that the meetings went nowhere.

The Feith memo is an example of cherry-picking—the selective use of intelligence. Fifty reports is less than a drop in the bucket for an intelligence target like bin Laden. In January 1998, when CTEG suggested that he was in Baghdad meeting with Tariq Aziz, there were probably scores of reports putting bin Laden in Afghanistan and perhaps a half a dozen other places. CTEG offers no suggestion of that complexity in the intelligence record, nor does it provide any reason to believe that the single report placing him in Baghdad was correct. Proving a report correct, or sufficiently corroborated to be considered plausible, requires a lot more work. Pulling the disparate pieces together and constructing a coherent picture—connecting the dots— requires a mastery of all the material. Raw intelligence has its value, especially for detecting an ongoing terrorist plot. But there is a reason why the intelligence community spends much time and energy putting out "finished product," the reports that evaluate a significant body of information to get the whole picture right. Making a judgment about any ties between Iraq and al Qaeda on the basis of the sections printed in *The Weekly Standard* would be like accepting a high school biology student's reading of a CAT scan.

But in the highest circles of the U.S. government—the White House, the vice president's office, the senior leadership at the Pentagon—the CTEG material appears to have been viewed as the more reliable version of the bin Laden–Saddam relationship. In January 2004, when Vice President Cheney was asked by a reporter from the *Rocky Mountain News* about the ties between al Qaeda and Iraq, he answered by saying that the *Weekly Standard* article was the "best source of information."[47] When confronted with this at a congressional hearing, George Tenet announced that when the CIA found out about the "uncoordinated" Feith letter in November 2003, it demanded that the Pentagon retract it because of concerns about inaccuracies. The retraction had obviously not reached the vice president; Tenet agreed that he would "talk to" Cheney about the memo.[48]

What could not be retracted, of course, was the impact on the American public of the numerous statements by Bush, Cheney, and others about the supposed links between al Qaeda and Iraq. Undoubtedly, Americans were inclined to believe that Saddam was behind the September 11 attacks. In the public mind, his face was associated with evildoing more than any other's, and in a poll taken on September 13, 2001, nearly 80 percent of Americans thought he was involved. After bin Laden's responsibility was established, most administration spokesmen—Cheney was a notable exception—were careful not to say that Saddam was specifically involved in the attacks. But they persistently linked him and bin Laden, and this had a powerful effect on public opinion. Long after Saddam was overthrown, approximately 70 percent of Americans continued to believe that he had been involved in the 9/11 attacks.[49] In 2005, almost as many continued to think that the Iraqi dictator and Saudi jihadists were in league.[50]

The story of CTEG lends credence to the contention of Colin Powell's aide Larry Wilkerson and others that the Iraq war was produced by an almost parallel foreign policy apparatus run not by the National Security Council but by the extraordinarily influential Office of the Vice President (OVP). Under Dick Cheney, the national security section of OVP has expanded enormously. In 2004, for example, a national security staff of fourteen served Cheney, many of them of high rank within the bureaucracy. His predecessor, Al Gore, by contrast, had a national security adviser, a deputy, and several mid-ranking military officers working for him. The connection between Cheney and his chief of staff, I. Lewis Libby, on the one hand, and the Pentagon team of Rumsfeld, Wolfowitz, and Feith on the other, also gave the OVP team a direct line to the Department of Defense.[51] Rumsfeld had been Cheney's first boss during the Nixon administration, when the former congressman from Illinois hired the young Wyoming native to work for him in the Office of Economic Opportunity. When Rumsfeld became White House chief of staff under President Gerald Ford, Cheney became his deputy and eventual successor. Libby had been a student of Paul Wolfowitz's at Yale. Feith had worked with both Cheney and Wolfowitz in earlier Republican administrations.

OVP has also seemed at times to be an independent intelligence agency: Cheney himself continued to suggest a collaboration between Saddam and al Qaeda long after others in the administration would make such a charge. Perhaps the most extreme examples were the continued references he made as late as June 2004 to an alleged meeting between Muhammad Atta and an Iraqi intelligence agent in Prague in April 2001—two years after the CIA and the FBI had investigated the matter and ruled out the possibility it could have occurred. When Colin Powell was preparing his crucial prewar speech before the United Nations Security Council in February 2003, he was first presented with a draft script from Cheney's office. Unwilling to accept it on faith, Powell spent four days at the CIA poring over the intelligence to decide what was credible. He quickly threw out the OVP script, calling it "bullshit." As Wilkerson recalls, the items came from "the kind of sources Feith would bring up. They were cherry-picked." In his speech before the UN, the secretary of state spent relatively little time on the Iraq–al Qaeda relationship, focusing instead on the issue of Iraqi weapons of mass destruction.

In this, as in so many other respects, Powell was the odd man out in the Bush administration. He was unwilling to join in the groupthink that was occurring, and he paid the price in being excluded or ignored on most major decisions. What has been impressive, however, is the degree to which most other members of the inner circle have retained their certainty about the links between al Qaeda and Iraq and the nature of the threat facing America. In a profile by Peter Boyer in *The New Yorker* in November 2004, Paul Wolfowitz returned to the Mylroie thesis, suggesting that the involvement of the Iraqi national Abdul Rahman Yasin in the first bombing of the World Trade Center pointed to an Iraqi-jihadist connection. "It would seem significant that one major figure in that event is still at large," Wolfowitz says. "It would seem significant that he was harbored in Iraq by Iraqi intelligence for ten years." But, Boyer notes, "Many intelligence analysts believe that the presence of Yasin in Iraq was not particularly meaningful . . . if he was being 'harbored,' the argument goes, it was only as a detainee that Saddam hoped to use as a bargaining chip with the United States."[52]

When the 9/11 Commission issued its verdict that Iraq and al Qaeda had no cooperative relationship, Dick Cheney announced that he had no major differences with the report, and yet he continued to maintain that "there clearly was a relationship" between Saddam and bin Laden and that "the evidence is overwhelming." He added that he "probably" had access to intelligence information not available to the commission and insisted that the story about the Atta meeting in Prague might be credible.[53] (Cheney later reversed himself and admitted that he did not have any intelligence reports that had not been given to the commission.) When asked about the report, President Bush was similarly resolute. "The reason I keep insisting that there was a relationship between Iraq and Saddam and al Qaeda," he said, is "because there was a relationship between Iraq and al Qaeda."[54]

While the Bush administration was preparing for war and making its case for a linkage between Iraq and al Qaeda, something it was not doing was considering how invading Iraq would affect the radical Islamist movement. Early on, there was strong foreboding within the intelligence community. A State Department official close to the issue says, "There was a sense in the community that this [going into Iraq] would be a poster child for the jihad." It might have seemed obvious, in the prewar planning, to inquire about the implications of an invasion for jihadists, but as one of the intelligence community's foremost experts on the region recalls, "We were not asked." This official recalls that in an effort to prod the policy makers to wakefulness, the CIA produced assessments "that said, yes, this would be a stimulant to the global jihad and a magnet for Islamic extremists. . . . We said that violence in Iraq would serve as an attraction to jihadists to get in on the action." It is questionable if these reports were even read. The official says he got virtually no feedback from the senior leadership, even though he saw them frequently. "I got one bit of senior level feedback that said, 'You guys are too pessimistic. You just don't see the larger regional opportunities.' "

In the summer before the war, CIA analysts expressed concerns that the "chaos after war would turn Iraq into a laboratory for terrorists."[55] A former counterterrorism official warned in a September 2002 op-ed article for the *New York Times* that "it is also worth considering how a war in Iraq might further the jihadist cause. . . . As images of the United States attacking another Muslim nation are beamed throughout the Middle East and South Asia, many will take it as confirmation of Mr. bin Laden's argument that America is at war with Islam." Recalling how bin Laden's own hatred for America was crystallized by Operation Desert Storm and the stationing of troops in Saudi Arabia, the writer warned, "The last war against Iraq was a catalytic event for the Islamists who formed al Qaeda. We should not be complacent and believe that the next one will be different, or that the jihadist violence cannot grow worse."[56] In the White House, however, such concerns were nowhere in evidence. As one former National Security Council official recalls, the question of whether the American presence in Iraq would galvanize radicals never came up: "I doubt Condi ever asked John Gordon," who was then the senior counterterrorism official at the NSC. "I doubt it occurred to her."

The failure is striking, not only because the Bush team was ignoring its own intelligence analysts but because it was ignoring what the jihadists were saying, even how they seemed to be licking their lips at the thought of

American troops coming to Iraq. In an audio statement issued in February 2003, bin Laden offered practical advice for the coming struggle: "We also recommend luring the enemy forces into a protracted, close, and exhausting fight, using the camouflaged defensive positions in plains, farms, mountains, and cities. The enemy fears city and street wars most, a war in which the enemy expects grave human losses."[57] Moreover, the message was not new. Bin Laden and other jihadist leaders had been singing the virtues of insurgency for years. In his 1996 fatwa, one of his first major statements, he spoke of the need to "initiate a guerrilla warfare . . . And as you know, it is wise, in the present circumstances, for the armed military forces not to be engaged in a conventional fighting with the forces of the crusader enemy."[58]

Curiously, the Bush team recognized that toppling Saddam would allow the United States to remove the 5,000 troops it had stationed in Saudi Arabia. It moved quickly to do so. The troops were withdrawn in August 2003, just four months after the end of major combat operations in Iraq. This, it was understood, would eliminate the anger often voiced by radical Islamists and even some moderate Saudis at having American troops in Arabia, where the Prophet had said "there should be no two religions."[59] Yet no one appears to have ever asked how the radicals, not to speak of hundreds of millions of Muslims around the world, would view the exchange of a few thousand troops in the Arabian desert for 150,000 GIs in and around Baghdad, the seat of the caliphate from 750 to 1258. Even more important are the raw memories of colonial occupation, especially by the British in Iraq and Palestine, which divided the Arab world into artificial states and is felt to have destroyed its unity. Those driving the U.S. engagement in Iraq did consider how an occupation would be viewed in the Muslim world but without regard for the colonial experience, which would predispose many to see Americans as intruders. The assumption that Americans would be received as liberators prevented the war planners from recognizing that our intervention would affirm perceptions that America seeks to occupy Muslim countries and subdue Islam.

They had failed the first test of military leadership. They did not know who their real enemy was.

8

THE PERSISTENCE OF ERROR

The decision to go to war in Iraq had serious consequences for the fight against al Qaeda. The United States effectively decided that it had a more important target than the group that had only months earlier killed 3,000 people on American soil. It is often said that with its $400-billion-a-year military and fifteen agencies in its intelligence community, the United States ought to be able to do many things at once. For the past decade, American defense planning has set as its central goal the ability to fight two regional wars almost simultaneously. The hypothetical wars would be in Iraq and on the Korean Peninsula. For two wars involving Muslims, most of them Arabic speaking, there would be shortfalls of specialists with area and language skills. Moreover, for two conflicts that involved tracking, apprehending, and destroying very specific, small targets—individual terrorists and weapons of mass destruction—intelligence assets would be in short supply. In practice, as opposed to the theory of planning documents, the military quickly runs low on "critical low-density high-demand assets," in the parlance of the Pentagon. These include satellite surveillance, airborne surveillance (such as the Predator drones and the Global Hawk unmanned vehicle, which flies at 65,000 feet and can stay aloft for thirty-five hours), the individuals and equipment to conduct signals intelligence and human intelligence—spies—and Special Operations forces.

By early 2002, many of these assets were being transferred for operations in and around Iraq. Some were taken from counterterrorism missions in Somalia and Yemen, where, according to military sources, at least 50 percent of the key assets were shipped out. Troops and materiel were taken from Afghanistan, an area of operations where much more was going on than in the Horn of Africa. The commando team that was charged with hunting for Usama bin Laden and other al Qaeda leaders reportedly shrank at times to less than a third of its initial size. In the first half of 2003, its equivalent unit in Iraq expanded to more than 200 troops to cope with a spreading insurgency and pursue the hunt for Saddam Hussein.[1] When replacements were sent to Afghanistan for the redeployed special forces, they were often reservists who were not nearly as sharp as the top "operators" who had departed.

On the intelligence side, the CIA postponed an $80 million plan to set up a new Afghanistan intelligence service and moved the Islamabad station chief to Washington to work on Iraq issues. As the *Washington Post*'s Barton Gellman has reported, "By the time war came in Iraq nearly 150 case officers filled the task force. . . . The Baghdad station became the largest since the Vietnam War, with more than 300."[2] According to one senior intelligence official, this was a "huge diversion of resources in terms of intelligence assets." The requirements of the two areas of operation meant that "when you consider the area and language expertise [available] in the ops world, there was a huge overlap," and Afghanistan lost. Of the more than 1,000 people who worked on the Iraq Survey Group, which conducted the postwar hunt for weapons of mass destruction, scores or more might have been working on counterterrorism instead—including some of the 900 people translating documents for the effort. But when terrorist activity near the Pakistani border flared up, requests from Kabul for additional personnel were turned down.

At the most practical level, these were not losses that could be made up by having the staff work longer hours. The crunch limited precisely those American units that were hunting terrorists. "The SOF [Special Operations] guys sent the A team to Iraq," says one individual who is deeply involved in the hunt for bin Laden. "They kept a capability but it wasn't the

A team." He adds, "There were very few Predators left in country. Seventy-five percent went over there [to Iraq] as well." The U.S. intelligence and military capability was further reduced by the scarcity of communications links between a command post and the field necessary to carry out an operation. "If you were looking for satellite relay to talk to guys on the ground—well, good luck," this official says. "It had shifted over there. Everyone knows that costs." In his view, the overall effect of these diversions of men and materiel directly contradicted the administration's goal of eliminating areas in which terrorists could operate: "Did anyone think about leaving a sanctuary in Afghanistan? I don't think so. I think our policies failed us and we have left them [al Qaeda] in place to plan from there."

The hiving off of assets for Iraq left some in the intelligence community and the military angry at the civilian leadership. "Were we finished in Afghanistan? Many people, me included, thought we were not finished—that defeat of the Taliban and al Qaeda was not sufficient. We needed their destruction," says Greg Newbold, the former chief of operations for the Joint Staff. "For those of us who wanted all the tools to destroy the terrorists, this was viewed as pedestrian thinking by Wolfowitz, Feith, and their counselors."

IN THE SPRING of 2002, the CIA and the Defense Department circulated intelligence about a burgeoning terrorist camp in the Kurdish zone in northern Iraq near a town called Khurmal, close to the Iranian border. The information was alarming enough for the military to begin drawing up plans for rapid action to destroy the camp.

The region was an anomaly. It was officially part of Iraq, but, after the refugee crisis following the Gulf War in 1991, it had effectively been detached from the rest of the country by the United States and its allies as a way of protecting the Kurdish population, which Saddam had persecuted viciously. American and British war jets patrolled the skies along the thirty-sixth parallel, the line of demarcation with the rest of Iraq, in what was called Operation Northern Watch. The enclave of 4 million people was governed primarily by the two major Kurdish political parties, the Patriotic Union of Kurdistan and the Kurdish Democratic Party, but their control was less than complete. In the northeastern corner of the region, radical Islamists associated with the group Ansar al-Islam had gathered. The group opposed the American-supported Kurdish parties.

What gave the issue of the Khurmal camp urgency was the reporting on what was going on there. Ansar al-Islam, a jihadist organization with predominantly Kurdish membership and links to al Qaeda, had recently swelled with an influx of jihadist fighters who had fled Afghanistan. Pentagon officials recount that the group was developing toxins—specifically ricin, which is made from castor beans and, if absorbed by the body in even tiny amounts, can kill. There were also indications of possible chemical and biological weapons development. The intelligence community's understanding was that the materials were being prepared for eventual use in Europe.

In addition, the Jordanian terrorist Abu Musab al-Zarqawi was known to be spending considerable amounts of time in the camp. Zarqawi was not yet a household name; he would first become known outside intelligence circles after the assassination of the American diplomat Lawrence Foley in Amman the following October. But already within the government, as one general who was deeply involved in hunting for terrorists recalls, "He was a big guy for us." The Joint Staff ordered military planners to draw up an option for destroying the Khurmal camp, including both air strikes and ground attacks. "This fit what we thought was American strategy," says Greg Newbold. "President Bush had said, 'They can run but can't hide,' and 'We'll destroy them where we find them.' We hadn't been finding them in Yemen or Somalia, and now we had found them. We thought they were very, very close to shipping the toxins." Within the Joint Staff, the preference was for an air strike, but all the options were sent forward with a recommendation for action by July 4, 2002.

At that point, everything began to slow down. Both the deputies committee and principals committee met to discuss Khurmal, but at the Joint Staff, nothing more was heard. As Newbold recalls, "A golden opportunity was passing. We expected the vans to pull up" and cart all the terrorists' materials away to a safer location. A former colleague of Newbold's confirms that the Joint Staff was eager to move: "We were all very frustrated. We knew they were making ricin and testing it on animals and, we thought, people. And the concern was: What happens if this is used on Americans?"

The July 4 deadline came and went. Later in the summer, the existence of the camp was leaked in a Turkish newspaper. In the second week of August, the vans did pull up, and soon the camp ceased to exist as a target.

Why did the Bush team fail to move against Khurmal? An NSC spokesman later explained, "Because there was never any real-time, actionable intelligence that placed Zarqawi at Khurmal, action taken against the facility would have been ineffective." But as Scot Paltrow of the *Wall Street Journal* reported in October 2004, "Former officials said the intelligence on Mr. Zarqawi's whereabouts was sound. In addition, retired Gen. John M. Keane, the U.S. Army's vice chief of staff when the strike was considered, said that because the camp was isolated in the thinly populated, mountainous borderlands of northeastern Iraq, the risk of collateral damage was minimal. . . . Gen. Keane characterized the camp 'as one of the best targets we ever had,' and questioned the decision not to attack it."[3]

Though they remain puzzled that the decision was made not to hit Khurmal, some of those in the military who were pushing for a strike offer a number of possible thoughts about why the decision went the way it did. Among the explanations that have been offered are that the White House, as one officer put it, "didn't want people to think we'd already gone to war and that this was the first shot" and that there was fear Saddam would see this as an opportunity to move against the Kurds, triggering a war before the Pentagon was ready to fight. This seems somewhat implausible since U.S. aircraft had been carrying out periodic strikes on Iraqi targets for years, and, of course, Khurmal was not in territory controlled by Baghdad.

Yet another theory that has been offered holds that the White House thought it would be more useful to point to a connection between Iraq and al Qaeda during the runup to war and afterward than to destroy the evidence with an air strike. This notion gains some support from the many times, beginning in October 2002, that administration leaders referred to Zarqawi's presence in the country as evidence of an Iraq–al Qaeda alliance, and the heavy emphasis Secretary of State Colin Powell placed on the camp itself in his February 2003 speech to the United Nations Security Council, one of the few points he made about the Iraq–al Qaeda relationship. He referred to Khurmal as a demonstration of the "sinister nexus between Iraq and the Al Qaida terrorist network," where "the Zarqawi network helped establish another poison and explosive training center camp." Powell underscored the danger of what was going on in the camp, which by this point had been reoccupied by Ansar al-Islam, by observing that "less than a pinch of ricin, eating just this amount in your food, would cause shock followed by circulatory failure. Death comes within 72 hours and there is no antidote, there is no cure. It is fatal." Although Powell acknowledged what other administration spokesmen usually glided over—that the camp lay in territory outside the control of the Iraqi government—he noted that "Baghdad has an agent in the most senior levels of the radical organization."[4] Powell left two facts unmentioned: First, that Ansar al-Islam was being supported by Iran as well as Iraq—two archenemies—because of their common opposition to the U.S.-backed Kurds; and second, that in the view of most intelligence analysts, the relationship between Baghdad and the group did not demonstrate a cooperative relationship that extended beyond the Kurdish zone.

Whatever the motivation behind the administration's inaction—the policy makers may, in the end, have judged the threat not to be significant—it is clear that Zarqawi and his group were a lower-tier concern than the Iraqi regime. On one and possibly two later occasions before the invasion of Iraq, the Joint Staff pressed for action against Khurmal, and in both cases the decision makers chose not to strike. Only after the war began was Khurmal finally destroyed.

Although there could be no certainty that a strike would have killed Zarqawi, the possibility that his career as a jihadist leader might have ended there is worth considering. After the invasion, Zarqawi initiated a wave of kidnappings and decapitations, beginning with the beheading of Nicholas Berg in May 2004. By the summer of 2005, he had orchestrated bombings and other attacks that had killed scores, if not hundreds, of Americans and many times that number of Iraqis. He has done as much as anyone to undermine the occupation and reconstruction of Iraq; his network has expanded into Germany, Spain, and Britain; and Usama bin Laden evidently believes that Zarqawi is the man who can attack the United States for him. In retrospect, the Bush team would have been well advised to at least take this jihadist more seriously.

*   *   *

IT IS AN open and probably unanswerable question whether the invasion of Iraq could have been done "right"—whether, that is, the United States could have toppled Saddam Hussein's regime, established public order, gotten reconstruction moving, and begun the work of establishing a new government well enough to preempt the insurgency that developed. But it is abundantly clear that the Bush administration's failure to do a better job at these tasks compounded its initial error of underestimating the jihadist threat. Had U.S. forces been deployed throughout the country in strength and had they clamped down on any early violence or disorder, it would have been harder for the insurgency to gain momentum. Instead, the administration created a wide-open field for the radicals. By failing to provide real security, the United States demonstrated a lack of concern for the fate of ordinary Iraqis, and as a result, some undoubtedly turned against us.[5] Through an overly ambitious de-Baathification program and the precipitous dissolution of the Iraqi army, America multiplied the number of those disgruntled by the fall of the regime, creating a large pool of tactical allies for the radicals. It seems that no one seriously contemplated the aftermath of the invasion going badly and the possibility of a real insurgency, or even the civil war that now appears to be looming, or how that would affect American standing in the Muslim world and, by extension, the effort to stem radicalization.

Why did the government fail to have the necessary forces and plans in place for the occupation of a country the size of California? The answer lies in a tangle of preconceptions and misunderstandings about how the war would unfold. Among these were the belief that the Iraqi people would welcome the American forces, that there would be minimal resistance, if any, that there would be a clean end to the fighting and a distinct transition to the post-conflict operations. It was also thought that America's key allies would be prepared to participate in the post-conflict peacekeeping, even if they had sat out the war.

These assumptions became fixed early in the planning for the invasion. Instead of preparing for a range of possible outcomes, the administration used these preconceptions as the basis for its postwar planning. These assumptions became a touchstone for administration credibility—in part because of ideological commitment and in part because they were woven into the administration's justification to the nation for going to war—and the Bush team did not deviate from them. In addition, because so much of the preparation for Iraq occurred outside established bureaucratic channels, the kind of scrutiny that such planning would ordinarily get was absent.

In a 2003 interview, Paul Wolfowitz discussed how the 9/11 hijackers were able to surprise the United States with their mass suicide attack. He explained that "probably the second greatest source of intelligence error is mirror imaging. . . . The greatest mistake is assuming that . . . people will be rational according to our definition of what is rational."[6] Yet this is precisely what the Bush administration did in expecting that American forces "will be greeted as liberators," as Vice President Cheney put it just before the invasion.[7] In their public comments, members of the Bush team were unrestrained in their optimism. Secretary Rumsfeld urged Americans to "think of the faces in Afghanistan when the people were liberated, when they moved out in the streets and they started singing and flying kites and women went to school and people were able to function and other countries were able to start interacting with them. That's what would happen in Iraq."[8] Wolfowitz himself echoed this claim, saying, "I think when the people of Basra no longer feel the threat of that regime, you are going to see an explosion of joy and relief."[9] As one State Department official later described the mind-set of the administration, "They thought Paris in 1944 was the precedent."

To be sure, most Iraqis saw Saddam as a tyrant whom they would be glad to be rid of. But just because U.S. planners in Washington believed that a people freed of a brutal dictator ought to be grateful and pliant did not necessarily mean that they would be, or, if they were, that the warmth would last long. In the event, whatever positive feelings Iraqis had for the United States were less durable than Cheney and other administration leaders expected. Since those planning for the occupation were certain that positive sentiments would dominate, no one prepared for the contingency of postwar looting and chaos from which the occupation never recovered.

One of the enduring mysteries about the postwar period in Iraq is why experienced, unsentimental practitioners of international politics such as Dick Cheney would believe that postwar Iraq would be a calm, relatively unproblematic place. Some of those who participated in prewar discussions of the invasion say that he and others were swayed by the arguments of the Iraqi exile Ahmed Chalabi. The scion of a wealthy Iraqi Shiite family, Chalabi emerged in the 1990s as a significant but controversial figure in the Iraqi exile community. He founded the Iraqi National Congress in 1992 as an umbrella group of Iraqi exiles, and he built a network of friends and supporters in the United States, especially among neoconservatives who shared his desire to topple the Baghdad regime and accepted his claims that the Iraqi people were eager for the Americans to come in and would greet them with flowers and candy. But there were at least as many people suspicious of Chalabi as there were supporters. A longtime resident of Jordan, Chalabi fled that country when his financial empire collapsed amid charges of fraud, and he continues to be wanted there for prosecution. His dealings with the CIA over a number of years had led the intelligence community to distance itself from him, reportedly because he was believed to be a fabricator of intelligence and had misused funds that had been given to him.

Although the CIA wanted nothing to do with Chalabi, the Defense Department, where the neoconservative movement was well represented by Wolfowitz, Feith, and others, established a close relationship with him. When the invasion came, some of his followers were armed and equipped by the Pentagon and flown into Iraq early in the fighting, leading many analysts to speculate that the Defense Department planned to install Chalabi as a successor to Saddam. It is unlikely that we will know the full extent of Chalabi's influence over the thinking of the Bush team for years—if ever—since official records and personal accounts will not be made public for some time. But this will be a critical piece of the puzzle of how America blundered so fatefully in Iraq.

The notion that we would be greeted with open arms might not have stood up to scrutiny within the administration if it had not dovetailed so neatly with a new vision of American military might that key members of the administration—in particular, the president and Secretary of Defense Rumsfeld—were propounding. At the heart of this vision were two linked concepts: the "Revolution in Military Affairs," and "Military Transformation." The first, often referred to by the acronym "RMA," describes a set of changes in warfare in the past two decades that have conferred an enormous advantage on cutting-edge militaries. These developments include the emergence of precision munitions and "net" warfare, which involves the linkage via electronic communications of computers and sensors on the battlefield to an array of intelligence assets including satellites, airplanes, and other means of "technical collection." This networking allows for the nearly instantaneous transmission of intelligence, targeting information, and guidance from commanders to combatants, all of which, its proponents claim, add up to a profound change in the nature of battle.

"Military Transformation" has become the code phrase for exploiting such RMA developments to further enhance American military might. It has been a goal of George W. Bush since he began his run for the presidency in 1999. In a speech at the Citadel that year, he declared:

> Power is increasingly defined, not by mass or size, but by mobility and swiftness. Influence is measured in information, safety is gained in stealth, and force is projected on the long arc of precision-guided weapons. This revolution perfectly matches the strengths of our country—the skill of our people and the superiority of our technology. The best way to keep the peace is to redefine war on our terms.[10]

The need to transform the American military to take advantage of technological change has been one that Bush has come back to time and again. In his first State of the Union address in February 2001, he announced, "Our military was shaped to confront the challenge of the past, so I have asked the Secretary of Defense to review America's armed forces and prepare to transform them to meet emerging threats."[11] A few months later, at the U.S. Naval Academy, he called for a "future force that is defined less by size and more by mobility and swiftness, one that is easier to deploy and sustain, one that relies more heavily on stealth, precision weaponry and information technology."[12] Much as with his commitment to a national missile defense, Bush's belief that technology can provide America with the solutions to its most urgent problems is deep and abiding.

That conviction has been widely shared among other senior members of the administration who see military power as the foremost tool of foreign policy. Donald Rumsfeld, in particular, joined Bush in seeing military transformation as a fundamental goal, and he has made clear that setting this process in motion will be the core of his legacy as secretary of defense.[13] For Rumsfeld, a central part of the argument about transformation has been that the U.S. military is already much more powerful than is commonly recognized. We are already midway into the RMA—witness the impact of precision munitions and computer integration to date— which means that the traditional American way of war, using massive troop deployments to overwhelm an opponent, is wasteful and unnecessary. In this view, the United States can already fight with great effectiveness with much lower troop numbers, given the firepower at our disposal.

A belief in the almost boundless power of the American military underlay the opening gambit in the war and, in a broader sense, the entire invasion. U.S. military sources told reporters that the initial attack on the regime would be unprecedented in its destructiveness. "There will not be a safe place in Baghdad," said one Pentagon official. "The sheer size of this has never been seen before, never been contemplated before."[14] This would be "shock and awe," a phrase that burst into the public consciousness in the weeks leading up to the invasion.[15] The principle behind shock and awe was that if appropriate tactics, overwhelming firepower, and the element of surprise were effectively combined, an enemy could be stunned into rapid submission. It is indicative of the approach that when General Tommy Franks briefed President Bush on the plans for Operation Iraqi Freedom, he emphasized that the campaign would use four times the amount of ordnance that was dropped on Iraq in 1991.[16]

The embrace of shock and awe seems to be a case in which the administration wanted to achieve through its actions what the terrorists accomplished on 9/11—the paralysis of the opponent through a stunning, almost otherworldly display of force. The administration also believed that the demonstration effect of American arms would be so overpowering that all potential enemies would simply give up the thought of resistance.[17] The problem was that shock and awe and the entire American war plan were focused exclusively on the Iraqi military, not the jihadist enemy who was lying in wait. As mentioned in chapter 2, the radicals had been reviewing U.S. military operations in Afghanistan, writing after-action reports and advising the insurgents in Iraq that they could ride out the air attacks and then inflict real damage once the ground troops appeared. This, moreover, was in keeping with nearly a decade of jihadist writing on the centrality of guerrilla operations against American or other Western militaries. As war approached, bin Laden exhorted Iraqis to take these lessons to heart, and other al Qaeda leaders, such as Saif al-Adel, supplemented bin Laden's rhetoric with online postings that contained more detailed instructions on guerrilla tactics.

It appears no one in the Department of Defense was paying attention to these communications. The U.S. military drove into the heart of the country with great speed, and there were relatively few engagements. Baghdad was taken quickly, but many Iraqi units, including much of the vaunted Republican Guard, melted into the countryside. And the jihadists began their work.

DONALD RUMSFELD, IT has been observed, is an unyielding competitor, a former college wrestler who has never lost his drive.[18] As Bob Woodward has documented—and government sources amply confirm—at the time of the U.S. victory in Afghanistan, Rumsfeld was angry and frustrated that the Pentagon had had no good war plans for that country and that the CIA had taken the lead in planning and executing the campaign there.[19] The CIA won great credit within the administration in the early days of the fighting for its ability to enlist the Afghan militias, coordinate them with U.S. airpower and special forces, and destroy the Taliban in a matter of weeks. Eventually, the Defense Department received public acclaim for the victory in Afghanistan, but, in a sense, the CIA had made Rumsfeld's point about the ability of the United States to fight in lighter, more agile, more innovative ways, and he appears not to have liked it.

So when it came time to plan for Iraq, Rumsfeld involved himself in revising the war plan in every respect to ensure that Central Command learned the CIA's lesson. The existing war plans called for a force of 500,000 troops, which would take months to assemble in the region. For Rumsfeld, this was the American military at its wasteful, lumbering worst. From the beginning of the planning effort that was spearheaded by General Franks, Rumsfeld incessantly demanded cuts in troop levels; in time, he personally began crossing units off the deployment list. In the end, Rumsfeld and Franks pared the force down to 165,000 American troops, with 45,000 more joining from the United Kingdom and other countries. More than 16,000 of these troops did not make it to Iraq in time for the invasion. When the Turkish Parliament voted against giving U.S. forces permission to invade northern Iraq through Turkish territory, it left the Fourth Infantry Division afloat on their transports in the Mediterranean.

By the standards of military practice, planning for the war in Iraq was an ad hoc affair. Not everyone in the Pentagon thought that Rumsfeld's approach was sound. Testifying before Congress in February 2003, General Eric Shinseki, the Army chief of staff, estimated the troop needs for occupying Iraq as "something on the order of several hundred thousand." Shinseki, himself one of the pioneer thinkers about military transformation, had based his number on the possibility of a variety of different postwar conditions. His remarks, however, were viewed as an affront to the civilian leadership, and Paul Wolfowitz slapped down the general publicly. "I am reasonably certain that they will greet us as liberators, and that will help us to keep requirements down," Wolfowitz said. "In short, we don't know what the requirement will be, but we can say with reasonable confidence that the notion of hundreds of thousands of American troops is way off the mark."[20] Looking back on how the war plan came to be, Joseph Collins, who served as deputy assistant secretary of defense for stability operations, remarked, "One of the worst things that happened was Rumsfeld crossing off those orders." Like many others who worked in the Pentagon at the time, Collins believes that the precedent of Afghanistan, where light and mobile fighters had shown their effectiveness, was central to the faulty preparations. "Whenever you see silly things done in Iraq, look to see if they were lessons learned from Afghanistan," he said. "There were a lot of people who were dizzy with success from Afghanistan."

On one level, though, Rumsfeld proved his point. The force that deployed to Iraq was a fraction of what "old think" commanders would have used, and it was sufficient to topple the Iraqi regime in virtually no time. The forces raced to Baghdad, and Saddam's regime was soon history. But the force was not properly sized to occupy Iraq and provide the security necessary for establishing public order.[21] Here, too, the assumptions about postwar Iraq were perfectly matched to the dismissive attitude within the Bush administration toward nation-building missions. Condoleezza Rice had set the tone for the administration in her 2000 *Foreign Affairs* article, in which she argued, "Using the American armed forces as the world's '911' will degrade capabilities [and] bog soldiers down in peacekeeping roles."[22]

And she later decried the absurdity of having "the 82nd Airborne escorting kids to kindergarten."[23] After taking office, Rumsfeld insisted that the Office of Peacekeeping Operations be renamed the Office of Stability Operations, and he sharply limited its activities. Testifying before the House Budget Committee in February 2003, Paul Wolfowitz expressed concisely the administration's inability to foresee the problems ahead of it: "First, it's hard to conceive that it would take more forces to provide stability in post-Saddam Iraq than it would take to conduct the war itself and to secure the surrender of Saddam's security forces and his army. Hard to imagine."[24]

The prejudice against peacekeeping was deeply held, and when events took a turn that had not been calculated into the prewar assumptions, Rumsfeld was again unwilling to examine his beliefs and change course. After looting broke out across Iraq and persisted for days, he brushed it off. "Freedom's untidy, and free people are free to make mistakes and commit crimes and do bad things," Rumsfeld said. "They're also free to live their lives and do wonderful things. And that's what's going to happen here." Looting, he added, occurred in countries in the midst of transitions, saying, "Stuff happens."[25] In the ensuing months, in an effort to preserve his military transformation agenda, Rumsfeld refused to send in more troops to quell the nascent insurgency. He claimed that the commanders in the field had not requested them, although such a request would have been unlikely, given his insistence during the planning process on sharply limiting the size of the military deployment. This refusal to deal with the evolving crisis helped doom the occupation.

IF THE PLANNING for the war-fighting was ad hoc, the preparations for the occupation were plainly chaotic. Planning efforts were undertaken in several different parts of the bureaucracy with little or no coordination. The attention of top policy makers was focused almost exclusively on the war, not on reconstruction. And the bureaucrats who had ultimate control were working "out of channels," issuing directives without ever having their plans scrubbed in the kind of tedious, iterative process that the government typically uses to make sure it is ready for any contingency. The story of all the things that went wrong is a sprawling tale, and much of it has been told elsewhere.²⁶ But a few key events indicate the major failures of the postwar planning effort.

Already, in 2002, preparations had begun in many different government agencies. The State Department began a wide-ranging "Future of Iraq Project," which would eventually produce a thirteen-volume document on an array of issues including governance, infrastructure, and relations among Iraq's Sunnis, Shiites, and Kurds. The U.S. Agency for International Development began work on reconstruction, and the Department of Defense also started examining what would be needed. There was, however, no integration.

The first government-wide effort to pull some of this work together was not held until November 2002 at the Pentagon's National Defense University in Washington. But from the start, the planners were hobbled by the Defense Department's insistence that all deliberations be based on a set of assumptions about what the situation on the ground would look like. At the top of the list was that the Iraqi people would greet American forces as liberators, and that the security situation would be assured. Another assumption was that there would be a clear moment when combat operations would end and the postwar stability operation would begin. A third was that the national infrastructure would be, for the most part, undamaged. A fourth was that most of the ministries of the Iraqi government would continue to function.

Historically, the first priority of all postwar operations has been to establish security.²⁷ But the planners were being told that they should not address any topic related to security because it would not be a problem. According to Paul Hughes, then a U.S. Army colonel, who organized the conference, "We were given the assumptions. We didn't assume anything. They came from OSD [Office of the Secretary of Defense] Policy, from Doug Feith's guy." There was little inclination to challenge these assumptions, Hughes says, because "Rumsfeld scared the shit out of people," and given the defense secretary's sharp handling of personnel since entering office, they feared for their jobs. Even so, the first recommendation in the paper that came out of the conference stated: "Given the potential for internal disorder and conflict, the *primary post-intervention focus of US military operations must be on establishing and maintaining a secure environment* in which all other post-intervention activities can operate."[28] (Emphasis in original.) But the group's marching orders from the Pentagon precluded it from examining some of the less rosy scenarios that might occur. They were not permitted to assess the possibility of jihadist violence. The paper was sent to the senior leadership of the Pentagon, but there was never any feedback.

In January 2003, President Bush broke with precedent and designated the Department of Defense as the lead agency for postwar reconstruction—in previous cases in which the United States engaged in reconstruction, the State Department had played that role. The directive he issued created the civilian Office for Reconstruction and Humanitarian Assistance (ORHA), which would report to Rumsfeld, and retired General Jay Garner was appointed to lead it. As they were taking primary responsibility in this area, the Pentagon leadership rejected requests from its planners to begin an interagency process to coordinate the effort among the many parts of the government that would inevitably be involved in administering postwar Iraq. Paul Hughes recalls being told by a member of Douglas Feith's staff that there was "no fucking way" that the Department of Defense was going to consult with other agencies. "We're going to tell the interagency what we need, and that's that," this staffer said. Indeed, the Pentagon did much more to shut out other agencies than to include them. The copious work of the Future of Iraq Project was largely ignored, and although it did not provide a clear plan for an occupation, it did contain a vast amount of useful information for dealing with the problems ahead. Excluding the State Department from influencing the planning became a high priority for the Pentagon's senior leadership and even for some in the White House. Garner, who was hired on January 20, 2003, did not find out about the Future of Iraq Project until a conference a full month later. He was impressed with Tom Warrick, the State Department official who ran the project, and offered him a job. Three days later Garner received a call from Rumsfeld telling him that he could not hire Warrick. The word apparently had come from Cheney's office that Warrick was unacceptable.[29]

When the United States invaded Iraq in March 2003, ORHA was barely up and running. Most of its efforts, understandably, were devoted to just getting people detailed to the organization. As a result, although planning for the war itself had begun sixteen months earlier, there was no document that set out what would happen in the country once its military was defeated. After the troops raced to Baghdad and toppled the regime, they had no instructions about what to do next. In its after-action report, the Third Infantry Division noted dispassionately, "Higher headquarters did not provide the Third Infantry Division (Mechanized) with a plan for Phase IV [postconflict operations]. As a result, Third Infantry Division transitioned into Phase IV in the absence of guidance."[30]

To the extent that anyone was thinking about postwar Iraq, the center of power was not in ORHA, the body constituted for the purpose. Instead, it lay in the Office of Special Plans (OSP), in Douglas Feith's Office of the Undersecretary of Defense for Policy. Run by Abram Shulsky, a graduate school friend of Paul Wolfowitz, the office had broad influence over the fundamental issues of the postwar period, such as de-Baathification and the organization of the postwar Iraqi governing authority. Former ORHA officials complain that they seldom had any interaction with OSP staff; they got their instructions through successive sets of briefing slides that were presented to them. These instructions had never gone through the long process of scrutiny and revision that is standard procedure for the U.S. military. To one general who was working on Iraq issues at the time, the failures of the occupation were largely due to the absence of such scrubbing. "Another organization (OSP) was given the tasking, but they weren't used to doing disciplined planning," he later ruefully observed. "We minimized the planning on the back side because of what we wanted it to look like." It did not help that throughout the preparations for the occupation and its early stages, the Pentagon declined to draw in the most capable people in the United States government. Instead, Feith's office, together with the White House Office of Personnel, vetted all candidates for work in Iraq for their political acceptability. Many had little or no government or foreign experience.[31]

For Jay Garner, the effort to get ORHA up and running in Iraq was a nightmare. Much of the organization had been deployed to Kuwait before its connections with the bureaucracy at home had been established, and then the staff was forced to sit and wait because of instability in Iraq. The first ORHA staff did not arrive in Baghdad until April 21, twelve days after Saddam Hussein's statue had been pulled down. Much of the looting had already been done, and there was deep discomfort in Washington. Three days later, Rumsfeld surprised Garner by telling him he was being replaced by former Ambassador L. Paul Bremer, who would become head of the new Coalition Provisional Authority.

On May 12, 2003, Bremer arrived in Baghdad. He had never run anything larger than the U.S. embassy in the Netherlands, where he had been posted in the early 1980s. The story of the months that followed, when U.S. forces and civilian authorities were surprised by the sudden growth of an insurgency for which they had not planned, has been well told in news accounts. Less well documented is the haphazard way the administration met these unexpected challenges. Key decisions continued to be made without the careful scrutiny that would be expected. To underscore this, administration officials point to the fact that the Principals Committee never met to discuss the disbanding of the Iraqi Army, which is now seen as one of the critical mistakes that has fed the insurgency. On May 23, eleven days after Bremer's arrival in Baghdad, the Coalition Provisional Authority issued the directive on the dissolution of Iraq's military. How the decision was made remains unclear.[32]

As Joseph Collins, the former deputy assistant secretary of defense for stability operations, would later say, "The worst thing that ever happened to us were those assumptions."

AS THE INSURGENCY ballooned, administration officials tried to deal with a bewildered American public by suggesting that it was to our advantage that the jihadists were coming to Iraq to attack U.S. forces. In articulating a kind of flypaper theory of counterterrorism, government spokesmen—up to and including the president—argued that our heavily armed forces would dispatch the radicals over there, reducing the threat to Americans at home. The most famous expression of this thought came in July 2003, when President Bush told reporters, "There are some who feel like . . . the conditions are such that they can attack us there. My answer is bring 'em on."[33]

There is, of course, merit to the notion of taking on terrorists far from America's vulnerable cities. The concept of finding jihadists, disrupting their operation, taking them off the street before they can attack the United States, its friends, and all of our foreign interests underlies the strategy for counterterrorism that intelligence and law enforcement services have embraced since the 1990s. But the administration's argument about fighting the terrorists in Iraq conceals some fallacies and questionable assumptions. It is, for example, hard to claim with assurance that if U.S. forces were not in Iraq, the jihadists who are attacking them would be able or motivated to attack Americans at home—especially given the studies showing that the foreign fighters who have come to Iraq had no background in terror.[34] More importantly, though, the argument is based on the same incorrect belief that lies behind the administration's emphasis on counting al Qaeda captures and kills—it assumes that the number of terrorists is limited. It also assumes that their lethality would be minimal and would not disrupt Iraqi reconstruction, and it assumes that this violence would not reverberate significantly outside of Iraq or overflow the nation's borders. More than two years later, with the tide of violence still rising in Iraq, the reconstruction crippled by violence, and terrorist attacks occurring in Western Europe, the weakness of these assumptions is clear.

PART THREE

The Road Not Taken

9

THE ELEMENTS OF A FOREIGN POLICY

If the record of the past four years is one of failure to stem the growth of the jihadist threat, then the question is: What would a successful strategy look like?

We need to start with first principles. A comprehensive counterterrorism strategy must be centered on four goals: First, stop terrorists from committing acts of violence by capturing them, disrupting their cells, or, if necessary, killing them. Second, keep the most dangerous weapons out of their hands. Third, recognizing that there is no way to prevent all attacks, protect those facilities in the United States that, if struck, would cause catastrophic damage. Fourth, halt the creation of new terrorists by dealing, to the extent possible, with those grievances that are driving radicalization.

In each of these areas, the United States can do better—in the last, we could hardly do worse. We can begin by recognizing how the nature of the problem dictates the tools that should be used for our response. So, for example, by acknowledging that jihadist terror is above all a phenomenon within countries, one whose units are individuals and small cells that burrow into societies and not armies that mass on borders, then it follows that the task of combating the terrorists is first and foremost one for intelligence and law enforcement authorities. That is not to say that we need to wait for an actual act of terror before issuing an indictment—the suggestion by

Vice President Cheney and other conservatives that this is what American counterterrorism policy was before 9/11 is a caricature. One can argue that some law enforcement authorities, the FBI above all, were insufficiently focused on intelligence gathering. But the U.S. counterterrorism effort was aimed at prevention and disruption, as it must continue to be.

There are times when the use of the military is appropriate for counterterrorism missions, particularly in the ungoverned or undergoverned regions, such as are found in Afghanistan, Yemen, Somalia, Central Asia, and the Philippines, where terrorist sanctuaries may exist. But the military possesses no tools for dealing with radical Islamists in Western Europe or in the cities of Saudi Arabia or Pakistan. The Bush administration has seriously overmilitarized the effort to stop jihadist terror. Military forces, which are designed to act quickly and with considerable violence, rarely penetrate terrorist networks, and using them in this way, as we have done in Iraq, too often ensures that the ratio of those captured and killed to those galvanized and recruited is the opposite of what is wanted. Although it is the jihadists' dream to control a country, which they could then use as a base for spreading their influence and ideas, the terrorists we face today seldom want to hold territory the way armies do. They are happy to slip away at the beginning of an attack against them and slip back when it is over—which is why the U.S. military is condemned to play "whack the mole" in Iraq for the foreseeable future. The terrorists evade us, they attract new recruits, they launch new attacks, and in the end we pay vastly more than we need to while enhancing the threat. (It is worth noting that our current defense budget is greater in real dollars than during the Cold War.) In October 2003, Secretary of Defense Donald Rumsfeld asked in a memo to his top civilian and military subordinates whether the war on terror had turned into a case in which "the harder we work, the behinder we get."[1] The answer is yes, in large measure because of the military tools we have used.

Because the problem of terrorism is transnational in nature, it follows that the United States has to develop the best possible cooperation with foreign intelligence and law enforcement agencies. After 9/11, many intelligence services, particularly in Europe, were embarrassed to see that they had underestimated a genuine threat. They moved quickly to redirect resources to deal with the new danger, and most agree that cooperation with their U.S. counterparts has been excellent. But comity at the level of intelligence and law enforcement can be insulated against corrosion at the political level for only so long. In an era in which every visit to Europe by the American president turns out hundreds of thousands of protesters, and polls show that sizable numbers of people in Western countries consider the United States to be the biggest threat to peace in the world, the kind of cooperation we need will be difficult to sustain. Washington's heedlessness of its allies on issues ranging from war and peace to the environment will eventually have a cost, one that we cannot afford.

The fact that our enemies are not armies but elusive individuals and cells also has implications for how we balance our counterterrorism efforts between offense and defense. The administration has taken the position that we must have a "forward strategy of freedom" and must fight the terrorists overseas so they cannot attack us here. To a certain extent, this makes sense: Any serious strategy will seek to preempt as many attacks as possible abroad. But it is a mistake to think that an aggressive offense eliminates the need for a strong defense, as the administration's haphazard and often negligent treatment of homeland security indicates. Some terrorists will get through. Or they may already live within the security perimeter in Europe or America that the Bush team is trying to construct. In either case, we need to be certain that they do not have fissile material with which to make a bomb or the ability to turn one of our chemical plants into an American Bhopal. In both the areas of locking up dangerous materials abroad and protecting key vulnerable sites at home, too little has been done, and too much time has been lost.

American foreign policy must also be reshaped to reflect the fact that we are fighting an ideology that holds real attraction for large numbers of people. Administration spokesmen frequently talk about ideology, as President Bush did after the London bombings, when he said, "We do know that terrorists murder in the name of a totalitarian ideology that hates freedom, rejects tolerance and despises all dissent. Their aim—the aim of the terrorists is to remake the Middle East in their own grim image of tyranny and oppression by toppling governments, by exporting terror, by forcing free nations to retreat and withdraw."[2] They acknowledge that the enemy is dispersed in numerous places and is not a massed army waiting to invade, and they often acknowledge that the struggle against terror is long term or "generational." But the chasm between the rhetoric and the policies remains wide. Thus far, we have been driving the fence-sitters of the Muslim world into the arms of our enemies. This must stop.

Although it came late to the realization that there needed to be a positive agenda for the Muslim world, the Bush administration now advocates democratization as a solution for the ills that drive radicalization. For this, it deserves some applause. President Bush's speeches have stirred the pot in many of the countries of the Muslim world and had a genuine effect on the terms of debate. Democracy as aspiration is more alive than it has been in many years. Unfortunately, in the current environment, many doubt our sincerity, but over the long term, an American push for democratization will help undermine the jihadist claim that the United States seeks to control Muslim countries through the "apostate" authoritarians now in power. Since this is one of bin Laden's core arguments, weakening it is essential. Democratization, a good in its own right, will bring other benefits as well, but democratization alone will not be sufficient to reduce the threat of terrorism without a far deeper, more thoroughgoing engagement with the countries of the Muslim world. Indeed, in light of the social, economic, and demographic conditions in many of those nations, it is questionable whether liberal democracy can even survive there without other far-reaching reforms as well as significant economic assistance.

Finally, we need to consider how we go about waging this campaign against the jihadist creed. Terrorism is the biggest security threat we face, but if we continue to approach it as the paramount, almost exclusive concern on our agenda, we will fail to improve our security. The war on terror has been given as a reason for trumping an array of other long-standing American values and priorities. At Guantánamo, we have cast aside our historic role as the world's foremost proponent of the rule of law. At Abu Ghraib, we have buried our reputation as the world's leading advocate of human rights. Through uncritical support of autocratic regimes, we have undermined our own campaign for democratization. America has become unrecognizable to many of its oldest, most devoted friends abroad. We need to reacquaint ourselves with some of the hard lessons of the Cold War, where we at times undercut our own long-term interests by making common cause with the wrong side simply because it was vocally anti-communist—think of Central America or Southeast Asia. When we make it so easy to hate us, we are also hastening the next attack.

TO CRAFT A foreign policy that will combat the terrorist threat and ultimately turn back the tide of radical Islam, we need first to identify the key points where the militancy is being generated. In public discussions of the threat, it is usually assumed that the problem is one centered in the Arab world, with other islands of trouble in Pakistan and Indonesia. This perception owes, no doubt, to the fact that most of the 9/11 hijackers were Saudis, and the rest were natives of various Arab countries, even though for the leadership of the operation, the radicalization that led them to carry out the attacks appears to have occurred while they were living in Europe. The sense that the challenges we face are located in the Arab world is heightened by the fact that Iraq has been transformed into "the central front in the war on terror," in the administration's phrase, as a result of the American invasion.

The true picture, as we have seen, is considerably more complicated. To be sure, American blunders have made Iraq the central arena of the global jihad, and the anger at the U.S. presence reverberates through the Muslim world. There are real problems in Pakistan, Saudi Arabia, Indonesia, and other countries. But as the Israeli scholar Emmanuel Sivan has argued, "al Qaeda is a problem of the Muslim diaspora," and while this may be an overstatement, the point is crucial.[3] The epicenter of the new *umma* is not in Egypt but in Europe, and while the online jihad is available to radicals everywhere, it stands to reason that its center of gravity is also in the West, given the higher level of computer use there. (Of course, radicalism nourished outside the states of the Arab world could well migrate back into those countries, and events in Iraq have likely accelerated that process.) It would be a mistake to suggest that the grievances of Muslims in the West are wholly detached from what goes on in their native countries; the Moroccans, Algerians, and Tunisians of France and Spain are, for example, deeply angered by the corrupt authoritarian governments in their home countries. And, to a large extent, they blame Western countries for propping up those regimes, rightly or wrongly. But home country concerns are only a part of their grievance, with the alienation and frustration of living as minorities in unfriendly countries also inspiring a great deal of their antipathy.

The Bush administration has constructed its foreign policy as though the new terrorism were a problem almost exclusively of the Arab world. It has prescribed two solutions: regime change through military force in Iraq, and vigorous advocacy of democracy in the rest of the region. But since much of the problem is elsewhere, the current policy is incomplete.

It is worth considering what else is needed. The rise of Islamic radicalism in the West is not something the United States can deal with militarily. At least in the world as it exists now, Washington will not be dispatching troops to fight in the Paris suburbs. But the growth of radicalism in Europe does require that the United States and its allies deepen their intelligence and law enforcement cooperation to the greatest possible extent to thwart terrorist operations. The record thus far has been good. But some aspects of the culture of intelligence services have not changed from the Cold War, when the CIA and other U.S. intelligence agencies limited information sharing to reduce the chances of Soviet infiltration. Now, the default position needs to be in favor of sharing intelligence. It is difficult to think of a major terrorist attack that occurred without any warning in the intelligence record. The ratio of such warnings to disrupted operations is excellent, but it needs to improve, and deeper cooperation is essential for achieving that goal.

Such cooperation regarding the jihadist threat is important for more than just tactical reasons; it is also a matter of long-term security policy. Washington cannot dictate to the democracies of Western Europe how they should work to integrate their Muslim minorities. But if the atmosphere were better—and if America had not done such a thorough job of aggravating its longtime partners—we would be in a better position to discuss with them the threat within their midst. Many European intelligence officials and a few individuals of ministerial rank recognize how ominous the situation has become. Europe's political leaders, however, have been slow to accept the gravity of the danger. Despite the Madrid bombings, they have been for the most part unwilling to challenge their publics to recognize the security and social problems they face, except for those whose response is to press for limits on immigration. Implicit in the aversion to rock the boat has been an unspoken assumption that the

United States remains the primary target for the terrorists, and these leaders do not want to be seen buying into the American worldview. As Madrid demonstrated, terrorists will be happy to punish Europeans for their alliance with America, and, as we saw in the van Gogh killing in the Netherlands, some will be satisfied to lash out locally against their global grievance. Europe will also likely remain the primary jumping-off point for terrorists who want to come to America, as it was for the leaders of the 9/11 conspiracy. Europeans are working hard on stopping attacks, but they have only begun to address the broader issues that underlie Islamist violence. Perhaps the reluctance to deal with these issues will diminish in the wake of the London Underground attacks. In the meantime, the United States cannot direct the countries of Europe to deal with the problems of their minorities, but with better relations, we might prod them to confront these challenges before it is too late. A Europe that is fully occupied with conflict between its communities is not in our interest.

The United States also needs to stop conducting the war on terror as a demonstration of unilateral force of will. For Washington, building a true global coalition has been more a matter of tamping down debate about its motives than anything else. Immediately after the 9/11 attacks, when NATO invoked for the first time Article V of its Charter, which designated the attack against one member as an attack against all members, the United States was barely gracious in spurning NATO's offer of assistance. From the outset, the Defense Department was concerned that any road to action through NATO would be a replay of its experience in Kosovo, where multinational operations proved cumbersome and constraining and required more coordination than the Pentagon thought was practical. At meetings in Brussels two weeks after the attacks, Deputy Secretary of Defense Paul Wolfowitz announced, "If we need collective action, we will ask for it; we don't anticipate that at the moment."[4] Although the Pentagon was more eager for support in the less popular mission in Iraq, this view of alliances as a source of entanglement and extra work—instead of as a means to build legitimacy and common cause—needs to change. The global insurgency is transnational; the United States cannot suppress it alone. The fight against terror must be a genuinely Western mission, with broad support from our traditional allies and a sustained effort to enlist better cooperation from those developing countries that face a jihadist threat.

One area in which joint effort is called for is in building the resources and skills of the intelligence services, police, prosecutors, and judges in those developing countries where jihadists have proven hard to wipe out. In Kenya, for example, the police crackdown after the 1998 bombing of the U.S. Embassy in Nairobi was inefficient enough that four years later, al Qaeda operatives could bomb a hotel filled with Israeli guests and fire missiles at an Israeli charter plane. Much more can be done, for example, to improve border controls, eliminate safe havens, and make travel documents more fraud resistant.

The international community has identified this agenda as a major need. When the United Nations Security Council convened after the 9/11 attacks, it passed a landmark resolution condemning the attacks and creating a mechanism that in theory would hold member countries responsible for meeting certain standards of counterterrorism effectiveness. It also envisioned that a new Counterterrorism Committee would provide a place for future assistance donors and recipients to be paired off. Nothing has come of this. The Group of Eight leading industrial countries tried the same thing, establishing a Counterterrorism Assistance Group in 2003. But it too has done nothing in this regard. Historically, the United States was the world's biggest provider of technical assistance and resources to improve poor countries' abilities in these areas, and after 9/11 the State Department, the Defense Department, and, reportedly, the CIA increased their assistance to a number of countries. But after a year or two, the funds and efforts began to decline. Budgetary strains and competing priorities have whittled down the State Department's annual budget for its Anti-Terrorism Assistance Program to less than $120 million—about the cost of a day's operations in Iraq and considerably smaller than is necessary to fulfill its mandate. At the same time, Washington is placing ever more onerous demands on other countries. For example, it has demanded the imposition of heightened financial controls and surveillance to restrict the terrorists' ability to raise and move money, but it has allocated just $10 million to be spread over dozens of countries. Military strategists speak of the need in war to "shape the battlefield," to create circumstances that favor one's forces. It is fair to say that we have done little to shape the battlefield with the terrorists.

Another area in which there is much that can be done to reduce the production of new terrorists involves tamping down the regional conflicts that feed the broad Muslim sense of embattlement and draw locals and foreign fighters into hostilities. Persistent conflict in such places as the Caucasus, Kashmir, Indonesia, and the southern Philippines provides a considerable amount of the fuel for the global insurgency.

But what can be done about this, especially while the fires rage in Iraq? After 9/11, when the United States was pushing terrorism to the top of the international agenda, many analysts and diplomats came to recognize in a new way that what goes on in distant corners affects us and others. This was a moment when like-minded nations might have impressed on Russia, Pakistan, India, Indonesia, and other countries that these low-level wars were too dangerous to be allowed to continue, and that the international community stood ready with diplomatic and financial assistance to help wind them down. There is no certainty that it would have worked— one could expect the Russians, for example, to say that they too were fighting radical Islam in Chechnya and needed no instruction on the dangers. But such a change of orientation might have started the wheels turning in different capitals, and it would have established a basis for pushing the claim that there are more interested parties than just those carrying weapons.

It may be too late to recapture that moment. But it certainly is worth a try. Again, the United States cannot make such a push alone—especially when our standing as an honest broker has been undercut by what is viewed abroad as the bad-faith diplomacy leading up to the war in Iraq. But if we were joined by the European Union, Japan, Australia, and other democracies, the possibility of achieving some progress, while remote, would be real.

As a source of Muslim grievance, few things surpass the Palestinian-Israeli conflict. Since the establishment of Israel in 1948 and especially after the 1967 war, the situation has been used by Arab regimes and their apologists to justify authoritarianism within and confrontation without. It has been so useful for these purposes precisely because of the sympathy for the Palestinians that is so deeply felt by Arab publics. Leaders may have been cynical, but the "street" was not. Although some analysts argue that Palestine is not very important to those not directly involved, most view the polling and anecdotal evidence of popular concern to be overwhelming.[5]

The Internet and satellite television have now ensured that the plight of Palestinians is at the forefront of Arab and Muslim grievances. The photo of Muhammad al-Durra, the Palestinian boy killed in Gaza in 2000, among other powerful images, has achieved iconic significance and generates real anger. Israeli military operations during the four years of the second intifada, especially its incursions into urban areas in the West Bank and Gaza, were broadcast incessantly on Arabic-language stations like al Jazeera and al Arabiyya. Because of America's close relationship with Israel and its support for Israel's current government, Arab and Muslim audiences do not distinguish between Israel and the United States. This has been crippling to our image and forms the mental backdrop against which Muslims experience our intervention in Iraq and gauge our pro-democracy rhetoric.

The administration could take an important step to change these perceptions simply by putting Palestine nearer the top of its diplomatic agenda. As a practical matter, this means appointing a senior envoy who has the confidence—and the ear—of the president, working intensively with the parties to rebuild confidence, assisting the Palestinian Authority to care for its citizens, and, above all, demonstrating to Muslim audiences that although we will always be Israel's close ally, we are committed to the establishment and support of a successful Palestinian state. This will not turn Islamist radicals into our friends, but it will take the sting out of jihadist propaganda and make it easier for Arab and Muslim governments to cooperate with us on terrorism and other vital issues, including Iraq.

The Bush administration holds the view that the Palestinians will make peace with Israel once Iraq is sorted out and change begins to permeate the region. Thus, America has sent as its representative to the two sides a succession of individuals with virtually no background in the region and little status in Washington. But this is an instance where the small, out-of-the-way places can have a powerful effect on our fortunes. Acting decisively will not only put a brake on the dynamic of radicalization in the Muslim world, it will also help us with most of our allies, especially in Europe, who have despaired of our ever recognizing this need. Since they will be called upon to provide much of the financial support that a fledgling Palestinian state will need, it is important that they be reassured of America's determination—and it is essential that we act now.

One final area in which we would see a tremendous premium paid for genuine solidarity is pressing a reform agenda in the Muslim world. The United States now advocates, in the words of Secretary of State Condoleezza Rice, a "transformational" strategy for the authoritarian regimes of the Muslim world. But in pressing this case, Washington is alone and out on a limb. When the Bush administration first began pushing for democratic and market reforms, it called the effort the "Greater Middle East Initiative." But when the draft initiative was leaked in February 2004 to *al Hayat,* the London-based Arabic newspaper, there was a backlash, with Arab countries denouncing the plan as an American diktat. (The name's similarity to Imperial Japan's 1940 plan for a "Greater East Asia Co-Prosperity Sphere" did not help, either. It was later changed to the "Broader Middle East and North Africa Initiative.") This, in turn, short-circuited the consultation process with our European allies and with countries in the region, leaving Washington on the defensive, explaining what the initiative was not, rather than what it was. For the Europeans and Arabs, the American approach was too broad-brush and did not take into account the country-by-country differences within the Arab world. They also believed that the Americans avoided the stark reality that reform cannot be imposed from outside but would have to come from within the region—a nettlesome point, particularly at a time when Americans were occupying Iraq. When Arab governments reacted indignantly, the Europeans distanced themselves, and the effort now languishes. It was an object lesson in how not to advocate reform in the Muslim world.

The Middle East Partnership Initiative, another administration program, was also intended to create more favorable conditions for reform in the Arab world. It was announced with great fanfare in 2002 as an essential part of the president's "forward strategy of freedom." This too has stalled because the efforts it funds are too timid, nibbling at the margins of the reform problem and, according to the Brookings Institution, supporting "a wide variety of uncontroversial programs and largely working within the boundaries set by Arab governments."[6] Its funding has also been shrinking—$75 million in fiscal year 2005, down from $100 million in fiscal year 2003. The gap between the resources we allocate to this daunting task and the rhetoric devoted to it is only getting wider. The administration is correct in highlighting the need for political reform, but its follow-through is lacking.

Former national security adviser Zbigniew Brzezinski cast the problem this way: "The simplistic notion that you talk a great deal about democracy and twist a few arms and it will somehow come magically on its own is absurd."[7] Money and sustained effort are required, and even then favorable outcomes are not guaranteed.

Yet some kind of reform agenda is necessary. It may be that "fixing" the ills of the Muslim world through the advocacy of democracy, economic reform, and a host of other changes is beyond the ability of any group of outside nations. The future, however, will only bring more discontent if these countries stay on their current trajectory of low or no economic growth, booming population growth and inadequate social services such as education and health care. Furthermore, the West, and the United States especially, needs to change how it is perceived by Muslims everywhere. With decades of anti-Western incitement already drummed into them and the jihadist argument gaining ground, changing minds will not be easy. Some will argue that the United States does not need to do anything in this regard—our policy has been self-interested but fair, and any revision will smack of appeasement. U.S. policy toward the Muslim world is something about which people can disagree, though it is noteworthy that President Bush and his top advisers have lamented that America and its allies did not encourage democracy in the Middle East a long time ago.[8] The important thing is to recognize that we cannot debate our way to greater security. There are too many people who are at risk of being radicalized. The need to demonstrate to the Muslim world that the aims of the West are beneficent—that we do not seek to steal the region's oil, oppress its people, or destroy their religion—is urgent. It is a matter of national security.

Freedom on the March

"These are incredibly exciting times. . . . They should be exciting times for everybody—because freedom is making unprecedented progress across the globe. In the last 18 months, we have witnessed revolutions of Rose, Orange, Purple, Tulip and Cedar—and these are just the beginnings. Across the Caucasus and Central Asia, hope is stirring at the prospect of change—and change will come. Across the broader Middle East, we are seeing the rise of a new generation whose hearts burn for freedom—and they will have it."[9] So spoke President George W. Bush in May 2005. The president's passion for democracy is admirable and no doubt sincere. He is also probably right in asserting that democratization can, given enough time and support, diminish the virulence and appeal of jihadism. Indeed, this insight is so fundamental and utterly seductive that it has tended to mask the towering obstacles to democratization in a region where there is such profound mistrust between regimes and opposition movements and where ruling elites can rely on resources—including American aid—that diminish their need for popular consent. The allure of the insight also obscures the uncomfortable truth that even in the most democratic states, individuals can still harbor militantly anti-American attitudes. The presumed inevitability of success and confidence in America's ability to bring this about also blinds believers from recognizing that our attempt to force democracy on Iraq has stripped us of our legitimacy as agents of change. It has also tarnished the idea of democracy itself in the minds of many who might have otherwise embraced it. Our enthusiasm for America's liberating mission has made it difficult to understand that the havoc we have caused in Iraq has strengthened the determination of regional rulers to keep a tight grip on power. At the same time, it has distracted us from the fact that we continue to rely on the police and intelligence services of authoritarian regimes, even as we have come to understand that it is the repressiveness of these regimes that has helped spawn the terrorism we are fighting. We can advance in the quest for democratization and in the fight against terrorists, but only by abandoning these intoxicating illusions.

Democracy may be the cure for tyranny, as the political scientist Samuel Huntington observed, but it does not necessarily provide the answer for a host of other social and economic ills, among them poverty and sectarianism. Nevertheless, the authors of the Arab Human Development Report, who contend that a "freedom and good governance deficit" and a "democracy deficit" has made Arab countries unpleasant places, are certainly right.[10] The connection between democratic political systems and good governance has spurred a virtual democratization industry over the past twenty years, which has now focused heavily on the Middle East and North

Africa. This machine now involves diplomats, bureaucrats, consultants, international civil servants, and a host of political activists, all casting about for ways to invigorate civil society: citizens' caucuses, unions, trade syndicates, and a vast array of interest groups deemed to be the essential intermediary between citizens and the power of the state and therefore the indispensable catalyst for fundamental political reform.[11] Authoritarian governments, which by definition do not depend on the people's consent to rule, aim to prevent groups that might challenge the state from coalescing around any but the most trivial issues. The emergence of civil society is, therefore, the indispensable bridge between the passivity of societies shattered by political repression and the vibrant activism that begets democracy. Civil society is said to serve this function by nurturing the social skills needed for collective action and, ultimately, good governance: give-and-take, inclusiveness, a sense of shared purpose, a willingness to compromise. The more mature—or "dense"—the civil society, the greater the pressure it will exert on authoritarian governments to democratize, and the more likely voters will be to make their democracy succeed.

The celebration of civil society and the profusion of programs meant to foster it stemmed from a number of interlocking factors. First, it did appear as though civil society groups facilitated the transition to democracy in Eastern Europe after the end of the Cold War.[12] Second, conservatives in the United States, who had long felt that Washington played too big a role in Americans' lives, felt comfortable with the small-scale, localized, community-centered values that underpinned the concept of civil society. Liberals also embraced the civil society approach because it provided a way around dealing with governments that were seen as morally objectionable. Third, for the nongovernmental organizations (NGOs) and their benefactors, aid programs for voluntary organizations proved to be a satisfying way of promoting democratization without taking overtly political positions that would directly challenge—and alienate—the repressive governments they were seeking to change, albeit slowly and indirectly. Thus, governments and NGOs implicitly recognized the limits of their power to effect change, but at least they were doing something.

Senior officials within the Bush administration have backed U.S. support for civil society organizations in the Middle East.[13] Yet the relatively meager funding that was actually provided for democracy programs—$120 million out of a total international development budget of $21.3 billion in 2005—revealed a more skeptical posture. A low level of effort was made to sustain the programs, in part for the good they might do at the margin, but also to keep the NGOs and their supporters at bay and, it was hoped, to deflect some European criticism of our foreign policy priorities.[14]

The administration's implicit view of grassroots democratization programs is that they are mundane and discredited tools. Swift democratization of the region, an urgent condition for American security in the years ahead, cannot be accomplished by subsidizing sewing circles. Democratization could, however, be jump-started through the use of military force against Iraq, which would unleash the yearning for freedom and participatory government intrinsic to the human spirit. Though the president conceded in his 2005 inaugural address that "the ultimate goal of ending tyranny in our world" was "not primarily the task of arms," the Middle East was clearly an exception for him and his team.[15]

In the administration's thinking, the war against Iraq would bring a kind of redemption. "America will seize every opportunity in pursuit of peace. And the end of the present regime in Iraq would create such an opportunity," the president declared. For the Arab world, the measured application of violence promised a profound reversal of fortune because "a liberated Iraq can show the power of freedom to transform that vital region, by bringing hope and progress into the lives of millions." Perhaps the greatest beneficiaries, after the Iraqis themselves, would be the beleaguered Palestinians: "Success in Iraq could also begin a new stage for Middle Eastern peace, and set in motion progress towards a truly democratic Palestinian state."[16]

Apparently, the administration sees signs that these transformations have come to pass. In the White House Rose Garden ceremony in March 2005, the president told a group of visiting Iraqi students, "Today, people in a long-troubled part of the world are standing up for their freedom. In the last few months, we've witnessed successful elections in Afghanistan, Iraq, and the Palestinian Territories; peaceful demonstrations on the streets of Beirut, and steps toward democratic reform in places like Egypt and Saudi Arabia. The trend is clear: Freedom is on the march."[17] The most revealing aspect of this statement is the way it imposes a clear, singular meaning on independent, largely coincidental events, all of which carry ambiguous implications for the inhabitants of the countries where they took place.

"We measure our success," Secretary Rice said, "in the democratic revolutions that have stunned the entire world: vibrant revolutions of rose and orange and purple and tulip and cedar. The destiny of the Middle East is bound up in this global expansion of freedom."[18] Such an interpretation of complex episodes might have been irresistible to any administration. But it was inaccurate.

Reality Therapy

There is no question that a cluster of intriguing regional events, large and small, have taken place since the United States intervened in Iraq in 2003. After decades of occupation, Syrian forces have departed from Lebanon, a welcome turn of events that the Lebanese themselves do not view as relating to democratization. (Most say that they have had a functioning democracy since 1990, but not full sovereignty, which is what the departure of Syrian troops may yet produce.) Syrian security agents are still active in the country, manipulating its politics and intimidating some of its leaders. In addition, a significant sector of Lebanon's population continues to see a Syrian role in their country as essential to its stability.[19] And while there was a shocking event that spurred the protests that led to Syria's troop withdrawal, it was not the destruction of Iraq's Baathist dictatorship; rather, it was the assassination of Rafik Hariri, a former prime minister, by agents linked to the regime in Damascus.[20]

The January 2005 election by the Palestinian Authority was likewise a welcome event, but it too was the result of another sui generis factor—the death of Yasir Arafat—and the exhaustion produced by four years of a brutal and losing fight against Israel. The race did not include the most important segment of the political opposition, Hamas, and the only major contender for the presidency, apart from Mahmoud Abbas, the protégé of Arafat, was serving a life sentence in an Israeli prison for murder. And so, while the election was free and well managed, an unusual occurrence in the region, the result was nevertheless predetermined.[21] Since that election occurred, the subsequent, pivotal vote on the makeup of the national assembly has been postponed by the government for fear of likely large opposition gains.[22] The emergence of true democracy in Palestine will result from generational change and a final status accord between a new state and Israel that leads to the withdrawal of Israeli forces and the establishment of an international border that the Palestinians accept.[23] It will not result from our intervention in Iraq.

In the case of Egypt and Saudi Arabia, meaningful reforms are not apparent. Egyptians are subject to an emergency law still in effect after twenty-three years, despite the fact that Egypt faces no plausible external threat and the insurgency that plagued the country until the mid-1990s has been crushed. The government of President Hosni Mubarak does not tolerate open dissent—it prevents even the moderate Islamist political opposition from organizing as a political party that can contest elections, and it routinely arrests and tries political opponents in special military courts.[24] The regime's reaction to increasing pressure from the United States, but also from domestic reformers, was to announce a referendum on a constitutional amendment that would permit wider participation in elections. The amendment set the bar for standing in elections so high, however, that it is not clear how it would actually expand the number of candidates eligible to run for office. The opposition Kefaya ("Enough!") Party protested this maneuver, but its members were beaten by police and pro-regime thugs.[25] Apart from these cosmetic measures, the remote possibility of near-term change has probably been delayed by events in Iraq, which have reinforced the caution of the ruling elite. As Mubarak told the Italian newspaper *La Repubblica* in March 2004, "Instant freedom and democracy can cause an earthquake in a country: For instance, what would happen if a majority of extremists were to win in parliament? You can put your money on it: We would be seeing Islamists in government in Egypt and in Iraq. But of course we will not allow any formula that might push us toward the catastrophe of anarchy, to be imposed on us from abroad."[26]

Saudi Arabia recently completed a long-planned election that allowed male subjects to contest half the seats on the kingdom's 178 municipal councils. The other half is appointed by the government, in essence, the al-Saud family. The municipal councils do not constitute a legislature and are

not empowered to pass laws or approve government budgets. Nevertheless, these elections do represent an expansion of the political process,
even if women are excluded and the powers of the municipal councils are
limited so they do not infringe on the prerogatives of the ruling family.
Though the elections were announced in October 2003, Crown Prince
Abdullah had been mulling the idea of municipal elections well before
they were actually scheduled. The trigger for the announcement was
the wave of jihadist violence that began in the spring of 2003, which convinced the royal family that a public promise of broadened political participation would strengthen its hand against the insurgents. In any case, it
is a stretch to construe these elections as the precursor of the sort of
sweeping change that the administration believes the intervention in Iraq
will set in motion.[27]

It is equally hard to identify the salutary effect of the Iraq invasion elsewhere in the region, let alone how the dramatic overthrow of the old
regime in Ukraine, so far outside the orbit of the Arab world, might have
been inspired by Operation Iraqi Freedom. Nearer Iraq, Bahrain began a
liberalization process in 2002, but it stalled almost immediately with the
imprisonment of a key human rights activist—he has since been
released—and its ruler has now been given the title "king," an improve-
ment, apparently, on his former title of emir.[28] Similarly, Qatar promul-
gated a new, more progressive constitution that afforded greater rights to
Qatari citizens, while nonetheless affirming the absolute power of its rulers.

One place where democracy does seem to be taking root is Afghanistan,
where the October 2004 presidential election was fairly free of manipula-
tion and turnout was high. This success, in which Americans can take
pride, was made possible by the overthrow of the Taliban, not Saddam,
and required the participation of our European allies as well as of the bor-
dering states, including Iran. In any case, the Afghan elections were an exception to the general rule that democratization does not result from a
deus ex machina.

On balance, the administration's assertive lobbying for democracy in
the region has had a positive effect. Putting the prestige of the United
States behind political liberalization was a bold thing to do, consistent
with the moral impulse that alongside strategic interest has traditionally
driven our foreign policy. Although the resources and energy necessary to

advance the process of democratization in the region—setting Iraq aside—have not been forthcoming, Washington's emphasis on the theme of reform has put the issue on the table for the first time. Precedent is important.

At the same time, the attempt to force democracy, as we have tried to do in Iraq, has undermined the moral authority the president brought to his passionate advocacy of reform. The war that was supposed to engender political transformation has turned out to be long and bloody, and a good deal of that blood has been Arab. The effort has also been tarnished by troop misconduct that, in an earlier era, would have had limited significance, but in a wired age exposed us to charges of hypocrisy and cruelty that made our defense of democracy appear illegitimate. Most crucially, the colonial experience of the region shaped the lens through which people in the region perceived the war and its liberal aims. Against this historical background, especially in Iraq, which emerged as a state under British rule, the United States was bound to be seen as another colonial power and therefore as a country with no right to speak of democratization.

The sad irony is that the war in Iraq itself is a barrier to democratization. The current chaos there confirms the fears of both the rulers and the ruled in the authoritarian states of the region that sudden political change is bound to let slip the dogs of civil war. Almost every state in the region, except perhaps Egypt, is riven by ethnic, religious, and linguistic divisions that can turn bloody. The slide toward civil war in Iraq has quickened these fears and cast a pall over the concept of democracy as a model of political organization. "What model?" asks Ahmed Aboul Gheit, Egypt's foreign minister. "Bombs are exploding everywhere and Iraqis are killed every day in the streets."[29] Amr Moussa, the secretary general of the Arab League, enlarged on this theme, warning that "those who use Iraq as an example are mistaken. One cannot build a country along ethnic, racial, or religious fault lines. Democracy is one voter one vote, it is not bargaining over feudal interests. If we insist on the differences between the Christians and the Muslims, or between the Shiites and the Sunnis, then we will be lifting the lid off another Pandora's Box."[30]

The other adverse implication of the war for regional democratization is the degree to which it has befouled the idea of democracy through its association with the chaos that we have created in Iraq. Even our good friends, like Saad Eddin Ibrahim, an Egyptian activist once jailed by Mubarak, have cautioned that America's credibility as a messenger of democratization is failing.[31] Marwan Muasher, the Jordanian foreign minister and strong supporter of the United States, agrees, cautioning that "we are faced with a situation today, where Arab [reformists] are being labeled as U.S. agents."[32]

There are powerful figures exploiting this theme. Sheikh Hassan Nasrallah, a leader of Hezbollah, gave a rousing speech in March 2004, televised throughout the region, that dripped with sarcasm. "The United States," he declared, "comes today to tell us about reform, democracy, elections, and human rights. This is the United States that had for decades installed in our Muslim region and world dictatorial regimes, and continues to support the most despicable dictatorial regimes. This is in the interest of the US plan to dominate the region with a new face, a new mask, and new, deceptive slogans—hence the US reform slogans. Sisters and brothers, the US reform in the Arab and Muslim countries will only replace a despot with another despot."[33] At this juncture, such arguments, however spurious, are getting harder to counter.

Relations between the United States and the Muslim and Arab world have never been problem free. Although in earlier times many Muslims and Arabs admired America as the embodiment of democratic ideals and material prosperity, relations were complicated by the Cold War, in which governments aligned with one or another of the superpowers to preserve their domestic political positions and secure their borders. The firm U.S. commitment to Israel's defense, perceived after 1967 among Arabs and Muslims as a bulwark for Israel's policies in the West Bank and Gaza, has also derailed American efforts to forge better ties with Arab publics. The first Gulf War, which we regarded as a triumph of arms and diplomacy over a vicious dictator, was perceived very differently in the region, as many Arabs saw the U.S. victory as an Arab humiliation. The ten years of UN sanctions on Iraq were widely—though erroneously—believed to have led to the deaths of millions of Iraqi children, which further hardened attitudes toward America. Then came Operation Iraqi Freedom, in which we have attempted to establish democracy through the barrel of a gun. The postwar chaos, the sense of personal insecurity, and the decline in living standards in Iraq have gutted our credibility in the region.

Any strategy for repairing the damage must therefore take Iraq into account. As of the summer of 2005, the public perception is that we have two broad options, neither very attractive. The first would be to deepen our commitment to securing the country, ensuring the safety of Iraqi citizens, restoring the country's economy, and creating and mentoring a professional bureaucracy capable of delivering government services. We would deploy more troops in order to seal and guard the country's borders and to force the necessary compromises on the different factions to establish stability and a working democracy. This way forward would entail years of anti-American violence, but if a successful Iraq emerged at the end of this bloody process, views of the United States just might be transformed as the altruism of our sacrifice became apparent. At that point, we would have a regional democratic ally and perhaps a rehabilitated relationship with the Muslim world.

The other course would resemble the one we are on. It would emphasize Iraqiization—that is, the rapid training and deployment of Iraqi security forces to maintain order; the formation of a predominantly Kurdish and Shiite military alliance against the Sunni rejectionists; the gradual drawdown of large U.S. military formations, first to cantonments to reduce their visibility and exposure to attack, and then out of the country, leaving a much smaller number of American troops in an advisory capacity.

The problem is that we have only the appearance of two options; the first one is no longer available to us. Ambassador James Dobbins, a retired diplomat known to colleagues as "our failed-state man" for his work in Haiti, Somalia, Bosnia, Kosovo, and Afghanistan, and now a leading analyst of America's role in Iraq, argues convincingly that we have lost the war for public opinion in Iraq—a judgment he makes on the basis of a range of polling data and wealth of reporting. He, like many other careful observers, questions the notion that deeper engagement will yield results. Moreover, the United States lacks the capacity to provide the forces necessary for this option. As a political matter, the risks of deeper involvement will likely make such a course unpalatable to a Republican Party facing midterm elections in 2006 and a general election two years after that.

The second option, therefore, is the only realistic one. We must accept the fact that a policy based on relatively rapid withdrawal is necessary to limit the damage we have already incurred. The question of pace is important. But there is a good chance that this course will carry its own penalties, especially because our departure will be trumpeted as a strategic defeat inflicted by jihadists on the American paper tiger. It will also be a tragedy for Iraq if, as seems likely, sectarian violence escalates as we draw down and Shiite and Kurdish militias begin the grisly task of destroying the Sunni resistance. While Iraq bleeds, the United States will be stigmatized throughout the Sunni world as a vile oppressor collaborating with a vengeful Shiite population. (Already, the prevailing view among Arabs is that the United States entered Iraq with the purpose of instigating a civil war as a way to weaken the *umma* and plunder Iraq's riches, another echo of bin Laden's argument.) The long-standing hostile U.S. policy toward Iran, however, ensures that we will get no benefit from this anti-Sunni alliance in Shiite public opinion. The bottom line is simply that perceptions of our aims and actions in Iraq will be difficult to reshape for the better and will likely get worse. We can expect that whatever we say about the desirability of democracy will be discounted at best or rejected at worst. Even in a best-case scenario that democratic institutions take root in Iraq, and a full-blown civil war is avoided, the United States is unlikely to get much credit—or warmth—from Iraqis and their neighbors.

Public diplomacy, the bureaucratic term for propaganda, is not the answer. The perceived gap between U.S. rhetoric and action is too wide to be bridged by slogans. In any case, we have been unable to get this balance right so far, in part because it has not been taken seriously by the Bush administration, which believed that Saddam's rapid defeat and the Iraqis' instant embrace of democracy would turn the United States into an object of emulation and gratitude among Arabs. Even assuming that persuasion was conceivable against the background of Guantánamo, Abu Ghraib, and the ruins of Fallujah, it would demand the talents of experienced, dedicated, highly knowledgeable individuals. Such officials would need regional credibility and the respect of the White House.

Instead, the individuals who have been given responsibility for outreach to the Muslim world have been Republican Party stalwarts with public relations or advertising experience. In the immediate aftermath of 9/11, Charlotte Beers, the retired CEO of the advertising firm J. Walter Thompson, was given this task with the rank of undersecretary of state.

Her career-making success had been an ad campaign she devised for Uncle Ben's Rice many years ago. When members of the Senate Foreign Relations Committee expressed their puzzlement about her appointment to Secretary of State Colin Powell, he shot back: "Well, guess what? She got me to buy Uncle Ben's Rice and so there is nothing wrong with getting somebody who knows how to sell something."[34]

Beers thought she had something uniquely valuable to work with. "The U.S. is an elegant brand," she explained, and the president and secretary of state are "symbols of the brand." (She also understood that Islam had a powerful appeal. In discussing a 30 percent increase in the conversion rate to Islam, she observed, "That would be a sales curve any company would love.") Her initial impulse was to seek out an appealing representative—a "great athlete . . . or singer"—to seduce foreign Muslims who were attracted to the message of Usama bin Laden. She had videos produced that depicted contented, if vapid, American Muslims talking about their lives in America. Some of these videos portrayed Muslim women in clothes that a conservative Muslim would judge immodest, and several countries refused to permit them to be broadcast to domestic audiences. Other videos focused on American Muslim women wearing robes and scarves; these were denounced by liberals as an official American endorsement of the subjugation of women and a blow for foreign reformers seeking a more pluralistic environment where they lived.

As one official said of Beers, "She didn't do anything that worked." This accurate, if harsh, judgment raises the question of whether she could have succeeded given that the White House Office of Global Communications, according to a senior official, had "been distancing itself from Charlotte since day one," and she had no influence over the two media outlets that count for something overseas, Voice of America and Radio Free Europe/Radio Liberty. When after eighteen months she left government service ostensibly for health reasons, the administration let it be known that it had "been looking for an honorable exit for some time."[35]

Her successor was Margaret Tutwiler, a political appointee in the administration of George H. W. Bush and a key member of Secretary of State James Baker's inner circle. Before her appointment, she had been ambassador to Morocco and therefore knew something about the Arab world, even if her career had been in public relations. She lasted less than a year, leaving amid rumors that she was frustrated that policy toward the Muslim world made it too hard to project a convincing, positive image of America. An appealing job offer to run public affairs for the New York Stock Exchange might have contributed to her decision to leave. Whatever the reason, her timing did the administration no favor, since her departure coincided with the scheduled handover of authority to the Iraqi interim government at the end of June 2004.

No replacement for Tutwiler was named for six months. Finally, in March 2005, Bush named his former public relations adviser, Karen Hughes, to head the outreach effort. She had no more relevant experience than her predecessors, but given her influence in the White House, the appointment was meant to convey the administration's seriousness about the task. That desire, though, was undercut by Hughes's announcement that she would not take up her new responsibilities until September.[36] Tellingly, four years after 9/11, there is not a single Muslim on her staff.

The administration's current approach has elicited the scorn of the professionals who have to make it work. "This is all feel-good mumbo jumbo," said one State Department official familiar with the public diplomacy efforts. "Particularly in light of Guantanamo Bay, it's unclear how this will make us safe. If this is so important, where's the money?"[37] The question was a good one. The U.S. Advisory Commission on Public Diplomacy reported in October 2004 that public diplomacy was "absurdly and dangerously underfunded."[38] Programs in the Muslim world received only a relatively small portion of the $685 million for public diplomacy in the State Department's 2004 budget. Education and cultural exchanges involving people from the Muslim world, a central part of the program, received $79 million, only slightly more than pre–9/11 levels. The scale of the effort is indicative: In the year after the Cold War ended, 5,000 exchanges were arranged with students and others from the former Soviet republics; in 2004, the first exchange program for Arab and Muslim high school students brought 170 students to the United States. That will grow to 1,000 in 2006 if the program is fully funded, but that is still a far cry from what is being accomplished with countries elsewhere in the world. Related enterprises, including Radio Sawa and Radio Farda and a television station called al Hurra, are lavishly funded, but they have not won the trust of Arab or Iranian audiences. According to Ned Walker, a former U.S.

ambassador to Israel and Egypt who is now head of the Middle East Institute, "The reaction to al Hurra has been very negative . . . people watch it once or twice and then turn to al-Jazeera or al-Arabiya—if they're inclined to look at news."[39]

Over the long run, changing the image of the United States, while reducing the influence of the jihadists, will require three things: a greater awareness of the gap between our expressed ideals and the way our actions are perceived by others; a sustained commitment by the White House along with substantial financial resources; and a keen eye for Muslims opposed to the claims made by the jihadists and their sympathizers, particularly about targeting of civilians. With the toll of Muslims killed by jihadists growing fast—especially in Iraq—America has an opening to win over the sympathies of those who are repulsed by such violence. But we can succeed in this only if we are seen as a fair-minded player and not the demon of jihadist mythology.

Why Do Democracies Happen?

The obstacles to democratization in the Middle East are formidable. This is not because Arabs are incapable of democracy, or because Islam is incompatible with it, although cultural factors do affect how democracy is practiced, as is the case in the rest of the world. Instead, it is the fundamental political and economic realities of the region that account for the failure of democracy to emerge. These conditions are deeply embedded in these societies. Any attempt on our part to change them should be made with some humility and an understanding that the results we want are not guaranteed.

We know from the emergence of democracies in Latin America, as well as the earlier establishment of democracy in Portugal and Spain in the 1970s, that the transition from authoritarian rule to democracy is usually slow and complicated. Sometimes this process can play out swiftly, especially when the old regime is unseated suddenly. This is what happened during the early 1980s in Argentina when a humiliating defeat in the Falklands War discredited the unpopular military junta, opening the door to a rapid transition to democracy. In Europe, Mikhail Gorbachev's

withdrawal of Soviet support for the regime in East Germany in 1989 pre-
cipitated that regime's rapid collapse, leading to the unification of Germany under the democratic institutions of its western half. But these are
exceptions to the rule.

The reason that the transformation from regime rule to democratic
governance usually takes a long time is that it requires the accumulation of
trust between reform-minded members of the regime in power and opposition activists prepared to compromise. This process requires proof of
good faith every step of the way, to dash long-standing suspicions. The
two sides need to convince each other that they are committed to a democratic outcome that will not have a draconian or vengeful outcome for either side and that they can keep their respective extremists in check. Thus,
reformers within the regime must convince the political opposition with
whom they are negotiating that the secret police and military will not
derail the deal and come after opposition figures. At the same time, the
leaders of the opposition must persuade their interlocutors that they can
keep the radicals in check, especially if some are committed to violence.
The complex and fragile nature of this interaction is easily disrupted and
often punctuated by reversals that put the outcome in doubt. When it
works, as it did in Poland after the fall of the Berlin Wall, the resulting
democracy can be sturdy.

One reason this process has not gotten off the ground in the Middle
East is that Islamists make up the opposition in almost every country. Although the Islamist oppositions have diverse agendas, they are united in
being the best organized and most plausible alternatives to the existing order. They have the regimes in power to thank for this enviable position because authoritarian rulers have precluded other kinds of opposition
movements and have often blocked the formation of political parties. As a
result, there is often just one major party in these countries, the one representing the regime itself. With political debate choked off, the only place
criticism can be expressed is the mosque, and the only critical language
that can be deployed is religious. At the same time, regional regimes—
Egypt and the Palestinian Authority are outstanding examples—have inadvertently strengthened the Islamist oppositions by failing to provide
good education, health care, and social services to the poor and lower
middle class. These tasks have been taken up by the Islamist oppositions,

which have become more popular as a result and even better organized. In the eyes of the ruling governments, the surging appeal of Islamist oppositions and the savagery that the militant wings of Islamist movements have demonstrated in the past have made them untrustworthy, and, in the case of some Islamist groups, there is reason to question whether they are committed to democracy or want to hold just one election that would allow them to take power. On the other hand, the Islamist experience with regimes that have used sweeping security laws, mass arrests, and detention of political moderates, as well as torture, make these movements exceptionally suspicious and reluctant to strike a deal. As long as trust remains elusive, the kind of deal making that has spurred democratic transitions in Europe and Latin America will not take place in the Middle East.

As if this were not enough to discourage those who support democracy in the region, the governments of the Arab Middle East have a relatively free hand to work around their citizens because they do not rely on them for direct tax revenue. Their motto might well be "no taxation, no representation." This has long been true of the oil-rich monarchies that own the country's resources; Saudi Arabia, after all, literally means "Arabia of the al-Saud family." This arrangement has benefited both sides. The population liked receiving basic services for free or buying commodities at subsidized prices, and was therefore willing, if reluctant, to forgo the right to vote. The ruling regime, on the other hand, did not object to sharing its profits from the country's oil revenues, if doing so meant not having to share power.

Not every Middle Eastern country is a major energy exporter, of course, but some can still achieve the same effect by extracting wealth from the United States or from other patrons instead of pulling it out of the ground in the form of oil.[40] Egypt has done this by trading peace with Israel, cooperation in the war on terrorism, and free passage for U.S. nuclear-powered warships through the Suez Canal in exchange for $2 billion per year in American cash, crucial diplomatic support, and a lenient attitude toward domestic repression. When these "profit-sharing" arrangements between rulers and ruled combine with the deep mistrust between regimes and opposition movements, the prospects for democratization become remote indeed.

Given these barriers, the Bush administration may be right in dismissing

civil society as the key to democratization even if it is wrong about its ability to trigger transformation through war. Egypt, for example, is reported
to have 19,000 civil society groups, yet it still represses political expression
and treats dissidents harshly. One explanation for this seeming
contradiction—a burgeoning civil society and the absence of political
reform—is that civil society groups have been co-opted by the government. Steven Cook, who tracks democratization in the Middle East for the
Council on Foreign Relations, explains that some civil society groups serve
as "window dressing" for the government's "predatory practices," and that
some of these organizations, like the Egyptian National Council for Human Rights, are actually established by the state to serve this purpose.[41]

Another reason to be cautious about a civil society approach to democratization is that not all civil society groups are committed to the liberal
values we would like to spread, particularly regarding women's rights and
religious pluralism. It is worth recalling that much of al Qaeda's funding
has come from charitable organizations that fit neatly under the rubric
of civil society. Nor should we forget that while democratization in the
Middle East would eventually reduce the threat of terrorism from that region, it would do little to curb Islamic extremism incubating in Western
Europe.

Thus we face an extraordinary challenge: The civil society approach to
democratization is probably too feeble to engender transformation from
below, prospects for trust between regime reformers and opposition
groups are slim, and the Iraq War has strengthened the determination of
the region's autocrats to push reform even further into the future. We are
going to have to rethink our approach. Whatever path we take, it must
make creative use of the middle ground between the two reflexes of current policy: dispatching the secretary of state to the Middle East to lecture
uncomprehending or resentful audiences about the virtues of democracy,
or imposing democracy by force of arms.

Plunging In?

If we are to be serious about promoting fundamental reform in pivotal
countries, we need to do more than hector them and sprinkle money on

small-scale initiatives. We must engage these societies deeply and dramatically. We have done this before. Decisive American action along these lines helped preserve democracy in Western Europe during the years after World War II, thereby laying the groundwork for the NATO alliance and eventual victory in the Cold War. Our tools then were the economic assistance of the Marshall Plan and, of course, military resolve in the face of a massive Soviet presence in Eastern Europe. The differences between Europe in 1945 and the Middle East today are huge, as are the differences between America then and now. Nevertheless, we did engage to a profound degree in other societies whose political development was crucial to our national security, and we were successful. Democracy in Western Europe flowered as European voters rejected the future promised by the Soviet Union.

What is more, there is already a contemporary model of deep engagement that can help point the way for us in the Middle East—the relationship between the European Union and Turkey. A decade ago, Turkey was effectively ruled by its military, which set limits to political dissent and Kurdish cultural self-expression. It was understood that the Turkish general staff could remove civilian governments from power and avoid oversight or criticism of its actions by the press or legislature. Today, Turkey's civil code has been overhauled, minority groups have been given cultural rights, the role of the military in the government has been significantly reduced, and basic freedoms—assembly, speech, and association—have been put on a sound footing. The party in power is Islamist, but it is committed to democracy and willing to abide by modern Turkey's legacy of secular government. These changes, as well as the speed with which they have taken hold, are nothing short of remarkable. That they happened at all is due to one thing: the prospect of membership in the European Union. The transformative potential this prospect has held has been clear to American policy makers for years, and, wisely, they have supported Turkey's bid consistently and vocally.

Turkey fastened onto the idea of EU membership because the Turks saw membership as the key to a dramatically better economic future. If Turkey were to be voted into the European community, EU funds would help to build a newer, better infrastructure, which in turn would improve economic performance. EU membership would ensure a steady flow of foreign direct investment essential to Turkey's development, which would reduce Turkey's need for loans and stabilize its crisis-ridden finances. Membership would also mean that, at least in the near term, there would be a bigger, more efficient market for Turkish workers and exports. Over the long term, greater prosperity at home would reduce the need for Turkish workers to seek employment outside of Turkey. In the meantime, the reforms Turkey has undertaken in order to qualify for membership have already created a more inviting environment for foreign investment and a more representative government.

Turkey's path to EU membership remains uncertain. The very reasons that Europe's Muslim communities face prejudice have fueled opposition within Europe to Turkey's accession, and some of the disarray in Europe since the defeat of the European Constitution in referenda in France and the Netherlands in the spring of 2005 owes to opposition to Turkish membership. Nevertheless, there is an important lesson in Turkey's transformation. The deep engagement of the EU in every aspect of Turkish society initiated and shaped a transformation of Turkish political institutions that few had thought possible.

The United States already uses conditional aid on a limited scale with a number of countries under the aegis of the Millennium Challenge Corporation, which promises financial assistance for governments that carry out economic reforms or measures that contribute indirectly to growth, such as improving institutions like courts and banks. This program, for which the Bush administration requested $2.5 billion from Congress in 2004, is not a favorite of Congress, which appropriated only half of what the White House wanted.[42] Even if the full amount had been appropriated, it still would have been far too small for the kind of dramatic initiative that circumstances require. For the past twenty-five years, the United States has given Egypt $1.2 billion in military aid and an average of $825 million in cash annually. Hosni Mubarak, Egypt's president during nearly all of that period, has used this "strategic rent" to postpone serious reform and has relied on the fact that Washington needs him more than he needs Washington to avoid cooperating more than absolutely necessary. If $2 billion per year for a generation has not been enough to get his attention, then $2.5 billion for a worldwide program of conditional aid seems unlikely to get better results. We will have to come closer to the dimensions of the bargain struck by Turkey and the EU.

This kind of "offer they can't refuse" would obviously not apply to countries that can go their own way, such as Saudi Arabia. But for countries treading water economically, the gains to be had from a package of large-scale, long-term financial and technical assistance combined with American backing for multilateral aid, inclusion in trade organizations, and eligibility for favorable trade arrangements might be enough to win their collaboration. Egypt is just such a country. The country currently has a 2 percent annual population growth rate and an economy growing at 3 percent per year, with unemployment estimated at 25 percent. Unemployment, however, is likely to worsen in the years to come. Foreign investment is at a twenty-year low. The bureaucratic and legal reforms needed to bring in urgently needed capital are advancing at a snail's pace. If any country would be tempted by a massive, but structured and highly conditional bailout, it would be a country like Egypt. The European Union is not going to offer Egypt membership in the foreseeable future, but it is within the power of the United States and its allies to offer a vision of a significantly better life through real integration with the global economy. Just the prospect of such a deal would help create the kind of broad and assertive constituency for a deal that might force the ruling regime to accept it.

Naturally, the benefits on offer would have to be as conditional as they were substantial. The conditions would include institutional reform, broadened political participation, and protection of human rights. The rulers of any country that enters such a bargain will need reassurance that they will not find themselves stripped of all their property, imprisoned, or worse. It will be equally challenging to structure this deal in a way that fosters a multiparty system and not the rapid ascendance of an Islamist opposition that only does lip service to democracy and is more than just vocally opposed to the United States.

In all likelihood, this admittedly ambitious process of deep engagement cannot be done by the United States alone. Politically and economically, EU participation will be essential, especially if we do not want the rulers of the recipient countries to identify other potential patrons that may provide an alternative to our "nonrefusable" offer. A partnership with the EU will also be vital for political cover, since the United States is not going to be viewed as a legitimate partner by the "street" or the elite in these countries as long as America remains embroiled in Iraq. But a grand bargain proffered in concert with Europe will increase the likelihood of it being accepted. At the same time, the United States needs to take steps to become a more acceptable partner for those countries that might be intrigued by such a deal. Recognizing that our presence in Iraq will remain a sore point about which we can do little in the near term, the most obvious action would be to devote more energy to resolving the Israeli-Palestinian problem and cultivate a more credible reputation for fairness toward the Palestinians.

The risks in an "offer they can't refuse" are considerable. We do not have a good record for making conditionality work, in part because we have typically lacked leverage and in part because domestic politics gets in the way. (In 2005, for example, American arms manufacturers lobbied Congress not to cut military aid to Egypt because it would result in lost business orders.) Withdrawing aid in the event that the recipient government reneges on the deal will have its own perils. When the United States threatened Egypt with suspension of a small portion of its annual aid transfer in 2002 to protest the imprisonment of a pro-democracy activist, Washington was vilified by every segment of Egyptian public opinion. Persuading the EU and others to embrace such a severe approach to conditionality will prove difficult, even if we think we are prepared to take such steps.

The overall feasibility of this course of action is, of course, debatable. Americans are generous when it comes to charitable giving but historically have been wary of foreign assistance. Moreover, U.S. fiscal and monetary policy, combined with the bills for the Iraq war—now running at $4.5 billion per month—have diminished our ability to make the kind of startlingly generous offer that would seize the attention of a Hosni Mubarak or Bashar al-Assad and captivate key constituencies in these countries. These are the opportunity costs of Iraq—we could have bought plenty of reform for the more than $300 billion the war has cost us this far.

But if the risks are high, so are the potential payoffs. The impact of tangible political reform in a country like Egypt on other authoritarian countries in the region would be immense. Showing the Muslim world that the West does indeed have a positive agenda to pursue with it and has the will to make real improvements in the lives of Muslims a reality would dramatically change the environment in which radical Islamists make their arguments. Conversely, if we continue to pursue democratization through rhetoric and force, we risk the chance that it will not happen or will happen in a way very much not to our liking. This choice seems clear.

10

SHORTCHANGING HOMELAND SECURITY

Our jihadist adversaries have a killing field in Iraq.[1] It offers them the opportunity to experiment with the latest in Islamist insurgent strategy. In "Managing the Barbarians," an influential treatise now making the rounds among jihadi theoreticians, the author, Abu Bakr al-Naji, explains that jihadists can turn carefully selected battlefields into truly Islamic states by creating and manipulating a state of chaos.[2] Unlike classic insurgencies, in which guerrillas wear uniforms and aim to occupy and rule larger slices of contested territory, al-Naji's disciples aim to create shifting pockets of anarchy and attack highly dispersed assets to force the enemy to spread himself too thinly to control the country. For the moment, this is their splendid little war.

At some point, the ambitious jihadists will carry their fight back to the United States. When this happens, we had better be ready. We will have to know what parts of our infrastructure are critical and ensure that they can survive an attack. Our transportation system, telecommunications and cyber networks, energy transmission grids, governmental and financial institutions, food and water supplies, emergency services, and health care delivery systems must be robust enough to get us through a potentially devastating assault. They must also be transformed in ways that prevent their use as a weapon by our enemies, as our commercial aircraft were used on 9/11. Moreover, we must have in place the laws and procedures to maintain civil and legal order in areas of the country that bear the direct effects of a successful attack.

We have been on notice since 9/11 that such protective measures are urgently needed. These defenses will require long lead times for implementation and, in some instances, radical changes to the way we did business in a simpler, less wired, and less interdependent age. Yet in the three and a half years since the jihad came to America—and we became aware that our enemy would use apocalyptic weapons against us—we have done little to reduce our vulnerability to an enemy strike or prepare to manage the consequences of such possibilities as a biological or radiological attack, or perhaps even a wave of suicide bombings. During that time, the combination of our heightened vigilance, the long cycle of al Qaeda planning, and the dispersal of jihadists from Afghanistan gave us the space to prepare. The interval between the carnage of 9/11 and today was a gift that we have squandered.

We failed to seize this precious time because we have overemphasized the offensive side of this war. Indeed, our approach is like the "cult of the offensive" that permeated the French general staff before World War I, leading it to believe that a spirited attack would overwhelm the most well-entrenched adversary. This belief nearly destroyed the French army in 1915–1916. Today, it has diverted the White House from the imperative of a sound defense.[3] Convinced that U.S. offensive military operations would destroy the terrorists on the outer perimeter before they got inside the wire, the administration has not devoted adequate attention to the technical, organizational, and political complexities of homeland defense. With defense relegated to the back burner, there has been little presidential and congressional oversight, weak departmental leadership, inadequate coordination between Washington and state and local governments, poor collaboration with the private sector, and only half-hearted attempts to reform entrenched interests, like the FBI, that had strong constituencies on Capitol Hill. Most regrettably, there was no perceived need for a strategy that would balance risk and resources to produce priorities for homeland defense, nor was there a vision of the end-state—of a secure America—and therefore no sense of how much would be effort enough to ensure that we could weather an attack without stalling economically, unraveling as a society, or failing to destroy our assailant.

It is not too late to develop a strategy that directs resources and American ingenuity to this urgent project. Popular support, though, will be essential. The fact that Iraq has displaced terrorist attack as a concern for Americans will make this support harder to gather.[4] For us to get this right, the president will have to shift his stance on the linkage between offense and defense and explain to Americans the continuing immediacy of our homeland security goals. Having taken this dramatic step, the president will then have to direct the work of identifying elements of our infrastructure that are both at risk and essential to our social cohesion and economic prosperity. He must then shepherd the cooperation of the public and private sectors in devising defenses and foster a comprehensive strategy that directs not only our defense efforts, but also the preparations we must make for the day our defenses fail us.

IN THE STOCKTAKING that took place in Washington and across the nation after September 11, people wanted to know how the attackers got through multiple layers of defense. Muhammad Atta and his crew, all foreigners, had entered the country by escaping the attention of immigration and intelligence officials, prepared for the attack unnoticed by federal and local law enforcement, and boarded four airplanes armed with unmistakable weapons despite airport security measures that had been inspired by the terrorist hijackings and airport attacks that plagued Europe during the 1970s and 1980s. Even more astonishingly, at least one of the hijackers had been spotted and correctly identified by the CIA prior to the attack, in a meeting with al Qaeda operatives in Malaysia in January 2000. Both he and a second attacker were known to have entered the United States before 9/11, while another would-be hijacker, who had taken flight lessons in the United States, had been taken into police custody because of his suspicious activities.[5] The public found it hard to believe that a team of nineteen amateurs could vault America's parapet and inflict such horrific damage. The failure of the Departments of Justice and State, the CIA, the National Security Agency, and the Federal Aviation Administration to share information that might have averted the attack compounded the sense of shock.

This consternation crystallized quickly into congressional demands that the White House take steps to strengthen American defenses and, in particular, to force the law enforcement and intelligence communities to exchange information vital to the nation's security. At first, the upshot of the policy debate was that the United States should establish a "vulnerability-based" or "capabilities-based" system of homeland security, which would involve huge investments in making the country as airtight as possible against terrorists and creating the capabilities to contain the full range of terrorist threats. Homeland security officials who served during that intense time remember no debate at all, only having to respond to what they called the "crisis du jour," but a number of decisive steps were taken. These included the swift creation of the Transportation Security Administration and the passage of the USA PATRIOT Act, which broke down some of the divisions between the FBI and the CIA regarding the collection and sharing of intelligence.

Competing visions about how to implement such a grand plan emerged on Capitol Hill, where some members of Congress agitated for an intelligence czar, on the model of the long-standing position of the drug czar, except that the intelligence version would have control over budgets and personnel. This prescription had surfaced before, mostly from CIA advocates, who argued that the director of Central Intelligence (DCI) had a great deal of responsibility but very little authority, since the bulk of the national intelligence budget was controlled by the Department of Defense. The problem with this arrangement was the Pentagon's preoccupation with collecting intelligence for combat commanders, force planners, and weapons developers. Although those requirements overlapped to some extent with intelligence priorities, they would not necessarily extend to include "collection targets" such as the rise of jihadism among Sunni Muslims. The DCI also did not have effective authority over senior appointments in those agencies under his formal jurisdiction but outside of his operational control. Particularly problematic was the DCI's relationship to the FBI, which was responsible for gathering terrorism-related intelligence within U.S. borders and using foreign intelligence leads collected overseas by the CIA to disrupt the growth of terrorist cells at home. The September 11 attacks transformed what had been an intense but narrowly confined policy debate about the organization of the intelligence community into an issue of urgent public concern.

Worries about homeland security erupted at the same time. The multiple anthrax attacks of October 2001, whose perpetrator still has not been identified, drew public attention to questions that, like intelligence reform, had been the province of a relatively small group of specialists during the preceding decade. In the mid-1990s, Congress had passed a law sponsored by Senators Sam Nunn, Richard Lugar, and Pete Domenici that required Washington to help state and local governments prepare to cope with the consequences of a terrorist attack involving weapons of mass destruction (WMD). At about that time, the Clinton administration issued a national security directive that assigned responsibility for preparedness efforts to specific agencies and began to include funds for "consequence management" in its budget requests. It was then, in 1995, that the term "homeland security" first entered the national security lexicon. These initiatives were haphazard, however, and never adequately funded. Before 9/11, most Americans, including those who managed the federal agencies responsible for disaster relief, were unable to imagine what a terrorist attack with a weapon of mass destruction would look like. Once they witnessed on television an attack that had the magnitude of a WMD event, they showed more interest.

In recent years, most of the public had understandably dismissed Cold War–style civil defense as futile for mitigating the holocaust of nuclear war, but now, against a new enemy that posed asymmetric WMD threats, civil defense had far greater appeal among laymen as well as experts. Various organizational proposals, such as one by former senators Gary Hart and Warren Rudman, had several common features: They generally had bipartisan support; they envisaged some combination of separate agencies and departments into a new, unified entity; and they provided for a cabinet-level head who would be confirmed by the Senate and therefore accountable for the performance of the new agency. They differed in the scope of integration and, importantly, whether or not they included the CIA and the FBI.

The Bush administration gave the cold shoulder to these proposals, however, and appointed Governor Tom Ridge of Pennsylvania, an old friend of the president, to be homeland security adviser, a staff position within the White House. The administration's disinclination to reorganize 170,000 people in twenty-two diverse agencies with a proposed total budget of $38 billion was understandable. David Walker, the head of the General Accounting Office, the federal government watchdog agency (now known as the Government Accountability Office), judged that the process of integrating so many different agencies with their own cultures, traditions, and objectives would take years and might never cohere. It was also true that the channels for sharing information among government agencies had been available prior to 9/11 but they had not been used because law enforcement and intelligence officers were unwilling to accommodate one another's concerns. The FBI was focused on criminal investigation and gathering evidence to win convictions in court, while the CIA was dedicated to collecting intelligence that might prove useful in understanding an adversary and planning covert operations to weaken the enemy. Both organizations prized their autonomy, but the FBI in particular acted as though sharing information would weaken its independence. Organizational fixes were unlikely to eliminate these cultural and psychological problems, which often pervaded entire institutions.

Combining agencies that lay outside the law enforcement and intelligence orbit into a single large entity had drawbacks as well. First, almost all the agencies, or the large units within them that have counterterrorism responsibilities, also do other things. The Coast Guard maintains our shore defenses, but it also handles maritime safety and carries out search-and-rescue operations. The Animal and Plant Health Inspection Service monitors the integrity of the food chain, but it also sets standards for treatment of animals in zoos and circuses. The mixture of terrorism-related work with activities that have nothing to do with the threat would necessarily divert the leadership of the new agency from their main responsibility. Second, consolidation would pit the cobbled-together elements of the new superagency against one another in a competition for resources, which would distract senior managers from their day-to-day responsibility for homeland security. Third, the very process of consolidation would inevitably devour resources that could otherwise have gone into the task of protecting American citizens.[6] New office space and equipment would have to be acquired, an enormous number of hours spent in planning and executing the transition, and employee morale and energy somehow sustained.[7]

For the Bush team there were yet other problems with the creation of a new government department. As a matter of ideology, the expansion of government was objectionable to many Republicans. While it was true that the proposals circulating in Congress did not make any of the individual components of the new agency any bigger—this whole was definitely not to be larger than the sum of its parts—the expansion of the cabinet suggested an expansion of government. Then there were the existing cabinet members to deal with, none of whom was likely to submit to having parts of their empires excised and delivered to a new cabinet secretary. In the universe of spying and policing, Bush could anticipate that Secretary of Defense Donald Rumsfeld would mobilize his congressional supporters to block the transfer of his budget authority over the sophisticated eavesdropping and surveillance assets the Pentagon controlled. Indeed, Rumsfeld had been eyeing an expansion of his own "humint" (human intelligence, or spying) and analytical capabilities. He was looking to expand his intelligence operations rather than have them pared down.[8] And there was nothing to suggest that the FBI's backers on the Hill would forsake the Bureau and allow it to be subordinated to an authority other than the attorney general.

Most important, though, there was the issue of need. As we saw in chapter 7, by late 2001 the White House was already preparing to take the war on terrorism to Iraq, where it would destroy a regime presumed to be supporting al Qaeda terrorists. Regime change in Iraq, the thinking went, would also cut off the terrorists' principal access to chemical, biological, and nuclear weapons and thus their ability to inflict mass casualty attacks within the United States. President Bush later summarized this strategy by saying that the United States was "aggressively striking the terrorists in Iraq, defeating them there so we will never have to face them in our own country."[9] Iraq, he would declare, "is now the central front in the war on terror. And we are rolling back the terrorist threat at the heart of its power." As the insurgency strengthened, he asserted that by taking on the Iraqi resistance, "Americans would not have to confront terrorists in the streets of our own cities."[10] He returned to this formulation repeatedly in speeches throughout the country beginning in the fall of 2003. In his 2005 State of the Union address, he went further still, predicting, or perhaps wishing, that "the victory of freedom in Iraq will strengthen a new ally in the war on terror."[11]

The statements by the president reflect the administration's resistance to a homeland security system centered on America's vulnerabilities. More compelling was a strategy of military preemption or prevention that in theory would push those borders out and leave the U.S. population well inside a safe buffer. The president's conviction that warfare against radicals in Iraq would obviate the risk of attacks on American homeland soil would have sufficed to explain the administration's hostility to the creation of a cumbersome new government agency—one designed to handle contingencies that would never arise if Iraq was managed well.[12] The combination of this strategic concept with an array of powerful bureaucratic, ideological, and political hurdles underlay White House opposition to creating a Department of Homeland Security in the winter of 2001 and the spring of 2002.

But in the spring of 2002, pressures were converging on the White House from the families of the 9/11 victims and from members of Congress who felt exposed on the homeland security issue.

In the face of these pressures, the White House changed course. The volte-face came unheralded.[13] In a remarkable display of discipline, administration officials said nothing about the start of an internal process to devise their own plan for a new department based on a bill that was being considered by Congress. The creators of the plan were four of Bush's senior advisers who met in the most secret place within the White House complex, the presidential Emergency Operations Center—the bunker to which the president is removed in an emergency if the Secret Service cannot get him to safety elsewhere.[14] Even the cabinet was uninformed until the plan was ready to be launched. Robert Mueller III, the FBI director, was apparently taken completely by surprise. When pressed by a congressional committee on whether he had been consulted, he said, "I believe I should not be forthcoming."

The Democrats were even more taken aback, especially since the White House proposal came with a grenade wrapped inside it, in the form of a provision allowing the new department to suspend the collective bargaining rights of its unionized employees. The White House plan was to use its tactical advantage to enact a union-busting provision, which the Democrats could not counter without being tarred with the charge of compromising national security for the sake of a "special interest." The

Democratic leadership nevertheless walked into the trap with eyes wide shut. They continued to press for the original bill, without the White House's provisions, but were filibustered by Senate Republicans, who depicted the Democrats as putting coffee breaks for loafing civil servants ahead of America's security. Mitch Daniels, a senior administration aide, declared that "where the safety of Americans is at stake, where speed, agility and flexibility will be literally life-or-death matters, it would be unconscionable to build in the processes that made the IRS and the Postal Service fodder for talk show humor." The rhetoric, if not the logic, was irrefutable, especially for the hapless and inarticulate Democratic opposition.

In fact, there was pressure on both sides to compromise. Republican and Democratic leaders in Congress had promised to get a homeland security bill to the president's desk by September 11, 2002, the first anniversary of the disaster. With midterm elections approaching, the Democrats found an early vote attractive since it meant more time to showcase domestic issues on which Republicans were thought to be vulnerable. For the Republicans, an early vote meant that the president could announce real progress toward a homeland security department on June 6—D-day—another important anniversary that would enhance the president's prestige and reinforce his carefully cultivated image as a war leader. The Democrats' anger got the better of their judgment, however, and they chose to fight a war of attrition over the bill's labor provisions. In the ensuing impasse, Republicans could not resist the temptation to lard the bill with special-interest provisions of their own, which fed already seething resentments. One provision ensured that Texas A&M University would receive a large amount of government funds to study terrorism. Another was meant to take Eli Lilly, the giant pharmaceutical manufacturer, off the hook for having sold a mercury-based vaccine that, according to litigants, had caused autism in children.[15] A vote on the bill was delayed until after the election, and Democrats paid a price for their principles, losing control of the Senate. Afterward, their attacks on the pork-barreling led to a barely face-saving compromise that enabled passage of the homeland security bill in the Senate on November 20, by a 90 to 9 vote.

Forced to embrace a new cabinet department, the White House faced the issue of managing it. Given the mountainous size of the new department, the diversity of its functions, and hundreds of entrenched interests that would be gathered under one roof, a strong leader, empowered by the president to take tough decisions and make them stick, would have been essential. The appointee, however, was Tom Ridge. As Bush's homeland security adviser, he had been given a $25 million budget, a West Wing office, and a staff that grew to nearly 100. President Bush described him as the counterpart to the national security adviser, Condoleezza Rice. Yet Ridge never seemed to get traction. He is now remembered mostly for his color-coded threat-advisory system, which led the late-night comic Jay Leno to ask him what he should do if the threat level changes when he is lounging at home in his underwear watching television. He is remembered as well for having mishandled the response to the anthrax attacks of October 2001, his first major challenge in the post.[16]

Unable to cope with the huge task of mobilizing and coordinating the array of agencies under his aegis, he spent much of his year on the job crisscrossing the country, telling local emergency service personnel, police, and firefighters that the federal government was there for them and that "if the hometown is secure, the homeland is secure." With no control over agency budget submissions and staffing and not really even in the chain of command, he could have set priorities and compelled tradeoffs only through force of personality backed by the clear support of the president. He had neither. Ridge is a genial man, whose beefy stature and air of authority mask an indecisive nature. He could not say no. In his time as governor of Pennsylvania, he never had to; the state ran budget surpluses and the Republican Party controlled both houses of the state legislature. His qualification for the job of Homeland Security adviser appeared to have been his loyalty and strong "brotherly" friendship with the president, with whom he campaigned for George H. W. Bush against Ronald Reagan in the 1980 Republican primaries.[17] His service as a combat soldier in Vietnam—he was awarded a Bronze Star—also lent him credibility in America's new war. Yet he never was able to draw strength from his relationship with the president or get the backing he would have needed to challenge the departmental barons who resisted him. In looking back at the year Ridge spent at the White House, senior aides said they were "unable to think of a bureaucratic battle he won."[18] Lawrence Korb, an expert on homeland security at the Council on Foreign Relations, may have been right in 2002 when he said that "you probably would have wanted someone who is tougher, who is willing to take unpopular stands and can take on the vested interests," but if the president was going to be indifferent to Ridge's battles, then cabinet and sub-cabinet officials were inevitably going to end-run him.[19] Despite this uninspiring performance, Bush chose Ridge to head the new department, where, if anything, the challenges would be exponentially greater.

The hardest of these multiple challenges was managing the huge amounts of money that were about to be dumped on the twenty-two agencies that made up the new Department of Homeland Security (DHS). The budget for these activities had been rising since the mid-1990s. In 1995, estimated spending for homeland security was $9 billion. Within five years it had risen to over $13 billion. Just before 9/11, the budget stood at $16 billion. These numbers rose sharply after the disaster—the result of intense public anxiety and a Congress and chief executive eager to show that something was being done. Two large supplemental appropriations were made in 2002 alone, totaling about $15 billion. These emergency sums brought the total appropriated for homeland security in 2002 to $34.5 billion. Ridge's first budget request as secretary of homeland security— $37.7 billion—brought the rate of increase down sharply. This was a significant amount of money, but American vulnerabilities as an open society were even bigger. Considering that nearly $7 billion of Ridge's request included funds for Defense Department homeland security costs and another $4.8 billion for the payroll costs of tens of thousands of screeners hired by the new Transportation Security Administration (TSA), the increase was not as big as it looked.

GIVEN WHAT IT would take to protect a large and complex transportation system, energy transmission grid, telecommunications network, and production and storage facilities for volatile fuels and toxic chemicals—and the linkages among these sectors—no amount of money will ever be enough. Priorities need to be established. Deciding on them requires a strategy that weighs vulnerability and risk and balances them against resources. Without a strategy, even the most well-intentioned of efforts will result in waste and lost opportunity. And without serious, hands-on management and presidential support, no such strategy can be implemented effectively. This is especially true of the crazy-quilt of roles, missions, and objectives that make up "homeland security."

But clear priorities were not set. The creation of the TSA was dictated by Congress very shortly after 9/11, when anxieties about the security of airports had reached stratospheric levels. The establishment of this new agency, the rapid hiring of 65,000 screeners and others, and the acquisition of expensive screening equipment for large airports took the initiative away from an administration that badly needed to think carefully through its plan. Although the sudden profusion of uniformed men and women milling around airport security stations and conducting intrusive searches might have deterred a second wave of hijackers—had there been one—the extraordinary expense and effort undercut more rational and systematic responses to 9/11.

The Department of Homeland Security under Tom Ridge never seemed to regain the initiative. Given what was known about America's vulnerabilities and the desires of the al Qaeda perfectionists who had dreamt up the 9/11 attacks, clear priorities for homeland defense could have been defined and put into practice. First was the need to secure ordinary infrastructure that could be turned into weapons, in much the same way that al Qaeda transformed airplanes into cruise missiles on 9/11, concentrating on those assets whose destruction could severely disrupt the nation's economy or pose a major threat to the health and safety of Americans. Second was the need to prevent deadly weapons, or weapons components like fissile material, from being smuggled into the country. Third was the need to prepare for a biological attack. And fourth was the need to know who was entering and leaving the United States and to monitor and disrupt terrorist cells that might be forming here at home.[20]

Neither these priorities nor any others were ever translated into a feasible national strategy. In part, this was because the department was staffed with "cops, spooks, and soldiers," as one former senior official described the situation. According to this observer, "These people simply lack a broad strategic view." To complicate matters, a comprehensive strategy required representation from the business world, because the burden of defending much of the infrastructure will fall on the private sector, which owns the majority of the infrastructure. But the intelligence, military, and law enforcement participants were simply not accustomed to taking suggestions from civilians outside of the national security establishment. They also failed at making themselves understood to the business community outside the defense sector.

The department's inability to convince the genuinely essential business sector to cooperate with Washington in protecting itself against terrorist attacks has contributed to its strategic failure.[21] High-profile commissions set up by the department, like the Homeland Security Advisory Council (HSAC), to elicit the cooperation of CEOs have failed because senior executives see them as charades at worst or pointless meetings with well-meaning but clueless bureaucrats at best. According to one prominent Washington consultant who operates as a liaison between government and industry, CEOs have described HSAC meetings as "a waste of time" and a "pile of shit." For these business leaders, DHS "dialogue" consists of demands for information about their physical and cyber assets for the purpose of compiling lists of facilities that are vital in the government's eyes, coupled with demands that businesses ensure on their own that they are defended from attack in the manner that the government stipulates.[22] From the perspective of these CEOs, the government should be asking them for their advice and working with industry to develop protective measures that companies will have to carry out, in some instances with government assistance and in some without. For government, cooperation has been a one-way street. The CEO of a top international delivery and freight service, who is understandably concerned that his company will inadvertently hire a terrorist, has asked the FBI for help in vetting employees. He has yet to have his call returned.[23]

These deficiencies might not have been decisive if Ridge had rejected the narrow, piecemeal perspective of the "cops, spooks, and soldiers" who worked for him, or had involved himself actively in policy development. It might also have made a difference if the White House leadership had been willing to insist upon a comprehensive strategic view in the department's planning. Instead, the White House seems to have discouraged such involvement on the part of its own staff. One person who worked in the White House Office of Homeland Security said that he and his colleagues tried repeatedly to get Ridge to concentrate on bigger issues, but Andrew Card, the president's chief of staff, would block these efforts, saying that Ridge should be allowed to go his own way. Since going his own way frequently meant backing down in favor of FBI and CIA prerogatives whenever they conflicted with the needs of his own agency, the Department of Homeland Security never got the access to intelligence or law enforcement information it needed to function. According to one participant in the process, Ridge "gave away the store every time." For the Information Assurance and Infrastructure Protection (IAIP) office that was supposed to map threat information against our vulnerabilities and share that data with the private sector, this was disabling. In high-level meetings, Ridge refused to push the CIA and the FBI to cooperate with the IAIP, which in turn consigned that key function to irrelevance. In part as a result of these routine capitulations, we are not as safe as we might have been, despite the gusher of dollars that has poured through DHS since the 9/11 attacks.

Preventing our enemies from ever turning our technology and infrastructure against us is probably an unattainable goal. There is simply too much to protect in any comprehensive way. We now know that with the right guidance system (a terrorist pilot) and explosive payload (a full tank of jet fuel), an aircraft can be transformed into a missile. Similarly, the Madrid attackers showed on 3/11 that trains can be turned into torpedoes. At the other end of the spectrum, an air conditioner perched on the roof of a building and the ductwork connected to it can be turned into a deadly weapon through the insertion of anthrax dust in the intake. Even our telecommunications system can be turned into a weapon, now that critical infrastructures are linked by and operated through the Internet. An enterprising hacker can corrupt the databases that underpin the management of critical blood supplies, scramble 911 call systems, launch devastating power outages, corrupt banking records, or infect computer systems in countless ways that would result not only in financial losses, but potentially large losses of life as well.

Recognizing that it is impossible to protect everything, a truly strategic approach would identify the critical assets that could and should be shielded. Cataloging has been done. As Matthew Brzezinski notes in his book *Fortress America*, the CIA has identified the top 100 targets within the United States, while governors have assembled their own list of 150 primary and 180 secondary targets.[24] Critical nodes, however, have not been appropriately identified and marked for protection, because DHS has not been able to agree internally on what these are. Not until February 2005, with the nomination of Ridge's replacement, Michael Chertoff, did the department publish an "interim" national infrastructure protection plan that attempted to take a strategic view.[25] This plan, which was congressionally mandated, had not been done on schedule and had to be produced as a rush job by an outside contractor, because Congress had made it clear to the White House that Chertoff would not be confirmed as the new secretary of homeland security until that organization figured out how to do its homework. Senior staff in the department believed that the interim report was inadequate, but they needed a product in a hurry and had no choice but to use it.

IN THE THREE and a half years since 9/11—the amount of time it took the United States to subdue Germany and Japan and lay the basis for the postwar order—and after the expenditure of $47.3 billion on homeland security in fiscal year 2005 alone, there are still alarming gaps in our defenses. This is due, in part, to personnel gaps. It is generally agreed that we should be developing the counterterrorism capacities of countries used by terrorists as transit stops, safe havens, or banks. Yet Cofer Black, the hard-charging CIA covert operations expert who had been given the job of making this happen as the State Department's counterterrorism coordinator, was not replaced for six months after his departure in late 2004.[26] John Gordon, the former deputy director of the CIA, had to wear two hats at the White House, one as deputy national security adviser for combating terrorism and the other as Ridge's successor as homeland security adviser. His replacement since May 2004, Frances Townsend, had the same two burdens until June 2005, when she selected Juan Zarate, a Treasury Department political appointee, to be her deputy for combating terrorism. On the NSC staff, the position of senior director for combating terrorism went unfilled for a year following Townsend's departure, when a thirty-two-year-old aide, Michele Malvesti, was finally tapped for the job. A number of key appointments to White House posts involving career civil servants with vital experience have been held up because of concerns about the political loyalties of the individuals—several candidates for these jobs report being flummoxed in their interviews by questions from

White House staff about who they voted for in the last election. In the Department of Homeland Security, the lack of focus on key personnel was evident in the initial selection of Bernard Kerik to succeed Ridge as secretary. Although he was never charged with any crime, Kerik had violated immigration and tax laws and was connected to a construction firm linked to organized crime. In the management rung just below, key IAIP positions went unfilled as well.[27]

In July 2005, the new secretary of homeland security, Michael Chertoff, announced a reorganization of the department. Chertoff, a former appellate judge, is said by those who know him to be intelligent and decisive, and his early actions reflect a more cogent set of priorities than any put forward by his predecessor. Cybersecurity, which languished under Ridge, will have a senior official in charge, raising the profile of this indispensable part of our national infrastructure. Similarly, the appointment of a chief medical officer should help redress the scattershot nature of policy making to deal with the bioterrorism threat. A chief intelligence officer will be appointed, too, which may help the department get the intelligence support it needs to do its job. Operational agencies under Chertoff's authority, including TSA, Customs and Border Protection, Immigration and Customs Enforcement, and the Federal Emergency Management Agency, will be regrouped and report directly to him. Whether this promising start yields results, and does not turn out merely to be an effort to "rearrange the deck chairs," as one official said, will depend crucially on the president's backing for the new secretary.[28]

In the meantime, serious dangers will not disappear while DHS figures out how to implement the secretary's instructions and Congress decides whether to authorize the new positions required by the reorganization. Aviation, for example, is still at risk. The proverbial little old lady is forced to take her shoes off, while trace machines that detect explosive residue on hand baggage merely get "limited undirected use," according to TSA inspectors, indicating that only the smallest percentage of carry-on bags are assessed.[29] And despite the huge increase in the number of screeners and many small miseries inflicted on travelers, weapons searches are still no more effective now than was the case shortly after September 11, 2001.[30] The cost of bomb detection machines that are used to screen checked luggage at 400 U.S. airports has doubled within eighteen months, from

$508 million to $1.2 billion. Despite the cost, they produce such a high false-alarm rate that their utility is questionable. More broadly, these expensive measures were all meant to address the challenges of the last war. Cargo and checked luggage are screened far less systematically than carry-on bags, which suggests that the best way for a terrorist to ensure that his bomb gets on the aircraft is to check it. Yet little progress has been made in filling this gap in aviation defense. In the meantime, terrorists seem to be looking for ways other than boarding aircraft to destroy them or turn them into flying bombs. In 2003, for example, the FBI handled over 500 cases relating to aviation; two were hijackings, both from Cuba. Most of the rest involved problems at airport checkpoints, no doubt caused by travelers maddened by security procedures, or abusive on-board behavior by drunks.[31] There were no hijacking attempts by Islamic terrorists. This does not mean attempts won't reoccur, only that terrorists are exploring other options.

The two threats that a strategic approach would already have addressed are the use of unsecured and unregulated general aviation to attack targets on the ground and the prospect of a shoulder-fired missile to shoot down an airplane on takeoff or landing. General aviation includes corporate jets, private planes, cargo aircraft, and other unscheduled flights. This vulnerability was widely recognized after 9/11, but was tossed into the "too-hard-to-do" bin by the new TSA, which had its hands full hiring in short order the thousands of screeners deemed necessary to prevent the attack that had already been carried out by Muhammad Atta's team. Any of these non-common-carrier planes could be turned into a cruise missile, like the 9/11 flights, without the attackers having to run the gauntlet of TSA guards at the gates of passenger carriers.

Even less regulated and more readily available to terrorist groups are kit and ultra-light airplanes, which could be used for manned or unmanned attacks. Terrorists are already adjusting to 9/11's positive effects on airport security. According to the director general of intelligence for Canada's armed forces, terrorist groups have purchased ultra-light aircraft and hang-gliders to avoid the need to hijack large commercial airliners for use as missiles. The appeal of using small aircraft lies primarily in the weak state of defenses against such low-flying objects. After Air

Force interceptors came within seconds of mistakenly shooting down the governor of Kentucky's official airplane as it was bound for President Reagan's funeral in Washington, D.C., on July 8, 2004, a congressional hearing disclosed the abysmal state of the nation's capacity to distinguish friend from foe. Flying at 3,000 feet—beneath the FAA's existing radar system—an attacker targeting Washington would face detection and interdiction only by Customs and Border Protection helicopters operating within a fifteen-mile radius around the White House. Other American cities, except perhaps for New York City, would be easy prey for such a low-level attack.[32]

The threat of shoulder-fired missiles is equally serious. In November 2002, al Qaeda came close to downing an Israeli-chartered airliner near Mombasa, Kenya, by just this method. At least 500,000 such weapons have been manufactured since the mid-1960s, and many were already missing from government stocks when the United States invaded Iraq. Since then, John Handy, the Air Force general who commands the U.S. Transportation Command, has spoken of the threat from "vast, unknown" quantities of antiaircraft weapons. In the fall of 2004, U.S. intelligence estimated that at least 4,000 missiles from Iraq's arsenal could not be accounted for, thus tripling the total number of such missiles that are believed to be out of government control worldwide.[33] Some intelligence officials put the number at 5,000. There are so many available on the global arms market that an early-generation missile can be had for only $5,000. The RAND Corporation studied this problem in 2004 and determined that if a single aircraft were destroyed by a missile, the direct economic cost to the United States would be $1 billion. The indirect cost, stemming from the shutdown of major airports while the authorities worked to determine who carried out the attack and whether there were more in store, would reach $15 billion. If the uncertainty lasted for a full year, or there was a second attack, associated costs would reach $50 billion.[34] By comparison, the full ten-year cost of developing, installing, operating, and maintaining laser jammers on America's fleet of 6,800 commercial passenger planes is estimated to be $40 billion. Thus, preventing a successful takedown of an airliner would appear to be economically prudent as well as technologically manageable. It would also be strategically essential. The RAND researchers,

while not backing immediate deployment of countermeasures, nevertheless concluded that:

> One or more successful attacks on American commercial aircraft would
> have profound strategic consequences for the United States and its part-
> ners in the fight against terrorist groups. America's enemies would gain a
> tremendous psychological boost from such attacks and would confront
> the world's population with serious doubts about not only the safety of
> air travel but also the viability of their governments' counter-terrorism
> efforts. A new front would be opened in the contest and the effects would
> be long-lasting: In the popular imagination, the terrorists would be cred-
> ited with having the capability to kill people on commercial aircraft more
> or less at will until such time as convincing policy solutions to the threat
> were implemented.[35]

If work had begun on this in 2001, the U.S. would be much closer to
equipping its commercial fleet with effective defenses against the threat of
missile attack.

Rail transportation is equally vulnerable, but not just because passengers are at risk, as they were in Madrid on 3/11. The shipping of hazardous
material is a looming problem. Chlorine, for example, is routinely shipped
in tank cars across the United States. Railway routes and the location of in-
dustries that use chlorine put these cargoes in close proximity to populous
areas. The Department of Homeland Security estimates that the detonation of one of these chlorine containers would kill 17,500 and injure
100,000.[36] Yet despite its own calamitous assessment of the risk and consequence of such an event, DHS continues to rely on the voluntary cooperation of the rail industry to reroute hazardous cargoes and make them
harder for terrorists to convert into a hell on wheels for an American city.
The security for passenger rail is shortchanged as well, with only $200
million having been allocated to it in fiscal year 2004 and no serious attempt being made to develop screening procedures.

Richard Falkenrath, President Bush's former deputy homeland security
adviser, told the *Washington Post* in November 2004 that "there's no area of
homeland security in which the administration has made more progress
than bioterrorism and none where we have further to go."[37] This is a sobering statement, in view of the accelerating availability of microbiology

technologies, jihadist interest in biological weapons, and the swift and stealthy way pathogens can spread before they are detected.[38] Unfortunately, Falkenrath is correct. There is no single government agency responsible for our bioterrorism defenses, and the White House has yet to play a commanding role. Blurred lines of authority between DHS and the Department of Health and Human Services have led to uncertainty about who would be the "lead agency" in a bioterror emergency. Apart from the scattered nature of the effort to develop detection devices and vaccines, American hospitals as well as state and local health agencies are not getting the resources they need to prepare for a biological attack, whether by ensuring that the large number of necessary beds will be available, distributing medication, or inoculating huge numbers of citizens clamoring for help. Perhaps the Chertoff reorganization will help, but it is too soon to say. Intra-governmental simulations of a crisis, where officials play the roles of cabinet members, have shown that the administration does not have a clear idea about how to cope with the massive exodus from stricken areas that could follow an attack. These impediments have existed for a decade, but nearly four years after 9/11 they should have been tackled.

This is not to say the administration is doing nothing. Funding has grown hugely.[39] But the problems are as much about organizational priorities as they are about budgets. One federal official involved in biodefense told reporters that "this issue has completely fallen through the cracks . . . no part of the federal government can deal with mass casualties." Shelley Hearne, the executive director of The Trust for America's Health, which is trying to get the crucial connections between federal and state governments untangled, cites "a lack of an overarching federal game plan in biodefense . . . nobody's in charge." There is just one player who can ensure that the system works when federal and state communications have broken down, intragovernmental lines of authority are confused, and industry needs to be brought into the picture: the president. Getting biodefense right means an engaged White House.

Port security offers the last chance to stop a weapon of mass destruction, or parts of such a weapon, from getting into the country. The number of containers entering the country is huge—as many as 9 million in 2004. Of these, 95 percent are not inspected. Whether this frequency of inspection would deter a terrorist group from entrusting their fissile material to a container ship bound for an American port is hard to say. But the odds of getting through are fairly good. And they will probably remain favorable, since the cost of securing U.S. ports will cost $7.3 billion over ten years—far exceeding the funds provided. Only $441 million has been distributed thus far to selected ports, and the total amount requested for fiscal year 2005 was $46 million. The failure to grapple with this problem is surprising, because at least some senior officials understand the seriousness of the risks involved. Robert C. Bonner, the combative commissioner of Customs and Border Protection, called the containers "the potential Trojan horse of the 21st century," saying that "a 40-foot container loaded with ammonium nitrate would create a huge blast 10 to 20 times that of the Oklahoma City bombing. But the sum of all fears is a 'nuke-in-a-box.' "[40]

The Container Security Initiative, under which cargoes are inspected in foreign ports before they depart for the United States, is a superb concept, but it lacks the kinds of arrangements that would enable U.S. officials to test whether foreign countries are complying with requirements and that would induce shippers to adopt the technical fixes that would make their containers tamper-proof. So far, there is also no workable plan to include ports in poor countries, from which terrorists are most likely to ship their cargoes.

The prevailing joke in Washington about this program is "Trust, don't verify," because only 597 of the 5,000 companies whose applications to the program have been accepted have actually been checked out. Customs authorities do not know whether the remaining 88 percent of "cleared" companies are taking the required measures. Senator Susan Collins, the Maine Republican who chairs the Homeland Security and Government Affairs Committee, detected the paradox inherent in this arrangement. "It is very troubling to me," she said. "If in fact it is a hollow program, then oddly enough that increases our vulnerability." Responding to the avalanche of skepticism directed at the program, Kristi M. Clemens, assistant commissioner at Customs and Border Protection, struck a rhetorical stance: "Are we perfect? . . . No."[41]

PROTECTING AMERICA'S CITIES, as well as critical infrastructure and key assets, amount to what the military calls "point defense." These are the searchlights, minefields, barbed-wire fences, and machine-gun nests that provide the last-ditch defense of an exposed position. As any soldier knows, it is better to counter the enemy well before he can test your point defenses. If the enemy gets that far, you're in trouble and your back is to the wall. In the homeland security domain, the tool that keeps the adversary at bay, well away from our point defenses, is intelligence about the enemy's identity, capabilities, actions, and intentions. Within our borders we depend largely on the FBI to acquire and interpret this intelligence and use it to prevent the enemy from getting a foothold in this country. The Bureau cannot collect all of this information itself. It must rely in some cases on what the CIA learns both overseas and at home and on data collected at the borders by immigration and customs authorities. Just as important, it must rely on the tens of thousands of beat cops on the streets of American cities for information that might be crucial to the disruption of enemy cells.

Before 9/11, the FBI essentially failed to do its job.[42] It is failing again, despite the intentions of Director Mueller and his attempts to reform the Bureau without restructuring it. The 9/11 Commission had already pointed to "gaps between some of the announced reforms and the reality in the field."[43] These gaps have not narrowed. The Bureau's culture remains committed to law enforcement, not intelligence gathering, and to combating crime rather than countering terrorist conspiracies. Power belongs to special agents from the criminal division who preside over the fifty-six field offices distributed throughout the United States. For the most part, their responsibilities are driven by the crime-busting needs of the localities where they are based. It is therefore not surprising that they insist that "bin Laden is never going to Des Moines."[44] In addition, dealing with crime is better for one's career at the FBI, where accomplishments that are easily measured—for example, the number of arrests an agent makes—count toward promotion, while the murkier tasks involved in counterterrorism do not lend themselves as easily to this box-checking process. Counterterrorism is therefore unlikely to migrate to the top of the typical agent's "to do" list.

Neither will intelligence analysis. In order to detect the formation of jihadist networks in the United States, infiltrate cells, and disrupt conspiracies, investigators need analytical support. This is important because

agents themselves do not have time, specialized knowledge, or skills to assemble all the scraps of information available to the FBI from many diverse sources into a coherent narrative. This can be done well only by
analysts with good language skills, a deep understanding of the way
the enemy thinks and operates, and close ties to analysts in other agencies,
especially the CIA, with whom they can compare notes and "hand off" intelligence targets. The FBI has had a hard time attracting and keeping such
analysts, however, because analysts have no status in its insular and hier-
archical culture, because they are not law enforcement officers. No gun, no
badge, no respect. John Gannon, an experienced CIA officer who was the
head of the National Intelligence Council from 1996 to 2001, puts it this
way: "If you're not an agent, you are furniture." He told the successor body
to the 9/11 Commission in June 2005 that the FBI "has not made an adequate investment" in a cadre of analysts who would have equal stature
within the Bureau.[45]

This is not merely the impression of one respected senior intelligence official. In May 2005, the FBI inspector general released a report on the treatment of analysts that verged on satire. Analysts, according to the report,
were made to spend much of their time on "escort, trash and watch duty . . .
as the name implies, escort duty is following visitors, such as contractors,
around the FBI office to ensure that they do not compromise security. Trash
duty involves collecting all 'official trash' to be incinerated. Watch duty involves answering phones."[46] All in all, the report described the work assigned to analysts as "demeaning," including repair jobs or doing simple
Internet searches or other tasks that, one analyst said, "don't require a college
education." Dismay over this is bipartisan. Senator Charles E. Grassley, Republican from Iowa, who sits on the Judiciary Committee, says, "The fact
that these experts who are supposed to be analyzing terrorist information
are taking out the trash or answering phones 50 percent of the time doesn't
seem to be a good use of anybody's talents in helping the FBI reach the highest standards." He concluded, "Little more than a dent has been made in the
FBI's analytical program in the 3½ years since September 11."[47]

The FBI's attempts to expand its analytical corps have not gotten off
the ground. Director Mueller has boasted about the 380 analysts the
bureau has hired since 2001—part of what the FBI's assistant director

called, without irony, "an unprecedented transformation"—but neglected to mention that 291 abandoned their positions during that period and most left the Bureau.[48] This is sensible behavior on the analysts' part given the burgeoning demand for this sort of talent throughout the national security bureaucracy. Why be abused when you can get respect at another agency, along with professional training that the FBI—according to the inspector general—has been unable and unwilling to provide?

Lacking its own analytical capability geared to the terrorist threat against America, the FBI should be cultivating cooperative ties to agencies that have an analytical capacity. In some ways, it has. Joint operations with the CIA have increased and the two agencies have worked together on "hard target" countries.[49] Nonetheless the perennial competition overseas between the CIA and the FBI continues, complicating recruitment of sources and creating problems with foreign governments. According to the 2005 report of the National Commission on Intelligence Capabilities, "Both agencies agree that lack of coordination has jeopardized ongoing intelligence activities."[50] This commission also reported that "officials from the CIA's Counterterrorism Center . . . have difficulty tracking down and obtaining information about terrorist cases after they hand them off to the FBI. . . . The failure of CIA and FBI to cooperate and share information adequately on such cases could potentially create a gap in the coverage of these threats, like the one the September 11 attack plotters were able to exploit."[51] The report highlights the efforts by the FBI to impede lawful information gathering by the CIA within the United States to retaliate for the CIA's control over source recruitment overseas, where conditions are obviously far more fraught than they are at home. In the commission's terse assessment, the FBI's proposals "are overly burdensome and counterproductive to effective intelligence gathering."[52]

Given these obstacles to coordinated intelligence collection and analysis, the ability of agents to reach into the FBI's rich case files to correlate emerging leads with archived information would be crucial. Unfortunately, it cannot be done. In the months following 9/11, Congress gave the FBI a blank check to replace its archaic and barely functional computers with an up-to-date system. This problem had plagued the few agents in the FBI that took the jihadist threat seriously, including John O'Neill, its head al Qaeda hunter until he ran afoul of the feckless director, Louis Freeh.[53] Thus far, the FBI has spent $581 million and is still not close to having a functioning system. Hardware purchases have been conducted smoothly, and secure communications networks have been set up to permit internal communications as well as communications with a small number of counterparts in other intelligence agencies. Unfortunately, the key software component of the new system, Virtual Case File, will have to be scrapped after an expenditure of $170 million because it does not work. The purpose of the software, which has been in development for about three years, was to enable agents and analysts to manage records, evidence, and other stored material and to collaborate on documents. This sort of automated access to case files is vital to "connecting the dots." Not unexpectedly, no one has taken the blame for this gargantuan waste.[54]

Faced with these cultural, organizational, and technological problems, the FBI is confined to picking the low-hanging fruit, which has resulted in the poor investigative results mentioned in chapter 5.[55] This reliance on a "round up the usual suspects" approach to counterterrorism is alienating Muslims without advancing our effort to find and dismantle terrorist cells that might be forming in the United States. The instrument of choice is immigration law, which is widely skirted by many entrants to the United States, including those from the Muslim world. This approach reduces the need for solid intelligence on the threat, or sophisticated investigative techniques, even as it sharply reduces the government's need to show that the individuals detained are guilty of a terrorism-related offense. There is no question that this tactic can and should be applied where there is good evidence that an individual is affiliated with a terrorist group, but where a trial would entail the disclosure of valuable intelligence. The problem is that it is used indiscriminately, in broad sweeps that delegitimize counterterrorism activities in precisely the community whose support Washington should be cultivating. This is a case where tactical experience endangers our strategic goals.[56]

These conditions will not be remedied overnight. Bassam Yousef, an FBI agent fluent in Arabic and an expert on Middle Eastern culture and politics, sued the FBI in 2004 for having sidelined him after 9/11, just when his rare skills would have made him useful. The trial testimony has highlighted the stubborn nature of the FBI's problems. In spurning

Yousef, who was described by the former CIA terrorism expert Dan Byman as "one of the government's most skilled terrorism fighters," senior FBI managers were working at cross-purposes to Mueller's pledge (at budget hearings in 2002) that "the FBI's shift toward terrorism prevention necessitates the building of a national level expertise and body of knowledge." Worse, it soon became clear that the FBI systematically downplayed knowledge of the Middle East and terrorism in the process of selecting, promoting, and deploying its senior counterterrorism managers. Asked about his own knowledge of these subjects, Gary Bald, the executive assistant FBI director in charge of counterterrorism, replied, "I wish that I had it. It would be nice," adding that "it is certainly not what I look for in selecting an official for a position in a counterterrorism position." According to the Associated Press, which obtained the testimony in the trial, Bald was not alone. FBI senior managers did not know that there was a difference between Sunni and Shiite Muslims, while at the top tier of management, officials did not know the most basic facts about al Qaeda.

At the same time, other FBI managers saw things differently. Paul Vick, a recently retired senior manager, conceded in testimony that Bassam Yousef had "many skills that were badly needed" after 9/11 and that the FBI's treatment of him was "inappropriate and a waste of a very important human resource." Nonetheless, it remains the case that many FBI officers, in the words of Dan Byman, "lack the skills to work with foreign governments or even their U.S. counterparts" when it comes to counterterrorism. Even Dale Watson, who headed the FBI's counterterrorism operation before and after 9/11, testified that he could not remember any discussion among senior managers about the skills or training that agents involved in counterterrorism might need. From Watson's perspective, terrorism was a crime, to be investigated like any other crime: "A bombing case is a bombing case," he said. "A crime scene in a bank robbery case is the same as a crime scene, you know, across the board."[57]

ALTHOUGH THE STORY in homeland security has been one of under-performance and dissipated energies, in some areas of counterterrorism operations, the Bush administration has been overly zealous. Perhaps the most obvious case involves the operations at the detention center at Guantánamo in Cuba, where approximately 600 detainees are kept in a legal gray zone, without real recourse to lawyers or a functioning judicial system. The problem of how to treat captured terrorists is a real one, but, as one senior intelligence official put it, the damage to America's reputation abroad, especially among Muslims, "so far outweighs the counterterrorism benefits in terms of intelligence gains" that keeping the detainees there no longer makes sense. Guantánamo has become a word that arouses rage for millions of Muslims, and in that sense, it is not serving our national security.

Another area in which the administration's aggressive stance is undercutting our broader efforts is its conduct of the intelligence operations known as renditions. Here, too, the approach has been so unrestrained that it has caused a public outcry not only in the Muslim world but also among America's allies and the American public. Renditions have historically been carried out for a number of purposes, but in this context, a rendition is the transfer of an individual involved in terrorist activities from one country to another without that person being formally extradited. There are a number of different forms of renditions. In 1995, Ramzi Yousef was apprehended by a group of American and Pakistani law enforcement officers in Islamabad and flown immediately to the United States, where he stood trial for his role in the first World Trade Center bombing. The government of Pakistan agreed to have Yousef moved in this way without legal proceedings, as it has done in many cases involving terrorists, out of a recognition that holding someone like Yousef for a protracted period of time would be politically difficult and the legal outcome would be uncertain. A second class of renditions involves the United States assisting in the transportation of someone involved in terrorist activity from one country to another, without the individual ever coming to America. Here, again, the transfer is agreed to by the host country and the destination country. A third class is called "extraordinary" rendition. There has been a great deal of misunderstanding of renditions, and many journalists have referred to all renditions as extraordinary. In fact, extraordinary renditions are the rarest of all, and involve an individual being removed from a country without the approval of a host government. Prior to 9/11, no extraordinary rendition was ever conducted, although if bin Laden had been captured in Afghanistan and brought back to face trial, the operation would have involved an extraordinary rendition.

Rendition is an invaluable tool. In the latter half of the 1990s, the use of renditions to third countries was one of the most important innovations by the intelligence community. Former CIA Director George Tenet has said that before 9/11, seventy suspected terrorists were rendered, and these actions undoubtedly thwarted a number of plots in the making.[58] U.S. courts have approved of the practice of rendition, and at least during the 1990s, renditions were overseen by the White House and a wide array of lawyers in different agencies, including the Defense Department, whose aircraft were occasionally used. In a perfect world, we would not need renditions. But the practice reflects the reality that some countries have poor or non-functioning judicial systems, and that a particular government's desire to avoid terrorist attack and cooperate with the United States needs to be shielded from domestic political pressure.

In the pre-9/11 period, the United States worked to ensure that it was living up to its laws and values in the rendition process. No one was rendered to any country that did not have an indictment or warrant or other legal proceeding of some kind against that person. The U.S. government required assurances from the governments to whom individuals were rendered that they would be treated in accordance with international human rights standards, and U.S. officials evaluated the practices of these countries to make certain their assurances were reliable. As one former CIA lawyer put it, "We never sent someone to a country where they would be tortured. We didn't do business with those people—it was off the table." Because the United States has ratified the United Nations Convention Against Torture, it is the law of the land, and sending someone to a country that practices torture would be, prima facie, a violation of the law.

After 9/11, the pace of renditions increased dramatically, according to intelligence officials. These operations are highly secretive, and it is difficult from outside the government to know what standards are being applied, though the president has stated that the United States does not condone torture in any way.[59] Nonetheless, press accounts now cast doubt on his assertion. There have been many allegations that individuals who were rendered were tortured, and the case of Maher Arar raises the most questions. A Syrian-born Canadian citizen, Arar was changing planes at New York's Kennedy Airport during a trip from Tunisia to Montreal when he was detained by U.S. authorities. He was then sent to Jordan for interrogation and then on to Syria, where he claims he was beaten. He was released after a year in custody by the Syrians, who evidently determined that he was not a terrorist, and he has returned to Canada. The seizure of Arar caused the Canadian government to protest, and his transfer to Syria, a country with an appalling record on human rights violations and torture, raises significant questions about whether Washington still abides by its obligations under the Torture Convention. "Before 9/11, I don't remember ever sending anyone to Syria," says the former CIA lawyer, who adds, "if they [the administration] are sending people to Syria now, yes, they are violating the Torture Convention."

There is a growing possibility that understandable public revulsion at abuses in renditions could result in the curtailment of the program by Congress. In the first half of 2005, Democrats repeatedly called for an investigation of rendition policy, and if many cases of abuse are uncovered, there will be pressure to get the United States out of this business. This would be a major loss and have a crippling effect in the fight against terror. It is easy to imagine the effect on those around the world who already question the legitimacy of this fight; it will be devastating if those doubts spread in America as well.

THE SEARCH FOR security at home is not impossible. But several conditions must be met if we are to succeed.

• *White House leadership.* With a strong staff, the president can set priorities and see that they are implemented. In the post–9/11 world, the president's assessment of the threat can still garner public and congressional support for these priorities.

• *Control over fissile material.* Terrorist use of a nuclear or radiological device could gravely damage social cohesion and political stability, especially given the carnage a nuclear yield would inflict on an American city. This threat makes it absolutely vital that errant fissile material be kept out of the United States. It also requires that such material, especially plutonium, be made unusable for weapons purposes. Russia, which has large quantities, would be a prime source for weapons fuel, but a deal to help them modify their plutonium was stymied by Undersecretary of State

John Bolton, who held up the deal (presumably with the support of the White House) by insisting that Moscow agree to accept legal liability for contingencies beyond Russian control. That a bargain so central to American security was blocked for so long and for so trivial a reason is incredible.[60] Control over fissile material is an urgent nonproliferation issue that demands adequate funding, active American diplomacy, and cooperation with other countries.[61]

• *Control of borders and ports.* The confusion that has characterized our efforts to know who and what enters the United States is not irremediable.

• *Prepare now for biological attack.* Deploy effective early warning systems and help states, local authorities, and health care delivery systems to prepare to manage such an attack. Much work has been done, but the state of our preparedness is woefully incomplete. With White House leadership, standards for state and local health care and emergency services can be developed and enforced. Only this will ensure that the system can cope with a crisis, should one occur.

• *Develop aviation defenses against missile attack.* We need to make up for lost time in learning more about the vulnerability of passenger aircraft to the threat of shoulder-fired missiles and deploying the most appropriate on-board defensive systems.

• *Control general aviation and remotely piloted aircraft.* Non-scheduled aircraft and remotely piloted planes can be turned into weapons. The gap in America's radar coverage below 3,000 feet needs to be closed and should be the responsibility of the Pentagon, not the FAA. Given the vested interests involved and the complexity of the dangers, this will require top-level attention.

• *Protect cyber systems.* The White House must direct the DHS to work closely with industry to develop the right kind of protection for these vulnerable but essential networks. In the latest reorganization of the DHS in 2005, this pivotal function was being downgraded. This is a strategic blunder.

• *Professionalize domestic counterterrorism.* As a country, we need a strong cadre of counterterrorism professionals to disrupt conspiracies and keep us safe. This requires a more elaborate set of skills than the investigative and managerial techniques that the FBI possesses.

• *Cultivate the cooperation of American Muslims.* Clumsy, ill-informed law enforcement, if it persists, will eventually try the patience of American

Muslims and perhaps even erode their patriotism. This is something that as a society we cannot afford.

• *Stop reorganizing.* Each time we re-jigger our bureaucracy, we diminish its focus while fooling ourselves that reformatting means better performance. The alternative to perpetual reorganization is the establishment of consistent, clear objectives and presidential leadership in pursuit of those objectives.

IN 1943, THE U.S. war production effort was a complete shambles. The military services were placing orders without coordinating with one another or with the War Department, production priorities were nonexistent, and there was no agreement on a sustainable balance between civilian consumption and military needs. Hearings chaired by Senator Harry S. Truman of Missouri highlighted these problems for an anxious public. Truman's instinct was to create a new government department to introduce order into the prevailing chaos. President Franklin D. Roosevelt's reaction was not to create a bigger bureaucracy. Instead, he looked to his good friend James F. Byrnes, a former senator and Supreme Court justice, to set up a small office in the West Wing of the White House. The space had only to be large enough to accommodate Byrnes himself and a staff of ten. Roosevelt issued an executive order establishing the Office of War Mobilization, appointed Byrnes as the director, and authorized him to take virtually whatever action he thought best for the purposes of mobilization and to issue directives to departments and agencies to carry out these actions. Roosevelt also explicitly obligated the heads of the departments to carry out Byrnes's directives. He wrote a letter to Byrnes, in which he said, "Your decision is my decision, and there is no appeal. For all practical purposes you will be assistant president."

With President Roosevelt's unequivocal backing, Byrnes used his power to order the service chiefs of staff to change production requirements where he thought it necessary, to command the Selective Service Board to raise the maximum draft age, and to cajole union leaders, industrial managers, and state and local politicians to work productively with one another and the federal government. By making clear to his cabinet that resistance to Byrnes was tantamount to submitting a resignation letter to the White House, Roosevelt empowered Byrnes to galvanize the war effort and help put America on the road to victory.[61]

Roosevelt grasped that the war could not be won solely by troops in the field. The home front was crucial and in some ways more complicated. True public-private partnerships were required, while every action had political reverberations at the local level and therefore in Washington as well. Consequently, Roosevelt committed his full prestige to the mobilization effort, picked the best man to manage it, and gave him the authority of the Oval Office to do what needed to be done. In contrast, the Bush administration's belief that striking terrorists in Iraq would remove the threat to Americans at home led the White House to leave the complex political and organizational challenges of the home front to officials without the necessary stature and authority. The result was lost opportunity and continued vulnerability.

11

FAITH AND WAR

Speaking in the ballroom of New York City's Sheraton Hotel in June 2005, Karl Rove, the president's top political adviser and deputy chief of staff, addressed himself to the subject of terrorism. The event was the annual dinner of the state's Conservative Party, and a huge American flag was fully extended across the wall behind Rove. With Governor George Pataki and Mayor Michael Bloomberg at the dais, Rove offered his characterization of how the two sides of the American political spectrum had responded to the attacks that had claimed nearly 3,000 lives just a few miles south of the midtown ballroom. "Conservatives," Rove said, "saw the savagery of 9/11 and the attacks and prepared for war. Liberals saw the savagery of the 9/11 attacks and wanted to prepare indictments and offer therapy and understanding to our attackers."

TO UNDERSTAND WHY the United States has failed to craft a strategy that reduces the long-term danger from terrorism, Rove's comments are an ideal place to start. We do need to attack terrorists with all the determination we would use to wage war. But as recent events have shown, *only* waging war makes for lousy counterterrorism performance. Rove implicitly rejects the basis of strategy, which is to use all the levers of power in pursuit of victory. He insists on an either/or approach to a long-term ideological conflict, for which we will need every asset at our disposal. By extolling the use of the military and, it seems, mocking diplomacy, tactical restraint, and influence, he illustrates the lopsidedness of the American war effort.

Four years after 9/11, the United States seems incapable of adapting to the new threat it faces and achieving a policy mix that will defend against the terrorists of today and prevent the emergence of the terrorists of tomorrow. We have asked the military to do a job for which it is not suited. We have failed to achieve the necessary balance between the offensive and defensive elements of our counterterrorism efforts, and we have failed to get our homeland security program up and running. Above all, we have failed so badly at keeping more Muslims from becoming radicalized, that we have likely prolonged the life of this threat into the distant future. What is missing is not therapy—Rove's partisan gibes are off the mark—but strategy, a plan that carries us from the subway bombs of today through the relationship of America and the Muslim world twenty or thirty years hence.

Why have we gotten this so wrong? After four years of retrograde motion in the fight against terror, it is worth asking whether the nation is capable of producing and implementing such a strategy. There are strong reasons to believe that the roots of the problem do not lie simply in the choices of the administration in office. At the deeper level of culture, we are headed in the wrong direction. We are becoming increasingly averse to acting in a way that distinguishes between the terrorists themselves and those who are at risk of embracing the jihadist ideology. The imperative of isolating the committed terrorists of today from their intended audience and the potential terrorists of tomorrow should be obvious. Yet we have failed, and to understand why, we need to look carefully at the forces ascendant in our society that may be thwarting us.

UNEXPECTED, OUTSIZED EVENTS like 9/11 are often described as having seismic effects on the intellectual life of a society. The word is apt: The conventional wisdom is overturned and large crevices yawn, venting strange ideas and flows of molten emotion. In the case of 9/11, the swift and spectacular murder of 3,000 people swept aside many long-held ideas about the security of the United States, our relationship with the Muslim world, and the nature of American power.

In Washington, the attacks created an opening for neoconservative strategists to push for radical solutions—as if the terrorists' spectacular demonstration of their power demanded a similar demonstration from the American side. At the far end of the spectrum were the recommendations published in December 2003 by Richard Perle, one-time head of the Pentagon's Defense Policy Board and an old friend of Paul Wolfowitz, and David Frum, a former White House speechwriter who had claimed credit for coining the phrase "axis of evil." The unabashedly utopian title of their book, *An End to Evil*, is indicative. Fittingly for two men who had strongly supported the invasion of Iraq, their work evinces little interest in what was new and distinctive about radical Islamist terror. Instead, al Qaeda is just another dark star in the constellation that included Iraq under Saddam Hussein, Iran, Libya, Syria, Saudi Arabia, Hamas, and Hezbollah. For Frum and Perle, the only way to meet the challenge of this new version of the "evil empire" is through the unflinching use of American military might. Running down through their to-do list to win the war on terror, they say of Iran, "The regime must go." The question about Syria is: "Why have we put up with it as long as we have?" The prescriptions are bold but short on detail and disregarded all the ways in which things can go wrong. Their recommendations can be summed up in their argument that "when it is in our power and our interest, we should toss dictators aside with no more compunction than a police sharpshooter feels when he downs a hostage-taker."[1] Perle's oft-repeated suggestion after the invasion of Iraq that American foreign policy could be reduced to the question "Who's next?" will echo in history as an example of how unhinged some became in this period.[2]

In a more serious and, according to administration insiders, more influential vein, the 9/11 attacks created an atmosphere in which the notion of remaking the Middle East through a bold stroke in Iraq could be aired seriously. In these circumstances, the influence of the distinguished historian Bernard Lewis became considerable. Lewis's argument was a variant on Machiavelli's theme of the preferability of fear over love. Speaking on C-SPAN after the 9/11 attacks, Lewis explained, "You can't be rich, strong, successful and loved, particularly by those who are not rich, not strong and not successful. So the hatred is something almost axiomatic. The question which we should be asking is why do they neither fear nor respect us?"[3]

In the period before the invasion of Iraq, Lewis appears to have become that rare thing—a scholar who swayed policy makers in real time, or at a minimum, articulated the reasons for a course of action that they had already chosen. At a time when a serious scholarly debate was taking place about whether America needed to take on an imperial role, Lewis pressed the idea in the White House. He believed that decisive military action in the Middle East would not only restore fear of the United States but would lead to the kind of radical reform the region needed. The notion that culture could be changed in a positive, predictable way by the use of force is something that it is hard to imagine being accepted by political leaders in a world other than the one created by 9/11.

After the debacle of Iraq, it seems unlikely that anyone will embrace that idea again any time soon. Since his reelection, President Bush has dismantled some of the neoconservative infrastructure in the Pentagon. Douglas Feith has resigned. Paul Wolfowitz was appointed president of the World Bank. As this is written, the Bush administration is in the midst of a review of its counterterrorism policy. It may well be that the neoconservative moment has passed, and that the United States will be more reluctant to use its military might as a tool of radical geopolitical transformation. (In light of the burdens of U.S. forces in Iraq, that may not even be possible.) But beneath the coming and going of neoconservatives, deeper currents continue to swirl around American policy making. The currents are among the strongest ones in our society—the religious beliefs that are held by millions of people.

AMERICAN SOCIETY IS evolving in ways that are undermining our efforts to subdue our adversary. As a society that is becoming more religious, we are increasingly inclined to look at our jihadist enemy from a theological perspective, grounded in a particular Christian identity. This is dangerous: The more we see this as a conflict between two faiths, the more likely we are to approach the battle emotionally rather than strategically.

The more we express our war aims and our conception of the adversary in the language of faith, the harder we make it to keep Muslims who are merely angry from siding with the killers—and the more we validate the jihadists' contention that America is waging war against Islam itself.

America has long been known for the ardor of its believers. In contrast to Europe, where religious affiliation has been dwindling, we have long stood out as the country of the most devoted churchgoers. The circumstances of the nation's settlement, and the early rejection of the notion of an established church, cleared the field for multiple religious movements to compete with one another for adherents. Spectacular revival movements from the time of Jonathan Edwards and the "Great Awakening" punctuated the eighteenth century and most of the nineteenth century, spreading religious fervor throughout the expanding frontier. The Massachusetts Bay Colony was founded as something akin to a theocracy, but the variety of different religious groups who settled in the future United States made tolerance a necessity, and out of that necessity grew some of the nation's greatest virtues.

Advances in science, the claims of Darwinism, and the new science of biblical study, which dealt with scripture as another ancient text to be deciphered, took some of the wind out of America's religious sails in the late nineteenth and early twentieth centuries. The Scopes "Monkey Trial" of 1925, in which a Tennessee biology teacher was prosecuted for teaching evolution, made the biblically oriented Christianity of the previous century seem out of step with the direction the country was headed. Many of the faithful did not capitulate to secularism; they turned inward and became an increasingly isolated community, permeated with a sense of embattlement. It was in these circumstances that fundamentalism was born—the term itself was coined to describe Protestant sects in the United States that emphasized returning to the fundamentals of faith and scripture. In the decades after the Scopes trial, American fundamentalists were generally reluctant to press matters of faith in the public sphere.

The vigorous expression of evangelical Protestantism was renewed by the Cold War and the challenge of a godless, communist adversary. The belief that a strong countervailing religious commitment was needed if America was going to survive gave preachers such as Billy Graham a cause to defend and an important political role to play. The social turbulence of

the 1960s loosened sexual mores and produced a subversive countercul-
ture, but it also spurred the desire of many Americans for a clear-cut faith
that would reaffirm traditional values, giving rise in the 1970s and 1980s to
a new politically active religious conservatism in the form of the Moral
Majority and the Christian Coalition. Since then, church attendance has
increased markedly, as has the personal dedication of Americans to a wel-
ter of evangelical and fundamentalist beliefs. About 60 percent of Americans say that religion "plays an important role in their lives" and four out
of five claim to have experienced "God's presence or a spiritual force."
Twenty-two percent report going to church more than once a week, while
three-quarters attend at least once a month. The number of Christians
who "agree strongly" with belief in God, judgment day, and the importance of prayer is increasing. In 1990, about 40 percent of American
Protestants described themselves as "born again"; more recent polls show
that this number has climbed to 50 percent.[4] Churches that emphasize the
individual believer's personal encounter with God and his or her personal
commitment to the faith have been growing if for no other reason than
demographics: Families belonging to conservative Christian denominations produce more children than those belonging to mainline groups.[5]
The growth of these denominations, however, is no longer a feature of
rural, low-income America, as it originally was. Their members are closing
the income and education gap with the mainline Protestant groups and
are establishing a larger presence on Ivy League campuses and in corporate boardrooms. Evangelical Christians are now firmly embedded in the
suburban landscape of America.[6]

As Americans have become more religious, their desire to see religious
values incorporated into public policy has strengthened. In a 2004 survey,
20 percent of respondents said that religion should "very much" influence
public policy; 41 percent think that religion should play "somewhat" of a
role. On the other side, a little more than one out of three rejected the idea
of religion informing policy choices. The results in the realm of domestic
policy are well known: an almost perpetual series of battles over abortion,
vouchers for religious schools, prayer in schools, stem cell research, and
the like. Less recognized is the extent to which foreign policy issues have
drawn the attention of religious groups. The treatment of Christians in
Saudi Arabia, the spread of sex trafficking, and the oppression of Sudanese

Christians and animists by the Muslim government have all drawn the ire of Christian denominations whose lobbying has led to more assertive action by the White House.

The most intense foreign policy focus of the religious right in America today involves the security and territorial integrity of Israel. An important reason for this is the way the doctrine of premillennial dispensationalism envisions the end of history and the thousand-year reign of Jesus Christ on earth.[7] For believers in this doctrine, an important strand of Christian theology that came to the United States from Britain in the late nineteenth century, the emergence of a modern state of Israel was proof of God's covenant with Abraham. This alone confers great metaphysical significance on the Jewish state. Believers look forward to the ingathering of the Jews to Israel and the expansion of Israel's borders to encompass all the land between the Nile and the Euphrates. The Jewish Temple must be reestablished on its original site, which will require that the Dome of the Rock, one of the holiest places in Islam, be razed. All of this is prelude: Israel will be the epicenter of God's intervention in history from this moment on. First, the Rapture will occur, in which the dead whom God wishes to redeem are resurrected, and the living who are selected for salvation are swept from earth to heaven. This is followed by the Second Coming of Christ and the annihilation of the Antichrist in the battle of Armageddon. Since all this action takes place in the territory that was ancient Israel, and since the Jews must rebuild the Temple for this to happen, there must be a Jewish state. So for those who hold this conception of history, what happens to modern Israel is a matter of profound importance—especially whether Israel maintains control over the West Bank, whose conquest in June 1967 is seen as a crucial sign that the process of redemption is under way. If the Jews do not control as much land as possible between Egypt and Iraq, or if they lose control over East Jerusalem, the location of the Temple Mount, then the very possibility of redemption is imperiled.

Obviously, their hopes for the future put dispensationalists at odds with America's avowed intention to seek peace in the Middle East. To strong believers, it is a threat to God's plan to mediate between Palestinians and Israelis in the hope of producing an Israeli withdrawal from the West Bank and the creation of a Palestinian state with its capital in

Jerusalem. Reverend Malcolm Hedding, whose International Christian Embassy is the headquarters for Christian Zionists in Jerusalem, believes that the pursuit of a final status accord between Israelis and Palestinians is pointless. "We stand for the right that all the land God gave under the Abrahamic covenant 4,000 years ago is Israel's," he said. "And He will regulate the affairs of how Israel comes into its allotment which is hers forever." Palestinian statehood is also irrelevant, he continued, since "there is no such thing as a Palestinian."[8] Similar views have become widespread in the United States, in part because of their advocacy in the "Left Behind" series of books by Tim LaHaye and Jerry B. Jenkins, which have set publishing records with sales of 58 million. These novels of the Rapture have, in turn, inspired dozens of millennialist Web sites and numerous television shows. A network of 200 grassroots organizations imbued with LaHaye/Jenkins theology has emerged in America.

Because of belief in the role it will play in the end-time, support for Israel is now common among these evangelicals. In 2003, the International Fellowship of Christians and Jews held an annual Day of Prayer for Israel in 18,000 churches. This group, which claims to have 350,000 donors, has raised $100 million for Israel, $20 million of it in 2003 and 2004. It has also sponsored the immigration to Israel of 100,000 Jews from Russia and Ethiopia to facilitate the ingathering of exiles that is essential for the redemption scenario to unfold. With their well-organized legions, these Christian Zionists enjoy excellent political access. Lobbying is channeled through several groups, including Christians' Israel Public Action Committee (CIPAC) and Stand for Israel, which is headed by the Republican strategist Ralph Reed. Congressional leaders take them seriously. Tom DeLay, the House majority leader, has been a key spokesman in Congress for Christian Zionists, and his role in this regard has become so pivotal that the White House reportedly asked for his clearance on President Bush's June 2002 speech outlining American policy in the Middle East and declaration of support for a Palestinian state. On key issues, DeLay's position is closer to that of the settlers on the West Bank than it is to much of the American Jewish community or, for that matter, to most Israelis. For example, on a visit to Israel, he said of the West Bank, "I don't see occupied territory; I see Israel."[9] Senator James Inhofe of Oklahoma, another legislator close to the Christian Zionists, echoed this conviction, telling his fellow senators that Israel was entitled to the land it occupied, "because God said so."[10] Dick Armey, the former House majority leader, endorsed "transporting" Palestinians to other countries that would take them.[11]

Despite the movement's clout, it does not win all its battles—the June 2002 declaration of U.S. support for a Palestinian state was deplored by the Christian Zionists, despite DeLay's involvement. But even when the movement falls short, it makes an impact. In 2002, when President Bush urged Israeli Prime Minister Ariel Sharon to pull military units out of Jenin, a city in the northern West Bank, the White House received 100,000 e-mails from pro-Israeli evangelicals protesting his intervention.[12] Gary Bauer, the conservative activist and president of the group American Values, recounted that President Bush reversed his criticism of Israel's June 2003 attempt to assassinate the head of Hamas, Abd al-Aziz al-Rantisi, because of pressure from the Christian Zionist lobby. "Several Evangelical leaders took issue with the president. . . . I got thousands of e-mails the next day that were copies of e-mails sent to the president. Within 24 hours, Bush had modified his remarks and emphasized Israel's right to defend itself."[13] When Israel killed al-Rantisi in April 2004, there was no criticism from the White House.

Dispensationalists are not the only source of Christian support for Israel. Richard Land, president of the Southern Baptist Convention's Ethics and Religious Liberty Commission, who rejects premillennial dispensationalism, argues that for many evangelical Christians the issue is their reverence for God's promise to Abraham to give the land of Israel to the Jews forever.[14] Among those evangelicals outside the dispensationalist camp are the Christian Allies Caucus, which includes John Hagee, pastor of the 17,000-member Cornerstone Church in San Antonio; Adrian Rogers, former head of the Southern Baptist Convention; and Edward McAteer, who chairs the Religious Roundtable, a group of influential religious, military, and civic leaders seeking to align public policy with Christian values.[15] The broad base of support for Israel has been underscored by Richard Cizik, vice president for government affairs for the National Association of Evangelicals, who explained to the *Washington Post* that "not all evangelicals agree [on theology], nor are all pro-Israeli positions alike," but evangelicals "are and will remain the staunchest supports of Israel."[16]

Jewish supporters of Israel who are right of center (in Israeli terms) have been delighted by the work of the Christian Zionist lobby, which not only amplifies their voice but helps give them a presence in congressional districts where there are too few Jews to have an electoral impact. Some might wonder about the Israeli government's encouragement of evangelicals, given that they view the return of Jews to Israel as "a stage-setting event for the tribulation period, when God's going to deal again with the Jewish people," in the words of pastor Mark Hitchcock of the Faith Bible Church in Edmond, Oklahoma. The coauthor of a book about end-time scenarios, Hitchcock believes that at the end of days the Jews in Israel will have to accept Christ as the messiah or be massacred. The government in Jerusalem, perhaps not surprisingly, has taken a position of accepting the evangelicals' support now and leaving end-time concerns for later.

Christian support for Israeli control of the West Bank is, to be sure, not the only reason that the Bush administration has steered clear of deep involvement in mediation between Israelis and Palestinians—many factors, including disgust with Yasir Arafat and his reliance on terror and, after Arafat's death, a desire to avoid betting presidential prestige on an uncertain outcome, have affected the policy makers' thinking. But the opposition of a politically vital constituency to a negotiated territorial settlement between Israelis and Palestinians is another powerful deterrent to taking diplomatic risks for a peace deal. Hence, there has been little follow-through on the 2002 endorsement of Palestinian statehood and the Roadmap for Peace, which the United States signed onto along with the European Union, the UN, and Russia. That is regrettable enough. In the larger and more urgent context of America's confrontation with jihadism, the opposition of Christian Zionists to U.S. action that might reduce one of the foremost Muslim grievances is plainly counterproductive.

THE CHALLENGE OF conducting an effective campaign against terror is made even more difficult by the growing polarization of attitudes within the fundamentalist community against all Muslims. In the wake of the 9/11 attacks, some of the leaders of the evangelical movement seized the opportunity to demonize Islam. Franklin Graham, who inherited the mantle of his father, Billy Graham, denounced Islam in August 2002 as a "wicked" and "evil" religion and "a greater threat than anyone's willing to speak." In his book, *The Name*, he characterizes Christianity and Islam as "eternal enemies," two faiths joined in a "classic struggle that will end with the second coming of Christ." Christians and Muslims do not worship the same God, he asserts; "the two are different as lightness and darkness." In his view, "the war on terrorism is just another conflict between evil and The Name," rather than a confrontation between jihadists and the United States.[17] Along similar lines, Pat Robertson, the Christian broadcaster and former presidential candidate, has branded Islam a "violent religion," and the prophet Muhammad as a "wild-eyed fanatic . . . a robber and brigand . . . a killer." Charles W. Colson, the Watergate conspirator who founded the Prison Fellowship, has said that Islam "breeds hatred," and Reverend Jerry Vines, the former president of the Southern Baptist Convention, has denounced Muhammad as a "demon-possessed pedophile," declaring that we should be killing jihadists "in the name of the Lord." Moral Majority founder Jerry Falwell called Muhammad a "terrorist" on *60 Minutes*, for which he subsequently apologized to "any sincere, law-abiding Muslim."[18]

The depth of feeling can be striking. Pastor Ted Haggard, the spiritual leader of the 11,000-member New Life megachurch in Colorado Springs, speaks openly of his dread of a Muslim conquest of America; he told *Harper's* magazine that his "fear is that my children will grow up in an Islamic state." Haggard, who claims to speak with the president or his advisers every Monday, also believes that Christians are embroiled in a spiritual war with evil that is mirrored in the physical contest between good and evil playing out now on the world stage.

Evangelical churches and seminaries today sponsor courses on Islam so that students might know the Muslim enemy and be better prepared to convert Muslims to Christianity. One of the organizations that devises and conducts these courses, the Arab International Ministry, says that it has taught 4,500 American Christians how to evangelize in the Muslim world. Don Richardson, a celebrity among missionaries, gives a good example of the kind of instructional materials on offer in his book, *The Secrets of the Koran*. Richardson's intention is to show that Christianity and Islam are unalterably opposed to each other, and he therefore tries hard to discount those parts of Muslim scripture that might appear consistent with the theology or ethics of Christianity. "The Koran's good verses," he explains, "are like the food an assassin adds to poison to disguise its deadly taste."[19]

It would be deeply unfair to suggest that all evangelical Christians are Islamophobes. Evangelicals are a diverse group, many of whom are tolerant and comfortable in a multiethnic society and in a world of many faiths. Bush's "warmhearted evangelicalism" fits this pattern. For him, the experience of transformation is what counts, rather than doctrine. This sort of evangelicalism differs from the "end time" beliefs of preachers like Pat Robertson. For inclusive evangelicals, like Bush, the experience of God's love is more important than one's denomination. It is why Bush was able to say that Muslims worship the same God he does, and why harderline evangelicals condemned him for saying it. Their covenant with God can shape their lives without necessitating that they press others to follow suit. Although they may believe that ethical behavior is guaranteed only in a world where religious values are present, they may be averse to using government to propagate these values. These believers can accept the need for conciliatory foreign policy initiatives that will help America surmount the challenge of radical Islam. And yet there are many evangelicals who do not fit this description and whose numbers and political activism give them considerable clout with an administration governing a divided country.

At stake is our ability both to craft an effective policy and bring along other nations to work with us. Many Muslims are alienated by the rising tide of religious sentiment and the extent to which it affects, or is believed to affect, Washington's actions. We also risk losing the allies we need to advance reform in the Muslim world and battle the jihadist ideology. As religion has become more a part of American political life, it has become less of a concern in particular for Europeans, who have been voicing increasing discontent on this issue. François Heisbourg, who has directed think tanks in London and Paris and is one of the pillars of the community of scholars and officials who have urged closer transatlantic cooperation, expressed exasperation on this issue during the Iraq crisis of 2003. "The biblical references in politics, the division of the world between good and evil, these are things that we simply don't get," he said. "In a number of areas, it seems that we are no longer part of the same civilization. You have a fairly religious society on one hand and generally secular societies on the other operating with different references. What would unite us does not seem to be in the forefront."[20] Peter Schneider, a German novelist who was one of the lonely few in his country to defend America during the 1991 Gulf War, noted recently, "In the United States a majority of respondents in recent years told pollsters that they believed in angels, while in Europe the issue was apparently considered so preposterous that no one even asked the question." He reflected widespread conviction when he observed, "When American commentators warn about a new fundamentalism, they generally mention only the Islamic one. European intellectuals include two other kinds: the Jewish and Christian variants."[21] The novelist John le Carré, who has been perhaps the most popular British novelist of the past forty years, declared in an article in *The Times* of London that fundamentalist Christianity has pushed America into a period of "historical madness."[22]

Americans do not need to apologize for their beliefs, but we do need to recognize our nation's place in the world and its strategic interests. The urgency of the situation demands that the leadership of America's evangelical churches shepherd their congregations toward an understanding of the perils of the next attack and of Washington's need for freedom of maneuver. Whether this is possible is open to question. As in the Muslim world, where the impulse of salafism has forced political leaders in the Middle East to accommodate a greater role for religion in public policy, clerical authority in the United States is fragmented. The dispersion of pastoral power is such that even if the head of a large denomination—say, the Southern Baptist Convention—were to argue that national security demands a less aggressive assertion of religious prerogatives, he might face real opposition from his fellow religious leaders. But someone has to try, because the alternative is clear. According to the *New York Times,* "At the grass roots of evangelical Christianity, many are now absorbing the antipathy for Islam that emerged . . . with incendiary comments of ministers."[23] The demonization of Islam has reinforced the message.

There is a danger in this, especially since the vilification of Muslims and Islam coincides with the increasingly widespread view that the government should take religious concerns into account when making policy decisions. The blending of these mutually reinforcing trends and the hazards they pose to our strategic interest are already visible in the U.S. military. In January 2003, William G. "Jerry" Boykin, a two-star general in charge of the hunt for Usama bin Laden and other "high value targets," spoke in uniform to a church group in Daytona Beach, Florida. In his remarks, he cast the United States in the role of a "Christian nation" locked in battle with Satan. He shared with his audiences the confidence he felt in combat against a Muslim foe, because, as he explained, "my God was bigger than his." In June, he told another church group in Sandy, Oregon, that the jihadists "will only be defeated if we come to them in the name of Jesus." He added that "George Bush was not elected by a majority of the voters in the United States. He was appointed by God."[24]

In the close community of the U.S. Special Forces, Boykin's patriotism and personal heroism are legend. From the failed Iranian hostage rescue mission in 1980 to later missions in Grenada, Panama, Colombia, and Somalia, he has demonstrated exemplary physical courage and inspired leadership. Yet his remarks caused immense damage to American interests by validating an image of the United States military as a Christian army warring with Muslims in the name of Jesus. For those U.S. officials whose job it was to win Muslim hearts and minds, Boykin was a nightmare. One senior official, who was traveling in the Middle East when the statements were reported, recalled, "It was the worst day of my life. It confirmed their conspiracy theory that the war on terrorism really is a war on Islam."[25] Precisely because such statements have that resonance, they are remembered by Muslim audiences long after the American media have gone on to the next news story. Harold C. Pachios, who serves on the State Department's Advisory Commission for Public Diplomacy, remarked that "if you took a poll in the United States, you might get 1% who know who Gen. Boykin is and what he said. If you took a poll in the Islamic world, a majority would know . . . and they would believe that he was speaking for the U.S. government."[26] Comments like Boykin's, with their overt religious language, are contributing to an evolution in Muslim thinking about America. John Esposito of Georgetown University, a leading expert on the Muslim world, has found "significant interest in the Muslim world in 'this thing called the Christian Right,' which has such an influence on Congress and the administration—and the tendency of those statements has been to reinforce the idea that this may be partly a Christian war."[27]

Perhaps as damaging as Boykin's statements was the fact that he was not immediately fired. However sympathetic one might be for someone who has devoted his life to making America secure, the only way to undo any of the harm would have been to dismiss him immediately. Instead, the Pentagon defended Boykin as a dedicated soldier and distanced itself from his remarks. The episode occurred shortly after Malaysia's former President Mahatir Mohammed had been criticized by President Bush for delivering an anti-Semitic speech at the Organization of the Islamic Conference. Few Americans linked the two events in their minds. Plenty of Muslims did.

Perceptions that the United States is engaged in a Christian crusade have been heightened by the arrival of American missionaries in Iraq. Between 2003 and 2004, nine evangelical churches opened in Baghdad alone. These churches have distributed large quantities of much-needed food and medical supplies as a way to attract people to the evangelicals' message. The food shipments have been accompanied by nearly a million bibles in Arabic. According to Tom Craig, one of missionaries, these evangelicals are in Iraq because "God and the president have given us an opportunity to bring Jesus Christ to the Middle East."[28] The executive administrator of the National Association of Evangelicals, Kyle Fisk, has a more expansive view. "Iraq will become the center for spreading the gospel of Jesus Christ to Iran, Libya, throughout the Middle East. . . . President Bush said democracy will spread from Iraq to nearby countries. A free Iraq also allows us to spread Jesus Christ's teachings even in nations where laws keep us out." This justification for regime change is disconcerting to some in Iraq, like the Shiite leader Sheikh Fatih Kashif Ghitaa, who observed that "Iraqis already see the American occupation as a religious war," and noted that he and his Sunni colleagues were weighing a fatwa against the missionaries. Some missionaries, like Todd Nettleton of the Oklahoma-based Voice of the Martyrs, acknowledge the problems that his activity can cause: "Yes, sharing Christ's love can cause conflict," he told the *Los Angeles Times*, "but the alternative is allowing people to go to Hell."[29]

THE AFFINITIES BETWEEN the views of evangelicals and the administration's response to terrorism need little elaboration. In some respects, the relationship is one of direct and powerful influence. For example, given the risks that missionary activity poses to American objectives in Iraq and the wider Muslim world, the administration might be expected to constrain it. But as John Green of the University of Akron, a distinguished analyst of religious politics in the United States, explained during the 2004 presidential campaign, "Many evangelicals feel war in Iraq is part of a broader religious mission . . . and the Bush campaign [sees the need] to mobilize that bloc. Evangelicals not only vote Republican, they produce a lot of activists that stuff envelopes, make phone calls—they are the grass roots."[30]

More than that, however, there is a deep similarity of worldview between the Bush administration and what may be its largest single constituency. The administration has depicted the fight against terror as a war in which we must exert sufficient will and appropriate force against "evil-doers," a word from the president's Bible-reading—Bush and others seldom use the words *radical Islamists* or *jihadists*. In this rhetoric, the fight against terror is a Manichean struggle. As Bush declared on the campaign stump in 2004, "America will continue to lead the world with confidence and moral clarity."[31] The theme of clear distinctions, of a war between good and evil, has been underscored since 9/11, most prominently in the 2002 State of the Union address, in which Bush divided the world, saying, "Either you are with us or you are with the terrorists."

Such certainties play well among the Christian right, and the effect was visible in the outcome of the 2004 presidential election. In fact, the exit polling suggests that Bush won the election because of the belief that he would handle the problem of terrorism better than his opponent, Senator John Kerry. Terrorism was the top concern of 19 percent of voters, and of that group, 86 percent voted for Bush. Although moral values was cited by even more voters—27 percent—as the most important issue, and the president won that group by a significant margin as well, there was little difference between how Bush was viewed in that regard and the view of him in 2000. What had changed was terrorism, and it seems likely that Bush's "moral clarity" in the war on terror translated into especially strong support among evangelicals.[32] After the election, James C. Dobson, the founder of the organization Focus on the Family and perhaps the most influential evangelical Christian leader in the nation, explained that a values voter was more than someone with a specific position on social issues such as abortion and gay marriage. Instead, it was someone with "a

Christian worldview who begins with the assumption that God is—that he not only exists, but he is the definer of right and wrong, and there are some things that are moral and some things that are immoral, some things that are evil and some things that are good." This clarity "is seen by many of us not as a negative but as a positive," Dobson said. "Here is a man who is simply committed to a system of beliefs."[33] In 2004, Bush won 78 percent of the white evangelical vote, up 10 percentage points from 2000.

The strong emphasis on offensive measures—to the virtual exclusion of defensive ones—also resonates. As Bush has declared so many times, "We're staying on the offensive. We'll strike the terrorists abroad so we do not have to face them here at home."[34] Pastor Ted Haggard communicates much the same message. "I teach a strong ideology of the use of power," he says, "of military might, as a public service." He is for preemptive war because he believes the Bible's exhortations against sin set a preemptive paradigm, and he is for ferocious war, because "the Bible's bloody. There's a lot about blood."[35]

TERRORISM, OF COURSE, is also bloody, and there is no escaping that. But to defeat the jihadists who use it against us, we will need to do more than shed blood. The outlines of what we must do to prevail are increasingly clear. We will need the right resources, organization, and, of course, the right plan. We will also need the right allies, and if we continue to be pulled by the currents shaping American culture today, we will drive away our friends in the West and moderate Muslims around the world. There is, however, a prior choice we need to make: We must decide whether we want a strategy for this conflict or a theology. How much blood will be shed depends at least in part upon that choice.

NOTES

Prologue

1. "Vice President Richard B. Cheney Delivers Remarks at Air Force Association National Conference," FDCH Political Transcripts, Washington, D.C., September 17, 2003.

2. Dana Priest and Spencer Hsu, "U.S. Sees Drop in Terrorist Threats; Al Qaeda Focusing Attacks in Iraq and Europe, Officials Say," *Washington Post*, May 1, 2005, A01.

3. Ivo Daalder, "The Return of Bush's Pre-9/11 Foreign Policy," May 3, 2005, http://www.americanprogress.org/site/pp.asp?c=biJRJ8OVF&b=640713.

4. Dana Milbank and Claudia Deane, "Poll Finds Dimmer View of Iraq War: 52% Say U.S. Has Not Become Safer," *Washington Post*, June 8, 2005; for exit poll data from the election, see CNN, "America Votes 2004: Exit Poll," http://www.cnn.com/ELECTION/2004/pages/results/states/US/P/00/epolls.0.html.

5. "Rumsfeld Warns on China Military. North Korea Seen as Worldwide Threat," June 4, 2005, http://www.cnn.com/2005/WORLD/asiapcf/06/04/rumsfeld.asia.ap/.

6. Thomas L. Friedman, *The World Is Flat: A Brief History of the Twenty-First Century* (New York: Farrar, Straus and Giroux, 2005), 391.

1. Terror's New Recruits

1. *The Koran*, revised translation by N. J. Dawood (London: Penguin, 1999), 43.

2. The details of the Madrid bombings of March 11, 2004, continue to be debated, and no authoritative account yet exists comparable to *The 9/11 Commission Report* in its treatment of the September 11 attacks. We have drawn on numerous sources to reconstruct the events of the period. Chief among them is the superb work of the Spanish daily newspaper *El Pais* and, in particular, its reporter Jose Maria Irujo. Many of the specifics we refer to are detailed in his book *El Agujero* (Madrid: Aguilar, 2005). Other sources include *Time* magazine, *New York Times, Washington Post,* and *Jane's*.

3. Assembly of WEU, The Interparliamentary European Security and Defence Assembly, "The Impact of the Iraq Crisis on Public Opinion in Europe," DOCUMENT A/1838, December 3, 2003, http://www.assembly-weu.org/en/documents/sessions_ordinaires/rpt/2003/1838.html.

4. This conclusion was not shared by the American intelligence community or by the investigators of the 9/11 Commission.

5. The outrage of Spanish Islamists at the authorities' crackdown has been much noted. For example, Reuven Paz, "Qa'idat al-Jihad, Iraq, and Madrid: The First Tile in the Domino Effect?" Project for the Research of Islamist Movements, Special Dispatch, vol. 2, no. 1 (March 13, 2004), http://www.e-prism.org/images/PRISM_Special_dispatch_no_1-2.pdf.

6. Al Jazeera, "Message to Iraqis October 2003," October 19, 2003, http://english.aljazeera.net/NR/exeres/ACB47241-D25F-46CB-B673-56FAB1C2837F.htm.

7. "Aljazeera Airs Purported bin Laden Audiotapes," October 19, 2003, http://www.cnn.com/2003/WORLD/meast/10/18/binladen.tape/.

8. Kanan Makiya and Hassan I. Mneimneh, "Manual for a 'Raid,'" in Striking Terror: America's New War, Robert B. Silvers and Barbara Epstein, eds. (New York: New York Review of Books, 2002), 319–27.

9. Reuven Paz, "A Message to the Spanish People: The Neglected Threat by Qa'idat al-Jihad," Project for the Research of Islamist Movements, Special Dispatch, vol. 2, no. 2 (March 18, 2004), http://www.e-prism.org/images/PRISM_Special_dispatch_no_2-2.pdf.

10. Quoted in Brynar Lia and Thomas Hegghammer, "Jihadi Strategic Studies: The Alleged Al Qaida Policy Study Preceding the Madrid Bombings," Studies in Conflict and Terrorism 27 (2004): 355–75.

2. From New York to Baghdad

1. "UK Bin Laden's Warning," October 7, 2001, http://news.bbc.co.uk/1/low/world/south_asia/1585636.stm.

2. The Pew Research Center, "America's Image Further Erodes; Europeans Want Weaker Ties but Post-War Iraq Will Be Better Off, Most Say," March 18, 2003, http://people-press.org/reports/display.php3?ReportID=175.

3. Al Jazeera, December 27, 2001.

4. Paul L. Hastert, "Operation Anaconda: Perception Meets Reality in the Hills of Afghanistan," Studies in Conflict and Terrorism 28, no. 1 (January–February 2005).

5. David Cook, "Radical Islam After the Taliban," in Terrorism and Political Violence 15 (Spring 2003): 31–56.

6. Ibid., 52–53.

7. Some of those apprehended were neither terrorists nor irregulars. See, for example, Greg Miller, "Many Held at Guantanamo Not Likely Terrorists," Los Angeles Times, December 22, 2002.

8. When Frances Fragos Townsend was "asked to elaborate, she said she would have to consult a list. White House spokeswoman Erin Healy referred follow-up questions to the FBI. Spokesmen for the FBI, the National Security Council, and the CIA did not respond to multiple telephone calls and e-mails." Barton Gellman and Dafna Linzer, "Afghanistan, Iraq: Two Wars Collide," Washington Post, October 22, 2004.

9. Secretary of Defense Donald Rumsfeld obliquely confirmed this in a press conference. Douglas Jehl and Eric Schmitt, "U.S. Suggests al Qaeda Cell in Iran Directed Saudi Bombings," New York Times, May 21, 2003.

10. Alison Pargeter, "The Islamist Movement in Morocco," *Terrorism Monitor* 3, no. 10 (May 19, 2005); Richard C. Paddock and Sebastian Rotella, "Experts See Major Shift in Al Qaeda's Strategy," *Los Angeles Times,* November 19, 2003.

11. Paddock and Rotella, "Experts See Major Shift."

12. Zahid Hussain and Jay Solomon, "Al Qaeda's Changing Face," *The Far Eastern Economic Review,* August 26, 2004; BBC Monitoring International Reports, "Arrested Pakistani Militants Reveal Plan of Attacking US Consulate, Other Targets," July 20, 2004.

13. Daniel Benjamin, "Saddam Hussein and Al Qaeda Are Not Allies," *New York Times,* September 30, 2002.

14. BBC News World Edition, "Bin Laden Tape," February 12, 2003, http://news.bbc.co.uk/2/hi/middle_east/2751019.stm.

15. BBC News World Edition, " 'Al Qaeda' Statement," May 21, 2003, http://64.233.161.104/search?q=cache:B5_1dSO2bRsJ:news.bbc.co.uk/2/hi/middle_east/3047903.stm+Zawahiri+and+Iraq+and+transcript&hl=en.

16. World Islamic Front Statement, "Jihad Against Jews and Crusaders," February 23, 1998, http://www.fas.org/irp/world/para/docs/980223-fatwa.htm.

17. BBC News World Edition, "Bin Laden Tape: Text," February 12, 2003, http://news.bbc.co.uk/2/hi/middle_east/2751019.stm.

18. James Bennet, "The Mystery of the Insurgency," *New York Times,* May 15, 2005, http://www.nytimes.com/2005/05/15/weekinreview/15bennet.html.

19. Ibid.

20. "U.S. Secretary of State Colin Powell Addresses the U.N. Security Council," transcript, February 5, 2003, http://www.whitehouse.gov/news/releases/2003/02/20030205-1.html.

21. The Central Intelligence Agency determined that there is no conclusive evidence Saddam Hussein's regime provided safe haven to Mr. Zarqawi in the months leading up to the American invasion of Iraq. This assessment follows a similar finding in June by the 9/11 Commission, which concluded that there was no "collaborative relationship" between al Qaeda and Saddam Hussein's regime. See also Don Van Natta Jr., "Who Is Abu Musab al-Zarqawi?," *New York Times,* October 10, 2004.

22. Toby Dodge, "Iraq's Future: The Aftermath of Regime Change," Adelphi Paper 372, The International Institute for Strategic Studies, London, 2005.

23. Iraqi Coalition Casualty Count, accessed at http://icasualties.org/oif/.

24. Andrew Cordesman, "Iraq's Evolving Insurgency," accessed at http://www.csis.org/features/050512_IraqInsurg.pdf.

25. Cf. http://www.iraqbodycount.net/.

26. Gilbert Burnham, Richard Garfield, Jamal Khudhairi, Riyadh Lafta, and Les Roberts, "Mortality Before and After the 2003 Invasion of Iraq: Cluster Sample Survey," *The Lancet,* 364, no. 9448 (2004).

27. Institute for the Analysis of Global Security, "Iraq Pipeline Watch: Attacks on Iraqi Pipelines, Oil Installations, and Oil Personnel," June 16, 2005, http://www.iags.org/iraqpipelinewatch.htm.

28. Energy Information Administration, "Iraq Country Brief," June 8, 2005, http://www.eia.doe.gov/emeu/cabs/iraq.html.

29. Energy Information Administration, "OPEC Revenues Fact Sheet," June 2005, http://www.eia.doe.gov/emeu/cabs/opecrev.html.

30. Caryle Murphy and Bassam Sebti, "Power Grid in Iraq Far from Fixed: New Government Inherits Huge Task," *Washington Post,* May 1, 2005.

31. Daniel Benjamin and Gabriel Weimann, "What the Terrorists Have in Mind," *New York Times,* October 27, 2004.

32. "Intissar al-Islam," http://www.ansarnet.ws/vb/showthread.php?t=14236. The authors are grateful to Reuven Paz for drawing our attention to this document. The mood of the insurgents and those who follow their progress in Iraq is, like that of any group in the midst of a struggle, prone to swing. After the Iraqi elections on January 30, 2005, which were reported as a positive event in the foreign media and a victory for democracy in Iraq, the insurgents were disgruntled. But in the spring, as elections gave way to a months-long logjam over appointing a cabinet, and a wave of bombings cost hundreds of lives, the high spirits returned.

33. ABC News, "This Week with George Stephanopoulos," transcript, September 19, 2004.

34. Mazzeti Mark, "Insurgents Are Mostly Iraqis, U.S. Military Says; Bush, Kerry and Allawi Have Cited Foreign Fighters as a Major Security Problem," *Los Angeles Times,* September 28, 2004.

35. ABC News, Daily Investigative Report, "News Report: Researcher Estimates over 2500 Saudis Left for Jihad in Iraq since 2003," May 9, 2005.

36. Carol J. Williams, "Suicide Attacks Rising Rapidly; Increasingly, the Bombers Are Iraqis Instead of Foreign Infiltrators," *Los Angeles Times,* June 2, 2005.

37. Ibid.; Dan Eggen and Scott Wilson, "Suicide Bombs Potent Tools of Terrorists," *Washington Post,* July 17, 2005.

38. Bryan Bender, "Study Cites Seed of Terror in Iraq," *Boston Globe,* July 17, 2005.

39. Ibid.

40. Mahan Abedin, "Post-Election Terrorist Trends in Iraq," *Terrorism Monitor* 3, no. 5 (2005), http://www.jamestown.org/publications_details.php?search=1&volume_id=411& issue_id=3258&article_id=2369397.

41. Williams, "Suicide Attacks Rising Rapidly."

42. Amatzia Baram, "Who Are the Insurgents?: Sunni Arab Rebels in Iraq," United States Institute of Peace, Special Report 134 (April 2005), 10, accessed at http://www.usip .org/pubs/ specialreports/sr134.pdf.

43. Ibid.

44. Mahan Abedin, "Anbar Province and Emerging Trends in the Iraqi Insurgency," *Jamestown Terrorism Monitor,* July 15, 2005, http://jamestown.org/terrorism/news/article. php?articleid=2369743.

45. Hannah Allam and Warren P. Strobel, "Amidst Doubts, CIA Hangs on to Control of Iraqi Intelligence Service," Knight Ridder Washington Bureau, May 8, 2005, http://www .realcities.com/mld/krwashington/11597494.htm.

46. "Iraq: Torture Continues at Hands of New Government, Police Systematically Abusing Detainees," Human Rights Watch, Baghdad, January 25, 2005, http://hrw.org/ english/docs/2005/01/26/iraq10053.htm.

47. Abedin, "Anbar Province."

48. That Iraq will become an enclave for terrorists for the long term was slyly confirmed by the National Intelligence Council, the CIA's in-house think tank, whose predictions about what the world will look like in 2020 appear in "Mapping the Global Future." The report observes, in the hedged language that is the vernacular of the intelligence community, "Iraq and other possible conflicts in the future could provide recruitment, training grounds, technical skills and language proficiency for a new class of terrorist who are 'professionalized' and for whom political violence becomes an end in itself." Some of those who participated in writing the study concede that the projection is already true today; they do not believe it will be untrue in fifteen years.

49. It appears the CIA has come to the same conclusion. Douglas Jehl, "Iraq May Be Prime Place for Training of Militants, C.I.A. Report Concludes," *New York Times,* June 22, 2005.

50. Cordesman, "Iraq's Evolving Insurgency."

51. Aqil Jabbar, "Merchant of Doom: Demolitions Expert Who Once Sold Explosives to Fishermen Says Guerrillas Now His Best Customers," Institute for War and Peace Reporting, ICR No. 76, July 28, 2004, http://www.iwpr.net/index.pl?archive/irq/irq_76_4_ eng.txt.

52. Gary Gambill, "Abu Musab al-Zarqawi: A Biographical Sketch," *Terrorism Monitor*, 2, no. 24 (2004), http://www.jamestown.org/publications_details.php?search=1&volume_ id=400&issue_id=3179&article_id=2369019.

53. Sami Yousafzai, Ron Moreau, and Mark Hosenball, "Tale of Two Terrorists," *Newsweek*, International Edition, April 11, 2005, http://msnbc.msn.com/id/7370375/site/ newsweek/.

54. David Ignatius, "Reading the Enemy," *Washington Post*, February 20, 2004.

55. Eric Lipton, "Bin Laden Aide Urged to Attack Outside Iraq," *New York Times*, March 1, 2005.

56. Iraq Survey Group, "Comprehensive Report of the Special Advisor to the DCI on Iraq's WMD," September 30, 2004, http://www.globalsecurity.org/wmd/library/report/ 2004/isg-final-report/.

57. N. Janardhan, "Kuwait Wakes Up to the Face of Militant Islam," *Terrorism Monitor* 3, no. 9 (May 6, 2005).

58. Intelligence and Terrorism Information Center at the Center for Special Studies (CSS), "The Kuwaiti Government's Struggle Against Radical Sunni Islamic Terrorist Supporters of Al-Qaeda," *Special Information Bulletin*, March 13, 2005, http://www.intelligence .org.il/eng/sib/4_05/kuwait.htm.

3. Jihad in the Age of Globalization

1. "U.S. Image Up Slightly, but Still Negative," Pew Global Attitudes Project, June 23, 2005, accessed at http://pewglobal.org/reports/display.php?ReportID=247.

2. Ibid.

3. The Pew findings are not sui generis. They are confirmed by other large-scale polling efforts carried out by Gallup in 2002, the U.S. Department of State in 2004–2005, and the University of Jordan in 2005.

4. Daniel Williams, "Anti-Americanism a Hit with Egyptian Audiences," *Washington Post*, August 20, 2004.

5. CNN, "Los Angeles Airport Shooting Kills 3," July 5, 2002, http://archives.cnn .com/2002/US/07/04/la.airport.shooting/.

6. "The President Will Also Meet with Moderate Muslim Leaders to Pay Tribute to the Tradition of Religious Tolerance in the World's Most Populous Muslim Nation." http:// www.whitehouse.gov/news/releases/2003/10/20031014-4.html.

7. Don Van Natta Jr. and Desmond Butler, "Threats and Responses: Terror Network. Anger on Iraq Seen as New Qaeda Recruiting Tool," *New York Times*, March 16, 2003, 1.

8. Bruce Crumley, Helen Gibson, and Jeff Israely, "After Istanbul, a Wave of Arrests," *Time Europe*, December 8, 2003. Syria has emerged as the hub for outsiders going to fight in Iraq. See Ghaith Abdul-Ahad, "Outside Iraq but Deep in the Fight: A Smuggler of Insurgents Reveals Syria's Influential, Changing Role," *Washington Post*, June 8, 2005, p. A01, accessed at http://www.washingtonpost.com/wpdyn/content/article/2005/06/07/AR20050607 02026.html.

9. Christopher Dickey, "Italy's Sleeper Cells; The Threat of an Al Qaeda Attack There Is Real—and Growing," *Newsweek*, August 20, 2004, accessed at http://www.msnbc.msn .com/id/5772911/.

10. U.S. Congress, Senate, Select Intelligence Committee Hearing: 109th Congress 1st session, Testimony of Porter Goss, February 16, 2005. Elsewhere in the testimony, Goss's efforts not to offend the White House led him into some verbal tangles, as when he declared, "The Iraq conflict, while not a cause of extremism, has become a cause for extremists."

11. Esther Dyson, George Gilder, George Keyworth, and Alvin Toffler, "Cyberspace and the American Dream: A Magna Carta for the Knowledge Age," *Progress and Freedom Foundation,* Release 1.2, August 22, 1994. The introduction notes that "this statement represents the cumulative wisdom and innovation of many dozens of people. It is based primarily on the thoughts of four 'co-authors': Ms. Esther Dyson; Mr. George Gilder; Dr. George Keyworth; and Dr. Alvin Toffler." http://www.pff.org/issues-pubs/futureinsights/fi1.2magnacarta.html.

12. David Talbot, "Terror's Server," *Technology Review,* February 2005.

13. Hamza Hendawi, "Real-life Horror Replaces Porn as Traumatized City's Preferred TV Viewing," Associated Press, September 26, 2004.

14. SITE Institute, trans., "Do Not Stop Slaughters for They Are Cure for the Hearts," December 22, 2004.

15. "Reactions to Sheikh Al-Qaradhawi's Fatwa Calling for the Abduction and Killing of American Civilians in Iraq," The Middle East Media Research Institute, Special Dispatch Series, no. 794, October 6, 2004, http://memri.org/bin/articles.cgi?Page=archives&Area=sd&ID=SP79404.

16. Cf. Daniel Benjamin and Steven Simon, *The Age of Sacred Terror* (New York: Random House, 2002), 38–94.

17. Peter Mandaville, "Digital Islam; Changing the Boundaries of Religious Knowledge?" *SIM Newsletter 2,* International Institute for the Study of Islam in the Modern World, March 1999, accessed at http://www.isim.nl/files/news_2.pdf.

18. Ibid.

19. Talar Nadir, "Kidnap Survivor Recounts Ordeal," *Institute for War and Peace Reporting,* February 24, 2005, http://www.iwpr.net/index.pl?archive/irq/irq_114_1_eng.txt.

20. Ibid.

21. See, for example, bin Laden's video appearance on the eve of the American presidential election.

22. Rajeev Syal, "Cleric Supports Targeting Children," *Sunday Telegraph,* September 5, 2004.

23. John Kelsay, "The New Jihad and Islamic Tradition," *FPRI Wire* 11, no. 3 (October 2003).

24. *Terrorism Monitor,* Jamestown Foundation, vol. 2, no. 14, July 22, 2005. Quotations cited by the Jamestown Foundation are from www.alsakifa.net.

25. Excerpt from www.al-fhd.net[8], Treatise "Ruling Regarding the Use of Weapons of Mass Destruction" [Against the Infidels] in Marie-Helene Boccara & Alex Greenberg, "Islamist Websites and their Hosts Part II: Clerics," Special Dispatch 11, The Middle East Media Research Institute, November 2004, http://memri.de/uebersetzungen_analysen/themen/islamistische_ideologie/isl_website_11_11_04.html.

26. Anonymous, *Imperial Hubris: Why the West Is Losing the War on Terror* (Dulles, Va.: Brassey's Inc., 2004), 154–55.

27. See the "MIPT Terrorism Knowledge Database," which incorporates the RAND Terrorism Chronology 1968–1997, RAND-MIPT Terrorism Incident Database 1998–present, the Terrorism Indictment Database (University of Arkansas), and DFI International's research on terrorist organizations at http://www.tkb.org/Home.jsp.

28. Dan Eggen and Scott Wilson, "Suicide Bombs Potent Tools of Terrorists," *Washington Post,* July 17, 2005.

29. Quran 4:33.

30. Farhad Khosrokhavar, *Suicide Bombers: Allah's New Martyrs*, trans. David Macey (London: Pluto Press, 2005).

31. Intel Center, "Al-Qaeda Targeting Guidance," April 1, 2004, http://www.asisonline .org/newsroom/aq.pdf.

32. The jihadist interest in using information technology to increase its capabilities is widespread. In early 2005, a Yemeni Islamist sheikh named Mohammed al-Moayad was tried in New York for fund-raising for Hamas and al Qaeda—he had been lured to Germany, where he was arrested, by a federal agent posing as someone who was interested in donating $2 million for the jihad. During the trial, prosecutors entered into evidence the transcripts of conversations between al-Moayad and his aide and fellow defendant, Mohammed Zayed, in which he expressed his desire to use the money to buy a set of military training software for Yemeni mujahedin.

33. Abu Obeid al-Qurashi, "America's Nightmares," *al Ansar* magazine, February 13, 2002.

34. Documents related to the British "Operation Contest," an effort to fight radicalism among British Muslims, indicate considerable concern on the part of Her Majesty's Government, noting that extremists "target middle class students and affluent professionals through schools and college campuses," http://www.times-archive.co.uk/onlinespecials/ cabinet1.pdf.

4. Radical Islam's Strategic Depth

1. Petter Nesser, "Jihad in Europe: A Survey of the Motivations for Sunni Islamist Terrorism in Post-millennium Europe," Norwegian Defence Research Establishment, April 13, 2004, p. 9, http://www.mil.no/multimedia/archive/00043/Jihad_in_Europe_43302a.pdf.

2. Daniel Benjamin and Steven Simon, *The Age of Sacred Terror: Radical Islam's War Against America* (New York: Random House, 2002).

3. ICM Muslims Poll, June 2002, accessed at http://www.icmresearch.co.uk/ reviews/2002/guardian-muslims-poll-june-2002.htm; Alan Travis, "The Need to Belong— but with a Strong Faith," *The Guardian,* June 17, 2002, accessed at http://www.guardian .co.uk/religion/Story/0,2763,738814,00.html.

4. Timothy M. Savage, "Europe and Islam: Crescent Waxing, Cultures Clashing," *The Washington Quarterly,* Summer 2004, p. 31.

5. Ibid., "U.S. Image Up Slightly, but Still Negative," The Pew Global Attitudes Project, June 23, 2005, p. 18, accessed at http://pewglobal.org/reports/display.php?ReportID=247.

6. Sebastian Rotella, "Europe's Boys of Jihad," *Los Angeles Times,* April 2, 2005.

7. Ibid.

8. Survey conducted April 3–4, 2002, by CSA Poll Institute and the weekly *Marianne* of 1,000 people aged over 18, accessed at http://www.crif.org/index.php?menu=5&dossier= 33&id_doss=2010&PHPSESSID=c344c; Timothy M. Savage, "Europe and Islam."

9. Jerome Cordelier, "IPSOS-LCI-LePoint Poll: Islam Is a Worry for the French," *Le Point,* May 16, 2003, cited in Timothy M. Savage, "Europe and Islam"; Paul Gallis, "France: Factors Shaping Foreign Policy and Issues in U.S. French Relations," Congressional Research Service, February 4, 2005, accessed at http://www.usembassy.it/pdf/other/ RL32464.pdf.

10. Tom Goeller, "Germans Intolerant of Immigrants," *Washington Times,* January 15, 2005; and Khaled Schmitt, "Islamophobia on Rise in Germany: Study," Islamonline.net, De-

cember 26, 2004, accessed at http://www.islamonline.net/English/News/2003-12/26/article 06.shtml, both citing the 2004 "German Conditions" survey conducted by the University of Bielefeld. "Anti-Muslim Bias 'Spreads' in EU," BBC, March 7, 2005, accessed at http://news .bbc.co.uk/1/hi/world/europe/4325225.stme00e7975de793c83239e4ebe215.

11. YouGov survey of a representative sample of 1,890 electors throughout Britain on-line on October 31 and November 1, 2002, commissioned by the Islamic Council of Great Britain, accessed at http://www.yougov.com/archives/bes_kelMain.asp?aId=10&sID=2& wID=0&UID=.

12. ICM Research, "Muslim Poll—November 2004," http://image.guardian.co.uk/sys-files/Guardian/documents/2004/11/30/Muslims-Nov041.pdf.

13. Robert Winnett and David Leppard, "Britain's Secret Plan to Win Muslim Hearts and Minds," *The Sunday Times*, May 30, 2004.

14. Steven Erlanger, "Italy's Premier Calls Western Civilization Superior to Islamic World," *New York Times*, September 27, 2001.

15. Hannah Cleaver, "We Must Show Our Opposition to Islam, Says Danish Queen," *Daily Telegraph*, April 15, 2005, http://www.telegraph.co.uk/news/main.jhtml?xml=/news/ 2005/04/15/wqueen15.xml&sSheet=/news/2005/04/15/ixworld.html.

16. UN Department of Economic and Social Affairs, Population Division, "Replace-ment Migration: Is It a Solution to Declining and Ageing Populations?" March 21, 2000, http://www.un.org/esa/population/publications/migration/migration. htm.

17. This is a UK Home Office estimate, but is generally cited by most analyses; see "Mi-gration: Its Present and Future Scale," *Migration Watch UK*, accessed at http://www.migra-tionwatchuk.org/pdfs/PresentFutureScaleofImmigration.pdf.

18. "A Civil War on Terrorism," *The Economist*, November 25, 2004, http://www.econo-mist.com/world/europe/displayStory.cfm?story_id=3427223.

19. Petter Nesser, "The Slaying of the Dutch Filmmaker—Religiously Motivated Vio-lence or Islamist Terrorism in the Name of Global Jihad?", *Norwegian Defence Research Es-tablishment*, FFI/RAPPORT-2005/00376, February 2005, p. 11.

20. Azzouz's story is recounted in David Crawford and Keith Johnson, "Home Grown New Terror Threat in EU; Extremists with Passports," *Wall Street Journal*, December 27, 2004, A1, accessed at http://www.letstalksense.com/w-agora/view.php?site=letstalksense &bn=letstalksense_politics&key=1104157267.

21. The text is a concatenation of verses from the Quran, Suras 80–81.

22. Toby Sterling, "Muslim Extremist Confesses in Court to Van Gogh Murder, Says He Would Do It Again," Associated Press, July 12, 2005.

23. Jason Burke, Antony Barnett, Martin Bright, Mark Townsend, Tariq Panja, and Tony Thompson, "Three Cities, Four Killers," *The Observer*, July 17, 2005, accessed at http:// observer.guardian.co.uk/uk_news/story/0,6903,1530265,00.html.

24. The use of converts is a key part of al Qaeda's strategy. They are less likely to be de-tected by law enforcement and border control authorities than those with darker skins or Arabic-sounding names. They also are more likely to have travel documents that facilitate entry into tightly controlled countries like the United States. In a logistical role, converts would find it easier than many other Muslims to rent safe houses, especially in the West, and carry out banking transactions and ship materiel without arousing suspicion. As individu-als who have embraced the faith as a matter of choice, their dedication to the cause is likely to be intense. Converts make a deliberate choice to cut themselves off from the religion, cul-ture, and society in which they were raised. Having made that decision, those who opt for jihad are likely to find it easier to strike what they have already rejected.

There are quite a few converts in the global jihad—Marc Sageman has noted that about

10 percent of those who have been arrested or killed are converts to Islam. (See *Report of the 9/11 Commission, Third Public Hearing, Terrorism, Al Qaeda, and the Muslim World,* Russell Senate Office Building, Washington, D.C., July 9, 2003.) French intelligence estimates that there are between 30,000 and 50,000 converts in France alone, so this ratio is not implausible. (Craig Smith, "Europe Fears Islamic Converts May Give Cover for Extremism," *New York Times,* July 19, 2004, accessed at http://www.theiraqmonitor.org/article/view/27312.html.)

Some of these conversions take place in prisons, such as those in the UK and France, where the Muslim population is disproportionately high. In some of these instances, conversion can be the key to survival. For some, like the British shoe bomber, Richard Reid, or the former American gang member Jose Padilla, it is less a short-term survival strategy than a powerful conviction and way of life. For others still, conversion is a way of protesting political or social conditions they reject, finding a sense of community and purpose, and accommodating to neighborhood peer pressure or even a new spouse. Some international Muslim organizations, like Tablighi Jamaat, fund trips for converts to Saudi Arabia or Pakistan, where they encounter militants who can have an outsized influence on them. John Walker Lindh, the American Taliban fighter captured by U.S. troops in 2002, was recruited by Tablighi Jamaat, as was Herve Loiseau, a French Taliban fighter who froze to death in the mountains of Tora Bora in 2001.

The utility of converts for jihad is evident in the pivotal roles that some converts have been given by the leadership of al Qaeda. Christian Ganczarski, who was arrested on June 2, 2005, in a joint U.S.–French–German operation, is a German metallurgist who was initially inspired by a Saudi cleric who toured Germany in the early 1990s. He subsequently got a scholarship to study Islam in Saudi Arabia, where he was radicalized. His next stop was Afghanistan, which he visited at least four times, training in al Qaeda camps and meeting bin Laden. He returned to Germany from his final trip to Afghanistan on September 2, 2001. Considered by American and French police and intelligence agencies to be "among the most important European al Qaeda figures alive," Ganczarski is known to have been in contact with the Djerba bombing ringleader just before that attack in April 2002 and with Khalid Sheikh Mohammed before his capture in 2003. According to intelligence officials, he was part of a systematic al Qaeda effort to recruit European converts and make them available for operational purposes. (Dana Priest, "Help from France in Covert Operations," *Washington Post,* July 3, 2005.)

The Courtailler brothers, Jerome and David, were similarly prominent. Jerome, along with two other converts, Johann Bonte and Jean-Marc Grandvisir, plotted to blow up the American embassy in Paris in 2001. Jerome converted to Islam in Britain, under the tutelage of a confessed al Qaeda member, Ahmad Beghal, around 1999. David converted to Islam earlier, in 1996, as a way to escape a downward spiral of drug use. "For David," explained his lawyer later, "Islam ordered his life." David's path from conversion to training camps in Afghanistan was nearly direct. From there he was put in contact with militants in Spain and Morocco, disappeared for a time, and resurfaced in Britain in 2000. While there, he is believed to have been involved in a plot that never came off to detonate a huge bomb, possibly in Birmingham, where his fake French driver's license was found in an apartment. Jerome and David were both ultimately arrested; Jerome is in a Dutch prison and David is nearly finished serving a four-year sentence in Britain. Although they were ultimately caught, the ease with which they crossed borders is explanation enough for their continuing role in a transnational jihad. (Smith, "Europe Fears.")

25. Marc Sageman, *Understanding Terror Networks* (Philadelphia: University of Pennsylvania Press, 2004).

26. *The 9/11 Commission Report: Final Report of the National Commission on Terrorist Attacks Upon the United States* (New York: W. W. Norton and Company, 2004).

27. Mark Kramer, "The Perils of Counterinsurgency: Russia's War in Chechnya," *International Security* 29, no. 3 (2005).

28. Ibid., 60.

29. Jamestown Foundation Eurasia Daily Monitor, vol. 2, no. 99.

30. Rajan Menon and Peter Reddaway, "The Real Crisis in Putin's Russia," *Newsweek International,* March 14, 2005.

31. Nesser, "Jihad in Europe."

32. Michael Scott Doran, personal e-mail.

33. Muhammad is reported to have said on his deathbed "akhraju al mushrikun min jazirat Muhammad," or "Expel the polytheists [Christians] from the isle of Muhammad." *Sawt al-Jihad* 1, 2003. Al-Muqrin's successors repeated this argument in subsequent issues of the bimonthly magazine.

34. CNN, "U.S. Worried about More al Qaeda Attacks: U.S., Saudis Suspect Terror Group in Riyadh Bombings," May 13, 2003, http://www.cnn.com/2003/WORLD/meast/05/13/saudi.blast/.

35. http://www.census.gov/ipc/idbsum/sasum.txt.

36. BBC, "Musharraf Declares War on Extremism," January 12, 2002, http://news.bbc.co.uk/1/hi/world/south_asia/1756965.stm.

37. Ibid.

38. Faced six plots: http://news.bbc.co.uk/2/hi/south_asia/4070296.stm; December 26 plot: http://news.bbc.co.uk/1/hi/world/south_asia/3347761.stm; re military involvement, http://www.cfr.org/publication.php?id=7743; CNN, "Musharraf Assassination Plot Foiled," September 18, 2002, www.cnn.com/2002/WORLD/asiapcf/south/09/19/pakistan.arrests.plot/; and "Musharraf Eludes Assassination Bid," CNN, December 14, 2002, accessed at http://www.cnn.com/2003/WORLD/asiapcf/12/14/blast.musharraf/.

39. BBC, "Parliament Suicide Attack Stuns India," December 13, 2001, http://news.bbc.co.uk/1/hi/world/south_asia/1708853.stm.

40. *Dawn,* February 9, 2005.

41. Statement of Stephen P. Cohen before the Senate Foreign Relations Committee, January 28, 2004, accessed at http://www.brookings.edu/views/testimony/cohens/20040128.pdf.

42. "A Year after the Iraq War," The Pew Research Center for the People and the Press, released March 16, 2004, accessed at http://people-press.org/reports/display.php3?ReportID=206.

43. C. Christine Fair, "Militant Recruitment in Pakistan: Implications for Al Qaeda and Other Organizations," *Studies in Conflict and Terrorism* 27, no. 6 (November–December 2004), 489–504.

44. See Benjamin and Simon, *The Age of Sacred Terror,* Chapter 5.

45. Abu Bakr Bashir is still the spiritual leader of the group, and has been on trial off and on during the three years since the Bali bombing, in which he is accused of playing a leading role. The Indonesian government is reluctant to convict him of charges that carry heavy penalties, for fear that this would create a backlash among salafist Muslims that would be hard to manage.

46. Occasionally, both technical and political guidance are said to be on offer. In April 2005, Singaporean officials were on the alert for two senior al Qaeda officers thought to be en route to the Philippines to advise the Abu Sayyaf Group. One was Muhsin Musa Mutawalli Atwah (a.k.a. Abd al Rahman al Muhajir), who is one of al Qaeda's most experienced explosives experts; the other was Rabi'a Abd al Halim Shuwayb (a.k.a. Hamza al Rabi), believed to be the successor to Khalid Sheikh Mohammed. See Stephen Ulph, "Peace Talks and Renewed Violence in the Philippines," *Terrorism Monitor,* Jamestown Foundation, April 21, 2005, accessed at http://www.jamestown.org/publications_details.php?volume_id=410&issue_id=3314&article_id=2369664.

47. "Huge Death Toll from Bali Bombing," BBC, October 13, 2002, http://news.bbc.co .uk/2/hi/asia-pacific/2323745.stm.

48. "Bomb Wrecks Top Jakarta Hotel," BBC, August 5, 2003, accessed at http://news .bbc.co.uk/2/hi/asia-pacific/3124919.stm.

49. "Massive Blast at Jakarta Embassy," BBC, September 9, 2004, accessed at http://news.bbc.co.uk/2/hi/asia-pacific/3639922.stm.

50. *9/11 Commission Report,* 490, note 26.

51. See for example the account of Philippine-Indonesian links in James Hookway, "A Dangerous New Alliance," *Far Eastern Economic Review,* May 6, 2004.

52. See "Southern Thailand: Insurgency, Not Jihad," *Asia Report* 98, International Crisis Group, May 18, 2005, accessed at http://crisisgroup.org/home/index.cfm?id=3436&i=1.

53. Roger Hardy, "Thailand: The Riddle of the South," BBC, February 15, 2005, accessed at http://newswww.bbc.net.uk/1/hi/world/asia-pacific/4264195.stm.

54. Ulph, "Peace Talks and Renewed Violence."

55. Ibid.

5. Muslims in America

1. CBS News, "Bin Laden Urges New U.S. Attacks," March 1, 2005, http://www. cbsnews.com/stories/2005/03/01/world/main677194.shtml.

2. *The 9/11 Commission Report: Final Report of the National Commission on Terrorist Attacks Upon the United States* (New York: W. W. Norton, 2004), 215–41.

3. See, for example, the testimony of Matthew Levitt on terrorist financing, U.S. Senate Committee on Banking, Housing and Urban Affairs, Hearing on Terrorist Financing, October 22, 2003.

4. Dan Eggen and Julie Tate, "U.S. Campaign Produces Few Convictions on Terrorism Charges; Statistics Often Count Lesser Crimes," *Washington Post,* June 12, 2005. See also Matthew Purdy and Todd Bergman, "Unclear Danger: Inside the Lackawanna Terror Case," *New York Times,* October 12, 2003.

5. The man who recruited the Lackawanna cell, Kamal Derwish, was killed in a Predator missile attack in Yemen in October 2002. See Matthew Purdy and Todd Bergman, "Unclear Danger."

6. The Center on Law and Security at NYU Law School, "Terrorist Trials: A Report Card," February 2005, http://www.law.nyu.edu/centers/lawsecurity/publications/terrorist trialreportcard.pdf.

7. No one is quite sure how many Muslims there are in America. The U.S. Bureau of the Census does not collect data on religious affiliation, so analysts must rely on self-identification, surname characteristics, and what can be gleaned regarding country of origin. All three indicators are prone to misinterpretation, while official information on geographic roots is normally available only for first-generation immigrants. To make matters worse, assertions about how many Muslims reside in the U.S. are often colored by political agendas. Muslims have an interest in inflating their numbers to create an impression of political clout and command the attention of legislators and policy makers, while Jewish groups are concerned to minimize the importance of the Muslim vote. In the absence of an authoritative count, the two sides have produced estimates ranging from 1.5 to 8 million Muslim Americans (including about 500,000 African-American Muslims). The best estimates appear to be around 2 million adults with a total household size of approximately 3 million. This is double the size of the Muslim population in 1990, with the South Asian component experiencing the most rapid growth.

8. "Muslims in the American Public Square: Shifting Political Winds and the Fallout from 9/11, Afghanistan, and Iraq," Georgetown University Project MAPS/Zogby International, October 2004, http://www.projectmaps.com/AMP2004report.pdf.

9. Matea Gold, "Lieberman to Meet Arab Americans: Democratic Vice Presidential Nominee Plans to Make a Key Gesture in Michigan, a State Expected to Be Hotly Contested in November," *Los Angeles Times,* August 27, 2000; Dana Calvo and Matea Gold, "Some Arab American Leaders Question Lieberman's Neutrality on Middle East," *Los Angeles Times,* October 14, 2000.

10. Mary Beth Sheridan, "U.S. Muslims Report More Hate Crimes: Islamic Group Blames 50 Percent Increase on the Lingering Effects of 9/11," *Washington Post,* May 12, 2005, http://www.washingtonpost.com/wp-dyn/content/article/2005/05/11/AR2005051101901.html.

11. Ihsan Bagby, "A Portrait of Detroit Mosques: Muslim Views on Policy Politics and Religion," Institute for Social Policy and Understanding (2004), http://www.ispu.us/pdfs/detroit_mosque_2.pdf.

12. Geneive Abdo, "Muslims Get in Touch with Their Faith, Culture," *Chicago Tribune,* September 14, 2003.

13. Barbara Brotman, "Muslim Youth Forge Own Path in America," *Chicago Tribune,* December 23, 2004.

14. Paul M. Barrett, "Student Journeys into the Secret Circle of Extremism: Muslim Movement Founded in Egypt Sent Tentacles to University in Knoxville," *Wall Street Journal,* December 23, 2003.

15. Eric Lichtblau, "Two Groups Charge Abuse of Witness Law," *New York Times,* June 27, 2005.

16. "John Ashcroft Holds News Conference," Federal Document Clearing House, Political Transcripts, October 4, 2002.

17. David Shepardson, "Ashcroft Sanctioned for Violating Gag Order in Detroit Terror Trial," *The Detroit News,* December 16, 2003.

18. Danny Hakim and Eric Lichtblau, "After Convictions, the Undoing of a US Terror Prosecution," *New York Times,* October 7, 2004.

19. Associated Press, "FBI Apologizes to Lawyer Detained in Madrid Bombings," May 25, 2004.

20. It is worth noting that majorities recognized Muslims' family-oriented lifestyle and that terrorists were "misusing" the teachings of Islam, while large pluralities acknowledged Islam's contribution to civilization and Muslims' contribution to the war on terrorism.

21. Eric C. Nisbet and James Shanahan, "MSRG Special Report: Restrictions on Civil Liberties, Views of Islam, and Muslim Americans," The Media and Society Research Group, Cornell University, December 2004, accessed at http://www.comm.cornell.edu/msrg/report1a.pdf.

22. Islam and Muslims: A Poll of American Public Opinion, Council on American-Islamic Relations, Project #04104, released August 2004, accessed at http://www.cairnet.org/downloads/pollresults.pdf. Also, see "Muslims in the American Public Square: Shifting Political Winds and the Fallout from 9/11, Afghanistan, and Iraq," Georgetown University Project MAPS/Zogby International, October 2004, http://www.projectmaps.com/AMP2004report.pdf.

23. Statistics in this paragraph derive from the MAPS 2004 study cited above.

24. Abdo's books include *There Is No God but God: Egypt and the Triumph of Islam* (New York: Oxford University Press, 2002) and, with Jonathan Lyons, *Answering Only to God: Faith and Freedom in Twenty-first Century Iran* (New York: Henry Holt, 2004).

25. John Tirman, "A Focus on Facts Ought to Dispel Mistrust of U.S. Muslims," *Christian Science Monitor,* January 31, 2005.

26. Jane Lampman, "US Muslims in a Quandary Over Charities," *Christian Science Monitor*, November 17, 2004, 11.

27. Paul M. Barrett, "Idaho Arrest Puts Muslim Students Under U.S. Scrutiny, Examination," *Wall Street Journal*, May 28, 2003, accessed at http://online.wsj.com/article/0,,SB105406885465552500-email,00.html.

28. Jerry Markon, "Muslim Lecturer Sentenced to Life; Followers Trained for Armed Jihad," *Washington Post*, July 14, 2005, accessed at http://www.washingtonpost.com/wp-dyn/content/article/2005/07/13/ AR2005071302169_pf.html.

6. The Measure of the Threat

1. Somini Sengupta and Salman Masood, "Guantánamo Comes to Define U.S. to Muslims," *New York Times*, May 21, 2005.

2. House Subcommittee on National Security, Emerging Threats, and International Relations, Committee on Government Reform, "Combating Terrorism: Chemical Plant Security," Testimony of John B. Stephenson, Director, Natural Resources and Environment, United States General Accounting Office, 108th Congress, 2nd session, February 23, 2004.

3. Richard A. Falkenrath, "We Could Breathe Easier: The Government Must Increase the Security of Toxic Chemicals in Transit," *Washington Post*, March 29, 2005.

4. Alessandro Andreoni and Charles D. Ferguson, "Radioactive Cesium Seizure in Thailand: Riddled with Uncertainties," Monterey Institute of International Studies, Research Story of the Week, July 17, 2003, http://cns.miis.edu/pubs/week/030717.htm.

5. In 1999, bin Laden declared in an interview with *Time* magazine that "acquiring weapons for the defense of Muslims is a religious duty. If I have indeed acquired these weapons, then I thank God for enabling me to do so," "Wrath of God: Osama bin Laden Lashes Out Against the West," *Time Asia*, January 11, 1999, accessed at http://www.time.com/time/asia/asia/magazine/1999/990111/osama1.html.

6. Adding to the natural dread this discovery caused for U.S. policy makers in the summer of 1998, al Qaeda operatives in the weeks before the 1998 bombings of two U.S. embassies in East Africa described an approaching operation as a "Hiroshima." Members used the same term shortly before 9/11.

7. For a detailed review of the intelligence and decision to bomb al-Shifa, see Daniel Benjamin and Steven Simon, *The Age of Sacred Terror* (New York: Random House, 2002), 256–60.

8. For a review of the documents, see David Albright, "Al Qaeda's Nuclear Program: Through the Window of Seized Documents," The Nautilus Institute, Special Forum 47, November 5, 2002, http://www.nautilus.org/archives/fora/Special-Policy-Forum/47_Albright.html.

9. Both bin Laden and al-Zawahiri have claimed in post–9/11 interviews that al Qaeda has nuclear weapons. Al-Zawahiri, perhaps playing on long-standing press and intelligence reports about al Qaeda acquiring a Russian tactical nuclear weapon, claimed that such weapons are "available for $30 million in the Caucasus."

10. "The Changing Face of Proliferation: The Role of Non-State Actors," Center for Strategic and International Studies, forthcoming.

11. Steve Coll, "What Bin Laden Sees in Hiroshima," *Washington Post*, February 6, 2005.

12. We are indebted to Richard Danzig for explaining the relative size of the different groups with different skill sets.

13. Alan Cullison and Andrew Higgins, "Files Found: A Computer in Kabul Yields a Chilling Array of al Qaeda Memos," *Wall Street Journal,* December 31, 2001.

14. Ibid. "As a first step, the memo suggests, militants must brush up on their reading. The memo gives a detailed precis of an American history of chemical and germ warfare. It lists a catalog of exotic killers, from anthrax to Rocky Mountain spotted fever."

15. Eric Lipton, "Al Qaeda Letters Are Said to Show Pre-9/11 Anthrax Plans," *New York Times,* May 21, 2005.

7. Threat Assessment

1. Condoleezza Rice, "Campaign 2000: Promoting the National Interest," *Foreign Affairs,* January–February 2000, 45.

2. Charles Krauthammer, "The New Unilateralism," *Washington Post,* June 8, 2001.

3. http://www.newamericancentury.org/iraqclintonletter.htm.

4. Michael Smith, "Blair Planned Iraq War from Start," *Sunday Times* (London), May 1, 2005.

5. Bob Woodward, *Bush at War* (New York: Simon and Schuster, 2002).

6. Richard Clarke, *Against All Enemies: Inside America's War on Terror* (New York: Free Press, 2004), 231–32.

7. Cf., for example, Laurie Mylroie, "Terrorism in Our Face," *The American Spectator,* April 1997; "The Method to Saddam's Madness," *Washington Times,* January 13, 1999. Mylroie's book, *Study of Revenge,* published in 2000 by the American Enterprise Institute, was revised and reissued as *The War Against America: Saddam Hussein and the World Trade Center Attacks* (New York: Regan Books, 2001).

8. For a spirited and thorough debunking of Mylroie's work, see "Armchair Provocateur," by al Qaeda expert Peter Bergen, *The Washington Monthly,* December 2003, and Jamie Glasov, "Symposium: The Saddam-Osama Connection," FrontPageMagazine.com, February 11, 2005, http://www.frontpagemag.com/Articles/ReadArticle.asp?ID=16985.

9. Ivo H. Daalder and James M. Lindsay, *America Unbound: The Bush Revolution in Foreign Policy* (Washington, D.C.: Brookings Institution Press, 2003), 99–100.

10. Bob Woodward, *Plan of Attack* (New York: Simon and Schuster, 2004), 24–26.

11. *The 9/11 Commission Report: Final Report of the National Commission on Terrorist Attacks Upon the United States* (New York: W. W. Norton, 2004), 559; Douglas J. Feith, "A War Plan That Cast a Wide Net," *Washington Post,* August 7, 2004.

12. Woodward, *Bush at War,* 99.

13. Ibid, 1.

14. Deputy Secretary of Defense Paul Wolfowitz, Department of Defense New Briefing, September 13, 2001, http://www.defenselink.mil/transcripts/2001/t09132001_t0913dsd.html.

15. President George W. Bush, State of the Union Address, Washington, D.C., January 29, 2002, http://www.whitehouse.gov/news/releases/2002/01/20020129-11.html.

16. CNN, "Late Edition with Wolf Blitzer," September 8, 2002, http://archives.cnn .com/2002/ALLPOLITICS/09/08/iraq.debate/.

17. Daalder and Lindsay, *America Unbound,* 85.

18. The Bush administration has contended that its discovery of a shipment of nuclear weapons–related material coupled with the demonstration of force in Iraq caused Libya to change its course. This is untrue. Libya had given up terrorist activity against the United States well before the Iraq War and had been cooperating with American counterterrorism efforts. Its sincerity in this regard is somewhat suspect since Libya was later implicated in an

effort to assassinate Saudi Crown Prince Abdullah. The regime of Moamar Qadhafi did give up its weapons of mass destruction program after the discovery of the nuclear shipments, but in the deal Washington made with Tripoli, a long-standing critical demand was taken off the table: Namely, the United States no longer insisted on Libya's assistance in pursuing the investigation of the Pan Am 103 bombing no matter how high in the government it went. By lifting this condition, Washington effectively removed the threat that such an investigation would pose to Qadhafi's hold on power. The deal may have been a sound one, but it was a deal nonetheless.

19. BBC News World Edition, "Gaza Bomb Hits US Convoy," October 15, 2003, http://news.bbc.co.uk/2/hi/middle_east/3194432.stm.

20. "Iraq planned and sponsored international terrorism in 2000. Although Baghdad focused on antidissident activity overseas, the regime continued to support various terrorist groups. The regime has not attempted an anti-Western terrorist attack since its failed plot to assassinate former President Bush in 1993 in Kuwait." "Patterns of Global Terrorism," 2000. The United States did not officially accuse Iraq of involvement in any other acts of anti-Western terror before the invasion in 2003.

21. It is an interesting question whether our opponents in the future will have the same respect for American intelligence capabilities after the debacle over Saddam's weapons of mass destruction. It would be deeply ironic if the push to war in Iraq weakened this aspect of our deterrence.

22. Apart from his aversion to secular tyrants, bin Laden has endorsed cooperation between sincere Muslims, even Shiites, against a common enemy. This position is one that separates him from *takfiris,* including Zarqawi.

23. *The 9/11 Commission Report,* 61.

24. Ibid., 66.

25. One of the authors had written speeches for President Bill Clinton on the issue, including a joint radio address he had delivered with British Prime Minister Tony Blair.

26. James Risen, "How Pair's Finding on Terror Led to Clash on Shaping Intelligence," *New York Times,* April 28, 2004.

27. James A. Baker III, with Thomas DeFrank, *The Politics of Diplomacy* (New York: G. P. Putnam and Sons, 1995), 359.

28. *The 9/11 Commission Report,* 472.

29. Thomas S. Kuhn, *The Structure of Scientific Revolutions* (Chicago: University of Chicago Press, 1970), 77.

30. Nicholas Lemann, "How It Came to War," *The New Yorker,* March 31, 2003, http://www.newyorker.com/fact/content/?030331fa_fact.

31. Barton Gellman and Dafna Linzer, "Afghanistan, Iraq: Two Wars Collide," *Washington Post,* October 22, 2004, http://www.washingtonpost.com/wp-dyn/articles/A52673-2004Oct21.html.

32. Barton Gellman and Susan Schmidt, "U.S., Pakistan Intensify the Search for Bin Laden; The Debate: To Kill or Capture," *Washington Post,* March 7, 2003.

33. Michael Elliot, "Why the War on Terror Will Never End: Bomb Attacks in Riyadh and Casablanca Suggest That Even on the Run, al-Qaeda Is a Resilient Threat to the West," *Time,* May 26, 2003. Interestingly, bin Laden uses similar imagery to describe the United States. Jamal al-Fadl, an al Qaeda defector, testified in U.S. federal court in 2001 that bin Laden had told his followers in the early 1990s that "the snake is America, and we have to stop them. We have to cut the head and stop them."

34. Gellman and Schmidt, "U.S., Pakistan Intensify the Search for Bin Laden."

35. Gellman and Linzer, "Two Wars Collide."

36. Ibid. See also chapter 2, note 8.

37. Dick Cheney, interview on Meet the Press, NBC News, March 16, 2003.

38. Speech of President George W. Bush at the National Endowment for Democracy, November 6, 2003, http://www.ned.org/events/anniversary/oct1603-Bush.html.

39. Jack Davis, "The Challenge of Managing Uncertainty: Paul Wolfowitz on Intelligence Policy-Relations," *Studies in Intelligence*, 39, no. 5 (1996), http://www.cia.gov/csi/studies/96unclass/davis.htm.

40. James Risen, "Clash on Shaping Intelligence."

41. Dana Priest, "Pentagon Shadow Loses Some Mystique: Feith's Shops Did Not Usurp Intelligence Agencies on Iraq, Hill Probers Find," *Washington Post*, March 13, 2004.

42. "It looked 'like a college term paper,' said one senior Pentagon official who saw the analysis. It was hundreds of connecting lines and dots footnoted with binders filled with signals intelligence, human source reporting and even third hand intelligence accounts of personal meetings between terrorists," Ibid.

43. For an indication of the prevalence of this view among neoconservatives, cf. David Frum and Richard Perle, *An End to Evil: How to Win the War on Terror* (New York: Random House, 2003).

44. Risen, "Clash on Shaping Intelligence."

45. U.S. Congress, Senate Committee on Armed Services Hearing, 108th Congress, 2nd session, March 9, 2004.

46. Stephen Hayes, "Case Closed," *The Weekly Standard* 9, no. 11 (2003), http://www.weeklystandard.com/Content/Public/Articles/000/000/003/378fmxyz.asp.

47. *Rocky Mountain News*, January 9, 2004. The vice president's comments surprised current and past government officials since it appeared to be a violation of the rule prohibiting comment on classified material that has appeared in public. For many years, officials were not allowed to mention the National Reconnaissance Organization, a multibillion-dollar agency that was reported in the press but whose existence was not acknowledged by the government.

48. Interestingly, the publication of the Feith memo prompted the *Washington Post*'s David Ignatius to report in his column that the United States and Britain had a highly placed informant in Iraqi intelligence "who told them before the war that in the late 1990s, Saddam Hussein had indeed considered such an operational relationship with bin Laden—and then decided against it." David Ignatius, "The Dubious Iraqi Link," *Washington Post*, March 15, 2002.

49. "Washington Post Poll: Saddam Hussein and the Sept. 11 Attacks," *Washington Post*, September 6, 2003, http://www.washingtonpost.com/wp-srv/politics/polls/vault/stories/data082303.htm.

50. "Iraq, 9/11, al Qaeda and Weapons of Mass Destruction: What the Public Believes Now, According to Latest Harris Poll," *Harris Interactive*, February 18, 2005, http://www.harrisinteractive.com/harris_poll/index.asp?PID=544.

51. Cf. James Mann, *The Rise of the Vulcans: The History of Bush's War Cabinet* (New York: Penguin Books, 2004), for a detailed examination of these relationships.

52. Peter J. Boyer, "The Believer: Paul Wolfowitz Defends His War," *The New Yorker*, November 1, 2004, http://www.newyorker.com/fact/content/?041101fa_fact.

53. Philip Shenon, "9/11 Report Is Said to Dismiss Iraq-Qaeda Alliance," *New York Times*, July 12, 2004.

54. David E. Sanger and Robin Toner, "Bush and Cheney Talk Strongly of Qaeda Links with Hussein," *New York Times*, June 18, 2004.

55. Walter Pincus, "Spy Agencies Warned of Iraq Resistance," *Washington Post,* September 9, 2003.

56. Daniel Benjamin, "Saddam Hussein and Al Qaeda Are Not Allies," *New York Times,* September 30, 2002.

57. BBC News World Edition, "Bin Laden Tape: Text," February 12, 2003, http://news.bbc.co.uk/2/hi/middle_east/2751019.stm.

58. *Online NewsHour with Jim Lehrer,* "Bin Laden's Fatwa," first published in *Al Quds Al Arabi,* London, August 1996: "Declaration of War against the Americans Occupying the Land of the Two Holy Places," http://www.pbs.org/newshour/terrorism/international/fatwa_1996.html.

59. "Deputy Secretary Wolfowitz Interview with Sam Tannenhaus," *Vanity Fair,* May 9, 2003, http://www.defenselink.mil/transcripts/2003/tr20030509-depsecdef0223.html.

8. The Persistence of Error

1. Late last year, the Defense Department merged the two commando teams and headquartered the reflagged Task Force 121 under Rear Adm. William H. McRaven in Baghdad. Barton Gellman and Dafna Linzer, "Afganistan, Iraq: Two Wars Collide," *Washington Post,* October 22, 2004, http://www.washingtonpost.com/wp-dyn/articles/A52673-2004Oct21.html.

2. Ibid.

3. Scot J. Paltrow, "Questions Mount over Failure to Hit Zarqawi's Camp," *Wall Street Journal,* October 25, 2004.

4. "U.S. Secretary of State Colin Powell Addresses the U.N. Security Council," February 5, 2003, http://www.whitehouse.gov/news/releases/2003/02/print20030205-1.html.

5. The only facility that the United States planned to protect after the invasion was the Iraqi Oil Ministry. For many Iraqis who were shocked to see the insurgency unfold without American intervention, this may have confirmed suspicions that America was, as radical Islamists claimed, interested in Iraq's oil, not the fate of its people.

6. "Deputy Secretary Wolfowitz Interview with Sam Tannenhaus, *Vanity Fair,*" *United States Department of Defense News,* transcript, May 9, 2003, http://www.defenselink.mil/transcripts/2003/tr20030509-depsecdef0223.html.

7. NBC News, *Meet the Press,* Interview with Vice President Dick Cheney, March 16, 2003.

8. "Donald H. Rumsfeld Holds a Media Roundtable with BBC and Voice of America (as released by Defense Department)," FDCH Political Transcripts, September 13, 2002.

9. Wolfowitz Tells BBC Iraqi Civilians Not a Target, March 25, 2003 (March 25 interview with BBC World Service), accessed at http://www.usembassy.it/file2003_03/alia/A3032509.htm.

10. President George W. Bush, address, "A Period of Consequences," The Citadel, South Carolina, Thursday, September 23, 1999, http://citadel.edu/pao/addresses/pres_bush.html.

11. President George W. Bush, Address to the Joint Session of Congress, February 27, 2001, http://www.whitehouse.gov/news/releases/2001/02/20010228.html.

12. President George W. Bush, Remarks at U.S. Naval Academy Commencement, May 25, 2001, http://www.whitehouse.gov/news/releases/2001/05/20010525-1.html.

13. Donald H. Rumsfeld, "Transforming the Military," *Foreign Affairs* (May–June 2002).

14. CBS News, "Iraq Faces Massive U.S. Missile Barrage," January 24, 2003.

15. The concept of "shock and awe" was developed in the mid-1990s by a study group led by military analyst Harlan Ullman in which Donald Rumsfeld participated.

16. Harlan Ullman, "Fair Test?: Shifting Goals Required a Change in Strategy, but That Doesn't Mean the 'Shock and Awe' Concept Was Flawed," *Los Angeles Times,* April 6, 2003.

17. The notion of shock and awe appears to have been on Rumsfeld's mind for some time. In April 1999, as the Clinton administration waged an air war against Serbian forces in Kosovo, Rumsfeld told CNN the assault might not be forceful enough. "There is always a risk in gradualism: It pacifies the hesitant and the tentative. What it doesn't do is shock and awe, and alter the calculations of the people you're dealing with." CNN, *Inside Politics,* "President Clinton Rejects Yugoslavia's Unilateral Cease-Fire, Promises to Press Ahead With Strikes Until Milosevic Meets NATO Demands," transcript, April 6, 1999.

18. James Mann, *The Rise of the Vulcans: The History of Bush's War Cabinet* (New York: Penguin Books, 2004).

19. Bob Woodward, *Bush at War* (New York: Simon and Schuster, 2002).

20. Shinseki, who, ironically, had been a pioneer in arguing for transformation, was punished for his refusal to agree with Rumsfeld. Rumsfeld later announced that General Pete Schoomaker would succeed Shinseki. Shinseki's retirement was still fourteen months off, and the announcement sent a clear sign of disfavor to the entire military. The petulance continued. At Shinseki's retirement ceremony at the Pentagon, no one above the rank of assistant secretary of defense attended from the civilian leadership, an unheard-of slight. In response, Secretary of State Colin Powell and Deputy Secretary Richard Armitage held a reception in the ornate Benjamin Franklin Room on the eighth floor of the State Department. Out of respect for Shinseki, both men stayed for the entire reception.

21. James Dobbins, who served as the U.S. special envoy for Somalia, Haiti, Bosnia, Kosovo, and Afghanistan, and a team at the RAND Corporation studied the history of nation building and, not surprisingly, found that a key variable affecting the success of a postwar mission was the ratio of military force to population. When they projected what Coalition troop levels in Iraq would be if the occupation began with the same force-to-population ratio as in Germany in 1945, the number came out to be 2.5 million. If the same ratio as occurred in Bosnia was used, the number would be 460,000; if extrapolating from the troop levels in Kosovo, almost 500,000. James Dobbins, John G. McGinn, Keith Crane, Seth G. Jones, Rollie Lal, Andrew Rathmell, Rachel Swanger, and Anga Timilsina, "America's Role in Nation-Building: From Germany to Iraq," RAND, 2004, http://www.rand.org/publications/MR/MR1753/.

22. Condoleezza Rice, "Campaign 2000: Promoting the National Interest," *Foreign Affairs* (January–February 2002).

23. Michael R. Gordon, "Bush Would Stop US Peacekeeping in Balkan Fights," *New York Times,* October 21, 2000.

24. House Budget Committee, U.S. Representative Jim Nussle Holds Hearing on FY 2004 Defense Budget Request, February 27, 2003.

25. CNN, "Rumsfeld on Looting in Iraq: 'Stuff Happens,'" April 12, 2003, http://www.cnn.com/2003/US/04/11/sprj.irq.pentagon/.

26. See Larry Diamond, *Squandered Victory: The American Occupation and the Bungled Effort to Bring Democracy to Iraq* (New York: Times Books, 2005), and David L. Phillips, *Losing Iraq: Inside the Postwar Reconstruction Fiasco* (New York: Westview Press, 2005).

27. James Fallows, "Blind into Baghdad," *The Atlantic Monthly,* January–February 2004.

28. "Workshop Report: Iraq: Looking Beyond Saddam's Rule," Institute for National Strategic Studies, November 20–21, 2002.

29. "Frontline: Truth, War and Consequences, Interview with General Jay Garner," http://www.pbs.org/wgbh/pages/frontline/shows/truth/interviews/garner.html; Peter Slevin and Dana Priest, "Wolfowitz Concedes Iraq Errors," *Washington Post,* July 24, 2003.

30. David Rieff, "Blueprint for a Mess," *New York Times,* November 1, 2003.

31. This fact is attested to by numerous State Department and other officials as well as David L. Phillips, *Losing Iraq: Inside the Postwar Reconstruction Fiasco* (New York: Westview Press, 2005).

32. Irregular, often inscrutable "process" is a criticism that a number of former senior officials level against the Bush administration. In this administration, as in past ones, it is customary to circulate a "Summary of Conclusions" after a Principals Committee meeting. Yet former officials complain that the "SOCs" they saw often were at odds with the discussions in the meetings themselves, suggesting that the White House was revising papers after the fact. As one observed, "It was often spooky how the SOCs changed."

33. CNN, "Bush Warns Militants Who Attack U.S. Troops in Iraq," July 3, 2003, http://www.cnn.com/2003/ALLPOLITICS/07/02/sprj.nitop.bush/.

34. Reuven Paz, "Arab Volunteers Killed in Iraq: An Analysis," Project for the Research of Islamic Movements, PRISM Series of Global Jihad, vol. 3, no. 1, March 2005, http://www.e-prism.org/images/PRISM_no_1_vol_3_-_Arabs_killed_in_Iraq.pdf. See also discussion on page 39 above.

9. The Elements of a Foreign Policy

1. For the full text of Rumsfeld's war-on-terror memo, see *USA Today,* October 16, 2003, at http://www.usatoday.com/news/washington/executive/rumsfeld-memo.htm.

2. "President Discusses War on Terror at FBI Academy, Quantico, Virginia," July 11, 2005, http://www.whitehouse.gov/news/releases/2005/07/20050711-1.html.

3. Emmanuel Sivan, "The Clash within Islam," *Survival* (Spring 2003).

4. "The reaction in Washington was quick and decisive—NATO could not be allowed to rein in any US response. According to a senior State Department official speaking to reporters after the first emergency meeting on 12 September, the United States was pushing for a resolution that would mention that the article could be invoked, without actually voting on the measure itself. A senior Administration official said that it was the Europeans who were 'desperately trying to give us political cover and the Pentagon was resisting it.' Eventually, Secretary of Defense Rumsfeld relented and agreed to accept the clause." Rebecca Johnson and Micah Zenko, "All Dressed Up and No Place to Go: Why NATO Should Be on the Front Lines in the War on Terror," *Parameters,* Winter 2002–03, 48–63. For an early critique of this approach, see Daniel Benjamin, "Get Those Allies into the Tent," *Time International,* December 3, 2001, 40.

5. For the minority view brilliantly argued, see Michael Scott Doran, "Palestine, Iraq and U.S. Strategy," *New York Times,* January 5, 2003, accessed at http://www.nytimes.com/cfr/international/1_FA_nift_030106_doran.html.

6. Quoted by Thomas Carothers, "A Better Way to Support Middle East Reform," Policy Brief, Carnegie Endowment, February 2005, accessed at http://www.carnegieendowment.org/files/PB33.carothers.FINAL.web.pdf.

7. Tyler Marshall, "Bush Foreign Policy Shifting," *Los Angeles Times,* June 5, 2005, accessed at http://politics.yahoo.com/s/latimests/bushsforeignpolicyshifting.

8. "Sixty years of Western nations excusing and accommodating the lack of freedom in the Middle East did nothing to make us safe—because in the long run, stability cannot be purchased at the expense of liberty. As long as the Middle East remains a place where freedom does not flourish, it will remain a place of stagnation, resentment, and violence

ready for export. And with the spread of weapons that can bring catastrophic harm to our country and to our friends, it would be reckless to accept the status quo." "President Bush Discusses Freedom in Iraq and Middle East," Remarks by the President at the 20th Anniversary of the National Endowment for Democracy, November 6, 2003, http://www.whitehouse.gov/news/releases/2003/11/20031106-2.html. See also Richard Haass's December 2002 speech at the Council on Foreign Relations, "Toward Greater Democracy," http://64.233.187.104/search?q=cache:OgRz8FhVX_YJ:www.cfr.org/pub5283/richard_n_haass/towards_greater_democracy_in_the_muslim_world.php+Richard+Haass+and+Council+on+Foreign+Relations+and+speech+and+democracy+and+Muslim&hl=en.

9. President Bush, Speech at the International Republican Institute Dinner, May 18, 2005, http://www.whitehouse.gov/news/releases/2005/05/20050518-2.html.

10. The 2004 report, released in 2005, can be downloaded at http://www.rbas.undp.org/ahdr2.cfm?menu=12.

11. For a detailed treatment of the interactions regarding civil society programs and NGOs and governments, see Alison Van Rooy, ed., *Civil Society and the Aid Industry* (London: Earthscan, 1998); Thomas Carothers, *Aiding Democracy Abroad: The Learning Curve* (Washington, D.C.: Carnegie Endowment for International Peace, 1999); and Thomas Carothers and Marina Ottoway, "The Burgeoning World of Civil Society Aid," in Carothers and Ottoway, eds., *Funding Virtue: Civil Society and Democracy Aid* (Washington, D.C.: Carnegie Endowment for International Peace, 2002). There are a number of seminal studies in this area, but the one that had the most impact in the United States, especially for a scholarly book, was Robert Putnam's *Bowling Alone: The Collapse and Revival of American Community* (New York: Simon and Schuster, 2000).

12. See Jan Kubik, *Rebellious Civil Society: Popular Protest and Democratic Consolidation in Poland, 1989–1993* (Ann Arbor: University of Michigan Press, 1999).

13. See "Confirmation Hearing of Condoleezza Rice, Transcript," *New York Times,* January 18, 2005. http://www.nytimes.com/2005/01/18/politics/18TEXT-RICE.html?ex=1118980800&en=834534b74f874b4f&ei=5070&oref=login&pagewanted=print&position=.

14. There was a debate over these programs, but it took place between the EU and the U.S. over the desirability of measures that could and should be taken to coerce the states in question to open up political space for civil society and take tangible steps toward political reform.

15. "There Is No Justice Without Freedom," the full text of the president's inaugural address, *Washington Post,* January 21, 2005, accessed at http://www.washingtonpost.com/wp-dyn/articles/A23747-2005Jan20.html.

16. "President Discusses the Future of Iraq," Washington Hilton Hotel, Washington, D.C., February 26, 2003, accessed at http://www.whitehouse.gov/news/releases/2003/02/20030226-11.html.

17. President Bush, Statement in the Rose Garden, March 29, 2005, accessed at http://www.whitehouse.gov/news/releases/2005/03/20050329.html.

18. Secretary Rice, Remarks at the AIPAC Annual Policy Conference, May 23, 2005, accessed at http://www.state.gov/secretary/rm/2005/46625.htm.

19. On Lebanon, see, for example, Dexter Filkins, "What Set Loose the Voice of the People," *New York Times,* March 27, 2005, and, for a more general sense of the complexity of regional politics and the insubstantial nature of the reforms that the administration sees as milestones, Neil MacFarquhar and Mona el-Naggar, "Unexpected Whiff of Freedom Proves Bracing for the Mideast," *New York Times,* March 6, 2005, accessed at http://www.nytimes.com/2005/03/06/international/middleeast/06mideast.html?ex=1121918400&en=a3087072bd4e8b39&ei=5070&hp&ex=1110085200&en=ed037f4802507fca&ei=5094&partner=homepage.

20. Leena Saidi, "Assassination of Hariri Stuns Nation," *International Herald Tribune,* February 15, 2005, accessed at http://www.iht.com/articles/2005/02/14/news/beirut.html.

21. "Abbas Achieves Landslide Poll Win," BBC, January 10, 2005, accessed at http://news.bbc.co.uk/1/hi/world/middle_east/4160171.stm.

22. "Abbas Postpones Palestinian Vote," BBC, June 4, 2005, accessed at http://news.bbc.co.uk/1/hi/world/middle_east/4609425.stm.

23. For a detailed analysis of the conditions for the emergence of durable democratic institutions in Palestine, see Glenn Robinson in Steven Simon et al., *Building a Successful Palestinian State* (Santa Monica: The RAND Corporation, 2005).

24. Charles Levinson, "$50 Billion Later, Taking Stock of US Aid to Egypt," *Christian Science Monitor,* April 12, 2004, accessed at http://www.csmonitor.com/2004/0412/p07s01-wome.html; and "Egypt: Calls for Reform Met with Brutality," Human Rights Watch, May 26, 2005, accessed at http://www.hrw.org/english/docs/2005/05/26/egypt11036.htm.

25. "Clashes Tarnish Egyptian Referendum," BBC, May 26, 2005, accessed at http://news.bbc.co.uk/2/hi/middle_east/4582469.stm.

26. Hosni Mubarak, interview with *La Repubblica,* March 05, 2004 (FBIS translated text).

27. For a revealing account of the elections, see Steve Coll, "Islamic Activists Sweep Saudi Council Elections," *Washington Post,* April 24, 2005, A17, accessed at http://www.washingtonpost.com/wp-dyn/articles/A12398-2005Apr23.html.

28. The process was kicked off well before Operation Iraqi Freedom via a referendum; see "Bahrain Backs Political Reform," BBC, February 15, 2001, accessed at http://news.bbc.co.uk/1/hi/world/middle_east/1171332.stm. Bahrain has other severe problems that have not been addressed by the slow pace of political reforms; see "Bahrain's Sectarian Challenge," International Crisis Group, May 6, 2005, accessed at http://www.crisisgroup.org/home/index.cfm?id=3404&l=1.

29. Interview with Ahmed Aboul Gheit, *Washington Post,* March 10, 2005.

30. Amr Mousa, in interview with *La Repubblica,* April 9, 2005 (FBIS translated text).

31. *Washington Post,* February 11, 2005.

32. *Daily Star,* April 3, 2004.

33. Hassan Nasrallah, speech commemorating Ashura, al Manar Television, March 2, 2004 (FBIS translated text).

34. Margaret Carlson, "Can Charlotte Beers Sell Uncle Sam?" *Time* magazine, Online Edition, November 14, 2001, http://www.time.com/time/columnist/klein/article/0,9565,184536,00.html.

35. "Bush's Muslim Propaganda Chief Quits; U.S. Official: 'She didn't do anything that worked,'" CNN, March 4, 2003, accessed at http://www.cnn.com/2003/US/03/03/state.resignation/.

36. Robin Wright and Al Kamen, "U.S. Outreach to Islamic World Gets Slow Start, Minus Leaders; Effort Involves No Muslims; Hughes Will Not Arrive Until Fall," *Washington Post,* April 18, 2005, accessed at http://www.washingtonpost.com/wp-dyn/articles/A61213-2005Apr17.html?nav=rss_politics.

37. Robin Wright, "U.S. Struggles to Win Hearts, Minds in the Muslim World: Diplomacy Efforts Lack Funds, Follow-Through," *Washington Post,* August 20, 2004, A01, http://www.washingtonpost.com/ac2/wp-dyn/A17134-2004Aug19?language=printer.

38. The commission's report can be downloaded at http://www.state.gov/documents/organization/36625.pdf.

39. Wright, "U.S. Struggles to Win Hearts, Minds."

40. Other examples are Jordan, which has extracted resources from the United States,

and Syria, which was supported by the Soviet Union—before its collapse—and by Saudi Arabia.

41. Steven A. Cook, "The Right Way to Promote Arab Reform," *Foreign Affairs,* March/April 2005, 91–102.

42. The FY 2005 and 2006 budget justifications submitted to Congress by the Millennium Challenge Corporation can be found at http://www.mca.gov/about_us/key_documents/FY06_Budget_Justification.pdf.

10. Shortchanging Homeland Security

1. Ghaith Abdul-Ahad, "Outside Iraq but Deep in the Fight: A Smuggler of Insurgents Reveals Syria's Influential, Changing Role," *Washington Post,* June 8, 2005, A01, accessed at http://www.washingtonpost.com/wp-dyn/content/article/2005/06/07/AR2005060702026.html.

2. Stephen Ulph, "New On-Line Book Lays Out al-Qaeda's Military Strategy," The Jamestown Foundation, March 18, 2005, accessed at http://jamestown.org/news_details.php?news_id=100.

3. See the classic essay on the hypnotic power of this belief, by Stephen Van Evera, "The Cult of the Offensive and Origins of the First World War," *International Security,* Summer 1984. For the way in which this conviction affected French fortunes, see the gripping history by Alistair Horne, *The Price of Glory: Verdun, 1916,* Revised Edition (London: Penguin, 1994).

4. Dana Milbank and Claudia Deane, "Poll Finds Dimmer View of Iraq War, 52% Say U.S. Has Not Become Safer," *Washington Post,* June 8, 2005, A01, accessed at http://www.washingtonpost.com/wp-dyn/content/article/2005/06/07/AR2005060700296.html.

5. The two conspirators, Khalid Al-Midhar and Nawaf Al-Hazmi, were not put on the State Department and Immigration and Naturalization Service watchlists until August 23, 2001, too late for them to be intercepted before the attacks. The individual Al-Midhar met with in Kuala Lumpur, Malaysia, in December 1999 was Tawfiz Al-Atash, who orchestrated the 1999 attack on the U.S.S. *Cole* in Yemen.

6. Philip Shenon, "Threats and Responses: The Reorganization Plan; Establishing New Agency Is Expected to Take Years and Could Divert It from Mission," *New York Times,* November 20, 2002, A14. It would be difficult to overstate how much chaos has surrounded the Department of Homeland Security even years after its creation. In early 2004, when DHS was already a year old, a representative of the department attended a conference at the Center for Strategic and International Studies (CSIS) and was introduced by a scholar from the host institution to a senior staff member from the National Security Agency, the nation's collector of communications intelligence. Several days later, the CSIS scholar received an e-mail from the NSA official asking for the phone number of the DHS representative. The CSIS staffer was astonished and e-mailed back, "You mean NSA can't find a DHS number??" The e-mail came back, "We have a really hard time connecting with them."

7. This has turned into a serious problem. In a December 2004 survey of over 10,000 Homeland Security employees conducted by the Office of Personnel Management, about half disagreed or strongly disagreed with the statement that promotions were based on merit; nearly half said that they did not have people, materials, or budget to get their job done; and only 28 percent were satisfied with the policies and practices of senior leaders.

These responses are markedly worse than the averages in government-wide opinion surveys. The perceptions revealed by this survey are illustrated in a comic way in the assessment of the results by the department's chief human capital officer: He was "encouraged" by the survey findings, which showed that workers "identify with the mission and understand what they do is important." See Stephen Barr, "Survey Has a Lot to Mull for Homeland Security Post," *Washington Post*, June 12, 2005, C02, accessed at http://www.washingtonpost.com/wp-dyn/content/article/2005/06/11/AR2005061100620_pf.html.

8. Seymour Hersh, "Selective Intelligence," *The New Yorker*, posted May 5, 2003, accessed at http://www.newyorker.com/fact/content/?030512fa_fact. See also Dana Priest, "Pentagon Shadow Loses Some Mystique. Feith's Shops Did Not Usurp Intelligence Agencies on Iraq, Hill Probers Find," *Washington Post*, March 13, 2004, A11, accessed at http://www.washingtonpost.com/wp-dyn/articles/A54569-2004Mar12.html?referrer=emailarticlepg.

9. Remarks by the president at Bush-Cheney 2004 Reception, St. Louis, January 5, 2004, accessed at http://www.whitehouse.gov/news/releases/2004/01/20040105-7.html.

10. Remarks regarding U.S. troops in radio address, http://www.whitehouse.gov/news/releases/2003/10/20031004.html, October 4, 2003: "Our military is confronting terrorists in Iraq and Afghanistan and in other places so our people will not have to confront terrorist violence in New York or St. Louis or Los Angeles."

11. February 2, 2005, State of the Union Address, http://web.lexis-nexis.com/universe/document?_m=b119ab16ee1b42bcef1badffbab9715b&_docnum=35&wchp=dglbvlb-zskvb&_md5=391d1bdd624b9765a71230c667b1d267. This conviction was so firmly embedded in President Bush's conception of strategic reality that he cast the rationale for the American presence in Iraq in just these terms during a September 2004 Rose Garden press conference with the Iraqi interim prime minister, Iyad Allawi, who must have wondered about the surreal impression the president's points were making back in Baghdad. Viewers there might well have interpreted his words to mean that the Iraqis dying at the hands of the insurgency were not as valuable as Americans.

12. It is conceivable that the administration's failure to get a handle on homeland security was a function of overload, rather than the logical implication of an explicit strategic concept. For the authors, however, this is too simple an explanation.

13. Dana Milbank, "Plan Was Formed in Utmost Secrecy; Final Proposal Came from 4 Top Bush Aides; Most Others out of the Loop," *Washington Post*, June 7, 2002, A1. See also William Safire, "The Plan from the PEOC," *New York Times*, June 10, 2002, 25.

14. The identity of only one of these is known, a senior director on the NSC staff and subsequently deputy homeland security adviser, Richard Falkenrath.

15. Helen Dewar, "Homeland Security Bill Faces Senate Test: Tight Vote Expected as Democrats try to Eliminate 'Special Interest' Provisions," *Washington Post*, November 19, 2002, A7.

16. See Stephen Labaton and Robert Pear, "Anthrax Menace Exposes Badly Coordinated Defense," *New York Times*, October 18, 2001, B7.

17. A White House official said that "the president sees Tom Ridge as family," and that Ridge had the "clout to go directly to the president to get things done." The official was certainly right about the first point. On the second, he was wide off the mark. See Philip Shenon, "Man in the News: A Man with Connections—Thomas Joseph Ridge," *Washington Post*, November 26, 2002, 17.

18. Mike Allen, "Ridge Faces Daunting Task in Homeland Office; Analysts Question Nominee's Record So Far and Whether He Can Win Bureaucratic Battles," *Washington Post*, November 26, 2002, A17.

19. Ibid.

20. Homeland security depends just as much on the impermeability of perimeter defenses, but these turn on the effectiveness of our foreign intelligence programs and diplomatic efforts, rather than the departments and agencies that constitute the homeland security bureaucracy and, of course, the FBI.

21. Some regard the Custom-Trade Partnership Against Terrorism (C-TPAT) as an exception to this rule in that importers and exporters have found the program to be useful and the Immigration and Customs Enforcement (ICE) to be attentive to their concerns. In this case, the exception proves the rule.

22. Ironically, the Homeland Security Department's reluctance to engage in joint planning is due to blowback from the vice president's 2001 energy task force imbroglio, in which Cheney and his staff engaged in secret talks with energy industry lobbyists, which were seen by critics as concealing unsavory logrolling. In unsuccessful court action to compel the White House to reveal what the task force had done, litigants claimed that Cheney was obligated by the Federal Advisory Committee Act (FACA) to do so. Even though this claim did not sway the Supreme Court, DHS officials fear that it may be invoked again, successfully, against them if they engage in planning with the private sector. The point here is that there are legal and procedural impediments to public–private cooperation that reinforce an a priori lack of understanding for the role of the private sector in homeland security. For details of the Cheney case, see Charles Lane, "High Court Backs Vice President; Energy Documents Shielded for Now," *Washington Post,* June 25, 2004, A01, accessed at http://www.washington-post.com/ac2/wp-dyn/A1988-2004Jun24?language=printer.

23. See Frederick W. Smith, "Securing America and the World, There's Much More CEOs Need to Achieve," *Chief Executive,* December 2004, no. 204, accessed at http://www.chiefexecutive.net/mag/204/index.html#1.

24. Matthew Brzezinski, *Fortress America: On the Front Lines of Homeland Security— An Inside Look at the Coming Surveillance State* (New York: Bantam Books, 2004), 7ff.

25. This report can be downloaded from multiple sites, including http://www.deq.state.mi.us/documents/deq-wb-wws-interim-nipp.pdf.

26. He was replaced in June 2005 by Hank Crumpton, the head of the CIA's national resources division.

27. On IAIP staffing, see "Testimony by Secretary Michael Chertoff Before the Homeland Security Subcommittee of the Senate Appropriations Committee," April 20, 2005, accessed at http://www.dhs.gov/dhspublic/display?theme=45&content=4475&print-true.

28. Spencer S. Hsu and Sara Kehaulani Goo, "Homeland Security to Be Restructured: Chertoff Aims to Address Criticism," *Washington Post,* July 13, 2005, A01, accessed at http://www.washingtonpost.com/wp-dyn/content/article/2005/07/12/AR2005071201563.html.

29. Eric Lipton, "Report Details Easy Ways to Fix Airline Security," *New York Times,* June 5, 2005.

30. Scott Higham and Robert O'Harrow, Jr., "Contracting Rush for Security Led to Waste, Abuse," *Washington Post,* May 22, 2005, A1.

31. Eric Lichtblau, "Report on U.S. Aviation Warns of Holes," *New York Times,* March 14, 2005, A1.

32. An unmanned aircraft, or UAV, would provide more than adequate space to deliver a biological agent or even a radiological contaminant such as cesium chloride. Moreover, even non-WMD attacks become attractive against certain civilian and industrial targets when one considers that a gasoline payload, mixed with air, releases fifteen times the energy as an equal weight of TNT. For an account of small aircraft threat, see Dennis M. Gormley, *On Not Confusing the Unfamiliar with the Improbable: Low-Technology Means of Delivering*

Weapons of Mass Destruction, Paper No. 25, prepared for the Weapons of Mass Destruction Commission, 2004, accessed at http://www.wmdcommission.org.

33. Douglas Jehl and David E. Sanger, "U.S. Expands List of Lost Missiles," *New York Times,* November 6, 2004.

34. James Chow et al., *Protecting Commercial Aviation Against the Shoulder Fired Missile Threat,* Occasional Paper, RAND Corporation, Santa Monica, 2005, 9.

35. Ibid.

36. DHS inadvertently released this and other nightmarish information to the public, but typically had no plan to manage the public reaction to the disclosure of frightening information. See Eric Lipton, "U.S. Report Lists Possibilities for Terrorist Attacks and Likely Toll," *New York Times,* March 16, 2005, A1.

37. John Mintz and Joby Warrick, "U.S. Unprepared Despite Progress, Experts Say," *Washington Post,* November 8, 2004, A1.

38. Regarding al Qaeda and WMD, see Tiina Tarvainen, "Al-Qaeda and WMD: A Primer," Jamestown.org, vol. 3, Issue 11, June 2, 2005, accessed at http://www.jamestown.org/publications_details.php?volume_id=411&issue_id=3354, and Jonathan Spyer, "The al Qaeda Network and Weapons of Mass Destruction," *Middle East Review of International Affairs,* 2004, issue 3, accessed at http://meria.idc.ac.il/journal/2004/issue3/spyer.pdf.

39. Funding increased from $414 million to $7.6 billion since 2001.

40. Remarks by Commissioner Robert C. Bonner, Council on Foreign Relations, New York, New York, January 11, 2005, accessed at http://www.customs.gov/xp/cgov/newsroom/commissioner/speeches_statements/01112005_foreign_rel.xml.

41. Eric Lipton, "Holes Seen in Port Safety; Homeland Security Attempt to Get Importers', Foreign Cities' Help Might Have Backfired, Investigation Finds," *New York Times,* May 25, 2005, accessed at http://www.ocregister.com/ocr/2005/05/25/sections/news/focus/article_532896.php.

42. See Daniel Benjamin and Steven Simon, *The Age of Sacred Terror* (New York: Random House, 2002). Also see Eric Lichtblau, "Report Details F.B.I.'s Failure on 2 Hijackers," *New York Times,* June 10, 2005, accessed at http://www.nytimes.com/2005/06/10/politics/10fbi.html.

43. *Final Report of the National Commission on Terrorist Attacks Upon the United States* (2004), 425, accessed at http://www.9-11commission.gov/report/911Report.pdf.

44. From a 2004 interview with a special agent in charge, quoted in *The Final Report of the Commission on Intelligence Capabilities of the United States Regarding Weapons of Mass Destruction,* March 31, 2005, 453.

45. For Gannon quotes, see Dan Eggen, "FBI Fails to Transform Itself, Panel Says; Former September 11 Commission 'Taken Aback' by Personnel, Technology Problems," *Washington Post,* June 7, 2005, A4.

46. Eric Lichtblau, "FBI Gets Mixed Review on Analysis," *New York Times,* May 5, 2005, A22.

47. Dan Eggen and Walter Pincus, "Report: FBI Analyst Jobs Remain Vacant; Rapid Turnover Highlights Bureau's Post-9/11 Struggle," *Washington Post,* May 5, 2005, A23.

48. Ibid.

49. See *The Final Report of the Commission on Intelligence Capabilities of the United States Regarding Weapons of Mass Destruction,* March 31, 2005, 469.

50. Ibid.

51. Ibid.

52. Ibid., 470.

53. One of the authors met with O'Neill shortly before 9/11 and his death in the North Tower. One of the conversation topics that preoccupied O'Neill was Freeh's dismissive attitude toward the Bureau's massive information technology problems and their impact on the FBI's ability to cope with its terrorism duties. During Freeh's tenure, the White House repeatedly increased the Bureau's budget request for these purposes, but the money was spent on other things, which neither the White House nor the appropriations committee staffs were able to identify.

54. For the history of the fiasco, see Richard B. Schmitt, "New FBI Software May Be Unusable," *Los Angeles Times*, January 13, 2005, A1.

55. Dan Eggen and Julie Tate, "Statistics Often Count Lesser Crimes," *Washington Post*, June 12, 2005, A01, accessed at http://www.washingtonpost.com/wp-dyn/content/article/2005/06/11/AR2005061100381_pf.html.

56. Mary Beth Sheridan, "Immigration Law as Anti-Terrorism Tool," *Washington Post*, June 13, 2005, A01, accessed at http://www.washingtonpost.com/wp-dyn/content/article/2005/06/12/AR2005061201441_pf.html.

57. This account of the Bassam Yousef trial is drawn from John Solomon, "FBI Managers Admit They Didn't Seek Out Terrorism Expertise After Sept. 11," Associated Press, June 19, 2005, accessed at http://ap.tbo.com/ap/breaking/MGBQ3ZUC5AE.html, and David Johnston, "F.B.I. Counterterror Officials Lack Experience, Lawyer Says," *New York Times*, June 20, 2005, accessed at http://www.nytimes.com/2005/06/20/politics/20terror.html.

58. Daniel Byman, "Reject the Abuses, Retain the Attack," *Washington Post*, April 17, 2005.

59. For details and background on this weird story, see Peter Baker and Dafna Linzer, "Policy Shifts Felt After Bolton's Departure from State Dept.," *Washington Post*, June 20, 2005, A02, accessed at http://www.washingtonpost.com/wp-dyn/content/article/2005/06/19/AR2005061900697_pf.html, and Barton Gellman and Dafna Linzer, "Unprecedented Peril Forces Tough Calls. President Faces a Multi-Front Battle Against Threats Known, Unknown," *Washington Post*, October 26, 2004, A01, accessed at http://www.washingtonpost.com/wp-dyn/articles/A62727-2004Oct25.html.

60. Programs for the control of fissile material are underfunded. See Matthew Bunn and Anthony Wier, "Securing the Bomb 2005: New Global Imperatives," *Nuclear Threat Initiative*, May 2005, accessed at http://nti.org/e_research/report_cnwmupdate2005.pdf.

61. Ernest May, "Small Office, Wide Authority," *New York Times*, October 30, 2001, accessed at http://bcsia.ksg.harvard.edu/publication.cfm?ctype=article&item_id=286.

11. Faith and War

1. Richard Perle and David Frum, *An End to Evil: How to Win the War on Terror* (New York: Random House, 2003).

2. "The Neo-Conservatives: Back in Their Pomp," *The Economist*, May 10, 2005.

3. Peter Waldman, "A Historian's Take on Islam Steers U.S. in Terrorism Fight: Bernard Lewis's Blueprint—Sowing Arab Democracy—Is Facing a Test in Iraq," *Wall Street Journal*, February 4, 2004, accessed at http://faculty-staff.ou.edu/L/Joshua.M.Landis-1/blogger/archive/2004_02_04_archive.

4. Brian C. Anderson, "Secular Europe, Religious America," *Public Interest* (Spring 2004), 143–56.

5. Michael Hout, Andrew Greeley, and Melissa J. Wilde, "The Demographic Imperative in Religious Change in the United States," *American Journal of Sociology* 107, no. 2 (September 2001): 468–502.

6. Laurie Goodstein and David D. Kirkpatrick, "On a Christian Mission to the Top; Class Matters," *New York Times*, May 22, 2005, 1A.

7. Dispensationalism—the idea that history advances through a series of dispensations, or stages—reached America from Britain, where it originated, in 1883. Each of these stages culminates in judgment. Adherents to this movement believe that mankind is now in the next-to-last dispensation, the church age, which will be followed by the millennium. The trigger for the millennium, according to dispensationalist doctrine, will be the Second Coming of Christ, who will establish a worldwide kingdom centered in the earthly Jerusalem. First, however, Christ's return will be marked by the Rapture in which the righteous dead and living believers are plucked from earth and instated in heaven. Those left behind will undergo the horrors of a seven-year tribulation, which will culminate in the battle of Armageddon, in Israel. Christ returns amid the slaughter and establishes his thousand-year rule. The centrality of the rebuilding of the Temple in this narrative as the precondition for Christ's return imparts a tremendous significance to the existence of a Jewish state with sovereignty over Jerusalem. Although dispensationalists took only sporadic steps to help Jews settle in Palestine before the Jews there won independence and carved out a state, the movement was spurred to take a more active posture by the 1967 war, which led to Israeli control of Judea and Samaria, the biblical term for the West Bank. Hal Lindsey's book, *The Late Great Planet Earth*, which was published at about that time, gave the movement even greater impetus.

8. Jane Lampman, "Mixing Prophecy and Politics," *Christian Science Monitor*, July 7, 2004, http://csmonitor.com/2004/0707/p15s01-lire.htm.

9. Roland Watson, "Texan Star Begins to Lose his Shine as Scandals Rattle Republican Allies," Times Online, April 9, 2005, http://www.timesonline.co.uk/article/0,,11069-1561077_2,00.html

10. Sen. James M. Inhofe, "America's Stake in Israel's War on Terrorism," Senate Floor Statement, December 4, 2001.

11. CNBC News, *Hardball with Chris Matthews*, transcript, "Republican Majority Leader Richard Armey Discusses Resolution Supporting Israel and War on Terrorism," May 1, 2002.

12. Jane Lampman, "The End of the World," *Christian Science Monitor*, February 18, 2004, 11.

13. Quotes on Christian Zionism are taken from Lampman, "Mixing Prophecy and Politics."

14. Jane Lampman, "New Scrutiny of Role of Religion in Bush's Policies; The President's Rhetoric Worries Even Some Evangelicals," *Christian Science Monitor*, March 17, 2003, 1. The biblical verse in question is in Genesis 35, "The lands I gave to Abraham and Isaac I also give to you, and I will give this land to your descendants after you."

15. Bill Broadway, "The Evangelical-Israeli Connection; Scripture Inspires Many Christians to Support Zionism Politically, Financially," *Washington Post*, March 27, 2004, B9.

16. Bill Broadway, "Backing Israel for Different Reasons," *Washington Post*, March 27, 2004, B9.

17. Hanna Rosin, "Younger Graham Diverges from Father's Image; Ministry's Patriarch Accepted Islam, but His Son Condemns the Religion," *Washington Post*, September 2, 2002, A3.

18. Ibid.

19. Laurie Goodstein, "Seeing Islam as 'Evil' Faith, Evangelicals Seek Converts," *New York Times,* May 27, 2003, A1.

20. Sebastian Rotella, "Rift with Europe Runs Deep; U.S. Views on War, Guns, Religion Strain the Alliance That Has Defined Western Democracy," *Los Angeles Times,* February 18, 2003.

21. Peter Schneider, "Across a Great Divide," *New York Times,* March 13, 2004.

22. Rotella, "Rift with Europe."

23. Goodstein, "Seeing Islam."

24. William M. Arkin, "Commentary; The Pentagon Unleashes a Holy Warrior; A Christian Extremist in a High Defense Post Can Only Set Back the U.S. Approach to the Muslim World," *Los Angeles Times,* October 16, 2003, B17.

25. Johanna Neuman, "Bush's Inaction over General's Islam Remarks Riles Two Faiths; Muslims Call for Rebuke of Boykin, but Such a Move Could Isolate Key Christian Supporters," *Los Angeles Times,* November 23, 2003, A24.

26. Ibid.

27. Jane Lampman, "Evangelicals Shift Approach to Muslims; They Cut Criticism and Offer New Guidelines for Dialogue," *Christian Science Monitor,* May 22, 2003.

28. Charles Duhigg, "Evangelicals Flock into Iraq on a Mission of Faith; Christian Missionaries Hope to Save Souls, but Risk Losing Their Lives and Weakening Stability," *Los Angeles Times,* March 18, 2004, A1, accessed at www.latimes.com/news/nationworld/world/la-fg-missionary18mar18,1,2483855.story?coll=la-headlines-world.

29. Ibid.

30. Ibid.

31. President Bush, "Global Messenger," remarks in Cincinnati, Ohio, August 17, 2004, http://www.whitehouse.gov/news/releases/2004/08/20040817.html.

32. As the political scientist Paul Freedman wrote in *Slate,* "Nationally, 49 percent of voters said they trusted Bush but not Kerry to handle terrorism; only 31 percent trusted Kerry but not Bush. This 18-point gap is particularly significant in that terrorism is strongly tied to vote choice: 99 percent of those who trusted only Kerry on the issue voted for him, and 97 percent of those who trusted only Bush voted for him. Terrorism was cited by 19 percent of voters as the most important issue, and these citizens gave their votes to the president by an even larger margin than morality voters: 86 percent for Bush, 14 percent for Kerry. Paul Freedman, "The Gay Marriage Myth," *Slate,* November 5, 2004, http://www.slate.com/id/2109275.

"These differences hold up at the state level even when each state's past Bush vote is taken into account. When you control for that variable, a 10-point increase in the percentage of voters citing terrorism as the most important problem translates into a 3-point Bush gain. A 10-point increase in morality voters, on the other hand, has no effect. Nor does putting an anti-gay-marriage measure on the ballot. So, if you want to understand why Bush was re-elected, stop obsessing about the morality gap and start looking at the terrorism gap."

33. Alan Cooperman and Thomas B. Edsall, "Evangelicals Say They Led Charge for the GOP," *Washington Post,* November 8, 2004.

34. George W. Bush Delivers Remarks at a Campaign Rally, Allentown, Pennsylvania, Friday, October 1, 2004, http://www.whitehouse.gov/news/releases/2004/10/20041001-10.html.

35. Jeff Sharlet, "Soldiers of Christ: 1. Inside America's Most Powerful Megachurch," *Harper's* May 2005.

ACKNOWLEDGMENTS

We have benefited from the assistance of many friends and colleagues in the course of writing this book. Michael Abramowitz, Steve Andreasen, John Kelsay, Vinca Lafleur, and Jonathan Stevenson read parts of the manuscript and provided important corrections and suggestions. Marc Sageman, Reuven Paz, Anthony Cordesman, Richard Danzig, Karen Greenberg, Richard Clarke, Mary DeRosa, Rick Barton, David Heyman, Alan Richards, Gabriel Weimann, Arnaud de Borchgrave, Elisa Avalos, Derek Mitchell, Robert Einhorn, Amy Smithson, Marvin Weinbaum, Michele Flournoy, and Tom Sanderson gave us the benefit of their expertise and time on a wide range of questions. Daniel Byman and Andrew Bacevich were kind enough to allow us to read the manuscripts of their excellent books, *Deadly Connections: States That Sponsor Terrorism* and *The New American Militarism: How Americans Are Seduced by War,* before their publication. We are particularly indebted to the SITE Institute and its director, Rita Katz, for allowing us to quote from its translations of material from the Web; in the short period of its existence, SITE has become an invaluable resource for anyone researching jihadist terror. Of course, all errors in the text are ours alone.

Some of the ideas we present in this book have appeared in different form in a number of publications. We wish to thank the editors who allowed us to grapple with these issues in their pages or on their Web sites:

David Shipley of *The New York Times,* Jacob Weisberg of *Slate,* and Nick Goldberg of the *Los Angles Times.*

We were especially fortunate that Paul Golob, the editorial director of Times Books, took on the project of *The Next Attack.* He has been all we could hope for in an editor, and his relentless attention to detail and organization as well as his encouragement have made this a much better book than it might otherwise have been. Our agent, Esther Newberg, has not only been a superb advocate but—what all writers crave—a source of support and good cheer every step of the way. We are also grateful to Jeffrey Smith, former general counsel of the CIA and now a partner at Arnold & Porter, for his careful review of the manuscript.

IN WORKING ON this book, I have incurred numerous personal debts. In particular, I want to thank the Center for Strategic and International Studies, its president, John Hamre, and its executive vice president, Robin Niblett, for their support and for making CSIS the ideal place to research and write. Among my colleagues and friends, no one has been more encouraging and dependably helpful at every stage than Kurt Campbell, CSIS's vice president and director of the International Security Program. Within the program, Julianne Smith and Tiffany Chan used their great ingenuity to clear obstacles and create the time and space for me to work. I have also been lucky to have superb help from my research assistant, Aidan Kirby, who worked long—and resourcefully—beyond the call of duty. CSIS interns Weimeng Yeo and Georges Chebib also provided invaluable research help. Alexandra Bradley and Sara Rioff translated essential materials with speed and precision.

Above all others, my wife, Henrike, made this book possible. During the nights, weekends, and vacations when much of the writing was done, she cheerfully handled the more taxing challenge posed by two young sons, Caleb and Jonah, both under the age of four. Her strong belief that the message of *The Next Attack* needed to be told was a source of sustenance; there are no thoughts in this book that have not been tried out on her first and refined by her insights. I owe her more than I could possibly say.

—*Daniel Benjamin*

WITHOUT MY WIFE, Virginia, I could not have participated in this project. Times Books gave us the go-ahead just as we were relocating to a derelict farm in the Blue Ridge. As I coped with both book writing and relentless travel demands, Virginia single-handedly managed multiple moves, the renovation of two old houses, and the containment of acres of poison ivy, while working on her own academic research and garden design business. She made this sacrifice because she too believed this story had to be told. Even more important, she was unstinting with her time and intellectual energy as I sought her views on the argument advanced by this book. I owe her a debt I cannot repay.

—Steven Simon

INDEX

ABOUT THE AUTHORS

DANIEL BENJAMIN is a senior fellow at the Center for Strategic and International Studies in Washington, D.C. He served from 1994 to 1999 on the National Security Council staff as a director for counterterrorism and, prior to that, as special assistant and foreign policy speechwriter for President Clinton. A graduate of Harvard and Oxford, he has been a foreign correspondent for *Time* and Berlin bureau chief for *The Wall Street Journal.*

STEVEN SIMON teaches at Georgetown University, having previously been assistant director of the International Institute for Strategic Studies in London. He served on the National Security Council staff for five years following a career at the U.S. Department of State in Middle Eastern security affairs. He holds degrees from Columbia, Harvard, and Princeton and was an international affairs fellow at Oxford.

Their first book, *The Age of Sacred Terror: Radical Islam's War Against America*, was published in 2002 and was awarded the Arthur Ross Book Prize by the Council on Foreign Relations.